W9-BSB-232

A GUIDE TO

TROLLOPE

BY

WINIFRED GREGORY GEROULD

AND JAMES THAYER GEROULD

DRAWINGS BY FLORENCE W. EWING

"There is a gallery of them, and of all in that gallery I may say that I know the tone of the voice, and the colour of the hair, every flame of the eye, and the very clothes they wear. Of each man I could assert whether he would have said these or the other words; of every woman, whether she would then have smiled or so have frowned."—Trollope, AN AUTOBIOGRAPHY, 2:12:50-51.

PRINCETON UNIVERSITY PRESS

PRINCETON, NEW JERSEY

Published by Princeton University Press, 41 William Street,
Princeton, New Jersey 08540

First Princeton Paperback printing, 1987

LCC 487405

ISBN 0-691-01441-8 (pbk.)

Printed in Great Britain

PREFACE

ANTHONY TROLLOPE today is in the ascendant both in England and America; he has emerged from a period of undeserved obscurity which followed the publication of his *Autobiography*. Frankness was unendurable to the Victorian, and Trollope's portrait of himself was hardly less rugged than that drawn by Cellini. A man who wrote so many hours, so many hundred words daily, assuredly could not have been an artist—so he passed below the horizon for years and many of his best novels were available only in the editions of the German Tauchnitz, which could not legally be brought into England. In recent years, however, the Barchester and the Parliamentary novels have been reprinted by Dodd, Mead and Company, as has also the so-called Manor House series, including *Is He Popenjoy?, John Caldigate, Orley Farm* and *The Vicar of Bullhampton*. Michael Sadleir has published the Shakespeare Head edition of the Barchester novels; the Oxford University Press has issued a large number of titles in their World Classics series, and there have been others. No complete record of all of the editions and reprints has been prepared, but our notes—too fragmentary for publication—show an astonishing number issued; for example, 47 separate issues of *The Warden*, and as many of *Barchester Towers*, 36 of *Framley Parsonage*, 32 of *The Small House at Allington* and others in lesser number.

The most devoted Trollopian will agree that Trollope wrote carelessly and that the correction of his proof was more careless still. Not infrequently he failed to remember the name by which he had baptized a character and provided another. The Rev. Mr. Armstrong in *The Kellys and the O'Kellys* is first Joseph, then George; Lady Linlithgow in *The Eustace Diamonds* is successively Penelope and Susanna, and occasionally the name is altogether changed, Flatfleece of the Beargarden Club becoming Fleeceflat; even the great Sir Omicron Pie is once spoken of as Sir Simon Omicron. Another amusing example of his carelessness is the case of the "lost children" of the Archdeacon and the Duke which has recently been the subject of spirited correspondence in the Literary Supplement of the (London) *Times*.

But with all his faults Trollope lives, and will live, for no one has surpassed him in portraying Victorian England. No other writer has depicted so clearly and so completely the virtues and the evils of the clerical and the political society of his day. It is doubtful if any Englishman of his time knew the countryside so well, for as a postal inspector he had penetrated into every corner of it. The breadth of his interests is reflected in his characterizations. He was an enthusiastic diner-out, a genial host in his own home, usually available for a game of whist at the Garrick, and wherever there were foxes he had ridden with the hounds. The poverty, the filth and the good humor of Ireland were familiar to him. His official duties made him a world traveler, and though he used that experience but sparingly in his novels, it forms the background for most of the short stories.

He was merciless in recording the grave inequities that had developed within the fabric of the Church of England. It disturbed him that the Rev. Vesey Stanhope, while living idly in Italy, could draw his £800 a year from parishes which for eleven years he had never visited, while the Vicar of Puddingdale supported a large family on half that sum, and Mr. Crawley of Hogglestock worked long and faithfully for only £130 annually. Nevertheless, he resented instinctively the changes made by the Ecclesiastical Commission. He was keenly aware of the injustice of the system of rotten boroughs and the corruption that attended parliamentary elections, but like a true Englishman, the old ways were very dear to him. He was a satirist but in no sense an iconoclast.

Although he moved easily among all sorts of men his characters are largely drawn from the upper classes; in all his novels there are few instances where workingmen play a major role. There is nothing of the democrat, in the modern sense, about Trollope. In dealing with his characters he was always kindly; however weak, however vicious he had made them, it is seldom that he did not hint at traits which relieved their blackness. In this he differs sharply from Dickens, whose whites and whose blacks were never shaded.

Trollopians will not agree as to his most unforgettable pages, but they will unite, we fancy, in counting among them, in the Barchester series: Dr. Grantly at his father's deathbed; Signora Neroni's entrance at Mrs. Proudie's party; Mr. Crawley's defiance of Mrs. Proudie in the Palace and the last days of Sir Roger Scatcherd; in the Parliamentary series: Lizzie Eustace's struggle to retain the diamonds; the scene between Plantagenet Palliser and Lady Glencora the morning after Lady Monk's party; the old Duke's love for Madame Max Goesler and the trial of Phineas Finn for the murder of Mr. Bonteen; in the lesser-known works: the contest between Dean Lovelace and the wicked Marquis in *Is He Popenjoy?*; the madness of Louis Trevelyan in *He Knew He Was*

Right; Mr. Scarborough's struggle to outwit the law of entail in *Mr. Scarborough's Family*; the trial of Lady Mason in *Orley Farm*; the debacle of Augustus Melmotte in *The Way We Live Now* and the picture of the famine of 1847 in *Castle Richmond*. Of the short stories little need be said. Aside from *Aaron Trow, Catherine Carmichael, Returning Home* and *The Spotted Dog*, most of them are very slight indeed, and appear to have been written to make use of notes accumulated on the author's extended travels.

The *Guide* is an alphabetical record of characters and places having a significant role in the novels and stories, and these are, in many cases, described in Trollope's own words. The citations of such quotations include volume, chapter and page in the first editions, and have been checked with the incomparable Parrish collection now in the Princeton University Library. So far as possible the chapters in which a given character appears are indicated. Since later editions of the original three-volume novels are frequently issued in one or two volumes, with resulting changes in chapter grouping, we have used an arbitrary chapter numbering, and append a table which will enable the reader to consult whatever edition he has at hand. Included in the alphabetical arrangement is a brief digest of the plot of each of the stories, along with Trollope's own estimate as given in his *Autobiography*, and occasional notes by his critics. As it may be of interest to students of Trollope, we have inserted in the list a grouping by names of the doctors, lawyers, moneylenders and Americans appearing in the novels, students of the various universities and colleges, hunting, election and courtroom scenes, and a list of the London streets and the shires in which the action of the novels is located. Trollope speaks of his characters as constituting a "gallery," and we have had this in mind in selecting the quotations which evoke them.

Mrs. William Ewing of Williamsburg, Virginia, has graciously permitted us to include her maps of the Trollope country, which she has based on a minute study of Trollope's own geographical indications.

We are indebted to Mr. Michael Sadleir for permission to use quotations from his monumental *Trollope: a Commentary*; to John Lane for similar permission to quote from Escott's *Anthony Trollope: His Public Services, Private Friends and Literary Originals*; and to the Macmillan Company for the opportunity to reprint sentences from Walpole's *Anthony Trollope* of the English Men of Letters series. Mr. Spencer Van Bokkelen Nichols has allowed us to coordinate his classification of the novels with our own, and with those of Sadleir and Walpole, and to quote his moving description of Archdeacon Grantly at the bedside of his dying father, from his *The Significance of Anthony Trollope*. Dr. R. W. Chapman of Oxford has read the proof and made valuable suggestions.

To Malcolm O. Young, Miss Julie Hudson and Miss Reba Cawley of the Princeton University Library we owe grateful thanks for the loan of books, and for assistance in checking references in the Parrish collection.

WILLIAMSBURG, VIRGINIA

W. G. G.
J. T. G.

CONTENTS

ILLUSTRATIONS

CHRONOLOGICAL LIST OF TROLLOPE'S NOVELS AND STORIES

WITH THE DATE OF THEIR PUBLICATION IN BOOK FORM

The Macdermots of Ballycloran. 3v. 1847
The Kellys and the O'Kellys; or, Landlords and Tenants. 3v. 1848
La Vendée; an Historical Romance. 3v. 1850
The Warden. 1v. 1855
Barchester Towers. 3v. 1857
The Three Clerks; a Novel. 3v. 1858
Doctor Thorne; a Novel. 3v. 1858
The Bertrams; a Novel. 3v. 1859
Castle Richmond; a Novel. 3v. 1860
Framley Parsonage. 3v. 1861
Tales of All Countries [First Series]. 1v. 1861
Contents: La Mère Bauche; The O'Conors of Castle Conor; John Bull on the Guadalquivir; Miss Sarah Jack of Spanish Town, Jamaica; The Courtship of Susan Bell; Relics of General Chassé; An Unprotected Female at the Pyramids; The Chateau of Prince Polignac
Orley Farm. 2v. 1862
The Struggles of Brown, Jones and Robinson; by One of the Firm. 1v. 1862
Tales of All Countries; Second Series. 1v. 1863
Contents: Aaron Trow; Mrs. General Talboys; The Parson's Daughter of Oxney Colne; George Walker at Suez; The Mistletoe Bough; Returning Home; A Ride Across Palestine; The House of Heine Brothers in Munich; The Man Who Kept His Money in a Box
Rachel Ray; a Novel. 2v. 1863
The Small House at Allington. 2v. 1864
Can You Forgive Her? 2v. 1864
Miss Mackenzie. 1v. 1865
The Belton Estate. 3v. 1866
Nina Balatka. 2v. 1867
The Last Chronicle of Barset. 2v. 1867
The Claverings. 2v. 1867

Lotta Schmidt and Other Stories. 1v. 1867

Contents: Lotta Schmidt; The Adventures of Fred Pickering (in this collection called "The Misfortunes of Fred Pickering"); The Two Generals; Father Giles of Ballymoy; Malachi's Cove; The Widow's Mite; The Last Austrian Who Left Venice; Miss Ophelia Gledd; The Journey to Panama

Linda Tressel. 1v. 1868

Phineas Finn; the Irish Member. 2v. 1869

He Knew He Was Right. 2v. 1869

Did He Steal It? A Comedy in Three Acts. 1v. 1869

The Vicar of Bullhampton. 1v. 1870

An Editor's Tales. 1v. 1870

Contents: The Turkish Bath; Mary Gresley; Josephine de Montmorenci; The Panjandrum; The Spotted Dog; Mrs. Brumby

Sir Harry Hotspur of Humblethwaite. 1v. 1871

Ralph the Heir. 3v. 1871

The Golden Lion of Granpère. 1v. 1872

The Eustace Diamonds. 3v. 1873

Phineas Redux. 2v. 1874

Lady Anna. 2v. 1874

Harry Heathcote of Gangoil; a Tale of Australian Bush Life. 1v. 1874

The Way We Live Now. 2v. 1875

The Prime Minister. 4v. 1876

The American Senator. 3v. 1877

Is He Popenjoy?; a Novel. 3v. 1878

An Eye for an Eye. 2v. 1879

John Caldigate. 3v. 1879

Cousin Henry; a Novel. 2v. 1879

The Duke's Children; a Novel. 3v. 1880

Dr. Wortle's School; a Novel. 2v. 1881

Ayala's Angel. 3v. 1881

Why Frau Frohmann Raised Her Prices; and Other Stories. 1v. 1882

Contents: Why Frau Frohmann Raised Her Prices; The Lady of Launay; Christmas at Thompson Hall; The Telegraph Girl; Alice Dugdale

Kept in the Dark; a Novel. 2v. 1882

Marion Fay; a Novel. 3v. 1882

The Fixed Period. 2v. 1882

Mr. Scarborough's Family. 3v. 1883

The Landleaguers. 3v. 1883
An Old Man's Love. 2v. 1884
The Noble Jilt [a Play]. 1v. 1923

STORIES PUBLISHED IN MAGAZINE FORM ONLY

Gentle Euphemia. 1866
Katchen's Caprices. 1866-67
Christmas Day at Kirkby Cottage. 1870
Never, Never,—Never, Never. 1875
Catherine Carmichael. 1878
Not If I Know It. 1882
The Two Heroines of Plumplington. 1882

MAJOR WORKS RELATING TO TROLLOPE

Dunn, Esther Cloudman, and Marion E. Dodd. *The Trollope Reader*. N.Y., Oxford University Press, 1947. 433p.

Contains an excellent introductory essay on Trollope.

Escott, T. H. S. *Anthony Trollope; his public services, private friends and literary originals*. London, Lane, 1913. 351p.

The first substantial discussion of Trollope's life and works, based on many years of friendship, notes of details supplied by Trollope himself, and on conversations with many of his surviving friends. It contains long summaries of the plots of many of the novels, and is supplemented by a bibliography of the first editions prepared by Margaret Lavington.

Irwin, Mary Leslie. *Anthony Trollope; a Bibliography*. N.Y., Wilson, 1926. 97p.

A brief record of first editions, serial publication, translations and contemporary reviews of all the novels and books of travel. The section on Biography and Criticism is marred by the inclusion of much unimportant material. Includes not only Trollope's books, but notes on poems, portraits, autographs, letters, maps; sales and prices, etc.

Nichols, Spencer Van Bokkelen. *The Significance of Anthony Trollope*. N.Y., McMurtrie, 1925. 59p. and folded map.

An admirable critical essay, including a map of Barsetshire based on Trollope's own descriptions, with the quotations given for each landmark. The map was executed by the author's friend, George F. Muendel.

Sadleir, Michael. *Anthony Trollope, 1815-1882*. In his *Excursions in Victorian Bibliography*. London, Chaundry and Cox, 1922. pp. 21-73.

Brief critical notes on the more important novels, with bibliographical details foreshadowing his later *Trollope: a Bibliography*. Characterized in a letter to the compilers as "prentice work."

Sadleir, Michael. *Trollope: a Bibliography*. An analysis of the history and structure of the works of Anthony Trollope, and a general survey of the effect of original publishing conditions on a book's subsequent rarity. London, Constable, 1928. 322p.

A monumental work, ranking with the best of similar bibliographical studies. Supplemented in 1934 by ten pages of Addenda and Corrigenda.

Sadleir, Michael. *Trollope: a Commentary*. London, Constable, 1927. 432p.

The Bible of all Trollopians, by the man who above all others is responsible for the renascence of interest in Trollope's work. J. L. Garvin in *The Observer* describes the book as a "loving and living biography."

Revised ed., N.Y., Farrar, Straus, 1947. 435p. Quotations in the *Guide* are from this edition.

STEBBINS, LUCY POATE, AND RICHARD POATE STEBBINS. *The Trollopes: the Chronicle of a Writing Family*. N.Y., Columbia University Press, 1945. 394p.

Contains much new material regarding the Trollope family, but is marred by what seems to be veiled contempt, particularly of Anthony, and an excessive reliance on Freudian psychology in the discussion of his characters.

TROLLOPE, ANTHONY. *An Autobiography*. Edinburgh and London, Blackwood, 1883. 2v.

A frank and factual record, with no self-glorification, practically nothing of his private life and with a modesty regarding his own work which estimates it far below its value.

TROLLOPE, THOMAS ADOLPHUS. *What I Remember*. N.Y., Harper, 1888. 546p.

Valuable for its side lights on his brother's career.

THE TROLLOPIAN: *A Journal of Victorian Fiction*. University of California Press. Summer 1945 to date.

Edited by Professor Bradford A. Booth. Semiannual, 1945-1946; quarterly, 1947 to date.

WALPOLE, HUGH. *Anthony Trollope*. (English Men of Letters series.) London, Macmillan, 1929. 205p.

A short but adequate and appreciative critical summary of Trollope's career and of his books, as they appeared to a fellow novelist.

Note: Professor Bradford A. Booth of the University of California at Los Angeles is editing a volume of Trollope letters which may be ready for publication in 1948.

CLASSIFICATION OF THE NOVELS AND STORIES

Nichols, Sadleir and Walpole have each published their classification schemes. The footnotes to this classification indicate their variations.

BARSETSHIRE NOVELS[1]
- The Warden
- Barchester Towers
- Doctor Thorne
- Framley Parsonage
- The Small House at Allington
- The Last Chronicle of Barset

POLITICAL NOVELS[2]
- Can You Forgive Her?
- Phineas Finn
- The Eustace Diamonds
- Phineas Redux
- The Prime Minister
- The Duke's Children

SOCIAL SATIRE[3]
- The Bertrams
- Mr. Scarborough's Family
- Miss Mackenzie
- Rachel Ray
- The Struggles of Brown, Jones and Robinson
- The Way We Live Now

PSYCHOLOGICAL ANALYSIS
- Cousin Henry*
- Dr. Wortle's School*
- An Eye for an Eye[4]
- He Knew He Was Right[5]
- Kept in the Dark*
- Mistletoe Bough
- An Old Man's Love*

OTHER NOVELS OF ENGLISH LIFE[6]
- Alice Dugdale
- The American Senator
- Ayala's Angel
- The Belton Estate
- Christmas Day at Kirkby Cottage
- The Claverings[7]
- Is He Popenjoy?
- Lady Anna
- The Lady of Launay
- Marion Fay
- Not If I Know It
- Orley Farm
- Ralph the Heir
- Sir Harry Hotspur of Humblethwaite
- The Telegraph Girl
- The Three Clerks
- Two Heroines of Plumplington
- The Vicar of Bullhampton

HISTORICAL ROMANCE
- La Vendée*†

FANTASTIC INCIDENT
- The Fixed Period*
- Gentle Euphemia

BURLESQUE
- Never, Never,—Never, Never

IRISH NOVELS AND STORIES[8]
- Castle Richmond
- Father Giles of Ballymoy
- The Kellys and the O'Kellys
- The Landleaguers
- The Macdermots of Ballycloran
- The O'Conors of Castle Conor

AUSTRALIAN NOVELS[9]
- Harry Heathcote of Gangoil
- John Caldigate

OTHER NOVELS AND STORIES WITH A FOREIGN SETTING
- Aaron Trow (Bermuda)
- Catherine Carmichael (New Zealand)
- The Chateau of Prince Polignac (France)
- The Courtship of Susan Bell (United States)
- George Walker at Suez (Egypt)
- The Golden Lion of Granpère (France)*†
- The House of Heine Brothers in Munich (Germany)
- John Bull on the Guadalquivir (Spain)
- The Journey to Panama (Panama)
- Katchen's Caprices (Austria)
- The Last Austrian Who Left Venice (Italy)

Linda Tressel (Germany)*†
Lotta Schmidt (Austria)
The Man Who Kept His Money in a Box (Italy)
La Mère Bauche (France)
Miss Ophelia Gledd (United States)
Miss Sarah Jack of Spanish Town (Jamaica)
Mrs. General Talboys (Italy)
Nina Balatka (Austria)*†
Relics of General Chassé (Belgium)
Returning Home (Costa Rica)
A Ride across Palestine (Palestine)
The Two Generals (United States)
An Unprotected Female at the Pyramids (Egypt)
Why Frau Frohmann Raised Her Prices (Austria)

PLAYS

Did He Steal It?
The Noble Jilt

SHORT STORIES

An Editor's Tales[10]
Lotta Schmidt and Other Stories
Tales of All Countries. First Series
Tales of All Countries. Second Series
Why Frau Frohmann Raised Her Prices and Other Stories

---

* Nichols under Stories of Contrast and Single Incident

† Sadleir and Walpole under Historical and Romantic Novels

[1] Nichols as Barsetshire Life; Sadleir and Walpole as Chronicles of Barsetshire

[2] Sadleir as Parliamentary Life

[3] Nichols as Satires on Social Life

[4] Nichols under Ireland

[5] Nichols under Satires on Social Life

[6] Nichols as Social Life; Sadleir as Novels of Manners, Convention and Social Dilemma; Walpole as Novels of Manners and Social Dilemma

[7] Nichols under Barchester Life

[8] Nichols as Ireland

[9] Nichols as Stories of Contrast and Single Incident. Colonial Life

[10] Nichols under Essays, etc.

ABBREVIATIONS

Used to Designate the Works in the *Guide*

Adventures.	Adventures of Fred Pickering
Allington.	Small House at Allington
Amer. Sen.	American Senator
Anna.	Lady Anna
Ayala.	Ayala's Angel
Barchester.	Barchester Towers
Bauche.	Mère Bauche
Belton.	Belton Estate
Bertrams.	The Bertrams
Brumby.	Mrs. Brumby
Caldigate.	John Caldigate
Can You.	Can You Forgive Her?
Carmichael.	Catherine Carmichael
Castle Rich.	Castle Richmond
Chateau.	Chateau of Prince Polignac
Christmas.	Christmas at Thompson Hall
Claverings.	The Claverings
Clerks.	Three Clerks
Courtship.	Courtship of Susan Bell
Cousin.	Cousin Henry
Did He.	Did He Steal It?
Dugdale.	Alice Dugdale
Duke.	Duke's Children
Euphemia.	Gentle Euphemia
Eustace.	Eustace Diamonds
Eye.	Eye for an Eye
Father Giles.	Father Giles of Ballymoy
Fay.	Marion Fay
Finn.	Phineas Finn
Fixed.	Fixed Period
Framley.	Framley Parsonage
Frohmann.	Why Frau Frohmann Raised Her Prices
Generals.	Two Generals
Gledd.	Miss Ophelia Gledd
Granpère.	Golden Lion of Granpère
Gresley.	Mary Gresley
He Knew.	He Knew He Was Right
Heathcote.	Harry Heathcote of Gangoil
Heine.	House of Heine Brothers in Munich
Hotspur.	Sir Harry Hotspur of Humblethwaite
Jilt.	Noble Jilt
John Bull.	John Bull on the Guadalquivir
Josephine.	Josephine de Montmorenci
Journey.	Journey to Panama
Katchen.	Katchen's Caprices
Kellys.	Kellys and the O'Kellys
Kept Dark.	Kept in the Dark
Kirkby.	Christmas Day at Kirkby Cottage

Land.	The Landleaguers
Last Aust.	Last Austrian Who Left Venice
Last Chron.	Last Chronicle of Barset
Launay.	Lady of Launay
Linda.	Linda Tressel
Lotta.	Lotta Schmidt
Macdermots.	Macdermots of Ballycloran
Mackenzie.	Miss Mackenzie
Malachi.	Malachi's Cove
Mistletoe.	Mistletoe Bough
Money.	Man Who Kept His Money in a Box
Never.	Never, Never,—Never, Never
Nina.	Nina Balatka
Not If.	Not If I Know It
O'Conors.	O'Conors of Castle Conor
Orley.	Orley Farm
Old Man.	Old Man's Love
Panjandrum.	Panjandrum
Parson.	Parson's Daughter of Oxney Colne
Plumplington.	Two Heroines of Plumplington
Popenjoy.	Is He Popenjoy?
Prime Min.	Prime Minister
Rachel.	Rachel Ray
Ralph.	Ralph the Heir
Redux.	Phineas Redux
Relics.	Relics of General Chassé
Returning.	Returning Home
Ride.	Ride across Palestine
Sarah.	Miss Sarah Jack of Spanish Town
Scarborough.	Mr. Scarborough's Family
Spotted.	Spotted Dog
Struggles.	Struggles of Brown, Jones and Robinson
Talboys.	Mrs. General Talboys
Telegraph.	Telegraph Girl
Thorne.	Doctor Thorne
Trow.	Aaron Trow
Turkish.	Turkish Bath
Unprotected.	Unprotected Female at the Pyramids
Vendée.	La Vendée
Vicar.	Vicar of Bullhampton
Walker.	George Walker at Suez
Warden.	The Warden
Way We Live.	Way We Live Now
Widow.	Widow's Mite
Wortle.	Dr. Wortle's School

ALPHABETICAL LIST

of the Works, with Abbreviations Used in the *Guide*

Aaron Trow. *Trow*
Adventures of Fred Pickering. *Adventures*
Alice Dugdale. *Dugdale*
American Senator. *Amer. Sen.*
Ayala's Angel. *Ayala*

Barchester Towers. *Barchester*
Belton Estate. *Belton*
Bertrams. *Bertrams*

Can You Forgive Her? *Can You*
Castle Richmond. *Castle Rich.*
Catherine Carmichael. *Carmichael*
Chateau of Prince Polignac. *Chateau*
Christmas at Thompson Hall. *Christmas*
Christmas Day at Kirkby Cottage. *Kirkby*
Claverings. *Claverings*
Courtship of Susan Bell. *Courtship*
Cousin Henry. *Cousin*

Did He Steal It? *Did He*
Doctor Thorne. *Thorne*
Dr. Wortle's School. *Wortle*
Duke's Children. *Duke*

Eustace Diamonds. *Eustace*
Eye for an Eye. *Eye*

Father Giles of Ballymoy. *Father Giles*
Fixed Period. *Fixed*
Framley Parsonage. *Framley*

Gentle Euphemia. *Euphemia*
George Walker at Suez. *Walker*
Golden Lion of Granpère. *Granpère*

Harry Heathcote of Gangoil. *Heathcote*
He Knew He Was Right. *He Knew*
House of Heine Brothers in Munich. *Heine*

Is He Popenjoy? *Popenjoy*

John Bull on the Guadalquivir. *John Bull*
John Caldigate. *Caldigate*
Josephine de Montmorenci. *Josephine*
Journey to Panama. *Journey*

Katchen's Caprices. *Katchen*
Kellys and the O'Kellys. *Kellys*
Kept in the Dark. *Kept Dark*

Lady Anna. *Anna*
Lady of Launay. *Launay*
Landleaguers. *Land*
Last Austrian Who Left Venice. *Last Aust.*
Last Chronicle of Barset. *Last Chron.*
Linda Tressel. *Linda*
Lotta Schmidt. *Lotta*

Macdermots of Ballycloran. *Macdermots*
Malachi's Cove. *Malachi*
Man Who Kept His Money in a Box. *Money*
Marion Fay. *Fay*
Mary Gresley. *Gresley*
Mère Bauche. *Bauche*
Miss Mackenzie. *Mackenzie*
Miss Ophelia Gledd. *Gledd*
Miss Sarah Jack. *Sarah*
Mr. Scarborough's Family. *Scarborough*
Mistletoe Bough. *Mistletoe*
Mrs. Brumby. *Brumby*
Mrs. General Talboys. *Talboys*

Never, Never,—Never, Never. *Never*
Nina Balatka. *Nina*
Noble Jilt. *Jilt*
Not If I Know It. *Not If*

O'Conors of Castle Conor. *O'Conors*
Old Man's Love. *Old Man*
Orley Farm. *Orley*

Panjandrum. *Panjandrum*
Parson's Daughter of Oxney Colne. *Parson*
Phineas Finn. *Finn*

Phineas Redux. *Redux*
Prime Minister. *Prime Min.*

Rachel Ray. *Rachel*
Ralph the Heir. *Ralph*
Relics of General Chassé. *Relics*
Returning Home. *Returning*
Ride across Palestine. *Ride*

Sir Harry Hotspur of Humblethwaite. *Hotspur*
Small House at Allington. *Allington*
Spotted Dog. *Spotted*
Struggles of Brown, Jones and Robinson. *Struggles*

Telegraph Girl. *Telegraph*
Three Clerks. *Clerks*
Turkish Bath. *Turkish*
Two Generals. *Generals*
Two Heroines of Plumplington. *Plumplington*

Unprotected Female at the Pyramids. *Unprotected*

La Vendée. *Vendée*
Vicar of Bullhampton. *Vicar*

The Warden. *Warden*
Way We Live Now. *Way We Live*
Why Frau Frohmann Raised Her Prices. *Frohmann*
Widow's Mite. *Widow*

CONVERSION TABLE

For the identification of citations in other than the first edition. The authors have used the volume, chapter and paging of the first edition for direct quotations, but for designating the appearance of characters or places, a continuous chapter numbering has been used.

TITLE	FIRST EDITION		DODD, MEAD ED.		ONE VOLUME ED.
The American Senator	1:1-27				1-80
	2:1-27	[28-54]			
	3:1-26	[55-80]			
Ayala's Angel	1:1-22				1-64
	2:23-43				
	3:44-64				
Barchester Towers	1:1-19		1:1-27		1-53
	2:1-15	[20-34]	2:1-26	[27-53]	
	3:1-19	[35-53]			
The Belton Estate	1:1-11		1:1-17		1-32
	2:1-10	[12-21]	2:1-15	[18-32]	
	3:1-10	[22-31]			
The Bertrams	1:1-15				1-47
	2:1-15	[16-30]			
	3:1-17	[31-47]			
Can You Forgive Her?	1:1-40		1:1-26		1-80
	2:1-40	[41-80]	2:1-26	[27-52]	
			3:1-27	[53-80]	
Castle Richmond	1:1-14				1-44
	2:1-15	[15-29]			
	3:1-15	[30-44]			
The Claverings	1:1-24				1-48
	2:1-24	[25-48]			
Cousin Henry	1:1-12				1-24
	2:1-12	[13-24]			
Doctor Thorne	1:1-14		1:1-23		1-47
	2:1-16	[15-30]	2:1-24	[24-47]	
	3:1-17	[31-47]			
Dr. Wortle's School	1:1-12				1-24
	2:1-12	[13-24]			
The Duke's Children	1:1-26		1:1-26		1-80
	2:1-27	[27-53]	2:1-27	[27-53]	
	3:1-27	[54-80]	3:1-27	[54-80]	
The Eustace Diamonds	1:1-26		1:1-38		1-80
	2:27-53		2:39-80		
	3:54-80				

CONVERSION TABLE

TITLE	FIRST EDITION	DODD, MEAD ED.	ONE VOLUME ED.
An Eye for an Eye	1:1-12		1-24
	2:1-12 [13-24]		
The Fixed Period	1:1-6		1-12
	2:7-12		
Framley Parsonage	1:1-16	1:1-24	1-48
	2:1-15 [17-31]	2:1-24 [25-48]	
	3:1-17 [32-48]		
He Knew He Was Right	1:1-49		1-99
	2:50-99		
Is He Popenjoy?	1:1-21	1:1-32	1-64
	2:1-20 [22-41]	2:1-32 [33-64]	
	3:1-23 [42-64]		
John Caldigate	1:1-21	1:1-32	1-64
	2:1-21 [22-42]	2:1-32 [33-64]	
	3:1-22 [43-64]		
The Kellys and the O'Kellys	1:1-12		1-40
	2:1-12 [13-24]		
	3:1-12 [25-36]		
Kept in the Dark	1:1-12		1-24
	2:13-24		
Lady Anna	1:1-24		1-48
	2:25-48		
Landleaguers	1:1-16		1-49
	2:17-32		
	3:33-49		
The Last Chronicle of Barset	1:1-43	1:1-29	1-84
	2:44-84	2:1-26 [30-55]	
		3:1-29 [56-84]	
The Macdermots of Ballycloran	1:1-12		1-36
	2:1-12 [13-24]		
	3:1-12 [25-36]		
Marion Fay	1:1-22		1-64
	2:1-21 [23-43]		
	3:1-21 [44-64]		
Miss Mackenzie	1:1-15		1-30
	2:1-15 [16-30]		
Mr. Scarborough's Family	1:1-21		1-64
	2:22-43		
	3:44-64		
Nina Balatka	1:1-8		1-16
	2:9-16		

TITLE	FIRST EDITION		DODD, MEAD ED.		ONE VOLUME ED.
An Old Man's Love	1:1-12				1-24
	2:13-24				
Orley Farm	1:1-40		1:1-27		1-80
	2:1-40	[41-80]	2:1-27	[28-44]	
			3:1-26	[45-80]	
Phineas Finn	1:1-37		1:1-25		1-76
	2:38-76		2:1-26	[26-51]	
			3:1-25	[52-76]	
Phineas Redux	1:1-40		1:1-27		1-80
	2:1-40	[41-80]	2:1-26	[28-53]	
			3:1-27	[54-80]	
The Prime Minister	1:1-20		1:1-27		1-80
	2:1-20	[21-40]	2:1-26	[28-53]	
	3:1-20	[41-60]	3:1-27	[54-80]	
	4:1-20	[61-80]			
Rachel Ray	1:1-15				1-30
	2:1-15	[16-30]			
Ralph the Heir	1:1-19				1-58
	2:1-19	[20-38]			
	3:1-20	[39-58]			
The Small House at Allington	1:1-30		1:1-20		1-60
	2:1-30	[31-60]	2:1-19	[20-39]	
			3:1-21	[40-60]	
The Three Clerks	1:1-16				1-48
	2:1-14	[17-30]			
	3:1-18	[31-48]			
La Vendée	1:1-9				1-34
	2:1-12	[10-21]			
	3:1-13	[22-34]			
The Vicar of Bullhampton	1-73		1:1-37		1-73
			2:1-36	[38-73]	
The Way We Live Now	1:1-50				1-100
	2:51-100				
An Autobiography	1:1-10		1-20		1-20
	2:11-20				

NOTE: The chapter divisions in a few later editions have been changed. See in this table *The Belton Estate; The Kellys and the O'Kellys*. In the 4th ed. of *La Vendée*, Chapman and Hall, 1875, chapter 9 is repeated, but with a total numbering of 34 chapters. There may be other variations in editions not examined.

A GUIDE TO TROLLOPE

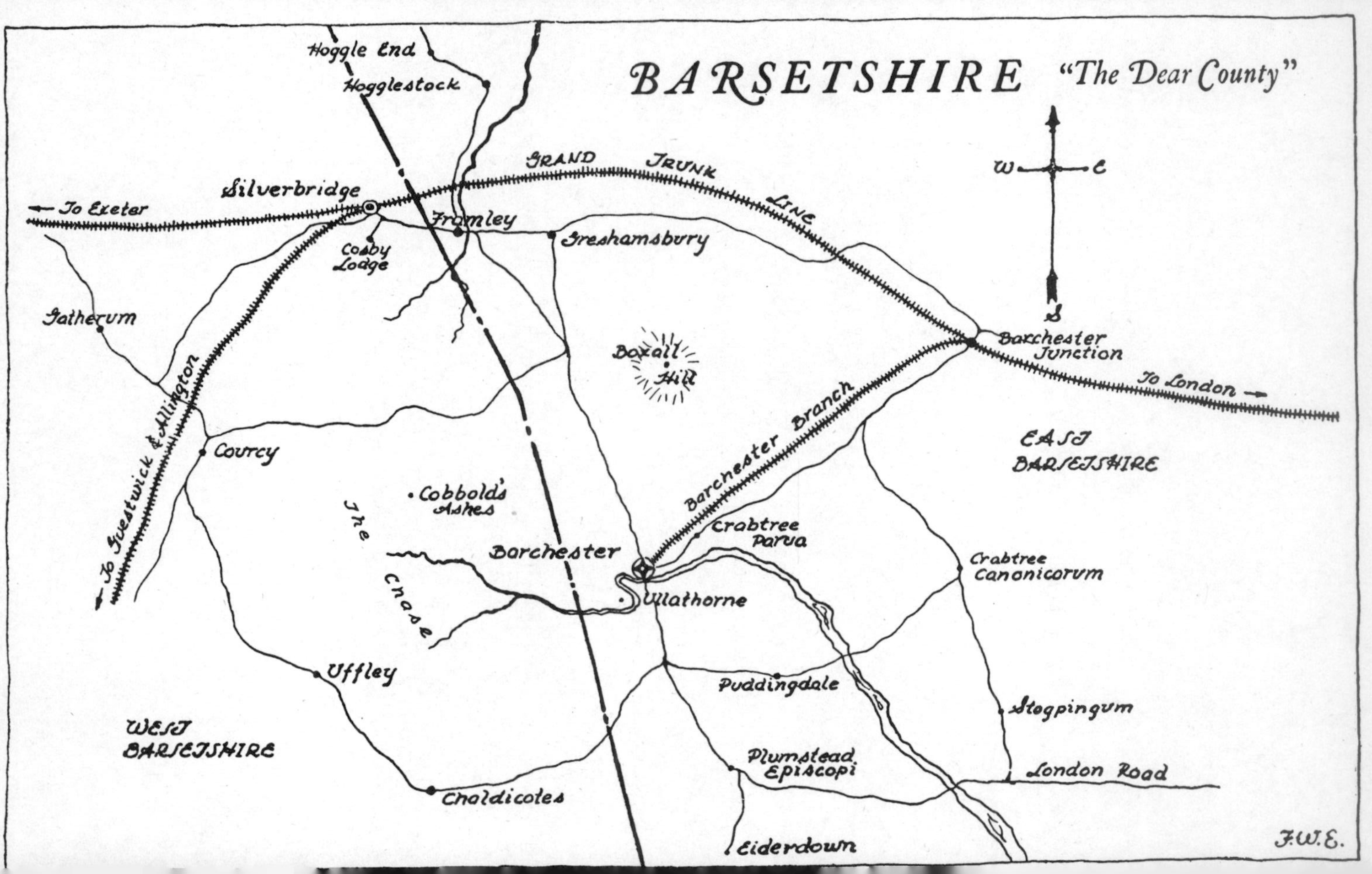
BARSETSHIRE "The Dear County"
W
E
S
Hoggle End
Hogglestock
Grand Trunk Line
Silverbridge
To Exeter
Fromley
Cosby Lodge
Greshamsbury
Gatherum
To Guestwick & Allington
Courcy
Boxall Hill
Barchester Junction
To London
Barchester Branch
East Barsetshire
Cobbold's Ashes
The Chase
Barchester
Crabtree Parva
Crabtree Canonicorum
Ullathorne
Uffley
Puddingdale
Stogpingum
West Barsetshire
Plumstead Episcopi
London Road
Choldicotes
Eiderdown
F.W.E.

A GUIDE TO TROLLOPE

AARON TROW. In *Tales of All Countries*, Second Series, 1863. Originally published in *Public Opinion*, Dec. 14, 21, 1861.

Plot. An English convict, Aaron Trow, was sent to the penal colony at Bermuda under a life sentence for murder. He escaped from prison and hid in a remote cave until search for him was abandoned. Driven by hunger, and fearing detection until he could find means to leave the island, he broke into the isolated cottage of Anastasia Bergen, demanding food and money. Terrified by his uncouth appearance and menacing manner, she prepared food for him, but when she failed to provide money he attacked, and nearly murdered her before help came. Caleb Morton, Anastasia's fiancé, at the risk of his life, cornered Trow in his cave and in a dramatic battle on the rocks and in the sea killed him.

ABCHURCH STREET. *See* London

ACORN, LAWRENCE. An accomplice of John Burrows in the murder of Farmer Trumbull. *Vicar* 46-47, 51, 69

ACROBATS (club). *See* London

ACTIVE SERVICE (club). *See* London

ADAM STREET. *See* London

ADAMSON, JACK. A mining partner of John Caldigate in New South Wales, who joined with Crinkett in a conspiracy against John, but later confessed his perjury. *Caldigate* 27-29, 41, 50, 55

ADVENTURES OF FRED PICKERING, The. In *Lotta Schmidt and Other Stories*, 1867. Originally published in *The Argosy*, Sept. 1866, under the title: *The Misfortunes of Fred Pickering*.

Plot. Fred Pickering, articled to a Manchester attorney, found the law distasteful and, because he had had a few poems printed, broke with his father, married a penniless girl and went to London where he hoped to make his living by writing. He gave up his first position because he considered it beneath his deserts and hunted in vain for a suitable one. A year later, his funds completely exhausted, he appealed to his father for help and returned to Manchester with his wife and baby, where he entered an attorney's office at thirty shillings a week.

AGRA, BISHOP OF. The Abbé de Folleville, who, for reasons never clearly understood, called himself the "Bishop of Agra." He appeared before the defeated and discouraged peasants at the battle of Saumur, and by his presence, his blessing and the celebration of the mass inspired them to fresh exertion. *Vendée* 9

AHALALA. A mining town in New South Wales, where John Caldigate made his fortune. *Caldigate* 11-12

AHASERAGH. The Irish village where Black Tom Daly had his kennels, which were later burned by the Landleaguers. *Land.* 9

AIREY FORCE. A waterfall near Humblethwaite, where George Hotspur proposed to Emily and was accepted. *Hotspur* 8

ALASCO. The tutor of Gentle Euphemia, who concocted the antidote for the poisoned arrow and so saved the life of the Lord of Mountfidget. *Euphemia*

ALBURY, SIR HARRY. The good-natured MFH of the Rufford and Ufford United pack, who entertained Ayala Dormer at his country place at

Stalham and loaned her his pony "Croppy" for the hunting. Appears frequently in *Ayala's Angel*.

ALBURY, ROSALINE, LADY. Sister of the Marchesa Baldoni, and cousin of Colonel Stubbs, whom she helped in his suit for Ayala Dormer's hand. Appears frequently in *Ayala's Angel*.

ALDERSHOT. Col. Jonathan Stubbs was a staff officer at Aldershot. *Ayala* 31

ALEXANDRINA COTTAGE. The home of the tailor Neefit and his daughter Polly, in Hendon. Mentioned frequently in *Ralph the Heir*.

ALF, FERDINAND. The editor of the "Evening Pulpit," and one of Lady Carbury's literary friends. He opposed Augustus Melmotte in the Westminster election, but was defeated. "He was a good-looking man, about forty years old, but carrying himself as though he was much younger, spare, below the middle height, with dark hair which would have shown a tinge of grey but for the dyer's art, with well-cut features, with a smile constantly on his mouth the pleasantness of which was always belied by the sharp severity of his eyes. He dressed with the utmost simplicity, but also with the utmost care" (1:1:6). Appears frequently in *The Way We Live Now*.

ALICE DUGDALE. In *Why Frau Frohmann Raised Her Prices and Other Stories*, 1882. Originally published in *Good Cheer*, Christmas number of *Good Words*, Dec. 1878.

PLOT. Alice Dugdale, the eldest daughter of a village doctor and a drudge and nursemaid for his second wife, had grown up with the vicar's son John Rossiter. When he returned from the wars a major, the villagers assumed that they would marry. However, Lady Wanless had selected John as a husband for her second daughter, Georgiana, and pursued him with more vigor than tact. John could not but compare the advantages of county as against village, but his love for Alice won over his ambition.

ALLAN, The REV. MR. A Wesleyan minister in New South Wales, who was alleged to have married John Caldigate and Euphemia Smith. *Caldigate* 29-30, 37, 41

ALLEWINDE, MR. A Dublin lawyer for the Crown at Thady Macdermot's trial for the murder of Myles Ussher. *Macdermots* 28-32

ALLINGTON. The parish in Barchester in which the Dales had lived for generations. There was no inn in the village but "a public-house, with a very nice clean bedroom," called the Red Lion. Most prominent in *The Small House at Allington*; mentioned frequently in *The Last Chronicle of Barset*.

"ALMSHOUSE." A novel by Mr. Popular Sentiment, whose theme was the injustice of the Ecclesiastical Courts in the handling of church endowments. It was aimed at the management of Hiram's Hospital and similar institutions. *Warden* 15

ALSTON. The assize town near Noningsby, the scene of the second Orley Farm trial. *Orley* 11, 64

ALSTON, LORD. An old friend of Sir Peregrine Orme, who remonstrated with him over his proposed marriage to Lady Mason. *Orley* 28, 44, 55, 76

ALTIFIORLA, FRANCESCA. A malicious busybody in Exeter, who discovered that when Cecilia Holt married George Western she did not tell him that she had jilted Sir Francis Geraldine. She and Sir Francis united to

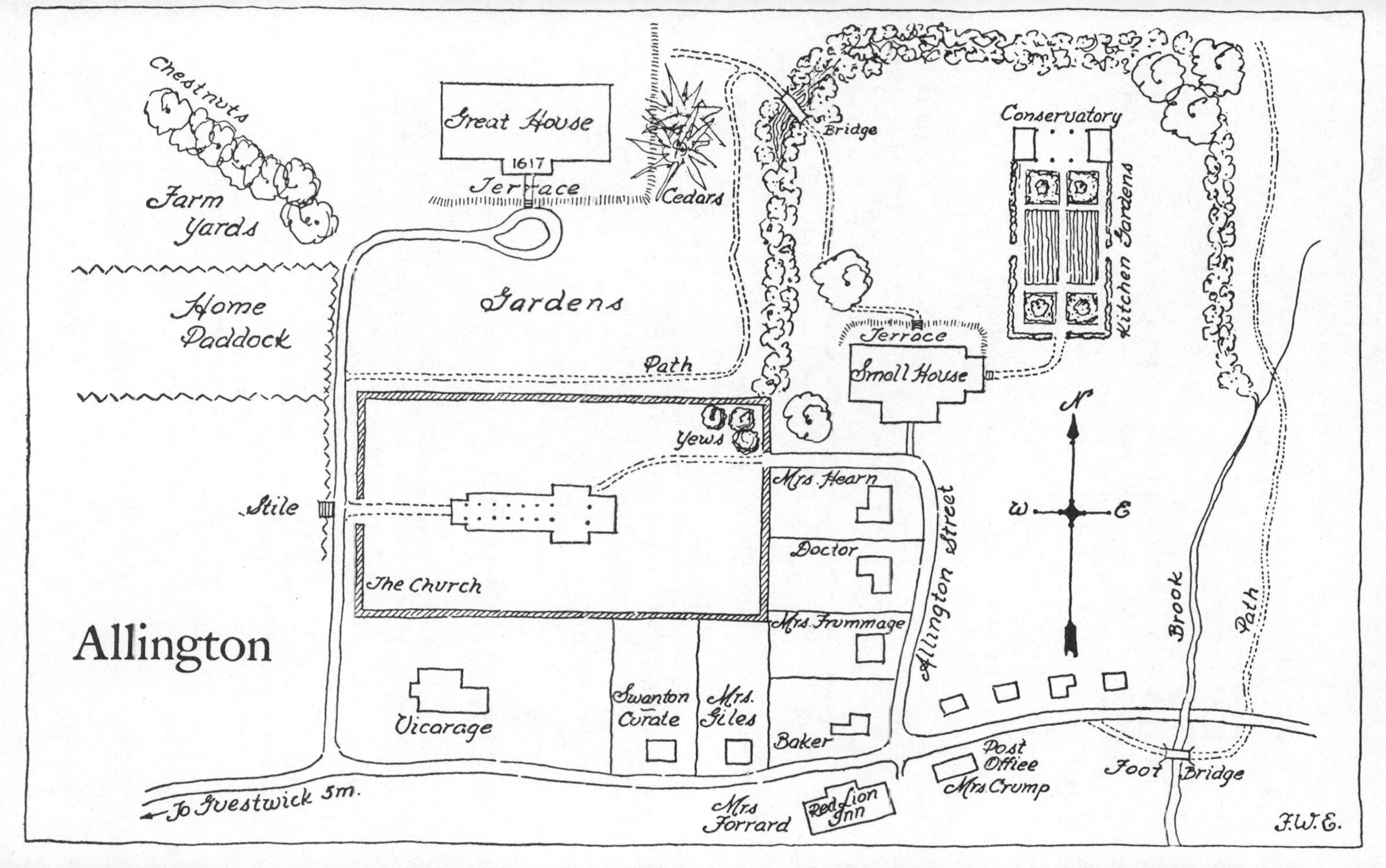
Chestnuts
Great House
1617
Terrace
Cedars
Bridge
Conservatory
Kitchen Gardens
Farm Yards
Home Paddock
Gardens
Path
Terrace
Small House
Yews
N
W
E
Stile
Mrs. Hearn
Doctor
The Church
Allington Street
Mrs. Frummage
Brook
Path
Allington
Vicarage
Swanton Curate
Mrs. Giles
Baker
Post Office
Mrs. Crump
Foot Bridge
To Guestwick 5m.
Mrs Forrard
Red Lion Inn
F.W.E.

make trouble for Cecilia that ended in her husband's desertion. Francesca failed, however, to ensnare Sir Francis for herself. One of the principal characters in *Kept in the Dark*.

ALTRINGHAM, EARL OF. A friend of George Hotspur, who understood his disposition well enough to refuse to lend him money. *Hotspur* 5-6

ALTRINGHAM, LADY. George Hotspur's sympathetic friend, who tried to help him win Emily Hotspur, although she knew that it was Emily's money he wanted. *Hotspur* 7, 9-10, 18, 20-22

AMAILLOU. A village in La Vendée, sacked and burned by Westermann, who was later attacked there by Larochejaquelin and Lescure and driven back. *Vendée* 16

AMBLETHWAITE, MR. MFH of the Braeside Harriers. *Fay* 12-14, 23

AMEDROZ, BERNARD. The life tenant of the Belton estate, and father of Clara and Charles. A hypochondriac, much broken by his son's suicide. "Mr. Amedroz was not a bad man,—as men are held to be bad in the world's esteem. He was not vicious,—was not a gambler or a drunkard,—was not self-indulgent to a degree that brought upon him any reproach; nor was he regardless of his children. But he was an idle, thriftless man, who, at the age of sixty-seven . . . had as yet done no good in the world whatever. . . . He was a large man, who had been very handsome, and who now, in his yellow leaf, was not without a certain beauty of manliness. He wore his hair and his beard long. . . . And though he stooped, there was still a dignity in his slow step" (1:1:1-2; 12-13). *Belton* 1-6, 12-13, 15-22

AMEDROZ, MRS. BERNARD (Winterfield). Mother of Charles and Clara, who died when they were children. Through her there was a relationship with Mrs. Winterfield of Perivale, who was supposed to have made Clara her heir. *Belton* 1

AMEDROZ, CHARLES. The heir to the Belton estate, who wasted both his own patrimony and that of his sister Clara. Expelled from Harrow and Trinity, he became a gambler and a frequenter of Newmarket until his debts led him to take his own life. At his death the estate reverted to Will Belton. *Belton* 1.

AMEDROZ, CLARA. Engaged for a time to marry the dashing Captain Aylmer, when he thought she was Mrs. Winterfield's heir. When he inherited the money, his changed attitude toward Clara convinced her of the unworthy motive of his proposal and she jilted him. Later she married Will Belton, a distant cousin, who had become owner of her old home.

". . . a handsome young woman, tall, well-made, active, and full of health. She carried herself as though she thought her limbs were made for use, and not simply for ease upon a sofa. Her head and neck stood well upon her shoulders, and her waist showed none of those waspish proportions of which ladies used to be more proud than I believe them to be now . . ." (1:4:87-88).

Heroine of *The Belton Estate*.

AMERICAN SENATOR, The. London, Chapman and Hall, 1877. 3v.

NOTES. "*The American Senator* will be read for the sake of its opening chapters, which set before the reader in a few pages the whole geographical and social pattern of an English county; for the sake of its hunting episodes, which are among the best not only in Trollope, but in the whole of English fiction; and for the sake of Arabella Trefoil, a masterly study of a girl without a heart, who may be compared with Molière's Célimène and even with Beatrix in *Esmond.*"—Sadleir, p. 397.

PLOT. The estate of Bragton Hall, for many years the property of the Morton family, came into the hands of John Morton, secretary of the British Legation in Washington. He returned to England accompanied by his fiancée Arabella Trefoil, her mother Lady Augustus and an American Senator, Elias Gotobed. The Senator was intent on a study of English life and John Morton undertook to introduce him to it. After a brief visit to Bragton Hall the party moved on to Rufford Hall, home of a wealthy, sporting bachelor, Lord Rufford.

Arabella, an unabashed fortune-hunter with numerous matrimonial adventures behind her, judged that a more profitable marriage might be arranged for herself with Lord Rufford than with John Morton, and schemed to make him propose to her. He indulged in a certain amount of philandering, gave her a riding horse, and she announced that he had asked for her hand. This he vigorously denied, but Lady Augustus charged him with a breach-of-promise, and demanded £8000 to soothe her daughter's broken heart. Arabella indignantly rejected this bargain, thinking that by skillful play the prize might yet be won. When John Morton, who still considered himself engaged to her, became seriously ill, she confessed her treachery to him and gave up her pursuit of Lord Rufford. John died, leaving her £5000, and with this legacy she married the recently appointed Ambassador to Patagonia, Mounser Green. To his cousin Reginald Morton, John left the estate.

Mary Masters, daughter of the Morton family attorney, had lived as a young girl at Bragton Hall with the cousins' aunt Lady Ushant, as her companion, and had loved Reginald since they were children there together. Lawrence Twentyman, a neighboring gentleman-farmer, was eager to make her his wife, with the backing of Mary's stepmother. When she refused him, her own home became unbearable to her and she again took refuge with Lady Ushant. Reginald followed and asked her to marry him.

The American Senator had formed his opinions of English rural life through his acquaintance with John Morton's friends, and concluded his visit to England with a lecture in St. James Hall in which he frankly but good-humoredly criticized English manners and customs. The speech was not well received by some of the audience, and the Senator was escorted out a back entrance for his own safety. On arriving in the United States he straightway lectured to his countrymen in praise of English institutions.

AMERICANS in Trollope's works. Although Trollope always felt that his mother's book, *The Domestic Manners of the Americans*, was somewhat less than generous, the American characters he portrayed in his own novels are far from eulogistic. Of the thirty-four who played any but incidental roles, Hamilton Fisker, Mahomet Moss and the Lefroy brothers were rogues, Gerald O'Mahony a loud-mouthed and irresponsible agitator; Phineas Beckard and Hetta Bell religious fanatics, narrow-minded and dictatorial; Olivia Q. Peabody, Wallachia Petrie and Rachel O'Mahony strong-minded women in search of a career—of the sort Trollope constantly decried; while Winifred Hurtle, Lucinda Roanoke, Madame Socani and Ella Peacocke were none of them equipped with a lily-white past. He notes one scholar, Ezekiel Boncassen, but deplores the fact that his father was "an American labouring man"; two diplomats, Elias Gotobed, who accepted English hospitality, the while criticizing his hosts and their society openly, and Jonas Spaulding, an ineffectual Ambassador to Italy. Miss

Ophelia Gledd, probably drawn from Kate Field, is described as having such an inferiority complex that, though she is shown as a favorite in Boston society, she feared that she would not be considered a "lady" in English society—an idea quite foreign to the real Kate Field. Isabel Boncassen is charming and beautiful, though her mental attainments are felt to be lower than would be desirable in the high position she is to occupy as the wife of Lord Silverbridge. All in all, Trollope's American portraits fall far short of his English ones. His very Britishness made any other result impossible.

Beckard, The Rev. Phineas. *Courtship*
Bell, Mrs., and her daughters, Hetta and Susan. *Courtship*
Boncassen, Ezekiel, his wife, and daughter Isabel. *Duke*
Dunn, Aaron. *Courtship*
Fisker, Hamilton. *Way We Live*
Fleabody, Olivia Q. *Popenjoy*
Forster, Ada. *Generals*
Frew, Frederic F. *Widow*
Gledd, Miss Ophelia. *Gledd*
Gotobed, Elias. *Amer. Sen., Duke*
Hoskins, Hannibal. *Gledd*
Hurtle, Mrs. Winifred. *Way We Live*
Ingram, Jefferson. *Unprotected*
Lefroy, Ferdinand and Robert. *Wortle*
Mackinnon, Mr. and Mrs. Conrad. *Talboys*
Moss, Mahomet M. *Land.*
O'Mahony, Gerald, and his daughter Rachel. *Land.*
Peacocke, Mrs. Ella. *Wortle*
Petrie, Wallachia. *He Knew*
Reckenthorpe, Major, and his two sons, Frank and Tom. *Generals*
Roanoke, Lucinda. *Eustace*
Socani, Madame. *Land.*
Spaulding, Jonas, and his nieces, Caroline and Olivia. *He Knew*
Unthank, Jackson. *He Knew*

AMSEL, HEINRICH. Implicated in the theft of Fritz Rosenheim's box. *Katchen*

AMSEL, LOTTA. Heinrich's mother. *Katchen*

ANDERSON, HUGH. The second secretary at the Brussels Legation, an unsuccessful suitor for the hand of Florence Mountjoy. Of minor importance, but appears frequently in *Mr. Scarborough's Family.*

ANGERS. Captured by the Vendeans under the leadership of Cathelineau, but evacuated because the peasants would not stand guard. Barrêre, Westermann and Santerre met there to plan the extermination of the Royalists. *Vendée* 15

ANNESLEY, The REV. and MRS. The Rector of Buston, and father of Harry, Fanny, Kate and Mary. Mrs. Annesley was the sister of Peter Prosper. Appear frequently in *Mr. Scarborough's Family.*

ANNESLEY, HARRY. The heir of his uncle Peter Prosper, the Squire of Buston, who because of his prospects grew up with no profession. In love with Florence Mountjoy, he was in complete disfavor with her mother because he had become innocently involved in the Scarborough plot. His uncle threatened to disown him, but the young lovers were not to be thwarted, and were finally permitted to marry. ". . . light-haired, with long silken beard, and bright eyes . . . there was usually present to his face a look of infinite joy, which was comfortable to all beholders" (3:61:268). One of the principal characters in *Mr. Scarborough's Family.*

ANTICANT, DR. PESSIMIST. A pamphleteer, whose publication "Modern Charity" held Mr. Harding up to scorn. Presumed to be a satirical portrait of Carlyle. *Warden* 15

ANTWERP. The setting for *Relics of General Chassé.*

APJOHN, MR. A Barchester attorney, one of the leading citizens, and favorably known to the old Duke of Omnium. *Thorne* 19

APJOHN, NICHOLAS. The lawyer for Indefer Jones and the maker of his many wills. Although he had quarreled with his client, he was confident that a will not of his drawing had been made, and persevered until it was found. *Cousin* 5-8, 10-14, 17-24

APPLEDOM, MR. One of Violet Effingham's many suitors, approved by Lady Baldock. ". . . one of the richest commoners in England, a fine Conservative too, with a seat in the House, and everything appropriate. He was fifty, but looked hardly more than thirty-five, and was . . . violently in love with Violet Effingham" (2:45:58). *Finn* 45

ARABIN, MRS. ELEANOR (Harding). The younger daughter of the Rev. Mr. Harding and much pursued by suitors, John Bold, Mr. Slope, Bertie Stanhope and Mr. Arabin. She married John Bold and had one child, Johnnie. Her second husband was Mr. Arabin, their children being Eleanor ("Ellie") and Susan, called "Posy."

"There was a quiet, enduring, grateful sweetness about her face. . . . Her loveliness was like that of many landscapes, which require to be often seen to be fully enjoyed. There was a depth of dark clear brightness in her eyes which was lost upon a quick observer, a character about her mouth which showed itself to those with whom she familiarly conversed, a glorious form of head the perfect symmetry of which required the eye of an artist for its appreciation" (*Barchester* 1:16:240-41).

Most prominent in *The Warden* and *Barchester Towers*; appears frequently in *Doctor Thorne, Framley Parsonage* and *The Last Chronicle of Barset.*

In the play *Did He Steal It?*, she is represented by Mrs. Lofty, and is described as "a benevolent old lady belonging to Silverbridge."

ARABIN, The REV. FRANCIS. Successively a Fellow at Lazarus, Vicar of St. Ewold's and Dean of the Cathedral of Barchester. He was a classmate and a constant friend of Mr. Crawley. He married Eleanor Harding Bold.

". . . the favoured disciple of the great Dr. Gwynne, a high churchman . . . a poet and also a polemical writer . . . an eloquent clergyman, a droll, odd, humourous, energetic, conscientious man . . . a thorough gentleman. . . . He was above the middle height, well made, and very active. His hair which had been jet black, was now tinged with gray, but his face bore no signs of years. . . . The cheek bones were rather too high for beauty, and the formation of the forehead too massive and heavy; but the eyes, nose and mouth were perfect. There was a continual play of lambent fire about his eyes, which gave promise of either pathos or humour whenever he essayed to speak, and that promise was rarely broken. There was a gentle play about his mouth which declared that his wit never descended to sarcasm, and that there was no ill-nature in his repartee" (*Barchester* 1:14:208; 2:1:11-12).

Most prominent in *Barchester Towers* and *The Last Chronicle of Barset*; appears frequently in *Framley Parsonage* and *Doctor Thorne.*

ARABIN, SUSAN ("Posy"). Mr. Harding's youngest granddaughter, a great delight and comfort to him in his old age. *Last Chron.* 49, 58, 67, 81

ARAM, SOLOMON. An attorney of rather dubious reputation, who acted for Lady Mason at the second trial of the Orley Farm case. *Orley* 53, 61-65, 67, 70-71, 75

ARBUTHNOT, MRS. ISABELLA (Staveley). The elder daughter of Judge Staveley, who, with her three children, was a guest at Noningsby during the Christmas holidays. *Orley* 22, 30, 57, 65

ARBUTHNOT, MARION. A charming young granddaughter of Judge Staveley, who was much attached to Felix Graham. *Orley* 22, 27-28

ARCHER, MAURICE. A young man just out of Oxford, in love with Isabel Lownd. "He had a snub nose; and a man so visaged can hardly be good-looking. . . . But he was a well-made young fellow, having a look of power about him, with dark-brown hair, cut very short, close-shorn, with clear but rather small blue eyes, and an expression of countenance which allowed no one for a moment to think that he was weak in character, or a fool" (1:3). One of the principal characters in *Christmas Day at Kirkby Cottage.*

ARDKILL COTTAGE. The home of Mrs. O'Hara and her daughter Kate, on a cliff overlooking the sea in County Clare, Ireland. The setting for much of *An Eye for an Eye*, described in chapter 5.

ARKWRIGHT, HARRY. A young English planter in Costa Rica, whose wife and child were drowned on the first lap of their return home to England. One of the principal characters in *Returning Home.*

ARMSTRONG, The REV. JOSEPH. The rector at Ballindine, who helped Lord Ballindine to make his peace with Lord Cashel, and to drive Barry Lynch out of the country. Sometimes called "George." "His children were helpless, uneducated, and improvident; his wife was nearly worn out with the labours of bringing them forth and afterwards catering for them; and a great portion of his own life was taken up in a hard battle with tradesmen and title-payers, creditors, and debtors" (2:7:157). *Kellys* 21, 26, 34-38

ARMSTRONG, MRS. JULIA (Brown). A horsy young woman, only daughter of Jonas Brown, whose behavior led her family "to fear she was coming out a little too fast; and that if they did not get rid of her now, she might in a short time become a card somewhat too hard to play. . . . Miss Julia could not only ride with her brothers in the morning, but . . . drink with them of an evening" (2:7:203). *Macdermots* 19

ARMSTRONG, TOBY. ". . . a squireen of three or four hundred a year," who was invited to Brown Hall for the purpose of inducing him to marry the unwanted Julia and ". . . not relishing pistols and coffee, made no objection to the young lady" (2:7:203-4). *Macdermots* 19

ARUNDEL STREET. *See* London

ASKERTON, COLONEL. A retired officer, who had been in the India service. He leased the shooting at Belton Castle and lived in seclusion at Belton Cottage. One of the principal characters in *The Belton Estate.*

ASKERTON, MRS. MARY. Wife of the Colonel, and the subject of malicious gossip in the neighborhood of Belton Cottage. As a young woman she had married Jack Berdmore, a drunkard who abused her. She left him in company with Colonel Askerton, but

Jack would not divorce her, and her marriage was postponed until after he drank himself to death. Her only intimate friend was Clara Amedroz. One of the principal characters in *The Belton Estate*.

AUGHACASHEL. A mountain near Ballycloran, where Thady Macdermot went into hiding after he had killed Myles Ussher. *Macdermots* 23

AULD REEKIE, MARCHIONESS OF. Helped to make the Melmottes socially accepted by attending Marie Melmotte's great coming-out ball. *Can You* 18; *Way We Live* 4

AULD REEKIE, MARQUIS OF. Uncle and guardian of Lady Glencora MacCluskie who arranged her marriage to Plantagenet Palliser. He insisted that his son Lord Nidderdale should try to marry Marie Melmotte for her money. *Allington* 55; *Can You* 18; *Way We Live* 4, 21, 29, 54, 57

AYALA'S ANGEL. London, Chapman and Hall, 1881. 3v.

Notes. ". . . possibly the most unjustly neglected of all Trollope's novels . . . and yet it is one of the most charming of all the long list. It is the lightest and airiest of them all, it has a gaiety and happiness and playfulness that Trollope, gay and happy though he often was, never exceeded. . . . what vigour of scene and creation, what vitality of action and dialogue it contains." —Walpole, p. 158.

Plot. The death of Egbert Dormer, a successful but improvident artist, left his two daughters, Lucy and Ayala, with no means of support. Their aunt had married a wealthy City banker, Sir Thomas Tringle, and their uncle Reginald Dosett had a meager income as an Admiralty clerk. Each offered a home to one of the sisters and Ayala, because she was charming and vivacious, was chosen by Lady Tringle. The two unattractive Tringle daughters soon became jealous of Ayala's social success, and the loutish son Tom promptly fell in love with her. Lady Tringle effected an exchange of wards, sending Ayala to the comparative poverty of the Dosett home.

Ayala's romantic nature, fostered by her happy, carefree childhood, adored by her father and admired by all his artistic circle, led her to expect a husband who would be an "Angel of light." Tom Tringle did not fit into that picture, nor did her second suitor, Captain Batsby. When Jonathan Stubbs, red-haired, red-faced, noisy but devoted, came, he did not seem at first to be her "Angel," but his persistence finally won her. Lucy, meantime, living in magnificence in the Tringle household, had engaged herself to a young sculptor and, with a generous dot from her uncle, they were able to marry.

Sir Thomas was not so fortunate in the marriages of his own daughters. The elder, Augusta, with a dowry of £120,000 ensnared the Honorable Septimus Traffic, an MP and son of Lord Boardotrade. Septimus, regardless of the dowry, was too parsimonious to provide a separate establishment for his wife and, despite all the urging of his irate father-in-law, they continued to live with the family. The amount of Augusta's dowry being known, the younger sister, Gertrude, was sought by the impecunious Frank Houston. Sir Thomas, angered by this obvious fortune-hunting, declared that Gertrude should have no fortune at all and Frank speedily withdrew. Gertrude was furious at her father's injustice and persuaded Captain Batsby to elope with her to Ostend, hoping that Sir Thomas would relent and support them. Tom's pursuit of Ayala led him into various escapades from which his father finally wearied of rescuing him, and he was shipped off on a long sea-voyage.

AYLMER, LADY. The domineering mistress of Aylmer Park, greatly feared and slavishly obeyed by family and servants. Sister of Mrs. Winterfield. "She had been a beauty on a large scale, and was still aware that she had much in her personal appearance which justified pride. She carried herself uprightly, with a commanding nose and broad forehead; and though the graces of her own hair had given way to a front, there was something even in the front which added to her dignity, if it did not make her a handsome woman" (2:6:146). *Belton* 17-19, 21-28

AYLMER, ANTHONY. Son and heir of Sir Anthony, but not on good terms with the family. *Belton* 17

AYLMER, SIR ANTHONY. Frederick's hen-pecked father, owner of Aylmer Park in Yorkshire, and Clara Amedroz' only friend in the family. "He was a heavy man, over seventy years of age, much afflicted with gout, and given to no pursuit on earth which was available for his comfort. . . . He was a big man, with a broad chest, and a red face, and a quantity of white hair, —and was much given to abusing his servants" (2:6:143). *Belton* 17, 19, 23, 25-28

AYLMER, BELINDA. Captain Aylmer's sister, completely dominated by her mother. ". . . as ignorant, meek, and stupid a poor woman as you shall find anywhere in Europe" (2:6:148). *Belton* 17, 19, 25-26

AYLMER, CAPT. FREDERICK FOLLIOTT. Son of Sir Anthony, and nephew and heir of Mrs. Winterfield. MP for Perivale. His engagement to Clara Amedroz was broken through the influence of his masterful mother, who had chosen Lady Emily Tagmaggert to be his wife. One of the principal characters in *The Belton Estate*.

AYLMER PARK. The home of the Aylmers, in Yorkshire, where Clara Amedroz, as the fiancée of Frederick, was entertained. She was severely snubbed by Lady Aylmer, who had other plans for her son's future. "The place was more distinguished for its style, and the number of its servants than for the quality and plentifulness of its food." *Belton* 17, 19-20, 25-26

BB HUNT. Included hunting men from Berkshire and Buckinghamshire, with headquarters at the Moonbeam in Barnfield. *Ralph* 27, 46

BABINGTON, HUMPHREY. Brother-in-law of Daniel Caldigate, and by him considered a "thick-headed fool." *Caldigate* 1, 16, 27, 32, 58

BABINGTON, JOHN. The eldest son and heir of Humphrey. *Caldigate* 1

BABINGTON, JULIA. *See* Smirkie, Mrs. Julia (Babington)

BABINGTON, MRS. MARY ANNE ("Aunt Polly"). John Caldigate's aunt, in whose home he spent much time when a boy. Her plan to marry him to her daughter Julia miscarried and she became his bitter enemy. Appears frequently in *John Caldigate*.

BABINGTON HOUSE. The home of the Babington family, in Suffolk, where John Caldigate spent much of his youth. The setting for many scenes in *John Caldigate*.

BACON, FRANCIS (real person). Sir Thomas Underwood spent many years gathering material for a life of Bacon which he never wrote. *Ralph* 40

BADEN-BADEN. Where the Countess de Courcy established herself after she had left her husband, and where Lady Alexandrina joined her ten weeks after her marriage with Adolphus Crosbie. Lady Alexandrina died there. *Allington* 56

BADGER and BLISTER. Mrs. Brumby's lawyers. *Brumby*

BAGGETT, MRS. A talkative but devoted housekeeper for Mr. Whittlestaff. One of the principal characters in *An Old Man's Love.*

BAGGETT, SERGEANT. The drunken husband of Mrs. Baggett, ". . . a most disreputable man with a wooden leg and a red nose." *Old Man* 10-12, 19, 22

BAGWAX, SAMUEL. A Post Office clerk, who, at the trial of John Caldigate, proved that the postmark on an envelope that was introduced as evidence was forged and that the stamp was issued at a later date. (One of the few instances where Trollope introduced his professional knowledge.) Sometimes called "Tom." He married Jemima Curlydown. *Caldigate* 47-48, 52-56, 64

BAILEY, CATHERINE. The fiancée of Mr. Whittlestaff in his youth, who jilted him and married Mr. Compas. *Old Man* 2

BAIRD, CATHERINE. *See* Carmichael, Mrs. Catherine (Baird)

BAKER, HENRY. A young friend of John de Courcy and Frank Gresham, interested chiefly in horses. A student at Cambridge, and a confidant of Frank in the affair of the thrashing of Mr. Moffat. *Thorne* 4-5, 21, 44

BAKER, MARY. Niece of George Bertram, Sr., who lived in lodgings at Littlebath with her niece Caroline Waddington. She met Sir Lionel Bertram when in Palestine with her old friend Miss Todd, and only escaped marriage with him because she had no fortune. One of the principal characters in *The Bertrams*; briefly in *Mackenzie* 3-5, 9-13

BAKER STREET. *See* London

BALATKA, JOSEF. A bankrupt and bed-ridden merchant of Prague, who was for a time a partner of the Jew Stephen Trendellsohn. The children of the two partners fell in love, and met opposition from both families. Josef was at first heartbroken at the thought of the marriage, but before his death became reconciled to it. *Nina* 1-5, 9, 13-14

BALATKA, NINA. The novel that bears her name begins: "Nina Balatka was a maiden of Prague, born of Christian parents, and herself a Christian—but she loved a Jew; and this is her story" (1:1:1). "Nina was fair, with grey eyes, and smooth brown hair which . . . did in truth add greatly to the sweet delicacy of her face; and she was soft in her gait, and appeared to be yielding and flexible in all the motions of her body" (1:7:180). Heroine of *Nina Balatka.*

BALDOCK, LADY. Violet Effingham's aunt and self-appointed guardian, who was violently opposed to Violet's marriage to Lord Chiltern. She was the mother of Gustavus, Lord Baldock and the Hon. Augusta Borcham. Most prominent in *Phineas Finn*; also mentioned, when she visited Violet and Lord Chiltern at Harrington, in *Redux* 2

BALDONI, BEATRICE, MARCHESA D'. A charming Englishwoman living with her titled husband and daughter in Rome. She befriended Ayala Dormer and introduced her to Colonel Stubbs, the Marchesa's cousin. Appears frequently in *Ayala's Angel.*

BALDONI, NINA. Daughter of the Marchesa, and a warm friend and confidante of Ayala Dormer. She married Lord George Bideford. Appears frequently in *Ayala's Angel.*

BALL, LADY. John's mother, who disapproved of his marriage with Margaret Mackenzie. One of the principal characters in *Miss Mackenzie.*

BALL, JOHN (later Sir John). A widower with nine children and no money, who felt cheated when the fortune he expected to inherit was left to his uncles. When Margaret Mackenzie fell heir to the money, he was persuaded by his domineering mother to ask her to marry him. He did so in a half-hearted way, but finally found himself in love with her. He was greatly depressed at her refusal, but after it was learned that he was the true heir, he persuaded her to marry him. One of the principal characters in *Miss Mackenzie.*

BALL, SIR JOHN. The cantankerous head of the Ball family, whose life was embittered by his brother Jonathan's perfidy in leaving his fortune to the Mackenzie brothers rather than to the younger John Ball. *Mackenzie* 1-2, 6-9, 16-23

BALL, JONATHAN. Brother of Sir John Ball, who, by leaving his fortune to his nephews, the Mackenzie brothers, was later discovered to have left money he did not possess. The wills, and the use of the money, are the background for *Miss Mackenzie.*

BALLINAMORE. A village in County Leitrim, headquarters of Captain Greenough, sub-inspector of police. *Macdermots* 4

BALLINASLOW ASYLUM. Where Barry Lynch hoped to have his sister Anty confined so that he could gain control of her fortune. *Kellys* 5

BALLINDINE, LORD, Francis John O'Kelly ("Frank"). The landlord and distant relative of Martin Kelly. His engagement to Fanny Wyndham was broken off by her guardian because of his horse-racing affiliations and his poverty. After Fanny refused to marry her guardian's son, her engagement to Frank was renewed.

"Frank was a very handsome fellow, full six feet high, with black hair, and jet-black silky whiskers, meeting under his chin. . . . He had an eye like a hawk, round, bright and bold; a mouth and chin almost too well-formed for a man; and that kind of broad forehead which conveys rather the idea of a generous, kind, open-hearted disposition, than of a deep mind or a commanding intellect" (1:2:39).

One of the two heroes in *The Kellys and the O'Kellys.*

BALLINTUBBER. A parish in County Galway originally owned by the Widow O'Dwyer, purchased by Philip Jones to add to his estate at Castle Morony. *Land.* 1

BALLYCLORAN. The home of the Macdermots, in County Leitrim. The setting for *The Macdermots of Ballycloran.*

BALLYGLASS. A town in County Mayo near Castle Conor. *O'Conors*

BALLYGLUNIN. A village in County Galway, near which Florian Jones was murdered while on his way to give evidence against the Landleaguers. *Land.* 30

BALLYMOY. A small village in County Galway. The setting for *Father Giles of Ballymoy.*

BALLYTOWNGAL. The seat of Sir Nicholas Bodkin, in County Galway. *Land.* 9-10

BALSAM, MR. The barrister selected to represent Henry Jones in his suit for libel. *Cousin* 17

BANGLES, PETER. The junior member of the firm of Burton and Bangles, wine-merchants in Hook Court, who married Madalina Desmolines. *Last Chron.* 75, 86

BANKS OF JORDAN (pub). *See* London

BANMANN, BARONESS. A Bavarian advocate of women's rights, who was brought to London to lecture at the "Disabilities." She lost the control of that organization to Dr. Olivia Q. Fleabody, an American exponent of the same reform. ". . . a very stout woman, about fifty, with a double chin, a considerable moustache, a low, broad forehead, and bright, round, black eyes, very far apart" (1:17:232). *Popenjoy* 16-18, 27, 30, 33, 51, 55-56, 60

BARCHESTER. The scene of all the novels in the Barchester series, and mentioned in a number of the other works, in particular *The Two Heroines of Plumplington.* While not identical at all points with Salisbury, Trollope says: "I visited Salisbury, and whilst wandering there one mid-summer evening round the purlieus of the cathedral, I conceived the story of *The Warden.* . . . I had stood for an hour on the little bridge at Salisbury, and had made out to my own satisfaction the spot on which Hiram's Hospital should stand."—*Autobiography,* 1:5:123.

BROWN BEAR INN. Mr. Reddypalm was the landlord, and cast the deciding vote in the election of Sir Roger Scatcherd to a seat in Parliament. *Thorne*

CATHEDRAL. All the stories of the Barchester series center around the Cathedral and Close. Bishop Grantly and later Bishop Proudie presided over the diocese.

DRAGON OF WANTLY INN AND POSTING HOUSE. Owned by John Bold, and later by Mrs. Arabin. The check Mr. Crawley was accused of stealing was for the rent of this inn. *Last Chron.*

GEORGE AND DRAGON (inn). The headquarters of Mr. Moffat when contesting the election with Sir Roger Scatcherd. *Thorne*

HIGH STREET. Where Mr. Harding took rooms above the chemist's shop after resigning as Warden of the Hospital. *Warden*

HIRAM'S HOSPITAL. The use of the funds to maintain this institution forms the plot of *The Warden.* Mr. Harding and later Mr. Quiverful were the incumbents.

PAKENHAM VILLAS. A group of houses built by John Bold near the Cathedral, in one of which he and his sister lived, and where after his marriage to Eleanor Harding she made her home. *Warden*

ST. CUTHBERT'S. The parish church of which Mr. Harding was rector. *Warden, Barchester*

BARCHESTER, BISHOP OF. *See* Grantly, Bishop; Proudie, Thomas, Bishop

BARCHESTER TOWERS. London, Longmans, 1857. 3v.

AUTHOR'S COMMENT. "In the writing of *Barchester Towers* I took great delight. The Bishop and Mrs. Proudie were very real to me, as were also the troubles of the archdeacon and the loves of Mr. Slope."—*Autobiography,* 1:6:137-38.

NOTES. "It is not . . . his greatest . . . nevertheless it remains as perhaps

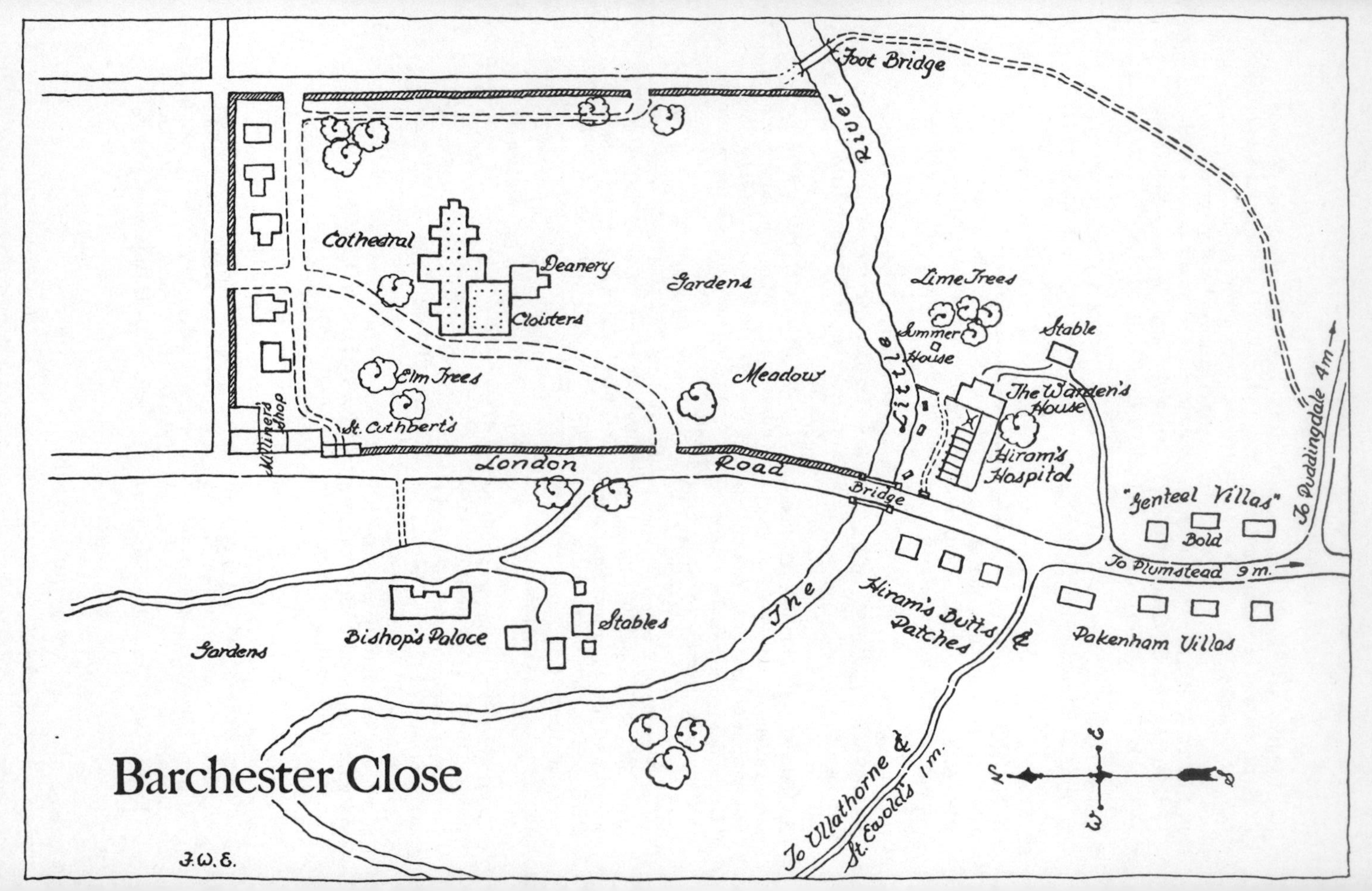
Foot Bridge
River
Little
Cathedral
Deanery
Cloisters
Gardens
Lime Trees
Summer House
Stable
Meadow
Elm Trees
St. Cuthbert's
Milliner's Shop
The Warden's House
Hiram's Hospital
London Road
Bridge
"Genteel Villas"
Bold
To Puddingdale 4m
To Plumstead 9 m.
The
Hiram's Butts & Patches
Pakenham Villas
Stables
Bishop's Palace
Gardens
To Ullathorne & St. Ewold's 1 m.
N
E
S
W
Barchester Close
J.W.E.

the type novel of all the Trollope family. It is the one book of them all that you would give to someone who said to you, 'Now what is Trollope really *like*? What *is* the point about Trollope?' This book introduces and exults over one of the greatest figures in the Barsetshire Chronicles—Mrs. Proudie. . . . The theme, slender as it is, is one eternally attractive—the theme of the biter bit, the bully bullied, the war between tyrants." —Walpole, pp. 48-49.

Plot. *Barchester Towers*, to which *The Warden* forms the prologue, is the story primarily of the contest between Mrs. Proudie, the Bishop's wife, and Mr. Slope, his chaplain, for primacy in the diocese. As an incident in this battle the wardenship of Hiram's Hospital was in question. Against the strenuous advice of his son-in-law Archdeacon Grantly, and following criticism of the administration of the hospital funds, Mr. Harding resigned as Warden. Mrs. Proudie and Mr. Slope united in warring against the high-church party that sought his reinstatement. Mr. Slope, without Mrs. Proudie's knowledge, had rashly offered the wardenship to Mr. Quiverful, but, upon learning that Mr. Harding's widowed daughter Eleanor Bold had an income of £1200, with an eye to the widow's favor he swung to the support of her father.

Not content with this demonstration of his independence, Mr. Slope secured the recall of the Rev. Dr. Vesey Stanhope, a prebendary of the Cathedral who had been living comfortably in Italy for the past twelve years on an income derived from parishes in the diocese. With Dr. Stanhope came his family, two daughters and a son, the latter a charming but worthless young man who joined in the quest for Eleanor Bold's fortune. The second daughter, calling herself Signora Vesey Neroni, although a cripple was yet so attractive as to bewitch almost every man whom she met. Her conquest of Mr. Slope so infuriated Mrs. Proudie that she secured his dismissal, although the Bishop had earlier acquiesced in his ambition to become Dean of the Cathedral.

Mr. Arabin, a brilliant young churchman from Oxford, and Vicar of St. Ewold's, married Eleanor Bold and was made Dean. Mr. Quiverful, Vicar of Puddingdale, became Warden.

BARHAM, FATHER JOHN. A Roman Catholic priest at Beccles, near Carbury Hall, very zealous in his attempt to secure converts, being himself a convert. "Father John was not above five feet nine in height, but so thin, so meagre, so wasted in appearance, that . . . he was taken to be tall. He had thick dark brown hair, which was cut short in accordance with the usage of his Church; but which he so constantly ruffled by the action of his hands, that, though short, it seemed to be wild and uncombed. . . . He had a high, broad forehead, enormous blue eyes, a thin, long nose, cheeks very thin and hollow, a handsome large mouth, and a strong square chin" (1:15:100). *Way We Live* 15, 19, 55-56, 87

BARRÊRE, BERTRAND (real person). A member of the Committee of Public Safety, who with Westermann and Santerre planned and executed the devastation of La Vendée. "He was a tall, well built, handsome man, about thirty years of age, with straight black hair, brushed upright from his forehead; his countenance gave the idea of eagerness and impetuosity, rather than cruelty or brutality. He was, however, essentially egotistical and insincere; he was republican, not from conviction, but from prudential motives. . . . It was he who demanded the murder of the Queen, when even Robespierre was willing to save her" (2:6:161-62). *Vendée* 15

BARRY, MR. Lawyer Grey's partner, and a suitor for his daughter. After Mr. Grey's retirement, Mr. Barry succeeded to the Scarborough business. Appears frequently in *Mr. Scarborough's Family.*

BARSETSHIRE. "I had it all in my mind,—its roads and railroads, its towns and parishes, its members of Parliament, and the different hunts which rode over it. I knew all the great lords and their castles, the squires and their parks, the rectors and their churches. . . . Throughout these stories there had been no name given to a fictitious site which does not represent to me a spot of which I know all the accessories, as though I had lived and wandered there."—*Autobiography*, 1:8: 204-5.

"There is a county in the West of England not so full of life, indeed, nor so widely spoken of as some of its manufacturing leviathan brethren in the north, but which is, nevertheless, very dear to those who know it well. Its green pastures, its waving wheat, its deep and shady and,—let us add—dirty lanes, its paths and stiles, its tawny-colored, well-built rural churches, its avenues of beeches, and frequent Tudor mansions, its constant country hunt, its social graces, and the general air of clanship that pervades it, has made it to its own inhabitants a favored land of Goshen" (*Thorne* 1:1:1-2).

Boxall Hill. Originally part of the Gresham property, purchased by Sir Roger Scatcherd, where he built an ostentatious house. *Thorne*

Chaldicotes. The property of Nathaniel Sowerby, which he lost. Miss Dunstable bought up the mortgages and after her marriage to Dr. Thorne made it their home. *Thorne*

Cosby Lodge. A small place taken by Major Grantly after his retirement from the army. *Last Chron.*

Courcy Castle. Home of the De Courcys. *Thorne*

Framley Court. Residence of Lady Lufton. *Framley*

Gatherum Castle. Estate of the Duke of Omnium. *Framley, Prime Min.* and others.

Greshamsbury. Estate of the Greshams. *Thorne*

Hogglestock Parish. Where Mr. Crawley was the perpetual curate. *Framley, Last Chron.*

Pakenham Villas. John Bold's home in Barchester. *Warden*

Plumplington. Home of the "two heroines." *Plumplington*

Plumstead. Archdeacon Grantly's estate, in the parishes of Plumstead and Eiderdown. *Warden, Barchester* and others.

Rosebank. Home of Farmer Lookaloft. *Barchester*

St. Ewold's. Church near Ullathorne, whose vicar was Mr. Arabin. *Barchester*

Ullathorne. Estate of Wilfred Thorne. *Warden, Barchester* and others.

BARSETSHIRE, EAST. Represented in Parliament by Mr. Western and Mr. Daubeny in *Phineas Finn*, and by John Newbold Gresham, Sir Roger Scatcherd, Gustavus Moffat and Francis Newbold Gresham in *Dr. Thorne.*

BARSETSHIRE, WEST. Represented in Parliament by Nathaniel Sowerby in *Framley Parsonage*, and by Arthur Fletcher in *The Duke's Children.*

BARTON, BISHOP, of Brotherton. ". . . not a general favorite, being strict, ascetic and utterly hostile to all compromise. . . . It was a law in the Close that Bishop Barton should never be allowed to interfere with the affairs of Brotherton Cathedral" (1:1:4; 1:4:48-49). *Popenjoy* 1, 4, 10, 44, 56-57

BASLE. The home of Armand Urmand, the linen-buyer who wished to marry Marie Bromar. *Granpère* 2

Where Alice, Kate and George Vavasor spent some time during their trip to Switzerland, and where Alice was won over to finance George's attempt to gain a seat in Parliament. *Can You* 5-6

BASLEHURST. "A town with a market, and hotels, and a big brewery, and a square, and street." The inns were the Dragon, to which Mr. Tappitt resorted more often than his wife approved, and the King's Head, which sought to rival the popularity of the Dragon. The setting for *Rachel Ray*.

BUNGALL AND TAPPITT'S BREWERY. "It was a sour and muddy stream that flowed from their vats; a beverage disagreeable to the palate, and very cold and uncomfortable to the stomach" (1:3:42). The contest for the control of the brewery is the subsidiary theme of *Rachel Ray*.

"BASLEHURST GAZETTE AND TOTNES CHRONICLE." A newspaper founded with Mr. Bungall's money, but critical of the quality of Bungall and Tappitt beer. *Rachel* 22, 25

BATES, MR. One of Harry Heathcote's herdsmen, formerly a squatter. Commonly known as "Old Bates." *Heathcote* 1, 5, 7, 9-10

BATH (real place). In both *Miss Mackenzie* and *The Bertrams* the city is called "Littlebath."

BATHERBOLT, The REV. MR. A country curate in the neighborhood of Caversham, calling himself a celibate, but unsuccessful in his attempt to remain so after Georgiana Longestaffe recognized in him her last chance at matrimony. *Way We Live* 95

BATSBY, CAPT. BENJAMIN. Half-brother of Sir Harry Albury, and one of Ayala Dormer's suitors. He later shifted his attentions to Gertrude Tringle in the hope that her father would provide a substantial dowry. *Ayala* 23-24, 39, 43, 45-63

BATTERSEA HAMLETS. Represented in Parliament by Sir Henry Harcourt. *Bertrams* 16, 19, 46

BATTLE, MR. The lawyer employed by Dean Lovelace in the Popenjoy affair. ". . . a very clever man, and perhaps a little sharp. . . . He was a handsome burly man, nearly sixty years of age, with gray hair and clean shorn face, with bright green eyes, and a well-formed nose and mouth—a prepossessing man" (2:5:70-71). *Popenjoy* 24-31, 36, 40

BATTLEAX, CAPTAIN. The commander of the "John Bright," which took the new President out to Britannula and brought the old President, Mr. Neverbend, home to England. *Fixed* 8-12

BAUCHE, ADOLPHE. Son of the innkeeper at the baths of Vernet, who callously deserted his sweetheart at his mother's insistence, saw her married to a man she hated and later found her dead body at the foot of a cliff. *Bauche*

BAUCHE, LA MÈRE. A stern and dominating innkeeper, who convinced her son that he could do better than marry his childhood sweetheart, and was indirectly the cause of her suicide. "She was about sixty years of age and was very stout and short in the neck. She wore her own gray hair. . . . Her eyebrows were large and bushy . . . serious in their effect, but not so serious as the pair of green spectacles which she always wore under them" (1:12). Principal character in *La Mère Bauche*.

BAWWAH, HERR. Tailor Neefit's cutter. *Ralph* 5, 8, 45

BAYSWATER ROAD. *See* London

BEAMINGHAM HALL. Ralph Newton's home, in Norfolk, described in chapter 49. *Ralph*

BEARGARDEN (club). *See* London

BEARSIDE, MR. An attorney retained by Mr. Gotobed, the American Senator, to act for Goarly in the matter of the poisoned foxes. The Senator paid dearly for his interference in the case, both in cash to the rascally attorney, and in loss of friendship with the outraged sportsmen. *Amer. Sen.* 3, 14, 16, 19, 29, 33, 52, 73, 79

BEAUFORT (club). *See* London

BECKARD, The REV. PHINEAS. The Baptist minister at Saratoga Springs, married to Hetta Bell. *Courtship*

BEDESMEN in Hiram Hospital. There were originally twelve, but only eight are named: Johnny Bell, Bunce, Jonathan Crumple, William Gazy, Abel Handy, Gregory Moody, Job Skulpit, Mathew Spriggs. *Warden* 1-5, 7, 10, 20-21; *Barchester* 2, 52

BEDFORD ROW. *See* London

BEDFORD SQUARE. *See* London

BEDFORD SQUARE HOTEL. *See* Tavistock

BEESWAX, SIR TIMOTHY. A Conservative who had held many offices. He was Solicitor-General under Mr. Daubeny and in the Coalition government, from which he retired. He was Leader of the House of Commons in both the Gresham and the Drummond governments. A bitter critic of the Duke of Omnium.

"He was industrious, patient, clear-sighted, intelligent, courageous and determined. . . . But there were drawbacks to the utility and beauty of Sir Timothy's character as a statesman. He had no idea as to the necessity or non-necessity of any measure whatever in reference to the well-being of the country. . . . No man was more warmly attached to parliamentary government . . . but he never cared much for legislation. Parliamentary management was his forte" (*Duke* 1:21:249-51).

Most prominent in *The Duke's Children* and *The Prime Minister.*

BEETHAM. A small town in the south of England, in which Dr. Dugdale was the doctor and the Rev. Mr. Rossiter the vicar. Most of the action of *Alice Dugdale* takes place there.

BEILBY, MR. The senior partner of Beilby and Burton, who managed the London business of the firm. *Claverings* 2

BEILBY and BURTON. Civil engineers with offices in London and Stratton, to whom Harry Clavering went for instruction in his chosen lifework. Mentioned frequently in *The Claverings.*

BELGRAVE SQUARE. *See* London

BELL, MRS. Mother of Hetta and Susan, who kept a boarding house in Saratoga Springs, N.Y. *Courtship*

BELL, HETTA. Susan's disagreeable sister, who married the Rev. Phineas Beckard, a Baptist minister, and unreasonably objected to Susan's marriage to Aaron Dunn. *Courtship*

BELL, SUSAN. Daughter of a widowed boardinghouse-keeper in Saratoga Springs, N.Y., with whom Aaron Dunn, one of the boarders, fell in love. Susan's sister Hetta was convinced that Aaron was a godless young man, and she and her narrow-minded husband tried vainly to separate the lovers. Heroine of *The Courtship of Susan Bell.*

BELLEROACHE, CAPTAIN. A friend of Mark Steinmark, and the successful suitor of Madame Brudo. One of the principal characters in *The Noble Jilt.*

In *Can You Forgive Her?*, represented by Captain Bellfield.

BELLFIELD, CAPT. GUSTAVUS. Mrs. Greenow's successful suitor. "He was a well-made man, nearly six feet high, with dark hair, but of that suspicious hue which to the observant beholder seems always to tell a tale of the hairdresser's shop. He was handsome, too, with well-arranged features,—but carrying, perhaps, in his nose some first symptoms of the effects of midnight amusements . . ." (1:8:59). One of the principal characters in *Can You Forgive Her?*

In *The Noble Jilt*, represented by Captain Belleroache.

BELTON, MARY. Will's crippled, invalid sister, who was his housekeeper at Plaistow Hall. *Belton* 13, 20, 27, 29-32

BELTON, WILL. A successful farmer living at Plaistow, who by the suicide of Charles Amedroz became the owner of Belton Castle and eventually married Clara Amedroz. ". . . a big man, over six feet high, broad in the shoulders, large limbed, with bright, quick grey eyes, a large mouth, teeth almost too perfect and a well-formed nose, with thick short brown hair and small whiskers which came but half-way down his cheeks—a decidedly handsome man with a florid face . . ." (1:3:56). Hero of *The Belton Estate.*

BELTON CASTLE. The ancestral home of the Beltons, in Somersetshire, not far from Taunton, where Bernard Amedroz, a life tenant, and his daughter Clara lived. The setting for many of the scenes in *The Belton Estate.*

BELTON ESTATE, The. London, Chapman and Hall, 1866. 3v.

Author's Comment. "It is readable, and contains scenes which are true to life; but it has no peculiar merits, and will add nothing to my reputation as a novelist."—*Autobiography*, 1:10:259.

Notes. "In no other novel is the essence of Trollope so concentrated. Using a cast of four principal and as few subsidiary characters, he fills three volumes with the matrimonial dilemma of Clara Amedroz, who has to choose between the uncouth farmer Will Belton—to whom has passed her thriftless father's estate—and the polished, self-seeking Captain Aylmer. . . . The theme is commonplace; the incidents unsensational; the treatment unassuming and serene. . . . To a reader in sympathy with the Trollopian method and mentality, the book is a delight for its smoothness, its subtlety and its faultless adjustment of character and circumstance."—Sadleir, p. 392-93.

Plot. By the suicide of the spendthrift son of Bernard Amedroz, the entail of Belton Castle passed to Will Belton, a distant cousin and a prosperous farmer in Norfolk. On his first visit to his new estate he fell in love with Clara Amedroz and impulsively proposed to her. She refused him as she was in love with Captain Aylmer, an MP distantly related to her wealthy aunt Mrs. Winterfield. Since her mother's death Clara had spent part of each year with her aunt, and it was generally supposed that she was her heir. However, when Mrs. Winterfield died, it was discovered that she had left her fortune to Captain Aylmer, after extracting from him a promise to marry Clara. His courtship was tepid, and when Clara visited Aylmer Hall as his fiancée, where she was severely snubbed by Lady Aylmer with no remonstrance from the Captain, she broke the engagement. Will Belton had never given up hope of winning Clara, and after he had taken over the management of the estate they were married.

A secondary plot deals with the story of Clara's friends the Askertons, who lived in a cottage on the estate.

BENDER, KARL. A German herder at Harry Heathcote's sheep ranch. *Heathcote* 2, 8-10

BENJAMIN, MR. *See* Harter and Benjamin

BENT, FANNY (real person). Said to be the original of the character Aunt Stanbury. Trollope's memories of visits to her home just outside the Close at Exeter were drawn on to describe Aunt Stanbury's home in *He Knew He Was Right.*

BERDMORE, JACK. An habitual drunkard, whose wife deserted him for Colonel Askerton, whom she married after Jack drank himself to death in India. *Belton* 5, 14, 16

BERGEN, MR. Father of Anastasia, a wood-merchant in Hamilton who lived on Crump Island, Bermuda. *Trow*

BERGEN, ANASTASIA. A young girl living with her father on a small Bermuda island. She was attacked by Aaron Trow, an escaped criminal, who broke into her home in search of food and money. Her fiancé, the Rev. Caleb Morton, discovered his hiding place, and, in a desperate fight, Trow was killed. Heroine of *Aaron Trow.*

BERKELEY SQUARE. *See* London

BERKSHIRE.

The hunting men of Berkshire and of Buckinghamshire united to form the BB Hunt. *Ralph*

BRAYBORO PARK. Seat of Sir George Eardham. *Ralph*

CRITERION. A small place owned by Sir Francis Geraldine. *Kept Dark*

DURTON LODGE. Home of Mr. and Mrs. Western. *Kept Dark*

HARDOVER LODGE. Home of Mrs. General Talboys. *Talboys*

BERMUDA. Crump Island, just off St. George's, Bermuda, is the scene of *Aaron Trow.*

BERRIER, PIERRE. The first conscript in St. Florent, whose refusal to fight for the Republic precipitated the Vendean revolt. *Vendée* 2, 4, 26

BERRYHILL. A village on the Castle Richmond property, where a mill was erected for grinding corn for the famine victims. *Castle Rich.* 8, 10-11, 25, 37

BERTRAM, GEORGE. Son of Sir Lionel Bertram, and nephew and presumably the heir of his uncle George, Sr. Lifelong friend of Arthur Wilkinson, and for some years engaged to marry Caroline Waddington. After a series of misunderstandings they agreed to part, but married after the death of Caroline's husband Sir Henry Harcourt.

"He was not a handsome boy, nor did he become a handsome man. His face was too solid, his cheeks too square, and his forehead too heavy; but his eyes, though small, were bright, and his mouth was wonderfully marked by intelligence. . . . He wore no beard, not even the slightest apology for a whisker, and this perhaps added to the apparent heaviness of his face; but . . . no face bore on it more legible marks of an acute mind" (1:1:11).

One of the principal characters in *The Bertrams.*

BERTRAM, GEORGE, SR. George's wealthy and cantankerous uncle, who distrusted his nephew's ability to handle money and bequeathed his large fortune to "Bertram College" for the education of children of London fishmongers. One of the principal characters in *The Bertrams.*

BERTRAM, SIR LIONEL. George's father, who neglected to provide for George's education and sponged on him whenever he could. He retired to Littlebath, where he weighed the monetary desirability of marrying Miss Todd or Miss Baker, and was eventually refused by both.

"... a soldier of fortune ... he held a quasi-military position in Persia ... an elderly gentleman, in a military frock, with a bald head, a hook nose, and a short allowance of teeth ... though elderly he was tall and upright; he was distinguished-looking ... not a little vain of his personal appearance ... but ... too clever to let his vanity show itself. ... He had been useful as a great oil-jar, from which oil for the quiescence of troubled waters might ever and anon be forthcoming. Expediency was his god, and he had ... worshipped it with a successful devotion" (1:9; 8:80).

One of the principal characters in *The Bertrams.*

BERTRAMS, The. London, Chapman and Hall, 1859. 3v.

AUTHOR'S COMMENT. "I do not know that I have ever heard it well spoken of even by my friends, and I cannot remember that there is any character in it that has dwelt in the minds of novel-readers."—*Autobiography*, 1:7:168.

NOTES. "... perhaps the most serious objection which can be brought against the book from the point of view of literature is that it is too much like life." —Algar Thorold, Introduction to the *New Pocket Library* edition, Lane, London, 1905.

PLOT. George Bertram's uncle, a wealthy City merchant, had sent him to Oxford where he made a brilliant record. Inclined toward the church and unwilling to follow his uncle's advice to adopt commerce as a career, he postponed his decision until after a visit to the Holy Land. In Jerusalem he met his father Sir Lionel Bertram, whom he had not seen since his boyhood and who had shown no interest in his upbringing. Sir Lionel held a minor military-diplomatic post that kept him in the East, and while personally charming was little better than a worthless spendthrift.

While in the Holy Land George met and fell in love with Caroline Waddington, granddaughter of George Bertram, Sr. She persuaded him to study for the Bar, but refused to marry him until he had acquired a suitable income. Their engagement dragged on for three years, George refusing to ask his uncle for financial aid and Caroline persisting in her original requirement. Finally, by mutual consent the engagement was broken, and Caroline soon married Sir Henry Harcourt, the brilliant and ambitious Solicitor-General. Although old Mr. Bertram tried to prevent the marriage, Sir Henry persisted, in the belief that his wife would be her grandfather's heir. He took a large house and entertained lavishly, but when he tried to compel Caroline to wheedle money from her grandfather to support his extravagance, she refused and left him, taking refuge at Hadley, her grandfather's gloomy country house where he lived alone, ill and moody. When the government fell Sir Henry was without a post. Harassed by debt, forsaken by his fair-weather friends and impotent to force Caroline to return to him, he committed suicide. After some time Caroline and George became reconciled and eventually married.

Sir Lionel Bertram, on his retirement to Littlebath, made a futile attempt to marry Miss Sally Todd for her fortune, but on her refusal was compelled to pare his expenses to his pension, plus such sums as he could extract from his son.

The secondary plot has to do with George's friend Arthur Wilkinson. To support his widowed mother and sisters he had become Vicar of Hurst Staple after unwisely agreeing to a stipulation of his patron that the major part of his salary should go to his mother. She soon came to regard the income as her own and was furious when Arthur wished to marry and occupy the vicarage. After some time she was forced to yield and Arthur married Adela Gauntlet.

BIDEAWHILE, MR. The junior member of the firm of London lawyers, Slow and Bideawhile, who refused to help Louis Trevelyan abduct his son and was stern in denouncing his client's behavior. *He Knew* 4, 14, 19, 33, 59, 75

BIDEFORD, LORD GEORGE. The young Englishman who married Nina Baldoni. *Ayala* 49-52

BIFFIN, MAJOR. A fellow traveler of George Bertram and Arthur Wilkinson from Suez to Southampton. He was in love with Mrs. Cox, who preferred flirting with George Bertram. "The major was a handsome man, with well-brushed hair, well-trimmed whiskers, a forehead rather low, but very symmetrical, a well-shaped nose, and a small, pursy mouth. The worst of his face was that you could by no means remember it" (3:9:168). *Bertrams* 39

BIGGS, MARTHA. An old friend and confidante of Mrs. Furnival, but heartily disliked by Mr. Furnival. *Orley* 21, 40-41, 49, 51, 55, 78

BILES, MISS. ". . . a thin, acrid, unmarried female friend" of Mrs. Morony, with whom she went on a shopping expedition to the store of Brown, Jones and Robinson. "Her nose was long, narrow and red; her eyes were set very near together; she was tall and skimpy in all her proportions." *Struggles* 14-15

BIRDBOTT, SERJEANT. Assistant to Mr. Chaffanbrass at Phineas Finn's trial for the murder of Mr. Bonteen. *Redux* 57

BIRMINGHAM. Where the International Legal Congress over which Lord Boanerges presided was held. *Orley* 17-18

BIRON, GENERAL (real person). One of the Republican generals fighting in La Vendée with an army made up of raw recruits "without discipline, and, in a great degree, without courage." *Vendée* 15
Full name: ARMAND-LOUIS DE BIRON.

BISHOPSGATE. *See* London

BLAKE, DR. A physician at Mohill, called to stand by on the occasion of the duel between Jonas Brown and Counsellor Webb. *Macdermots* 26-27

BLAKE, The REV. MONTAGU. The young curate at Little Alresford, who had been at Oxford with John Gordon. *Old Man* 9, 12-17, 20, 22-24

BLAKE, The REV. SEPTIMUS. The curate to whose care Sir Felix Carbury was entrusted during his exile in Germany. *Way We Live* 99

BLAKE, THOMAS. An Irish gentleman living at Carnlough in County Galway, to whom Philip Jones went for advice in bringing Pat Carroll to justice for flooding his fields. *Land.* 4, 30

BLAKE, WALTER ("Dot"). A clever gambler and sportsman, a friend of Frank Ballindine, living at Handicap Lodge and devoted entirely to making money for Dot Blake. ". . . an effeminate-looking, slight-made man, about thirty or thirty-three years of age; good looking and gentlemanlike. . . . He had a cold, quiet grey eye, and a thin lip. . . . On matters connected with racing, his word was infallible . . . a finished gambler" (1:3:49-50). *Kellys* 3, 10, 15-16, 26, 34, 39

BLANKENBERG. "A little fishing-town some twelve miles distant from Bruges," where Lord Chiltern and Phineas Finn fought a duel because of Violet Effingham. *Finn* 38

BLOCK and CURLING. The family lawyers of the Marrable family, who acted for Walter against his father. *Vicar* 13-14, 16, 18, 21, 33

BLOCKS, PILES and COFFERDAM. The engineering firm interested in building Limehouse Bridge, and the only ones who made any money out of it. *Clerks* 32, 34

BLOOMSBURY SQUARE. *See* London

BLUE DRAGON INN. *See* Tavistock

BLUE POSTS (restaurant). *See* London

BLUESTONE, MRS. Serjeant Bluestone's wife, who befriended Lady Anna Lovel when her mother turned her out of doors because of her refusal to marry the young Earl. Appears frequently in *Lady Anna.*

BLUESTONE, ALICE. Serjeant Bluestone's youngest daughter, and Lady Anna's only friend, who nevertheless urged her not to marry the tailor Daniel Thwaite and to accept Earl Lovel. *Anna* 22, 26-27, 36

BLUESTONE, SERJEANT. The leading counsel in the interest of the Countess Lovel. ". . . a very violent man, taking up all his cases as though the very holding of a brief opposite to him was an insult to himself" (1:5:59). Appears frequently in *Lady Anna.*

BOANERGES, LORD. One of the old Duke of Omnium's guests at Gatherum. ". . . an old man who would have his own way in everything, and who was regarded by all men . . . as an intellectual king, by no means of the constitutional kind—as an intellectual emperor, rather, who took upon himself to rule all questions of mind without the assistance of any ministers whatever. . . ." But not all the time at Gatherum was spent on politics, for ". . . the all-venerable and all-wise Lord Boanerges . . . spent the morning . . . in teaching Miss Dunstable to blow soap bubbles on scientific principles" (*Framley* 1:8:141-42, 59-60). Briefly in *Framley* 6, 8; *Bertrams* 28, 33; and, as President of the International Legal Congress, in *Orley* 17

BOARDOTRADE, LORD. Father of Septimus Traffic. *Ayala* 5, 12-13, 18

BOBSBOROUGH. Frank Greystock represented the borough in Parliament. *Eustace* 3-4, 35

BOBSBOROUGH CATHEDRAL. Bishop Eustace of Bobsborough was uncle of Sir Florian Eustace, and Dean Greystock was uncle of Lizzie, Sir Florian's wife. *Eustace* 1

BOBTAILED FOX (inn). *See* Egham

BOCAGE. A district in the center of which was the chateau of Durbellière, the seat of the Larochejaquelin family. Mentioned frequently in *La Vendée*.

BODKIN, SIR BOREAS. The Secretary of the Post Office, familiarly known as "Aeolus." Appears frequently in *Marion Fay*.

BODKIN, SIR NICHOLAS. The sporting owner of Ballytowngal. *Land*. 9-11

BODKIN, PETER. The eldest son of Sir Nicholas. Although a Catholic, he was a warm friend of Black Daly and sided with him in his fight with the Landleaguers. *Land*. 9-11

BOFFIN, MR. He worked with Sir Orlando Drought against the leadership of the Duke of Omnium. ". . . a gentleman who had belonged to the late Ministry, but had somewhat out-Heroded Herod in his Conservatism, so as to have been considered to be unfit for the Coalition. . . . He was a labourious, honest man,—but hardly of calibre sufficient not to regret his own honesty in such an emergency as the present" (1:11:175-76). *Prime Min*. 9, 11, 20, 41

BOGEN, MRS. FANNY (Heise). A childhood friend and near neighbor of Linda Tressel in Nuremberg, whose happy and carefree life was in complete contrast to Linda's. After her marriage to Max Bogen she moved to Augsburg, where she later befriended Linda. *Linda* 12

BOGEN, MAX. A lawyer in Augsburg, who married Linda Tressel's best friend, Fanny Heise. *Linda* 12

BOLD, MRS. ELEANOR. *See* Arabin, Mrs. Eleanor (Harding).

BOLD, JOHN. The young surgeon of Barchester who brought suit for an accounting of the revenues of Hiram's Hospital, and was called an "impious demagogue" by Dr. Grantly. His love for Eleanor Harding, whose father, the Warden, resigned his position because of the publicity attending the suit, led him to withdraw it. He and Eleanor were married, but he died soon after. ". . . a strong reformer. His passion is the reform of all abuses; state abuses, church abuses, corporation abuses . . . abuses in medical practice, and general abuses in the world at large" (2:18). *Warden* 2-3, 5-15, 21

BOLD, JOHNNIE. The only child of John Bold and Eleanor Harding, described in great detail in his infancy, but only briefly mentioned as he grew older. *Barchester* 2, 16, 44

BOLD, MARY. Sister of John Bold, and a devoted friend of Eleanor Harding, later her sister-in-law. *Warden* 2, 6, 10-11; *Barchester* 2, 8, 10, 16, 31, 44

BOLLUM, RICHARD. The partner of Tom Crinkett, who induced John Caldigate to refund part of the purchase price of his mine to the conspirators who were trying to prove him a bigamist. *Caldigate* 38-40

BOLSTER, MRS. BRIDGET. A witness of Sir Joseph Mason's will, who appeared at both trials of the Orley Farm case. *Orley* 32, 62, 67, 71, 77

BOLT, SIR SIMON. MFH of the Brotherton Hunt for fifteen years. ". . . so well known that no sporting pen and no sporting tongue in England ever called him more than Sir Simon" (1:7:91). *Popenjoy* 7-8

BOLTBY, JOHN. Sir Harry Hotspur's family lawyer, who discovered the facts about George Hotspur's gambling debts, his shady companions and his mistress, and advised his client not to let Emily marry him. *Hotspur* 10, 12, 15-18, 22-23

BOLTON, DANIEL. Nicholas Bolton's second son, a partner in his father's bank in Cambridge. He and his wife are frequently mentioned in *John Caldigate*.

BOLTON, HESTER. *See* Caldigate, Mrs. Hester (Bolton)

BOLTON, MRS. MARY. Hester Bolton's mother, a religious fanatic, insanely jealous of her daughter's love for John Caldigate. One of the principal characters in *John Caldigate*.

BOLTON, NICHOLAS. A banker living at Cambridge, and an old friend of Daniel Caldigate. He arranged the details of John Caldigate's sale of the reversion of the estate and, after John's return from New South Wales, settled the mortgages. He was devoted to his only daughter, Hester, but was very much in subjection to Hester's mother, his second wife. His four sons were all successful men, the two eldest partners in the Cambridge bank, and the two youngest, lawyers. One of the principal characters in *John Caldigate*.

BOLTON, NICHOLAS, JR. The eldest son of the rich Cambridge banker. He and his wife, almost as fanatical as old Mrs. Bolton, appear frequently throughout *John Caldigate*.

BOLTON, ROBERT. An attorney in Cambridge, who, realizing the abnormal home life of Hester with her half-crazed mother, advised her marriage to John Caldigate. Later, when John was accused of bigamy, he bitterly denounced him and attempted to remove his sister from her husband's home. Both he and his wife Margaret are important characters in *John Caldigate*.

BOLTON, WILLIAM. The barrister, living in London, who finally succeeded in reconciling Hester's parents to her marriage with John Caldigate. One of the principal characters in *John Caldigate*.

BOLTON ABBEY. At a picnic near the Abbey, Earl Lovel renewed his proposal of marriage to Lady Anna. *Anna* 15

BOLTON STREET. *See* London

BONCASSEN, EZEKIEL. An American scholar in London with his wife and his daughter Isabel. ". . . an American who had nothing to do with politics and nothing to do with trade. He was a man of wealth and a man of letters. . . . He was a tall, straight, ungainly man, who always wore black clothes. He had dark, stiff, short hair, a long nose, and a forehead that was both high and broad" (2:2:11; 2:6:62). *Duke* 28, 32-33, 46-47, 52-53, 76

BONCASSEN, MRS. EZEKIEL. Isabel's mother, overawed by the grandeur to which her daughter's marriage had raised her. *Duke* 31-33, 52-53, 68

BONCASSEN, ISABEL. An American girl of great beauty, who married Lord Silverbridge. "She was slight, without that look of slimness which is common to girls, and especially to American girls. That her figure was perfect the reader must believe on my word, as any detailed description of her arms, feet, bust, and waist, would be altogether ineffective. Her hair was dark brown and plentiful; but it added but little to her charms, which depended on other matters. . . . It was . . . the vitality of her countenance,—the way in which she could speak with every feature, the command which she had of pathos, of humour, of sympathy, of satire, the assurance which she gave by every glance of her eye, every elevation of her brow, every curl of her lip, that she was alive to all that was going on,—it was all this rather than those feminine charms which can be catalogued and labelled that made all acknowledge that she was beautiful" (2:2:12-13). One of the principal characters in *The Duke's Children.*

BONCHAMPS, CHARLES, MARQUIS DE (real person). A professional soldier and an ardent Royalist, who fought in the La Vendée campaign and was mortally wounded at Cholet. *Vendée* 3-4, 6, 9, 11, 25

BOND STREET. *See* London

"BONEBREAKER." A violent and unmanageable horse belonging to Lord Chiltern, which he loaned to Phineas Finn for the Brake Hunt. *Finn* 19, 24

BONN, UNIVERSITY OF. Where Ferdinand Lopez was educated. *Prime Min.* 3

BONNER, MARY. Niece of Sir Thomas Underwood, who refused to marry Ralph, the heir, because she was in love with the other Ralph, Ralph Newton. "She was tall and somewhat large, with fair hair . . . with dark eyes, and perfect eyebrows, and a face which, either for colour or lines of beauty, might have been taken as a model for any female saint or martyr. There was a perfection of symmetry about it,—and an assertion of intelligence combined with the loveliness . . ." (1:4:61). One of the principal characters in *Ralph the Heir.*

BONTEEN, MR. Accepted in the higher parliamentary circles as a useful party man, he had held various posts in the government. He incurred the enmity of Mr. Emilius by attempting to prove that the latter's marriage to Lizzie Eustace was bigamous. After a quarrel at the Club with Phineas Finn, he was found murdered. Mr. Emilius was at first accused, but having a perfect (though, as it turned out, a fraudulent) alibi, the crime was charged to Phineas Finn, who was acquitted after a sensational trial. Most prominent in *Phineas Finn* and *Phineas Redux*; briefly in *Eustace* 47, 54-55, 80

BONTEEN, MRS. An unpleasant, gossiping woman, who singled out her husband's enemies for her most vigorous attacks. Her demands that Phineas Finn should be convicted for the murder of her husband were incessant and groundless. Lady Laura Standish said of her: "I hate that woman like poison. . . . She is always playing a game, and it is such a small game that she plays! And she contributes so little to society. She is not witty nor well-informed,—not even sufficiently ignorant or ridiculous to be a laughing-stock" (*Finn* 1: 36:305). Most prominent in *Phineas Finn* and *Phineas Redux*; briefly in *Eustace* 47, 54-55, 80

BOOBY and MOGGS. A firm of master-bootmakers in West End trade. Since Mr. Booby was dead, the firm consisted of Moggs and his son Ontario. *Ralph* 8, 16, 47

BOODLE, CAPTAIN ("Doodles"). A horsy friend of Archie Clavering, who advised Archie as to his wooing of Lady Ongar. Doodles became much interested in the "Russian spy," Madame Gordeloup, and finally followed her to the continent. ". . . wore a cut-away coat, a coloured shirt with a fogle round his neck, old brown trowsers that fitted very tightly round his legs . . . a man with a small bullet head, who wore his hair cut very short and had no other beard than a slight appendage on his lower chin" (*Claverings* 2:6:69). *Clav-*

erings 17-19, 24, 30, 34-35, 39, 46; *Redux* 69

BOOKER, ALFRED. The editor of the "Literary Chronicle," who was not above writing favorable reviews of inferior books in exchange for similar favors for his own. *Way We Live* 1, 11, 30, 35, 62; *Prime Min.* 11

BOOLABONG. A cattle ranch belonging to the Brownbies, near Harry Heathcote's home at Gangoil. *Heathcote* 6

BOOTHBY, MESSRS. The London lawyers of Lord Trowbridge, with offices in Lincoln's Inn. *Vicar* 56-57

BOREHAM, The HON. AUGUSTA. *See* Veronica John, Sister

BOSCOBEL. One of Harry Heathcote's workmen, whom he discharged for just cause and who joined the Brownbie gang in an attempt to burn Heathcote out. *Heathcote* 5-6, 9, 11

BOSTON, Mass. The setting for *Miss Ophelia Gledd.*

BOTSEY, NED and FRANK. Good-natured brewers in Norrington, who hunted with the URU. Frequently mentioned in *The American Senator*; briefly in *Ayala* 23

BOTT, MR. An MP in the following of Plantagenet Palliser, whom Lady Glencora found most objectionable, as he constituted himself her guardian and reported to her husband all her shortcomings. He later married Mrs. Marsham. "He was a tall, wiry, strong man, with a bald head and bristly red beard, which, however, was cut off from his upper and lower lip. This was unfortunate, as had he hidden his mouth he would not have been in so marked a degree an ugly man. His upper lip was long, and his mouth was mean" (1:24: 191). Appears frequently in *Can You Forgive Her?*

BOUNCER, MR. A novelist and member of the Universe Club, who was present during the quarrel between Phineas Finn and Mr. Bonteen on the night of Mr. Bonteen's murder, and was one of the witnesses at the trial. *Redux* 46, 61

BOURBOTTE, PIERRE (real person). A Republican general, fighting under Santerre in La Vendée. *Vendée* 15, 17

BOW STREET POLICE COURT. *See* London

BOWES LODGE. The seat of the Marquis of Stapledean, in Westmoreland. *Bertrams* 3, 43

BOWICK SCHOOL. A preparatory school for Eton, the background for *Dr. Wortle's School.*

BOXALL HILL. Originally a part of the Greshamsbury estate, halfway between Greshamsbury and Barchester. It was sold to Sir Roger Scatcherd, in part payment for mortgages he held against the estate, and there he built a pretentious mansion where both he and his son died. It was later occupied by Frank Gresham after his marriage to Mary Thorne. Repeatedly mentioned in *Doctor Thorne* and *Framley Parsonage.*

BOYCE, The REV. MR. The Vicar of Allington, with a large family: Jane, Charles, Florence, Bessy, Minnie, Dick and others unnamed. *Allington* 10; *Last Chron.* 6, 16, 35

BOZZLE, SAMUEL. A rascally ex-policeman, hired by Louis Trevelyan as a detective to spy on his wife and to make arrangements for the abduction

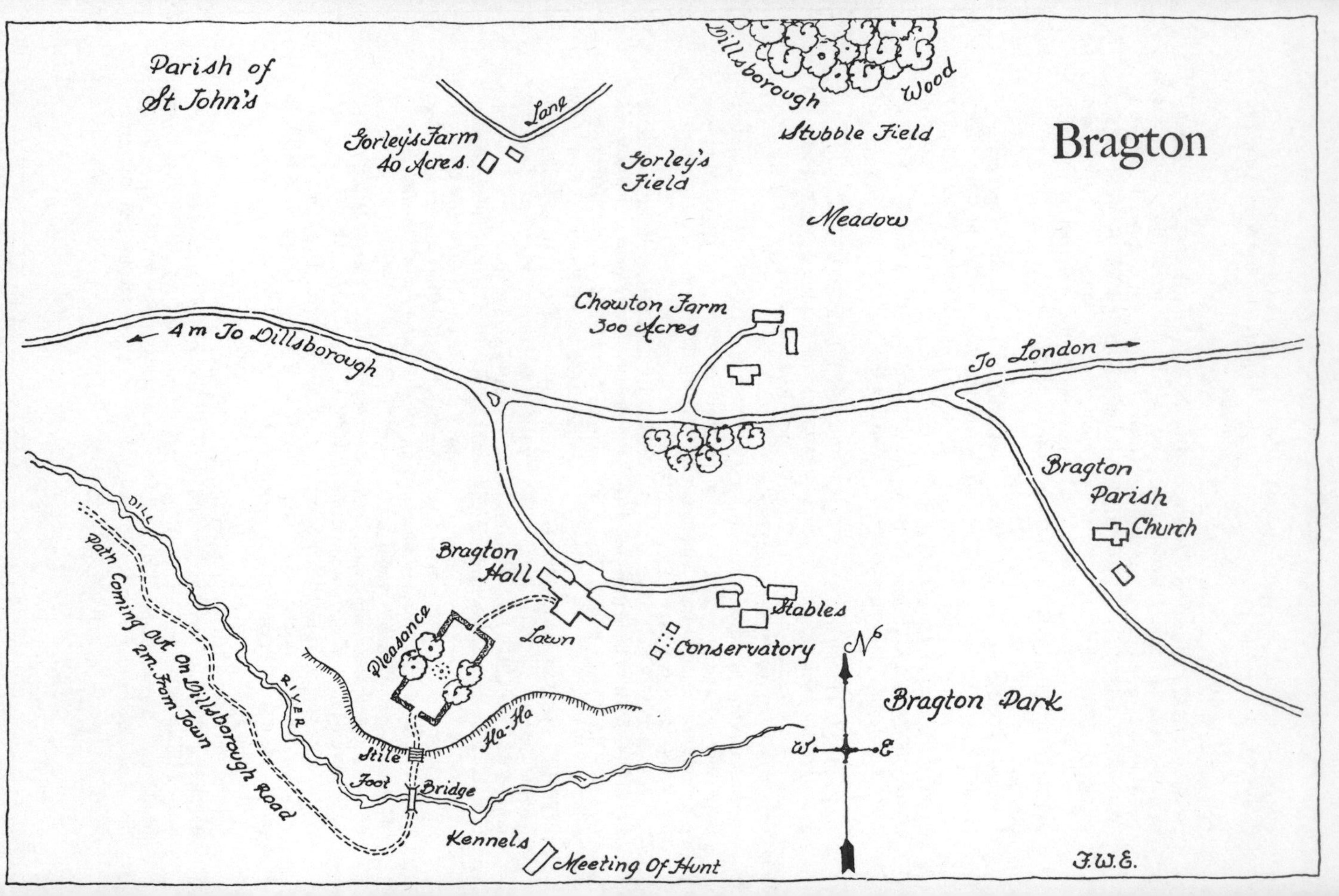

Bragton
Parish of St John's
Lane
Gorley's Farm 40 Acres.
Dillsborough Wood
Stubble Field
Gorley's Field
Meadow
Chowton Farm 300 Acres
← 4 m To Dillsborough
To London →
Bragton Parish
Church
Bragton Hall
Stables
Lawn
Conservatory
Pleasance
N
Bragton Park
W
E
Dill
River
Ha-Ha
Stile
Foot Bridge
Path Coming Out On Dillsborough Road
2m. From Town
Kennels
Meeting Of Hunt
F.W.E.

of his child. Appears frequently in *He Knew He Was Right.*

BRABAZON, LADY. An elderly relative of the Germains, living in London. *Popenjoy* 12, 28, 36, 59-60

BRABAZON, HERMIONE. *See* Clavering, Hermione (Brabazon), Lady

BRABAZON, JULIA. *See* Ongar, Julia (Brabazon), Lady

BRACY, EARL. Father of Lord Carstairs, and friend of Dr. Wortle. *Wortle* 6, 12, 20, 22

BRADY, MARY. *See* McGovery, Mrs. Mary (Brady)

BRADY, PAT. The confidential servant of Thady Macdermot, who became a stool-pigeon for Thady's bitterest enemy, Hyacinth Keegan, and whose testimony resulted in Thady's conviction. "He was strong-built, round-shouldered, bow-legged, about five feet six in height, and he had that kind of external respectability about him, which a tolerably decent hat, strong brogues, and worsted stockings give to a man, when those among whom he lives are without such luxuries" (1:3:27). One of the principal characters in *The Macdermots of Ballycloran.*

BRAESIDE HARRIERS. The hunt club in Cumberland with which Lord Hampstead rode. *Fay* 12-13, 23, 39-40

BRAGG'S END. The cottage at Cawston where Mrs. Ray and her daughters lived. The setting for much of *Rachel Ray.*

BRAGTON HALL. The seat of the Morton family, who "had possessed the property and lived on it for the last three centuries." It was here John Morton entertained the American Senator, Arabella Trefoil and her mother. *Amer. Sen.* 2, 8-13, 53-54

BRAKE HUNT. Lord Chiltern was the MFH, and many of his friends hunted with the Brake: Madame Goesler and Phineas Finn, Adelaide Palliser and Gerard Maule (*Redux* 15-17); Silverbridge and Frank Tregear (*Duke* 62-63).

BRAMBER, MR. JUSTICE. The judge in the bigamy case against John Caldigate, who believed the prisoner to be guilty. *Caldigate* 41, 43, 53-55, 59, 64

BRATTLE, CARRY. The "fallen woman" in *The Vicar of Bullhampton.* "I have endeavoured to endow her with qualities that may create sympathy, and I have brought her back at last from degradation, at least to decency. . . . She is introduced as a poor, abased creature, who hardly knows how false were her dreams . . . but with an intense horror of the sufferings of her position."—*Autobiography*, 2:18:177, 180.

"Carry had been her father's darling. . . . Fair she had been; with laughing eyes, and floating curls; strong in health, generous in temper, though now and again with something of her father's humour. . . . To her father she had been as bright and beautiful as the harvest moon" (5:33).

One of the principal characters in *The Vicar of Bullhampton.*

BRATTLE, FANNY. The second daughter of Jacob Brattle, ". . . a girl as good as gold, the glory and joy and mainstay of her mother, whom even the miller could not scold,—whom all Bullhampton loved. But she was a plain girl, brown and somewhat hard-visaged;—a morsel of fruit as sweet as any in the garden, but one that the eye would not select for its outside grace, colour, and roundness" (5:33). Appears frequently in *The Vicar of Bullhampton.*

BRATTLE, GEORGE. The eldest son of Jacob Brattle, who lived at Startup Farm. *Vicar* 15, 19, 38, 40-41, 47

BRATTLE, JACOB. The miller at Bullhampton, a tenant of Squire Gilmore. Father of Sam, Fanny, Carry, George and Mrs. Jay. ". . . had ever been a hardworking, sober, honest man. But he was cross-grained, litigious, moody and tyrannical . . . a low, thickset man, with an appearance of great strength, which was now submitting itself, very slowly, to the hand of time. He had sharp green eyes, and shaggy eyebrows, with thin lips, and a square chin, a nose which, though its shape was aquiline, protruded but little from his face. His forehead was low and broad. . . . His hair and very scanty whiskers were grey. . . . He was a silent, sad, meditative man, thinking always of the evil things that had been done to him" (5:30, 34).

"Best figure in the book is Jacob Brattle, one of the truest rustics in English fiction. He stands out indeed against those autumn and winter backgrounds . . . half animal, half human, as obstinate as he is gloomy, as gloomy as he is courageous, hemmed in by troubles—moral, financial, domestic—that he cannot understand, but is too proud to question."—Walpole, p. 140.

One of the principal characters in *The Vicar of Bullhampton.*

BRATTLE, MRS. MAGGIE. Wife of Jacob Brattle, ". . . one of those loving, patient, self-denying, almost heavenly human beings, one or two of whom may come across one's path, and who, when found, are generally found in that sphere of life to which this woman belonged" (5:32). Appears frequently in *The Vicar of Bullhampton.*

BRATTLE, SAM. The youngest son of the miller. Suspected of Farmer Trumbull's murder, he became morose and distrustful, even of the Vicar who steadfastly befriended him. Through the Vicar's efforts he was eventually freed of complicity in the murder and returned to the mill. One of the principal characters in *The Vicar of Bullhampton.*

BRAWL, BARON. One of the guests at the dinner party given by Sir Henry Harcourt, who apologized to his wife for inviting him by saying, "He's loud and arrogant . . . but he's not loud and arrogant about nothing, as some men are" (3:3:55). *Bertrams* 33

Also mentioned as a guest at Gatherum at the Duke of Omnium's dinner. *Framley* 8

BRAYBORO PARK. Sir George Eardham's estate, in Berkshire. *Ralph* 52

BREGHERT, EZEKIEL. A Jewish banker in the City, a widower with five or six grown children, who became involved in the financial downfall of Augustus Melmotte. Believing him wealthy and willing to provide a house in London, Georgiana Longestaffe tried to marry him, but when the house did not seem to be forthcoming, she dismissed him. *Way We Live* 45, 53, 60-61, 65, 78-82, 88

BRENTFORD, EARL OF. Father of Lady Laura Standish and Lord Chiltern, at whose town house Phineas Finn met most of the distinguished men of the day. He was for a time Privy Seal, and through his daughter's influence helped to forward the ambitions of her young friend. After Lady Laura's marriage with Mr. Kennedy went on the rocks, he accompanied her to Dresden, and from brooding over her troubles returned to Saulsby a broken man.

Most prominent in *Phineas Finn*; but appears frequently in *Phineas Redux*.

"BRIEN BORU." The race horse owned by Lord Ballindine that won renown on the English turf. Lord Ballindine's preoccupation with racing was one of the reasons given by Lord Cashel for breaking off his ward's engagement. Sometimes spelled "Brian Boru." *Kellys* 2, 10, 26, 39

BRISKET, WILLIAM. The mercenary butcher who wished to marry Maryanne Brown on condition that her dowry was £500. One of the principal characters in *The Struggles of Brown, Jones and Robinson.*

BRITANNULA. An imaginary self-governing island near Australia, the setting for *The Fixed Period.*

BRITTANY. After the battle at Cholet, the Vendean Royalists fell back to Brittany, where they fought the battle of Laval. *Vendée* 29-32

BROCK, LORD. The Prime Minister who was succeeded by Lord de Terrier. *Framley* 17-20, 23; *Can You* 42, 44, 59

BRODERICK, MR. Isabel's father, an attorney at Hereford. *Cousin* 4, 11, 16, 19, 21-22

BRODERICK, MRS. Isabel's stepmother, who ". . . preferred her own babies to Isabel." *Cousin* 11-12, 16

BRODERICK, ISABEL. Niece of Indefer Jones, with whom she lived, and to whom he wished to bequeath his estate, although he desired also that it should go to a Jones. By the last of several wills it was left to her and, when she married, her husband took the name of Indefer Jones. "In appearance she was one calculated to attract attention,—somewhat tall, well set on her limbs, active and of good figure; her brow was broad and fine, her grey eyes were bright and full of intelligence, her nose and mouth were well formed, and there was not a mean feature in her face" (1:2:33). Heroine of *Cousin Henry.*

BRODERICK, SIR WILLIAM. A London physician attending John Scarborough. *Scarborough* 7, 9-10, 19, 21, 38, 53, 58

BROMAR, MARIE. The theme of the novel in which Marie Bromar appears is her love for George Voss, son of the owner of the Golden Lion of Granpère. ". . . she was very pretty, with rich brown hair that would not allow itself to be brushed out of its crisp half-curls in front, and which she always wore cut short behind, curling round her straight, well-formed neck. Her eyes were grey, with a strong shade indeed of green, but were very bright and pleasant, full of intelligence, telling stories by their glances of her whole inward disposition, of her activity, quickness, and desire to have a hand in everything that was being done" (1:18). Heroine of *The Golden Lion of Granpère.*

BROMLEY, The REV. THOMAS. The rector of Utterden parish near Folking, who never wavered in supporting John Caldigate during his bigamy trial. *Caldigate* 23, 27, 32, 37, 44, 51, 58, 62

BROMPTON ROAD. *See* London

BROOK PARK. The home of Sir Walter Wanless and his numerous daughters. *Dugdale*

BROOK STREET. *See* London

BROOKS'S (club). *See* London

BROSNAN, FATHER. The curate to Father Giles at Tuam, who pledged Florian Jones by an oath not to reveal to his father what he knew about the Landleaguers. *Land.* 2-4

BROTHERTON. ". . . a most interesting little city . . . full of architectural excellencies, given to literature, and fond of hospitality." The center of the action in *Is He Popenjoy?*.

BROTHERTON, DOWAGER MARCHIONESS OF. Mother of the Marquis. A complaining, ill-tempered old woman, sure that the head of the house could do no wrong, and bitter toward her other children who dared to oppose his will. One of the principal characters in *Is He Popenjoy?*.

BROTHERTON, FREDERICK AUGUSTUS, MARQUIS OF. The "wicked Marquis," who abused his family, neglected his duties as a landlord, produced an ailing heir of doubtful legitimacy and made himself generally obnoxious. "He was an idle, self-indulgent, ill-conditioned man, who found that it suited his tastes better to live in Italy, where his means were ample, than on his own property, where he would have been comparatively a poor man" (1:1:5). One of the principal characters in *Is He Popenjoy?*.

BROUGHTON. A town near Bowick School, where Robert Lefroy stayed when he followed the Peacockes to England in an attempt to blackmail them. Mentioned frequently in *Dr. Wortle's School*.

BROUGHTON, BISHOP OF. *See* Rolland, The Right Rev. Mr.

BROUGHTON, DOBBS. A partner with Augustus Musselboro and Mrs. Van Siever in moneylending and stockbroking of an unsavory kind. At the last, bankrupt and discredited, he killed himself. Appears frequently in *The Last Chronicle of Barset.*

BROUGHTON, CAPT. JOHN. The wealthy nephew of Miss Le Smyrger, who became engaged to Patience Woolsworthy, the rector's daughter, but lost her when he tried to teach her how exalted would be her position as his wife. *Parson*

BROUGHTON, MRS. MARIA (Clutterbuck). She was painted by Conroy Dalrymple as a Grace. After the death of her stockbroker husband, she married his partner, Augustus Musselboro. ". . . a very beautiful woman, who certainly was not yet thirty-five, let her worst enemies say what they might" (1:24:204). Appears frequently in *The Last Chronicle of Barset.*

"BROUGHTON GAZETTE." A diocesan newspaper that published an article attacking Dr. Wortle for his support of Mr. Peacocke. *Wortle* 13, 24

BROUNE, NICHOLAS. The editor of the "Morning Breakfast Table." He became a friend of Lady Carbury through his publication of her writings, and, despite his clear understanding of her nature, he came to admire her and they were eventually married. Most prominent in *The Way We Live Now*; briefly, with his wife, as a guest at Gatherum, in *Prime Min.* 11

BROWBOROUGH, MR. Represented Tankerville in Parliament for many years until defeated by Phineas Finn. He was tried for bribery, but though obviously guilty was acquitted. *Redux* 1-2, 4, 13, 44

BROWN, MR. A retired butter dealer, who lost his fortune in attempting to establish himself in a haberdashery business. Senior partner of the firm in *The*

Struggles of Brown, Jones and Robinson.

BROWN, CHARLES. An unwilling traveler from the south of France to spend Christmas with his wife's relatives at Thompson Hall. When Mrs. Brown put the mustard plaster intended for him on Mr. Jones, he attempted to make a suitable apology, which was somewhat ungraciously received. *Christmas*

BROWN, SIR FERDINANDO. The governor sent to Britannula to supersede President Neverbend. *Fixed* 9-12

BROWN, FRED. Heir to Brown Hall, and a willing disciple to his father's training for his two sons: ". . . to consider sport their only business—horses and dogs their only care—grooms and trainers the only persons necessary to attend to—and the mysteries of the field and the stable the only pursuits which were worthy being cultivated with industry, or learnt with precision" (2:7: 201). *Macdermots* 19, 26, 29

BROWN, GEORGE. A "gentleman jockey," who rode his own horse "Conqueror" at the Carrick races. *Macdermots* 17, 19, 26

BROWN, JONAS. ". . . an irritable, overbearing magistrate, a greedy landlord and an unprincipled father. . . . He was a stern, hard, cruel man, with no sympathy for any one and was actuated by the most superlative contempt for the poor, from whom he drew his whole income. He was a clever, clear-headed, avaricious man; and he knew that the only means of keeping the poor in their present utterly helpless and dependent state, was to deny them education, and to oppose every scheme for their improvement and welfare" (2:7: 201; 3:1:22-23). *Macdermots* 19, 25-26

BROWN, JULIA. *See* Armstrong, Mrs. Julia (Brown)

BROWN, MRS. MARY (Thompson). Spending a night in a Paris hotel on her way to her old home for the Christmas festivities, Mrs. Brown made a mustard plaster in the salon to cure her husband's sore throat. Mistaking the room number, she placed the poultice on the throat of a stranger who, as the story develops, was her sister's fiancé, also on his way to spend Christmas at Thompson Hall. *Christmas*

BROWN, MARYANNE. The younger daughter of Mr. Brown, sought in marriage by the butcher Brisket, if with dowry, and by George Robinson, even without it. One of the principal characters in *The Struggles of Brown, Jones and Robinson.*

BROWN, SEPTIMUS. A permanent official at the Home Office, to whom Daniel Caldigate appealed for his son's freedom. *Caldigate* 57-59, 61

BROWN BEAR INN. *See* Barchester

BROWNBIES of Boolabong. A family of cattle herders, consisting of a father, a former convict, and six sons, most of whom had spent some time in prison for various misdemeanors. They lived mostly by horse and cattle stealing and, though they kept no sheep, their principal diet was sheep and lamb. *Heathcote* 3-9, 11

BROWNLOW, MRS. The widowed sister of Sir Gregory Marrable's late wife, who, with her daughter Edith, lived with Sir Gregory at Dunripple. *Vicar* 44-45, 54, 58, 71

BROWNLOW, MRS. A friend and distant relative of the Underwood family, who lived at Bolsover House, not far from Popham Villa. ". . . a very little old woman, very pretty, very grey, very nicely dressed, and just a little deaf" (1:12:211). *Ralph* 12, 18, 32-33, 50

BROWNLOW, EDITH. A favorite of Sir Gregory Marrable, who tried unsuccessfully to marry her first to his son and then to Walter Marrable. ". . . she was pretty, soft, ladylike, with a sweet dash of quiet pleasant humour" (44: 285). *Vicar* 44-45, 54, 58, 67, 71

BROWNRIGGS. One of the farms in the Newton Priory estate, leased to Mr. Walker. *Ralph* 18

BROWN'S HOTEL. *See* London

BRUDO, MADAME. Margaret de Wynter's aunt, a wealthy widow who, still weeping, was not insensible to the charms of love. One of the principal characters in *The Noble Jilt*.

In *Can You Forgive Her?*, represented by Mrs. Greenow.

BRUGES. Bruges in 1792 is the scene of the play *The Noble Jilt*.

BRUHL, ADELA. A young Viennese girl, with whom Fritz Planken danced too often to suit his sweetheart Lotta Schmidt. Coming at the end of a series of misunderstandings between the two, this precipitated Lotta's decision to marry Herr Crippel. *Lotta*

BRUMBY, MRS. A would-be authoress, who made life miserable for the Editor because he refused to publish her worthless writings. *Brumby*

BRUNNENTHAL VALLEY. Frau Frohmann's inn was in the Brunnenthal Valley in the Tyrol. *Frohmann*

BRUSSELS. Florence Mountjoy's uncle Sir Magnus Mountjoy was British Minister at Brussels, and it was to his home that Florence was taken to separate her from Harry Annesley. *Scarborough* 14-15, 30-32

BRUTON STREET. *See* London

BUCKINGHAMSHIRE. The hunting men of Buckinghamshire united with the men of Berkshire to form the BB Hunt. *Ralph* 27, 46

BUCKISH, LORD. Nephew of Lady Arabella Gresham, a minor diplomat in the Embassy in Paris. Frank Gresham was sent to live with him for a year, in the hope that he would outgrow his attachment for Mary Thorne. *Thorne* 30

BUDCOMBE. A parish on the Launay property, of which Mrs. Miles was the patron, and the Rev. Alexander Morrison the rector. *Launay*

BUFFLE, SIR RAFFLE. The fussy, bureaucratic head of the Income Tax Office who was Johnny Eames's chief. ". . . was intended to represent a type, not a man; but the man for the picture was soon chosen, and I was often assured that the portrait was very like. I have never seen the gentleman with whom I am supposed to have taken the liberty." — *Autobiography,* 1:10:239. Most prominent in *The Small House at Allington* and *The Last Chronicle of Barset.*

BUGGINS, MR. The office boy for Lord Petty Bag, who resigned at 60 as he resented having the office held by a commoner. "I don't think it ain't constitutional for the Petty Bag to be in the Commons." *Thorne* 18

BUGGINS, MRS. Margaret Mackenzie's old servant on Arundel Street, with whom she lived for a time after she lost her fortune. *Mackenzie* 23, 25-26

BULL INN. *See* Leeds

BULLBEAN, MR. One of George Hotspur's most objectionable gambling associates, who was willing to testify that he cheated at cards. *Hotspur* 15, 18-19, 22

BULLHAMPTON. A parish seventeen miles from Salisbury, in the gift of St. John's College, Oxford. The setting for *The Vicar of Bullhampton.*

BUMPWELL, DR. An old doctor in Barchester. *Barchester* 23

BUNCE. The senior bedesman at Hiram's Hospital, and one of Mr. Harding's personal friends. "He was one on whose large frame many years, for he was over eighty, had made small havoc, —he was still an upright, burly, handsome figure, with an open, ponderous brow, round which clung a few, though very few, thin grey locks. The coarse black gown of the hospital, the breeches and buckled shoes became him well. . . . This man was certainly the pride of the hospital" (*Warden* 3:34). Briefly in *Warden* and *Barchester*; his death noted in *Last Chron.* 81

BUNCE, JACOB. Phineas Finn's London landlord, who considered himself something of an authority on law because of his work as a journeyman copyist in a legal stationer's office. He lived with his wife Jane, and eight children in Great Marlborough Street. A stout defender of Phineas Finn at his trial for murder. *Finn* 7, 13, 17, 25-26, 28, 44; *Redux* 6, 22

BUNDLESHAM. The home of the Primero family, neighbors of Roger Carbury, in Sussex. *Way We Live* 6

BUNFIT, MR. A detective engaged in the search for the stolen Eustace diamonds. *Eustace* 48-49, 51, 57, 61

BUNGALL and TAPPITT'S BREWERY. *See* Baslehurst.

BUNRATTY, MARQUIS OF. Father of Lord Kilfenora. *Can You* 12-13, 41

BUNTINGFORD. The home of the Thoroughbungs, in Hertfordshire. Mentioned frequently throughout *Mr. Scarborough's Family.*

BUNTINGFORD, LORD. The eldest son of the Duchess of Stevenage, who was prevailed upon to stand up with Marie Melmotte in the quadrille that opened her mother's great ball. He "objected mildly, being a young man devoted to business, fond of his own order, rather shy" (1:4:24). *Way We Live* 4

BURGESS, BARTHOLOMEW. Brother of the Brooke Burgess from whom Miss Stanbury inherited her money. ". . . a tall, thin, ill-tempered old man, as well-known in Exeter as the cathedral, and respected after a fashion. . . . But he was a discontented sour old man, who believed himself to have been injured by all his friends . . . and whose strongest passion it was to hate Miss Stanbury of the Close" (1:35:270-71). *He Knew* 35, 44, 51, 57, 88-89, 97

BURGESS, BROOKE. Nephew of the Brooke Burgess who left his fortune to Miss Stanbury, and her heir. Married Dorothy Stanbury. ". . . a good-looking man, with black whiskers and black hair . . . and pleasant small bright eyes. . . . He was rather below the middle height, and somewhat inclined to be stout. . . . He had a well-cut nose, not quite aquiline, but tending that way, a chin with a dimple on it, and as sweet a mouth as ever declared the excellence of a man's temper" (1:31:243-44). One of the principal characters in *He Knew He Was Right.*

BURKE, THOMAS HENRY (real person). Undersecretary to Lord Spencer, the Lord Lieutenant of Ireland. During the Landleaguer disturbances in 1882 he was "hacked to death in front of the Viceregal Lodge." *Land.* 39

BURMISTON, MR. Son of a rich brewer, whom Lady Wanless had captured for her third daughter, Edith. When it became apparent that the plan to marry her second daughter, Georgiana, to Major Rossiter was not working out, she promoted Mr. Burmiston to the honor of Georgiana's hand, as she thought the girls should marry in the order of their age. *Dugdale*

BURNABY, SERJEANT. The barrister who defended Sir Thomas Underwood at the time of the Percycross petition. *Ralph* 44

BURROWS, MRS. Mother of "Jack the Grinder." A disreputable old woman who kept an "establishment for brandy-balls" at Pycroft Common. The Vicar found Carry Brattle living with her after she had been turned out of her own home by her father. *Vicar* 25

BURROWS, JOHN ("Jack the Grinder"). Convicted of the murder of Farmer Trumbull. He ". . . had been in every prison in Wiltshire and Somersetshire . . ." (10:59). *Vicar* 10, 14-15, 22, 25, 27, 46-48, 51, 69

BURSLEM, The REV. MR. The prebendary at Barchester Cathedral whose place, at his death, was offered by Mr. Sowerby to Mark Robarts. *Framley* 18

BURTON, MR. Junior partner of Beilby and Burton, civil engineers, who managed the Stratton office for the firm. The father of a large family, whose sons were all civil engineers and whose daughters had all married into the same profession. Appears frequently in *The Claverings.*

BURTON, MRS. A practical and understanding mother, who had successfully married off three daughters and was determined that the fourth, Florence, should be as happy as the others. Appears frequently in *The Claverings.*

BURTON, MRS. CECILIA. The charming wife of Theodore Burton, and mother of Cissy, Sophie ("Miss Pert") and Theodore, Jr. A firm friend to Harry Clavering when the rest of the Burton family were very doubtful of him. "She was tall and slight, with large brown eyes, and well-defined eyebrows, with an oval face, and the sweetest, kindest mouth that ever graced a woman. Her dark brown hair was quite plain, having been brushed simply smooth across the forehead, and then collected in a knot behind" (1:8:94-95). *Claverings* 8, 17, 26, 28, 31-34, 37-43

BURTON, FLORENCE. Daughter of Harry Clavering's chief, with whom Harry fell in love after his dismissal by Julia Brabazon. Although severely tried by his continued attentions to his former love, she never lost faith in him. Heroine of *The Claverings.*

BURTON, THEODORE. The oldest of the Burton sons, destined to succeed his father in the firm. "A very hard-working, steady, intelligent man . . . with a bald head, a high forehead, and that look of constant work about him which such men obtain" (1:7:78). *Claverings* 7-8, 26, 28, 31-32, 40-44

BURTON and BANGLES. Wine-merchants with offices in Hook Court. *Last Chron.* 37, 43, 75, 84

BURTON CRESCENT. *See* London

BUSH INN. *See* Dillsborough

BUSTON HALL. The estate of Peter Prosper, in Hertfordshire, which, after his vain attempt to marry Mathilda Thoroughbung and beget an heir, was left to Harry Annesley. Mentioned frequently throughout *Mr. Scarborough's Family*.

BUTTERWELL, MR. When he was promoted to a seat on the Board of Commissioners, Adolphus Crosbie became the Secretary of the General Committee Office. ". . . a pleasant, handsome man of about fifty, who had never yet set the Thames on fire, and had never attempted to do so. . . . He knew that he was not very clever, but he knew also how to use those who were clever" (*Allington* 1:28:282). *Allington* 28, 35, 45, 48, 60; *Last Chron.* 43-44

CAIRO. Where Arthur Wilkinson, accompanied by George Bertram, went for his health. *Bertrams* 38

CALDIGATE, DANIEL. The Squire of Folking, who quarreled with his only son, John, because of his losses at Newmarket, but was reconciled with him when he returned with a fortune from New South Wales. One of the principal characters in *John Caldigate*.

CALDIGATE, GEORGE. Nephew of Daniel Caldigate, who at one time was thought to be the heir to Folking. *Caldigate* 1, 23

CALDIGATE, MRS. HESTER (Bolton). The only child of the second marriage of Nicholas Bolton, completely dominated in her youth by her fanatically religious mother. She married John Caldigate against her mother's wishes and refused to be parted from him when he was falsely indicted for bigamy. Heroine of *John Caldigate*.

CALDIGATE, JOHN. Disinherited by his father after sowing wild oats at Newmarket and elsewhere, he emigrated to New South Wales where he made a fortune in gold-mining. On his return to England he became reconciled with his father and married Hester Bolton. Former mining associates attempted to blackmail him by alleging an earlier marriage in New South Wales. Unable to confute their story, he was tried and sentenced for bigamy. Soon after the trial one of the conspirators turned against her confederates, and when it was proved that the evidence against him was forged, he was pardoned. Hero of *John Caldigate*.

CALIFORNIA. Seeking wealth, Paul Montague invested his small fortune with his uncle and Hamilton K. Fisker in California. On his return to England he was induced to join with Augustus Melmotte in promoting Fisker's fictitious South Central Pacific and Mexican Railway. *Way We Live* 6
See also San Francisco

CALVERT, MARIE. An orphan adopted by La Mère Bauche, who grew to womanhood loving and feeling herself beloved by the son of the house. When his mother forbade the marriage and forced Marie to marry an elderly suitor, she threw herself from the top of a cliff and was killed. Heroine of *La Mère Bauche*.

CAMBOURNE ARMS. *See* Polpenno

CAMBRIDGE. The scene of much of the action in *John Caldigate*, but rarely mentioned as a university town.

CAMBRIDGE UNIVERSITY STUDENTS.
- Annesley, Harry, at St. John's. *Scarborough*
- Baker, Henry, at St. John's. *Thorne*
- Caldigate, John. *Caldigate*
- Clavering, Harry, "a Fellow at his college." *Claverings*
- Cruse, Mr., at Trinity. *Bertrams*
- Gresham, Frank. *Thorne*

Mackenzie, Julius. *Spotted*
Mason, John. *Orley*
Onslow, Herbert. *Heine*
Palliser, Gerald, at Trinity. *Duke*
Scarborough, Augustus. *Scarborough*
Scatcherd, Louis, at Trinity. *Thorne*
Shand, Dick. *Caldigate*
Slope, Josiah. *Barchester*
Trefoil, Dean. *Barchester*

CAMBRIDGESHIRE.

Folking. Home of Daniel Caldigate. *Caldigate*

Nethercoats. John Grey's place near Ely. *Can You*

Puritan Grange. Where the Bolton family lived. *Caldigate*

Twopenny Farm. Leased by Ralph Holt from the Caldigates. *Caldigate*

CAMPAN, THEODORE. An elderly boarder at the inn owned by La Mère Bauche, who connived with her to marry her ward Marie Calvert, although they both knew that she was in love with the innkeeper's son. Immediately after the ceremony Marie jumped from a high cliff and was killed. "He was a tall, well-looking man; always dressed in black garments . . . perhaps fifty years of age, and conspicuous for the rigid uprightness of his back—and for a black wooden leg" (1:18). One of the principal figures in *La Mère Bauche*.

CAMPERDOWN, JOHN. Son of Samuel, and junior member in the firm of Camperdown and Son. *Eustace* 28; *Redux* 59-60

CAMPERDOWN, SAMUEL. The Eustace family lawyer, who was determined that Lizzie must be made to restore the heirloom diamonds to the family estate. ". . . a man turned sixty, handsome, gray-haired, healthy, somewhat florid, and carrying in his face and person external signs of prosperity and that kind of self-assertion which prosperity always produces. . . . The interests of his clients were his own interests, and the legal rights of the properties of which he had the legal charge, were as dear to him as his own blood" (2:28:15-16). Appears frequently in *The Eustace Diamonds*.

CAN YOU FORGIVE HER? London, Chapman and Hall, 1864. 2v.

Author's Comment. "Of *Can You Forgive Her?* I cannot speak with too great affection, though I do not know that of itself it did very much to increase my reputation. As regards the story, it was formed chiefly on that of the play . . . 'The Noble Jilt.' . . . The humourous characters, which are also taken from the play . . . are well done. But that which endears the book to me is the first presentation which I made in it of Plantagenet Palliser, with his wife, Lady Glencora."—*Autobiography*, 1:10:239-40.

Notes. "*Can You Forgive Her?* forms a link uniting Trollope's purely social stories with those which were political as well. Now, for the first time, the shadow of . . . the Duke of Omnium throws itself over the incidents and personages so far as these belong to politics. . . . Today, *Can You Forgive Her?* acquires a new interest from the fact of its showing its author as a pioneer of the problem novel, the point of which generally comes to this—how to act in the conflict between passion or self-indulgence and the laws of good behavior."—Escott, pp. 208-9.

Plot. After the conclusion of a stormy engagement with her reckless and selfish cousin George, Alice Vavasor, a young woman with an independent fortune, engaged herself to a country gentleman, John Grey. The marriage was approved by her father and her highly placed relatives, but George's sister Kate persuaded her that she was not adapted to the quiet life of the country, and she broke her engagement.

Kate was anxious that Alice should marry George to assist him in a parliamentary career, and she weakly consented to renew her engagement, although with a stipulation that the marriage should be postponed for a year.

George's grandfather, whose death he had been eagerly anticipating, disinherited him, and in his disappointment and anger he demanded that Alice furnish the funds to pay his election bills. Mr. Grey learned of this and provided £4000, presumably from Alice's account. George won the election and took his seat, but shortly after was compelled to contest again and lost. When he learned of Mr. Grey's intervention, he was so furiously angry that he tried to kill him. Finally, finding himself without friends or funds, he emigrated to America.

Interwoven with this plot is the story of Plantagenet Palliser and Lady Glencora. Glencora, a wealthy heiress in love with the worthless but charming Burgo Fitzgerald, had been coerced into a loveless marriage with the heir to the Duke of Omnium. His austerity and preoccupation with politics made her life seem dreary and purposeless. Burgo felt that she still loved him, and almost persuaded her to elope with him from a ball given by his scheming aunt Lady Monk, who had provided not only the occasion, but also the funds for her nephew's venture. Mr. Palliser, warned of his wife's danger, arrived at the ball and took Glencora home, where she frankly told him that she still loved Burgo, and begged him to let her go so that he might marry again and have an heir. Although he had just been offered the eagerly anticipated post of Chancellor of the Exchequer, he refused it and took Glencora on an extended European journey.

Alice Vavasor, who was Lady Glencora's cousin and confidante, accompanied them and they were later joined by John Grey, who finally persuaded Alice to renew their engagement. On their return to England they were married at Matching Priory, and Mr. Grey became MP from the Palliser pocket-borough, Silverbridge.

Lady Glencora and her husband were made happy by the birth of a son, Lord Silverbridge, who would become the future Duke of Omnium.

CANE, BETSY. Jilted by Denis McGovery because the cow, a part of her dowry, did not have a calf. *Macdermots* 5

CANEBACK, MAJOR. A sporting friend of Lord Rufford, who was killed by a fall on the hunting field at Rufford Hall. ". . . known to all the world as one of the dullest of men and best riders across country that England had ever produced" (1:11:110). *Amer. Sen.* 11, 22-23; *Ayala's Angel* 23

CANN, BILLY. Accused as one of the thieves who attempted to steal the Eustace diamonds at Carlisle. ". . . that most diminutive of full-grown thieves" (2:49:300). *Eustace* 49, 57, 74, 78

CANOLIN, FATHER. A friend and counselor of Frau Frohmann, who agreed with her, not without an eye to his own comfort, that life at her inn should be cheap, simple and the food plentiful. *Frohmann*

CANTOR, JOSEPH (father and son). Farmers on the estate of Indefer Jones, who witnessed his last will, and through whose testimony it was eventually found. *Cousin* 5-6, 8, 10, 12, 14, 17, 24

CANTRIP, LADY. After the death of the Duchess of Omnium, she acted for a time as duenna to Lady Mary Palliser. Most prominent in *The Duke's Children*; briefly in *Finn* 40, 68; *Redux* 63; and *Prime Min.* 27

CANTRIP, LORD. A Liberal statesman, under whom Phineas Finn served in the Colonial Office. He and his wife were close friends of the Duke and Duchess of Omnium. For meritorious services to the Crown, he was made Knight of the Garter. Prominent in *Phineas Finn, Phineas Redux*, and *The Prime Minister*; briefly in *Duke* 22, 35

CARBOTTLE, MR. The Liberal candidate in opposition to Frank Tregear at the election at Polpenno. *Duke* 55

CARBUNCLE, MRS. JANE. Aunt of Lucinda Roanoke, and confidante and at one time housemate of Lizzie Eustace. Of uncertain past, but seeming present prosperity, she was a hanger-on of wealthy and titled London society.

". . . certainly a handsome woman. She was full-faced,—with bold eyes, rather far apart, perfect black eyebrows, a well-formed broad nose, thick lips, and regular teeth. Her chin was round and short, with, perhaps, a little bearing toward a double chin . . . the wonder of her face was its complexion. . . . But, though that too-brilliant colour was almost always there, covering the cheeks but never touching the forehead or the neck, it would at certain moments shift, change, and even depart. There was no chemistry on Mrs. Carbuncle's cheek, and yet it was a tint so brilliant and so transparent, as almost to justify a conviction that it could not be genuine" (1:36:126).

One of the principal characters in *The Eustace Diamonds*.

CARBURY, SIR FELIX. Trollope's most perfect picture of a cad. After spending his own fortune, he beggared his mother and sister, and as a last resort planned to elope with Marie Melmotte. He gambled away the money she stole from her father for their expenses, and failed to keep his tryst. Through the interest of Lady Carbury's friends he was finally sent off to Germany in charge of a parson, with no means allowed him for his return.

"His heart was a stone. But he was beautiful to look at, ready-witted, and intelligent. He was very dark, with that soft olive complexion which so generally gives to young men an appearance of aristocratic breeding. His hair, which was never allowed to become long, was nearly black, and was soft and silky. . . . His eyes were long, brown in colour, and were made beautiful by the perfect arch of the perfect eyebrow. But perhaps the glory of the face was due more to the finished moulding and fine symmetry of the nose and mouth than to his other features. . . . The form of his chin too was perfect. . . . He was about five feet nine in height, and was as excellent in figure as in face" (1:2:12).

One of the principal characters in *The Way We Live Now*.

CARBURY, HENRIETTA. Daughter of Lady Carbury, who was loved devotedly by her cousin Roger, but, in spite of her mother's insistence, persevered in her attachment for Roger's friend Paul Montague, whom she married. "She, also was very lovely, being like her brother; but somewhat less dark and with features less absolutely regular. . . . She had in her countenance a full measure of that sweetness of expression which seems to imply that consideration of self is subordinated to consideration for others. . . . Her face was a true index of her character" (1:2:13-14). One of the principal characters in *The Way We Live Now*.

CARBURY, MATILDA, LADY. An aspiring but unsuccessful author, fatuously devoted to her disreputable son Sir Felix, and determined to settle her daughter in marriage with her cousin Roger, regardless of her wishes. After Felix was sent to Germany in disgrace, she married Nicholas Broune. "She could write after a glib, commonplace, sprightly fashion, and had already acquired the knack of spreading all she knew very thin, so that it might cover a vast surface. She had no ambition to write a good book, but was painfully anxious to write a book that the critics should say was good" (*Way We Live* 1: 2:11-12). Most prominent in *The Way We Live Now*; briefly, as a guest with her husband at Gatherum, in *Prime Min.* 11

CARBURY, ROGER. Head of the Carbury family, and Squire of Carbury Hall, Suffolk. A second cousin of Felix and of Henrietta, whom he wished to marry. Trollope used him as a mouthpiece for his own denunciation of the hollowness and evil practices of certain phases of English society life.

"At present he was not much short of forty years of age, and was still unmarried. He was a stout, good-looking man, with a firmly set square face, with features finely cut, a small mouth, good teeth, and well-formed chin. His hair was red, curling round his head, which was now partly bald on top. He wore no other beard than small, almost unnoticeable whiskers. His eyes were small, but bright, and very cheery when his humour was good. He was about five feet nine in height, having the appearance of great strength and perfect health. A more manly man to the eye was never seen" (1:6:35).

One of the principal characters in *The Way We Live Now.*

CAREY, MR. The Newton family lawyer. *Ralph* 22, 31, 47

CARLISLE. Where Lizzie Eustace's party spent the night, returning from Portray Castle to London, and where the strong box supposed to contain the diamonds was stolen from her hotel room. *Eustace* 44

CARLTON CLUB. *See* London

CARLTON GARDENS. *See* London

CARLTON TERRACE. *See* London

CARLYLE, THOMAS (real person). Supposed by some critics to have been the original of Dr. Pessimist Anticant. *Warden* 15

CARMARTHEN, Wales. The market town nearest Llanfeare, frequently mentioned in *Cousin Henry.*

"CARMARTHEN HERALD." The newspaper that, by a series of articles regarding the Indefer Jones will, forced Henry Jones to sue it for libel so that he might be brought into court and questioned. *Cousin* 13-14, 16-17, 22

CARMICHAEL, MRS. CATHERINE (Baird). Wife of Peter, whom she hated. After his death she married his cousin John. *Carmichael*

CARMICHAEL, JOHN. A young Australian, who helped manage his cousin Peter's sheep ranch. He was too poor to marry Catherine Baird, and she had married Peter whom she soon came to hate. After Peter's death she refused his estate and turned it over to John, who accepted it on condition that she would marry him. *Carmichael*

CARMICHAEL, PETER. The wealthy owner of a sheep ranch in New Zealand, so harsh and stingy that his young wife hated him. Returning from the town, where he had taken his cousin John after turning him out of his house, he was drowned. *Carmichael*

CARNLOUGH. The home of Thomas Blake, in County Galway. *Land.* 4, 30

CARRARA, Italy. Where Ethelbert Stanhope had a studio for four years, to which he returned after Eleanor Harding refused to marry and support him. *Barchester* 9, 45

CARRICK-ON-SHANNON. The assize town of County Leitrim, where Thady Macdermot was tried and executed for the murder of Myles Ussher. The setting for many of the scenes in *The Macdermots of Ballycloran.*

CARRICK RACES. Where Major McDonnel attempted to assume a sportsmanlike air with an eye on the next election, and where Mr. McKeon took responsibility for making the races an event of note. *Macdermots* 17, 19

CARROLL, PAT. The ringleader of the Landleaguers in County Galway, who refused to pay his rent to Philip Jones, his landlord, and led the gang that flooded the Lough Corrib fields. As it seemed impossible to convict him in his own county, the trial was removed to Dublin, where he was sentenced. One of the principal characters in *The Landleaguers.*

CARROLL, CAPT. PATRICK. An improvident worthless Irishman, who lived on the bounty of his brother-in-law Mr. Grey. The family consisted of a nagging wife and four daughters: Amelia, "a forward, flirting, tricky girl of seventeen"; Sophy, who had delusions of her own importance in the world; Georgiana, "possessed of terrible vitality"; and the youngest, Minna. *Scarborough* 16, 18, 34-35, 62

CARROLL, TERRY. Brother of Pat Carroll. He went to the trial to give evidence against his brother, and was killed in the courtroom. *Land.* 31

CARRUTHERS, LORD GEORGE DE BRUCE. A soldier of fortune living by his wits, who was one of the guests of Lizzie Eustace at Portray and was suspected of being implicated in the theft of the diamonds. After Lizzie was freed from Mr. Emilius, they were married. ". . . he was a long-legged, long-bodied, long-faced man, with rough whiskers and a rough beard on his upper lip, but with a shorn chin. His eyes were very deep set in his head, and his cheeks were hollow and sallow. . . . He had large hands, which seemed to be all bone, and long arms, and a neck which looked to be long; because he so wore his shirt that much of his throat was always bare" (2:36:132). One of the principal characters in *The Eustace Diamonds*; briefly in *Redux* 80

CARSTAIRS, LORD. The eldest son of Lord Bracy, a special student at the Bowick School, where he fell in love with Mary Wortle, the master's daughter, and married her. *Wortle* 6, 10, 16, 20, 22-24

CARTER, The REV. MR. An English Protestant clergyman, who went to County Cork at the time of the famine to administer relief donated by English sympathizers. "Mr. Carter was a tall, thin, austere-looking man; one, seemingly, who had macerated himself inwardly and outwardly by hard living. He had a high, narrow forehead, a sparse amount of animal development, thin lips, and a piercing, sharp, gray eye. . . . He always wore new black gloves, and a very long black coat which never degenerated to rust, black cloth trousers, a high black silk waistcoat, and a new black hat" (3:8:154-55). *Castle Rich.* 37

CARTWRIGHT, MR. An English guest, with his wife and daughter, at Frau Frohmann's inn, who vainly endeavored to teach her the value of money. *Frohmann*

CASALUNGA. Louis Trevelyan's retreat near Siena, where he hid himself after abducting his son. *He Knew* 78-79, 84, 86, 92-93

CASHEL, LADY. Mother of Lord Kilcullen and Lady Selina Grey, and aunt of Fanny Wyndham. A tiresome old lady, dominated by her husband, ignored by her son and despised by her daughter. ". . . a very good-natured old woman, who slept the greatest portion of her time, and knitted through the rest of her existence" (1:12:282-83). *Kellys* 11-14, 29-31, 36-39

CASHEL, LORD. Uncle and guardian of Fanny Wyndham, who, when she became an heiress, tried to break off her engagement to Lord Ballindine, and to persuade her to marry his own son Lord Kilcullen. ". . . a man of about sixty-three, with considerable external dignity of appearance, though without any personal advantage, either in face, figure or manner. He had been an earl, with a large income, for thirty years; and in that time he had learned to look collected, even when his ideas were confused" (1:9:223). One of the principal figures in *The Kellys and the O'Kellys.*

CASSEWARY, MISS. ". . . a certain elderly lady, reported to be in some distant way a cousin of the family . . . who, in the matter of looking after Lady Mab [Grex], did what was supposed to be absolutely necessary. . . . [she] was a great politician, and was one of those who are always foreseeing the ruin of their country" (1:9:108-9). *Duke* 9, 16, 20, 28-29, 31, 34

CASTLE CORRY. The Earl of Altringham's place in Scotland, where George Hotspur visited. *Hotspur* 5, 10

CASTLE MORONY. The home of Philip Jones and his family, in County Galway. The setting for most of *The Landleaguers.*

CASTLE QUIN. The seat of the Earl of Kilfenora, near Liscannor, County Clare. *Eye* 2, 5

CASTLE REEKIE. The home of the Marquis of Auld Reekie, in Scotland. *Can You* 18

CASTLE RICHMOND. The residence of Sir Thomas Fitzgerald and his family, near Kanturk, County Cork, and the setting for *Castle Richmond.*

CASTLE RICHMOND. London, Chapman and Hall, 1860. 3v.

AUTHOR'S COMMENT. "The scene is laid in Ireland, during the famine. . . . This novel . . . is of itself a weak production. The characters do not excite sympathy. The heroine has two lovers, one of whom is a scamp and the other a prig. . . . The dialogue is often lively, and some of the incidents are well told; but the story as a whole was a failure." —*Autobiography*, 1:9:208-9.

PLOT. Sir Thomas Fitzgerald, a wealthy landowner living at Castle Richmond, County Cork, married Mary Wainright, whose former husband was believed to have died in Paris. There were three children, Herbert, Emmeline and Mary. Nearby lived the Countess of Desmond, with her daughter Clara and her young son Patrick. Owen Fitzgerald, a relative of Sir Thomas, and his heir after Herbert, lived at Hap House not far away. Owen was in love with Lady Clara and considered himself engaged to her, but the Countess would not acknowledge the engagement, giving as her reason the unconventional life Owen was supposed to live in his bachelor quarters. Her real reason was that she herself was in love with him.

For some time before the story opens, Matthew Mollett, representing himself to be Lady Fitzgerald's first husband, had been blackmailing Sir Thomas, threatening an exposure that would make their children illegitimate and give the estate to Owen. Mr. Prendergast, the family lawyer, urged a frank acceptance of the situation. Sir Thomas died, broken-hearted, and the family were preparing to leave the Castle when the lawyer discovered that Mollett had been married before he met Mary Wainright and that consequently her marriage to Sir Thomas was a legal one. Herbert succeeded to the estate and married Lady Clara Desmond. Throughout the book there are moving descriptions of the famine of 1846-47.

CASTLEMORRIS. The estate of the Earl of Tulla, Phineas Finn's patron, in County Clare. *Finn* 1-2

CASTLEWELL, LORD. A wealthy patron of the opera, who secured Rachel O'Mahony's engagement at Covent Garden, and wished to marry her. *Land*. 26-28, 32, 34-38, 42

CAT AND WHISTLE (pub). *See* London

CATHELINEAU, MME. FRANÇOISE. Mother of Jacques, who tried vainly to keep him from joining the Royalist revolt. *Vendée* 28

CATHELINEAU, JACQUES (real person). The postilion in St. Florent who struck the first blow in the resistance to the Republican forces. He won the respect and admiration of the Vendeans, and was made their first general-in-chief. He loved Agatha Larochejaquelin, who was present at his death, after he received a fatal wound at Nantes.

"... a very good-looking man, about thirty-five years of age; his hair was very dark, and curled in short, thick clusters; his whiskers were large and bushy, and met beneath his face; his upper lip was short, his mouth was beautifully formed, and there was a deep dimple on his chin; but the charm of his face was in the soft, benignant expression of his eyes; he looked as though he loved his fellow-creatures ..." (1:4:105-6). *Vendée* 2, 4, 6, 9-14

CATHERINE CARMICHAEL; *or* Three Years Running. In *Masonic Magazine*, Christmas number, 1878, pp. 2-16. Never reprinted.

Plot. The orphaned daughter of a drunken and shiftless gold miner in New Zealand, Catherine Baird, was induced to marry a former associate of her father, old Peter Carmichael, owner of a sheep ranch in another part of the colony. At the time of her father's death she met Peter's young cousin John and fell in love with him, but as he had no means of supporting her he gave no sign of wishing to marry her. Peter was wealthy but so harsh and niggardly, so demanding and unfeeling, that Catherine soon hated him. A few months after their marriage he hired his cousin to come to the ranch to assist in its management. His presence was torture to Catherine, torn as she was by hatred of her husband and love for John. The situation became unendurable, and she demanded that he be sent away. Returning from town where he had taken John for the beginning of his journey, Peter was drowned. Although all his property was left to her, her hatred was so great that she refused to accept it and sent for John to turn it over to him. Upon his arrival, sympathizing with her scruples, he accepted the property on the condition that she was to give herself with it.

CAULD-KALE CASTLE. The Aberdeenshire home of Lord Gaberlunzie. Sometimes spelled "Cauldkail Castle." *Clerks* 8, 35

CAVENDISH, LORD FREDERICK CHARLES (real person). An English statesman appointed as Chief Secretary to Lord Spencer, Lord Lieutenant of Ireland in 1882. On his first day in office, in company with Thomas Henry

Burke against whom a plot had been laid, he was "hacked to death in front of the Viceregal Lodge." *Land.* 39

CAVENDISH SQUARE. *See* London

CAVERSHAM. The Longestaffe country place in Suffolk, near Carbury Hall. *Way We Live* 13, 78

CAWSTON. A parish about two miles from Baslehurst, where Mrs. Ray and her daughter Rachel lived. The Rev. Mr. Comfort was the rector. The setting for *Rachel Ray.*

CECIL STREET. *See* London

CEDARS, Twickenham. The estate of Sir John Ball, just outside London. *Mackenzie* 6

CENTURY, DR., of Silverbridge. Called by Dr. Thorne one of his "learned enemies." *Thorne* 7-8, 31

CETTINI, Mademoiselle. *See* Smith, Mrs. Euphemia

CHADWICK, JOHN. The steward of the Bishop of Barchester, and in charge of the financial affairs of Hiram's Hospital. "The present Mr. Chadwick was a worthy scion of a worthy stock, and the tenants on the butts and patches, as well as those on the wide episcopal domains of the see, were well pleased to have to do with so worthy and liberal a steward" (*Warden* 1:5-6). Most prominent in *The Warden* 1-3, 5, 8-9, 21; briefly in *Barchester* 1, 10; *Framley* 6; and *Last Chron.* 34

CHAFFANBRASS. MR. The Old Bailey barrister who is Trollope's most famous attorney, ". . . than whom no barrister living or dead ever rescued more culprits from the fangs of the law" (*Redux* 3:4:40).

"He confined his practice almost entirely to one class of work, the defence namely of criminals arraigned for heavy crimes. . . . To such a perfection had he carried his skill and power of fence, so certain was he in attack, so invulnerable when attacked, that few men cared to come within reach of his forensic flail. . . . To apply the thumbscrew, the boot, and the rack to the victim before him was the work of Mr. Chaffanbrass's life. . . . a little man, and a very dirty little man. He has all manner of nasty tricks about him, which make him a disagreeable neighbour to barristers sitting near to him. He is profuse with snuff, and very generous with his handkerchief. He is always at work upon his teeth, which do not do much credit to his industry. His wig is never at ease upon his head, but is poked about by him, sometimes over one ear, sometimes over the other, now on the back of his head, and then on his nose; and it is impossible to say in which guise he looks most cruel, most sharp, and most intolerable. His linen is never clean, his hands never washed, and his clothes apparently never new" (*Clerks* 3:11:195, 97, 99-200).

Appears first in *Clerks* 40-41, 44, at the trial of Alaric Tudor; later in *Orley* 34, 64-65, 67-72, 75, defending Lady Mason; and finally in *Redux* 57, 60-67 defending Phineas Finn.

CHALDICOTES. The estate of Nathaniel Sowerby, which he mortgaged heavily to maintain a racing stable and sumptuous London quarters. Martha Dunstable bought up the mortgages and it became her home after her marriage to Dr. Thorne. ". . . a place of very considerable pretension . . . a large stone building, probably of the time of Charles the Second." Mentioned frequently in *Framley Parsonage* and *The Last Chronicle of Barset.*

CHAMBERLAINE, The REV. HENRY FITZACKERLY. A prebendary of Salisbury Cathedral, and uncle of Harry Gilmore. ". . . a gentleman of about fifty-five years of age, unmarried, possessed of a comfortable private independence. . . . He was a very handsome man, about six feet high, with large light grey eyes, a straight nose, and a well cut chin. His lips were thin, but his teeth were perfect,—only that they had been supplied by a dentist. His grey hair encircled his head, coming round upon his forehead in little wavy curls, in a manner that had conquered the hearts of spinsters by the dozen in the cathedral" (24:148-49). *Vicar* 1, 24-25, 27, 42, 56

CHAPEAU, JACQUES. ". . . valet, groom, and confidential factotum to Larochejaquelin." He became a Royalist recruiting sergeant, survived the Vendean revolt, married Annot Stein, and retired to Paris to be a barber. One of the principal characters in *La Vendée.*

CHAPTER HOTEL AND COFFEE HOUSE. *See* London

CHARETTE DE LA CONTRIE, FRANÇOIS (real person). A friend of Henri Larochejaquelin, and one of the leaders in the Vendean revolt. Second in command at the Royalist defeat at Nantes. *Vendée* 1-2, 4, 6, 11-12, 14, 33

CHARLEYS, SIR THOMAS, of Charlicoats. The magistrate at Hytesbury at the murder trial of "Jack the Grinder." *Vicar* 15, 17, 19, 47, 51

CHASE OF CHALDICOTES. An old forest, mostly Crown property, near Chaldicotes, ". . . of aged hollow oaks, centuries old, and wide-spreading withered beeches." *Thorne* 2

CHASSÉ, GENERAL. A Dutch general defeated at the siege of Antwerp, whose trousers, kept in a museum in the city, narrowly escaped being cut up as souvenirs by a group of English tourists. *Relics*

CHATEAU OF PRINCE POLIGNAC. A beautiful ruin near Le Puy, where M. Lacordaire took Mrs. Thompson and her two daughters for an excursion, and proposed marriage to Mrs. Thompson. *Chateau*

CHATEAU OF PRINCE POLIGNAC, The. In *Tales of All Countries* [First Series], 1861. Originally published in *Cassell's Illustrated Family Paper*, Oct. 20, 27, 1860.

PLOT. Mrs. Thompson, widow of an English civil servant in India, had placed her older daughter Lillian in a boarding school in Le Puy, and with her younger child Mimmy went there to be near her. At their hotel was a courteous and sympathetic Frenchman, M. Lacordaire, whom she took to be the local banker, and whom she came to love. On a sight-seeing trip to the Chateau of Prince Polignac he asked her to marry him, explaining that he was the village tailor, and although she was distressed at his lack of position, she accepted him.

CHÂTILLON. The meeting place of the Vendean generals after the recapture of the Chateau of Durbellière. It was eventually sacked, the inhabitants murdered, and the whole town burned by the Republicans. *Vendée* 24

CHEEKEY, JOHN. A London lawyer, known as "Supercilious Jack" for his terrifying attitude when cross-questioning. He was retained by Gregory Evans, editor of the "Carmarthen Herald," to represent him at Henry Jones's trial. *Cousin* 17-22

CHEESACRE, SAMUEL. Mrs. Greenow's unsuccessful suitor, whom she induced to marry Charlie Fairstairs. ". . . a fat Norfolk farmer, with not an idea beyond the virtues of stall-feeding. He was a stout, florid man, of about forty-five, a bachelor, apparently much attached to ladies' society, bearing no sign of age except that he was rather bald, and that grey hairs had mixed themselves with his whiskers, very fond of his farming, and yet somewhat ashamed of it when he found himself in what he considered to be polite circles. And he was, moreover, a little inclined to seek the honour which comes from a well-filled and liberally-opened purse" (1:8:58). Most prominent in *Can You Forgive Her?*.

In *The Noble Jilt*, represented by Herr von Hoppen.

CHELSEA DISTRICTS. Represented in Parliament successively by Lord Kilfenora, George Vavasor and Mr. Travers. *Can You* 4, 12, 44, 71-72

CHELTENHAM. Alice Vavasor, when a child, lived with her aunt Lady Macleod at No. 3, Paramount Crescent. *Can You* 1

The home of Mrs. Mountjoy and her daughter Florence. *Scarborough* 2

Where Mary Masters visited Lady Ushant. *Amer. Sen.* 30

CHELTENHAM COLLEGE. Lawrence Twentyman's school. *Amer. Sen.* 1

CHESHIRE. The location of the parish of Plumstock, where the Rev. Mr. Granger was rector. *Widow*

CHESHIRE CHEESE. *See* London

CHESTERTON. A village near Cambridge, the home of the Bolton family. *Caldigate* 2

"CHEVALIER, LE PETIT." *See* Mondyon, Arthur

CHILTERN, OSWALD STANDISH, LORD. Son of the Earl of Brentford, and brother of Lady Laura Standish. Violent in temper and undisciplined in conduct, tarred with a reputation for wildness that he did nothing to refute, he was sent down from Oxford for good cause, and devoted his time almost equally between gambling at cards and the Newmarket races. He squandered the whole of Lady Laura's fortune, and was refused by Violet Effingham, although she loved him dearly. He and Phineas Finn had a duel because of Violet, who finally decided to marry him to reform him. The marriage was a happy one, and they retired to a small country place where Lord Chiltern expended his energies in acting as Master of the Hounds for the Brake Hunt, and became a model country gentleman.

". . . an admirable figure of the English gentleman-savage who hunts ferociously, loves madly, fights violently, and is a good fellow at heart."—Walpole, p. 108.

". . . really represents Trollope's snapshot at the Lord Hartington of his own day, who died eighth Duke of Devonshire."—Escott, p. 259.

"Lord Chiltern was a red man, and that peculiarity of his personal appearance was certainly the first to strike a stranger. It imparted a certain look of ferocity to him. . . . His beard was red, and was clipped, so as to have none of the softness of waving hair. The hair on his head also was kept short, and was very red,—and the colour of his face was red. Nevertheless he was a handsome man, with well-cut features, not tall, but very strongly built, and with a certain curl in the corner of his eyelids which gave him a look of resolution,—which perhaps he did not possess. He was known to be a clever man, and when very young had had the reputation of being a scholar" (*Finn* 1:11:88).

Most prominent in *Phineas Finn* and *Phineas Redux*; briefly in *Prime Min.* 20; *Duke* 62-63; and *Eustace* 17, 47, 80

CHILTERN, VIOLET (Effingham), LADY. The most intimate friend of Lady Laura Standish. Loved and courted successively by Lord Faun, Mr. Appledom, Phineas Finn, and continuously by Lord Chiltern, whom she finally married.

". . . an orphan, an heiress, and a beauty. . . . She was small, with light crispy hair, which seemed to be ever on the flutter round her brows, and which yet was never a hair astray. She had sweet, soft grey eyes. . . . Her cheek was the softest thing in nature, and the colour of it, when its colour was fixed enough to be told, was a shade of pink so faint and creamy that you would hardly dare to call it by its name. Her mouth was perfect . . . almost divine, with the temptation of its full, rich, ruby lips. Her teeth, which she but seldom showed, were very even and very white, and there rested on her chin the dearest dimple that ever acted as a loadstar to men's eyes. . . . In figure she was small. . . . Her feet and hands were delicately fine, and there was a softness about her whole person, an apparent compressibility, which seemed to indicate that she might go into very small compass" (*Finn* 1:10: 80-81).

Most prominent in *Phineas Finn*, but in some degree in each of the six novels in the Parliamentary series. Also briefly, as a guest of Mistletoe, in *Amer. Sen.* 36, 37, 39-40; and, as a guest of Lady Glencora, in *Eustace* 17, 47, 80

CHILTERN HUNDREDS. By a convention in Parliament, the acceptance of the stewardship of the Chiltern Hundreds is equivalent to a resignation of the member's seat. Often referred to in the Parliamentary novels.

CHINA, EMPEROR OF. On his visit to England, he was entertained at a great dinner by Augustus Melmotte. *Way We Live* 35, 53-62

CHISWICK GARDENS. *See* London

CHOLET, BATTLE OF. A severe Royalist defeat, in which D'Elbée was killed and Beauchamps and Charles de Lescure mortally wounded. *Vendée* 25

CHOUANS. Insurgent peasants, largely from Brittany—the outgrowth of the organization formed by Adolphe Denot, called "La Petite Vendée." *Vendée* 34

CHOUARDIN, GENERAL. A Republican general under Santerre. *Vendée* 15

CHOWTON FARM. A 300-acre farm owned by Lawrence Twentyman, a gentleman-farmer. It was originally part of the Morton estate, and was just opposite the front gate of Bragton Hall. *Amer. Sen.* 1, 35

"CHRISTIAN EXAMINER." An Evangelical newspaper published in Littlebath, which printed the Rev. Mr. Maguire's attack on John Ball under the heading "The Lion and the Lamb." *Mackenzie* 24-25, 28, 30

CHRISTMAS AT THOMPSON HALL. N.Y., Harper, 1877. Originally published in *The Graphic*, Christmas number, 1876. Later collected in *Why Frau Frohmann Raised Her Prices and Other Stories*, 1882. An English edition with the title: *Thompson Hall*, was published by Sampson Low, 1885.

PLOT. Mrs. Brown, journeying with her husband from the south of France to her old home in England for the Christmas holidays, spent the night in Paris where Mr. Brown developed a sore throat. Thinking to make a mustard poultice from a pot of mustard she had seen in the salon, Mrs. Brown lost her way on her return and, entering the wrong room, discovered after the poultice had been applied that the patient was not her husband. Traced next morning by the handkerchief she had used, her husband made as satisfactory an explanation as was possible to the aggrieved and blistered Mr. Jones. During the remainder of their journey the Browns found themselves accompanied by this same gentleman, whom on their arrival they discovered to be the intended husband of Mrs. Brown's sister

Jane, who had been invited there to meet them.

CHRISTMAS DAY AT KIRKBY COTTAGE. In *Routledge's Christmas Annual*, 1870, pp. 1-25.

PLOT. Isabel Lownd quarreled with her lover Maurice Archer, because he had said that Christmas was a bore. On Christmas Day after the sermon he explained that it was the observance and not the spirit that annoyed him, and he was forgiven.

CLADY. A village near Desmond Court, where Lady Desmond tried, with insufficient means, to establish a soup kitchen for the famine sufferers. *Castle Rich.* 7-9, 11, 16, 33

CLANDIDLEM, LADY. One of the gossips at the De Courcy house party, who was certain that Plantagenet Palliser intended to elope with Lady Dumbello. *Allington* 17-18, 26, 43

CLARKSON, MR. A money-lender, who tried to collect Laurence Fitzgibbon's "little bill" which Phineas Finn had endorsed. *Finn* 21-22, 27-28, 31

CLAVERING, ARCHIBALD. Brother of Sir Hugh, and cousin of Harry, lazy and stupid in everything but subjects connected with horse-racing. He tried to gain the hand of Lady Ongar, after ascertaining that her money did not revert on a second marriage.

"He was not bad-looking, though his face was unprepossessing to a judge of character. He was slight and well made, about five feet nine in height, with light brown hair, which had already left the top of his head bald, with slight whiskers, and a well-formed moustache. . . . His eyebrows were light-coloured and very slight, and this was made more apparent by the skin above the eyes, which was loose and hung down over the outside corners of them, giving him a look of cunning which was disagreeable" (1:11:131).

One of the principal characters in *The Claverings.*

CLAVERING, FANNY. The younger daughter of the Rev. Henry Clavering, much interested in church and school affairs, who fell in love with her father's unprepossessing curate, Mr. Saul. "She was a pretty, gay-spirited girl, with bright eyes and dark brown hair, which fell in two curls behind her ears" (1:2:24). *Claverings* 1-7, 23-24, 33-34, 44

CLAVERING, HARRY. Son of the Rev. Henry Clavering. Attractive, brilliant and impulsive, he was yet so weak that when Lady Ongar, who had once jilted him, offered herself to him when she became a rich widow, he was almost unequal to telling her that he was engaged to Florence Burton. On the death of his two uncles he came into the estate and title, and married Florence. Hero of *The Claverings.*

CLAVERING, MRS. HENRY. The efficient and amiable wife of the Rev. Henry Clavering. Appears frequently throughout *The Claverings.*

CLAVERING, The REV. HENRY. The rector of Clavering parish, and father of Harry, Mary and Fanny. "He was a kind, soft-hearted, gracious man, tender to his wife, whom he ever regarded as the angel of his house, indulgent to his daughters, whom he idolized, ever patient with his parishioners, and awake,—though not widely awake,—to the responsibilities of his calling. The world had been too comfortable for him, and also too narrow; so that he had sunk into idleness" (1:2:17-18). *Claverings* 1-6, 10-11, 20, 33-35, 41, 44

CLAVERING, HERMIONE (Brabazon), LADY. Completely dominated by her husband Sir Hugh, and without courage to rebel against him. Sister of Lady Ongar. Appears frequently in *The Claverings.*

CLAVERING, SIR HUGH. A brutal tyrant in his own home, and in no sense popular outside it. "The eleventh baronet of that name . . . handsome, every inch an English gentleman . . . given to few words, proud of his name, and rank, and place, well versed in the business of the world, a match for most men in money matters, not ignorant, though he rarely opened a book, selfish, and utterly regardless of the feelings of those with whom he came in contact" (1:11:132). One of the principal characters in *The Claverings.*

CLAVERING, MARY. The elder daughter of the Rev. Henry Clavering, who married a neighboring rector, the Rev. Edward Fielding. *Claverings* 1-7, 44

CLAVERING PARK. The country place of Sir Hugh Clavering, uncomfortable, neglected and cordially hated as a residence by Sir Hugh. The setting for many of the scenes in *The Claverings.*

CLAVERINGS, THE. London, Smith, Elder and Co., 1867. 2v. Originally published in *The Cornhill Magazine*, Feb. 1866-May 1867.

AUTHOR'S COMMENT. "I consider the story as a whole to be good, though I am not aware that the public ever corroborated that verdict."—*Autobiography*, 2:11:2.

NOTES. "*The Claverings* is the best wrought of the novels designed for the *Cornhill*, and as surely conceived as any book he ever wrote."—Sadleir, p. 391.

"It is a novel of atmosphere, and the atmosphere is of that sort very dangerous for the English novelist, the atmosphere captured so supremely well by Thackeray; the green-lighted, close-scented gambling rooms, the shabby adventures of half-deserted spas, the shelving beaches of foreign watering-places, concealed accents, stolen passports, impoverished counts and impertinent ladies' maids. . . . Trollope's most serious attempt to escape from his own personality."—Walpole, p. 131.

PLOT. Harry Clavering, after a brilliant career at Oxford, was jilted by Julia Brabazon in favor of a wealthy old debauchee, Lord Ongar. After an unhappy year on the Continent, culminating in the death of her husband, the wealthy widow, accompanied by the sycophant Sophie Gordeloup and her brother Count Pateroff, established herself in London.

Harry had become a civil engineer and was engaged to Florence Burton, daughter of a member of his firm. Assuming incorrectly that Lady Ongar knew of his engagement, he allowed himself to be again drawn into her circle until it became clear that she wished to renew their old engagement. The temptation was great but he resisted it. About this time Sir Hugh Clavering and his brother were drowned in a storm off the coast of Norway and Harry became the heir to the estate and married Florence.

CLAYTON, CAPT. YORKE. The leader of the fight against the Landleaguers, in hourly peril of his life. Married Edith Jones. ". . . he had small but comfortable private means; he was remarkable among all men for his good looks; and he lacked nothing necessary to make life happy" (1:15:246). One of the principal characters in *The Landleaguers.*

CLEEVE, THE. The home of Sir Peregrine Orme. The setting for much of the action in *Orley Farm.*

CLIFFORD, LADY ANNE. The widowed mother of two boys in Dr. Wortle's school, who, despite her affection and trust both in Dr. and Mrs. Wortle, was induced by her relatives to remove her sons from the school in protest over the presence of Mr. and Mrs. Peacocke. *Wortle* 12, 14

CLISSON, CHATEAU OF. The estate of the De Lescure family, which was sacked and burned by Westermann. *Vendée* 5-6, 17

CLOSERSTIL, MR. Engaged by Sir Roger Scatcherd to forward his parliamentary ambitions. *Thorne* 15-17, 22, 25

Acted for Martha Dunstable in getting possession of Chaldicotes. *Framley* 37

CLOUDESDALE. Sir Harry Hotspur's old butler. *Hotspur* 1, 19

CLUTTERBUCK, MARIA. *See* Broughton, Mrs. Maria (Clutterbuck)

COBBE, FRANCES POWER (real person). Trollope is supposed to have used her as a model for Miss Todd, in *The Bertrams* and *Miss Mackenzie.*

COBBOLD'S ASHES. Hunting country, halfway between Framley and Chaldicotes. *Framley* 14

COCKCHAFFINGTON. A village near Exeter visited by Colonel Osborne, as an excuse for calling on Mrs. Trevelyan. *He Knew* 19-21

COGAN. Under pretense of buying illicit whiskey from the makers and selling it for his own profit, he learned where the stills were and sold the information to Myles Ussher. *Macdermots* 4

COHENLUPE, SAMUEL. The MP for Staines, and associate of Augustus Melmotte in his stockjobbing operations. He disappeared when Melmotte was proved to be a scoundrel. Appears frequently in *The Way We Live Now.*

COLDSTREAM GUARDS. Mountjoy Scarborough was a cornet in the Coldstream Guards. *Scarborough* 1

COLLEGES. *See* Schools and colleges

COLLIGAN, DR. While treating Anty Lynch in her illness, he was approached by Anty's brother Barry with a bribe to murder her. Although recognized as a good doctor, "... he was excessively dirty in his person and practice: he carried a considerable territory beneath his nails; smelt equally strongly of the laboratory and the stable; would wipe his hands on his patient's sheets, and wherever he went left horrid marks of his whereabouts; he was very fond of good eating and much drinking, and would neglect the best customer that ever was sick, when tempted by the fascination of a game of loo" (2:9:204). *Kellys* 23-24, 27, 34-35

COLMAR. The Alsatian town in which George Voss managed the Hôtel de la Poste after he had quarreled with his father. *Granpère* 3

COLZA, MISS. A boarder at Mrs. Tom Mackenzie's house, who spied on Margaret Mackenzie and passed on her information to the Rev. Mr. Maguire as material for his articles, "The Lion and the Lamb," attacking John Ball. She finally married him, after he had lost all hope of marrying Margaret. "... a young lady somewhat older than Miss Mackenzie; but the circumstances of her life had induced her to retain many of the propensities of her girlhood. She was as young looking as curls and pink bows could make her" (1:8:150). *Mackenzie* 8, 18-25, 30

COMFORT, The REV. CHARLES. The rector of Cawston, and a friend and frequent adviser of Mrs. Ray. "Mr. Comfort had been regarded as a Calvinist when he was young, as Evangelical in middle life, and was still known as a Low Churchman in his old age" (1:4:82). *Rachel* 1, 5, 18-19

COMFORT, PATTY. *See* Cornbury, Mrs. Patty (Comfort)

CONDUIT STREET. *See* London

CONG. A village not far from Castle Morony, near which Captain Clayton was shot. The center of the violence in *The Landleaguers. Land.* 46

CONNAUGHT. The district in Ireland in which *The Kellys and the O'Kellys* has its setting.

CONSTANTINOPLE. The setting for chapters 11-12 of *The Bertrams.*

CORDWAINERS' ARMS INN. *See* Percycross

CORK. The Kanturk Hotel, "... that very unsavoury public-house in South Main Street" owned by Mr. O'Dwyer, and presided over by his daughter Fanny, was in Cork. Matthew Mollett and his son Aby made the hotel their headquarters while engaged in blackmailing Sir Thomas Fitzgerald. *Castle Rich.* 6, 13, 15, 23

CORKSCREW, VERAX ("Screwy"). A "navvy" friend of Charley Tudor's in the Internal Navigation Office. *Clerks* 18, 28, 46

CORNBURY, BUTLER. Son of the Squire of Cornbury Grange. His campaign to represent Baslehurst in Parliament is one of Trollope's best descriptions, drawn from his own experience in contesting Beverley. *Rachel* 17-18, 24-26

CORNBURY, MRS. PATTY (Comfort). Wife of Butler Cornbury, and mother of five children. A good electioneer for her husband, and a staunch friend to Rachel Ray in her matrimonial difficulties. "She was bright, well-featured, with speaking lustrous eyes, with perfect complexion, and full bust, with head of glorious shape and figure like a Juno;—and yet with all her beauty she had ever about her an air of homeliness which made the sweetness of her womanhood almost more attractive than the loveliness of her personal charms" (1:7:129). *Rachel* 1, 5-8, 17-18, 23, 26, 30

CORNBURY, WALTER. Cousin of Butler Cornbury, who at Patty's suggestion paid complimentary attention to Rachel Ray at her first ball. *Rachel* 7-8

CORNWALL.

MALACHI'S COVE. Where Mahalla Tringlos and her grandfather lived. *Malachi*

POLWENNING. Frank Tregear's home. *Duke*

TREGOTHNAN HALL. Home of the Docimers. *Ayala*

COSBY LODGE. A small place near Barchester, where Major Grantly lived after his retirement from the army. *Last Chron.* 2, 22, 36, 57-58

COSTA RICA. The setting for *Returning Home.*

COUNTIES, IRISH. *See* Ireland

COURCY. A small town in West Barsetshire near Courcy Castle. It had been an important center in coaching days and still maintained the old inn, the Red Lion. Mentioned frequently in *Doctor Thorne* and *The Small House at Allington.*

COURCY CASTLE. The seat of the De Courcy family in Barsetshire, "... a huge brick pile, built in the days of William III." Frequently mentioned in *Doctor Thorne, Framley Parsonage* and *The Small House at Allington.*

COURTON, JOHN. The guardian of the young Earl Ongar, who tried to purchase Lady Ongar's interest in Ongar Park for his ward. *Claverings* 38

COURTROOM SCENES in Trollope's works, and the characters involved.

Brattle, Sam. *Vicar* 32
Browborough, Mr. *Redux* 44

Caldigate, John. *Caldigate* 41-43
Carroll, Pat. *Land.* 31
Eustace, Lizzie. *Eustace* 74, 78
Finn, Phineas. *Redux* 61-67
Lovel, Countess. *Anna* 28-29, 31
Macdermot, Thady. *Macdermots* 29-32
Mason, Lady. *Orley* 68-69, 71-72, 75
O'Connell, Daniel. *Kellys* 1
Tudor, Alaric. *Clerks* 40-41

COURTSHIP OF SUSAN BELL, The. In *Tales of All Countries* [First Series], 1861. Originally published in *Harper's New Monthly Magazine*, August 1860.

NOTES. A dress rehearsal for the longer story *Rachel Ray*, the chief characters being the same weak mother, the fanatically religious older sister and, as heroine, the younger sister who knew what she wanted.

PLOT. Susan Bell, younger daughter of a widowed boarding-house keeper at Saratoga Springs, N.Y., was courted by Aaron Dunn, a rising young engineer. Susan's dominating sister and her sanctimonious husband, the Rev. Phineas Beckard, professed to find Aaron unsuitable, as too worldly, but opposed the marriage unsuccessfully.

COUSIN HENRY. London, Chapman and Hall, 1879. 2v. Originally published simultaneously in *The Manchester Weekly Times*, Supplement, March 8-May 24, 1879, and in *The North British Weekly Mail.*

NOTES. "*Cousin Henry* paints a shrewd portrait of a mean but pathetic man, not strong enough either for villainy or generosity; tortured in mind; suspected and insulted by his neighbors; but clinging with the obstinate tenacity of weakness to his unhappy secret."—Sadleir, p. 394.

PLOT. As Indefer Jones, the owner of Llanfeare, grew old, he was beset by doubts as to his proper heir. He wished the estate to go to his favorite niece Isabel Broderick, but he also wished that it remain in the hands of a Jones. His only relative of that name was his nephew Henry Jones, living in London, whom he heartily disliked. He made a series of wills, declaring as his heir first Isabel, then Henry, and finally, just before his death, Isabel again. The last-named document was not found and the will giving the property to Henry was proved. Henry, however, knew of the existence of the latter will as he had found it between the pages of a book of sermons that his uncle was reading shortly before he died. For weeks he sat in the library where the book rested on the shelves, fearing its discovery but lacking courage to destroy it.

In Carmarthen and about the estate the belief grew that Henry knew of the existence of the will, and that he knew where it was. The local paper published a series of articles expressing this suspicion. The family lawyer Mr. Apjohn, in order to bring Henry into court for questioning, insisted that he sue the paper for libel, and finally forced him to bring the action. Before the case came into court, the house was again searched and the will found. As no clear case of fraud could be made against Henry, he was allowed to return to London. Indefer Jones's two wishes were finally fulfilled, as Isabel Broderick received the property, and, when she married, her husband took the old man's name.

COVENT GARDEN. *See* London

COVERDALE, KATE and PATTY. Two young cousins of Elizabeth Garrow, who were guests at Thwaite Hall for Christmas. *Mistletoe*

COX, LIEUTENANT. A friend of Ralph, the heir, at the Moonbeam, Barnfield. *Ralph* 8-9, 21, 27, 42, 46

COX, MRS. ". . . a divinely perfect" young widow on the boat from Suez to Southampton, who flirted with George Bertram until she discovered that he had no money, and then returned to her old love, Major Biffin. *Bertrams* 39-40

COX and CUMMINS. London attorneys for Mr. Chadwick, steward of Hiram's Hospital, with chambers in Lincoln's Inn. *Warden* 2-3, 5, 19

CRABSTICK, PATIENCE. Lizzie Eustace's personal maid, who connived in the burglary of the diamonds from the London house, and later married the detective who persuaded her to turn state's evidence. *Eustace* 44-45, 52-53, 58-68, 74, 78

CRABTREE CANONICORUM. A parish in the Barchester diocese, whose rector was the Rev. Dr. Vesey Stanhope. *Warden* 9

CRABTREE PARVA. The small living held by Mr. Harding as a minor canon, and later served by his curate Mr. Smith. *Warden* 13, 16, 21

CRABWITZ, MR. Mr. Furnival's clerk. ". . . a genteel looking man . . . very careful as to his gloves, hat, and umbrella, and not a little particular as to his associates . . . had now been with Mr. Furnival for the last fifteen years, and . . . considered that no inconsiderable portion of the barrister's success had been attributable to his own energy and genius" (1:12:89). Appears frequently in *Orley Farm.*

CRADELL, JOSEPH. A brother clerk of Johnny Eames, who also lived at Mrs. Roper's boardinghouse. After Amelia Roper failed to marry Johnny, she turned to Joseph with better success. Most prominent in *The Small House at Allington*; briefly in *Last Chron.* 15, 48

CRANBOURN HOUSE. Miss Dunstable's London house, ". . . one of those abnormal mansions. . . . It had been built by an eccentric millionaire at an enormous cost, and the eccentric millionaire, after living in it for twelve months, had declared that it did not possess a single comfort, and that it was deficient in most of those details, which . . . are necessary to the very existence of man. . . . The world at large very generally called it Ointment Hall" (2:13:243). *Framley* 13, 29

CRASWELLER, EVA. Daughter and heir of Gabriel Crasweller, ". . . the most perfect piece . . . of youthful feminine beauty . . . perfect in symmetry, in features, in complexion, and in simplicity of manners" (1:2:31-32). Heroine of *The Fixed Period.*

CRASWELLER, GABRIEL. An old friend of President Neverbend of Britannula, and an advocate of the Fixed Period until it came time for him to be "deposited" in the "college" to await his end. ". . . a remarkably handsome man. . . . He was tall, robust, and broad, and [at sixty-seven] there was no beginning even of a stoop about him" (1:2:37). One of the principal characters in *The Fixed Period*

CRAUCHER, SERJEANT. A Republican soldier under Westermann, who attempted to seize Marie de Lescure at Clisson, and was killed by Henri Larochejaquelin. *Vendée* 17

CRAWLEY, BOB. The only living son of the Rev. Josiah Crawley. Dean Arabin was his godfather and sent him to Marlborough School to prepare for Cambridge. Briefly, as an infant, in *Framley* 22, 36; and, as a schoolboy, in *Last Chron.* 1

CRAWLEY, GRACE. The eldest daughter of Josiah Crawley, who married Major Henry Grantly, son of the Archdeacon. ". . . there were those who said that, in spite of her poverty, her shabby outward apparel, and a certain thin, unfledged, unrounded form of person, a want of fulness in the lines of her figure, she was the prettiest girl in that part of the world. . . . No girl ever lived with any beauty belonging to her who had a smaller knowledge of her possession. . . . Nor had she the slightest pride in her own acquirements. That she had been taught in many things more than had been taught to other girls, had come of her poverty and of the desolation of her home. She had learned to read Greek and Italian because there had been nothing else for her to do in that sad house" (*Last Chron.* 1:1:6; 1:30:255). Most prominent in *The Last Chronicle of Barset*; briefly, as a child, in *Framley* 22, 26, 34, 36, 46

She is also one of the characters in the play *Did He Steal It?*

CRAWLEY, JANE. Mr. Crawley's younger daughter. Most prominent in *The Last Chronicle of Barset*; briefly in *Framley* 36

CRAWLEY, The REV. JOSIAH. An Oxford classmate of Dean Arabin, whose life had been embittered by a combination of his own unbending pride and financial difficulties. His work in Cornwall, and later as perpetual curate of Hogglestock parish, had been among the most miserable of men. Though moody, unhappy and disappointed, he was hard-working, conscientious and gave his whole strength to his work. In his abject need he grudgingly received aid from Dean Arabin, and in so doing became possessed of a check that he could not account for. The plot of *The Last Chronicle of Barset* concerns the accusations made against him of stealing the check, and his vindication. He finally became Vicar of St. Ewold's.

"I claim to have portrayed the mind of the unfortunate man with great accuracy and greater delicacy. The pride, the humility, the manliness, the weakness, the conscientious rectitude and bitter prejudices . . . were, I feel, true to nature and well described."—*Autobiography*, 2:15:107.

"He was a man who when seen could hardly be forgotten. The deep angry remonstrant eyes, the shaggy eyebrows, telling tales of frequent anger,—of anger frequent but generally silent,—the repressed indignation of the habitual frown, the large nose and large powerful mouth, the deep furrows on the cheek, and the general look of thought and suffering, all combined to make the appearance of the man remarkable, and to describe to the beholders at once his true character" (*Last Chron.* 1:18:155).

Most prominent in *The Last Chronicle of Barset* and *Framley Parsonage*.

His story, slightly altered, but using his name, is the basis for the play *Did He Steal It?*.

CRAWLEY, MRS. MARY. Wife of the Rev. Mr. Crawley, whose fight to keep her husband and children fed and clothed was unending. ". . . she had endured with him and on his behalf the miseries of poverty, and the troubles of a life which had known no smiles. . . . In all the terrible troubles of their life her courage had been higher than his. The metal of which she was made had been tempered to a steel which was very rare and fine" (*Last Chron.* 1:1:65-66). Most prominent in *The Last Chronicle of Barset* and *Framley Parsonage.*

Appears also in the play *Did He Steal It?*

CREAGH, The REV. COLOMB. A most unpopular priest, quarrelsome and unkempt, who was assistant to Father McCarthy. *Castle Rich.* 18, 25, 32

CREAMCLOTTED HALL. The home of Squire Crowdy, in Devonshire. *Framley* 10

CREW JUNCTION. A borough in

West Barsetshire represented in Parliament by Green Walker. *Framley* 8

"CRIMINAL QUEENS OF THE WORLD." Lady Carbury's book, which was not well received by the critics despite her attempts to wheedle or bribe in order to receive favorable reviews. *Way We Live* 11

CRINKETT, TIMOTHY. A mine owner in Nobble, New South Wales, and one of John Caldigate's partners in the Polyeuka mine, who followed him to England in an attempt to blackmail him. Sometimes referred to as "Thomas." *Caldigate* 8-10, 24-29, 55-64

CRINOLA, DUCA DI. George Roden's uncle, the Italian Minister of Education, who acknowledged George's right to the title, which George, however, refused to use. *Fay* 43-44

"CRINOLINE AND MACASSAR." A short story written by Charley Tudor for publication in the "Daily Delight." *Clerks* 19, 21-23, 26, 46

CRIPPEL, HERR. The elderly violinist and leader of the orchestra at the Vienna Volksgarten whom Lotta Schmidt married. One of the principal characters in *Lotta Schmidt*.

CRITERION. A small place in Berkshire belonging to Sir Francis Geraldine. *Kept Dark* 9-10

CROCKER, SAMUEL. A Post Office clerk who made himself offensive to everyone, but particularly to George Roden and Lord Hampstead. Appears frequently in *Marion Fay*.

CROFTS, DR. JAMES. The physician at Guestwick near the Small House at Allington. Although he had but a small practice and a meager income, he won the hand of Lily Dale's sister Bell. ". . . a slight, spare man, about five feet nine in height, with very bright dark eyes, a broad forehead, with dark hair that almost curled . . . with a thin well-cut nose, and a mouth that would have been perfect had the lips been a little fuller. The lower part of his face, when seen alone, had in it something of sternness, which, however, was redeemed by the brightness of his eyes" (*Allington* 1:9:88). Most prominent in *The Small House at Allington*; briefly in *Last Chron.* 16, 35

CROKER'S HALL. The home of Mr. Whittlestaff, in Hampshire, and the setting for *An Old Man's Love*.

CROLL, MR. Augustus Melmotte's confidential clerk, who married Madame Melmotte after her husband's suicide and emigrated with her to America. *Way We Live* 77, 81-82, 86, 88, 92, 97-98

CROOK, SIR WILLIAM. A friend of Harry Annesley, who offered Harry a post as his private secretary, when Peter Prosper seemed about to disinherit him. *Scarborough* 45

CROPPER and BURGESS. Bankers in Exeter; the firm of which Bartholomew Burgess had been a partner, and in which Brooke Burgess succeeded him. *He Knew* 88

CROSBIE, ADOLPHUS. A socially ambitious young government official, who jilted Lily Dale to marry Lady Alexandrina de Courcy. His marriage was unhappy and after the death of his wife he attempted to renew his courtship of Lily, with no success. "He was a tall, well-looking man, with pleasant eyes and an expressive mouth,—a man whom you would probably observe in whatever room you might meet him. And he knew how to talk, and had in him something which justified talking . . . had his opinions on things,—on politics, on religion, on the philanthropic tendencies of the age, and had read something here and there as he formed his opinion" (*Allington* 1:2:12-13). Most prominent in *The Small House at Allington*; appears frequently in *The Last Chronicle of Barset*.

CROSBIE, LADY ALEXANDRINA (de Courcy). After two broken engagements because of difficulties over marriage settlements, she married Adolphus Crosbie, but was soon separated from him and retired to Baden-Baden with her mother, where she died.

"Alexandrina was the beauty of the family. . . . She had, perhaps, counted too much on her beauty, which had been beauty according to law rather than beauty according to taste, and had looked, probably, for too bounteous a harvest. That her forehead, and nose, and cheeks, and chin were well formed, no man could deny. Her hair was soft and plentiful. Her teeth were good, and her eyes were long and oval. But the fault of her face was this,—that when you left her, you could not remember it" (*Allington* 1:17:165).

Most prominent in *The Small House at Allington*; briefly in *Barchester* 37; and *Thorne* 4

CROSS HALL. The dower house on the Brotherton property, leased to a gentleman-farmer and ardent huntsman, Mr. Price, except for the few months when the Dowager and her daughters were driven from Manor Cross and lived there. *Popenjoy* 6-7

CROSSTREES, LIEUTENANT. The second in command on the "John Bright." *Fixed* 9, 12

CROWDY, MRS. BLANCHE (Robarts). Sister of Mark Robarts. "Blanche had a bright complexion, and a fine neck, and a noble bust . . . a true goddess. . . . Blanche, too was noted for fine teeth. They were white and regular and lofty as a new row of houses in a French city" (1:10:83). *Framley* 10, 26

CROWDY, SQUIRE. Blanche's husband, and owner of Creamclotted Hall. *Framley* 10, 26

CROWE, MR. An attorney at Ennis, who was in the confidence of Fred Neville, and succeeded in buying off Captain O'Hara after Fred had repudiated the Captain's daughter Kate. *Eye* 17, 21

CRUMB, JOHN. The inarticulate miller in Bungay who was in love with Ruby Ruggles. When she ran away to London in search of Sir Felix Carbury, John followed her, thrashed Sir Felix soundly and persuaded Ruby to return to the mill with him. Appears frequently in *The Way We Live Now*.

CRUMBIE, JUDGE. The presiding judge in the case of the Percycross petition. *Ralph* 44

CRUMMIE-TODDY. ". . . an enormous acreage of so-called forest and moor" in the west of Perthshire, about twelve miles from Killancodlem. The shooting was taken by Lord Popplecourt and Reginald Dobbs, and Lord Silverbridge and his brother were their guests. *Duke* 38-40, 42

CRUMP, MR. The landlord of the Bull, at Leeds. *Orley* 6, 9

CRUMP, MRS. The postmistress at Allington. *Allington* 21

CRUMP, JONAS. A violent and uncouth man, brother of Mrs. French, to whose tender care she confided Camilla after her engagement to Mr. Gibson had been broken. *He Knew* 82-83

CRUMP ISLAND. Where Anastasia Bergen and her father lived, near St.

George's, Bermuda. The setting for *Aaron Trow*.

CRUMPLE, JONATHAN. One of the bedesmen at Hiram's Hospital. *Warden*

CRUSE, The REV. MR. Tutor to Mr. Pott, with whom he was taking the grand tour. He made one of Miss Todd's picnic party to the Valley of Jehoshaphat. ". . . educated at Trinity College, Cambridge, and piqued himself much on being far removed from the dangers of Puseyism. . . . He was good-looking, unmarried, not without some talent, and seemed to receive from the ladies . . . more attention than his merits altogether deserved" (1:9:89). *Bertrams* 8-11

CULLEN, FATHER. The curate of Father John. "He was educated at Maynooth, was the son of a little farmer in the neighbourhood, was perfectly illiterate, but chiefly showed his dissimilarity to the parish priest by his dirt and untidiness. He was a violent politician. . . . He was as zealous for his religion as for his politics. A disciple less likely to make converts than Father Cullen it would be difficult to imagine; in language most violent and ungrammatical—in appearance most uncouth —in argument most unfair" (1:5:71-72). *Macdermots* 5, 7, 14, 33

CULPEPPER, CAPTAIN. A hunting companion of Lord Lufton's, ". . . a man with an enormous moustache, and a great aptitude for slaughtering game." *Framley* 11

CUMBERLAND.

The Braeside Harriers Hunt Club was in Cumberland. *Fay*

HUMBLETHWAITE HALL. Estate of Sir Harry Hotspur. *Hotspur*

LOVEL GRANGE. Home of the Earl of Lovel. *Anna*

CUMBERLOW GREEN HUNT. A hunt near Buntingford. *Scarborough* 28-29

CUMBERLY GREEN. A hamlet in the parish of Clavering, where a small chapel was erected chiefly through the efforts of the Rev. Mr. Saul. *Claverings* 2, 6

CUMMINGS, MR. The Marquis of Kingsbury's London lawyer, who handled with great discretion the problem of Mr. Greenwood's blackmailing letters to Lady Kingsbury. *Fay* 63

CUMMINGS, MAURICE. The proprietor of Mount Pleasant, a run-down coffee and sugar plantation in Jamaica. His love for Marian Leslie forms the plot of *Miss Sarah Jack of Spanish Town*.

CURATES AID SOCIETY. The society for which Bishop Yeld secured a large contribution from Augustus Melmotte, and in consequence defended him against all criticism. *Way We Live* 55

CURLING, MR. A Barchester attorney, to whom Mark Robarts went in his trouble with Mr. Sowerby. *Framley* 42-43

CURLYDOWN, MR. The Post Office clerk who testified at the bigamy trial of John Caldigate. *Caldigate* 47-48, 52

CURLYDOWN, JEMIMA. The irrepressible daughter of the Post Office clerk, engaged to Samuel Bagwax. *Caldigate* 52-53, 64

CURRAGH RACE COURSE. Where Dot Blake and Lord Ballindine trained their horses. *Kellys* 2

CURRY HALL. The home of Mrs. Montacute Jones, in Gloucestershire, where she exercised her gift for matchmaking. *Popenjoy*

CURZON STREET. *See* London

CUSTINS. Lady Cantrip's country place, in Dorsetshire, to which the Duke of Omnium banished his daughter Mary Palliser, to keep her away from Frank Tregear. *Duke* 35, 46-48

CUTTWATER, CAPT. BARTHOLOMEW ("Uncle Bat"). A retired navy officer, uncle of Mrs. Woodward, who lived with her at Surbiton Cottage, Hampton. "In person Captain Cuttwater was a tall, heavy man, on whose iron constitution hogsheads of Hollands and water seemed to have had no very powerful effect. He was much given to profane oaths. . . . All that was really remarkable in Uncle Bat's appearance was included in his nose. It had always been a generous, weighty, self-confident nose, inviting to itself more observation than any of its brother features demanded. But in latter years it had spread itself out in soft, porous red excrescences, to such an extent as to make it really deserving of considerable attention" (1:4:67-68). Appears frequently in *The Three Clerks*.

DAGUILAR, MARIE. The only daughter of Mr. Pomfret's Spanish partner, whom John Pomfret traveled down the Guadalquivir to marry. *John Bull*

"DAILY DELIGHT." "A newly projected publication," to which Charley Tudor sent his short stories. *Clerks* 19, 22, 26-27, 46

"DAILY JUPITER." *See* "Jupiter"

"DAILY RECORD." The penny sheet for which Hugh Stanbury wrote, and thereby infuriated his Aunt Stanbury. *He Knew* 4, 6-7, 19, 63, 70

DALE, BELL (Isabella). Lily's older sister and the favorite of her uncle, who wished her to marry his heir Bernard and reign as mistress at the Great House at Allington. Bell was in love with a young doctor in the neighboring town of Guestwick, and married him. One of the principal characters in *The Small House at Allington*.

DALE, BELL and LILY. "They were fair-haired girls, very like each other. . . . They were something below the usual height, being slight and slender in all their proportions. . . . The two girls were very fair, so that the soft tint of colour which relieved the whiteness of their complexion was rather acknowledged than distinctly seen. . . . Their eyes were brightly blue; but Bell's were long, and soft, and tender, often hardly daring to raise themselves to your face; while those of Lily were rounder, but brighter, and seldom kept by any want of courage from fixing themselves where they pleased. . . . There was about them a dignity of demeanour devoid of all stiffness or pride, and a maidenly modesty which gave itself no airs" (*Allington* 1:6:49-50).

DALE, BERNARD. Nephew and heir of the old Squire, who wished him to marry his cousin Bell and offered him £800 a year if he succeeded. After Bell married Dr. Crofts, Bernard married Emily Dunstable. "He was a small slight man, smaller than his uncle, but in face very like him. . . . On the whole he was not ill-looking and . . . carried with him an air of self-assurance and a confident balance, which in itself gives a grace to a young man" (*Allington* 1:2:11). Most prominent in *The Small House at Allington*; briefly in *Last Chron.* 9, 35, 45, 52, 59

DALE, CHRISTOPHER. The old Squire of Allington, uncle of Bell and Lily Dale, whose heir was Capt. Bernard Dale.

"A constant, upright, and by no means insincere man . . . thin and meagre in his mental attributes, by no means even understanding the fulness of a full man, with power of eye-sight very limited in seeing aught which was above him, but yet worthy of regard in that he realized a path of duty and did endeavour to walk therein. . . . In person, he was a plain, dry man, with short grizzled hair and thick grizzled eyebrows. Of beard, he had very little, carrying the smallest possible grey whiskers, which hardly fell below the points of his ears. His eyes were sharp and expressive, and his nose was straight and well-formed,—as was also his chin. But the nobility of his face was destroyed by a mean mouth with thin lips; and his forehead, which was high and narrow, though it forbade you to take Mr. Dale for a fool, forbade you also to take him for a man of great parts, or of wide capacity" (*Allington* 1:1:4-5).

Most prominent in *The Small House at Allington*; briefly in *Last Chron.* 9, 16, 28, 45, 52

DALE, LILY. Her love for the social-climber Adolphus Crosbie and Johnny Eames's unrequited love for her form the plot of *The Small House at Allington.*

". . . one of the characters which readers of my novels have liked the best. . . . I have been continually honoured with letters, the purport of which has always been to beg me to marry Lily Dale to Johnny Eames. Had I done so, however, Lily would never have so endeared herself to these people."—*Autobiography,* 1:10:238.

"Lily Dale . . . was, by inference, the novelist's own ideal, and many readers worship in his company. Certainly Lily is perfect—whether, as at first, she is blithely mischievous; whether . . . she is reserved and watchful; whether . . . she walks with head bravely high, but with a broken heart."—Sadleir, p. 383-84.

Heroine of *The Small House at Allington*; and prominent in *The Last Chronicle of Barset.*

Caricatured as Mary Tomkins in the burlesque *Never, Never,—Never, Never.*

DALE, MRS. MARY. Widow of Squire Dale's youngest brother, whose marriage the Squire never forgave. For the sake of the two daughters, Bell and Lily, the Small House at Allington was put at her disposal. ". . . she was a lady, inwards and outwards, from the crown of her head to the sole of her feet, in head, in heart, and in mind, a lady by education and a lady by nature. . . . And the Squire, though he had no special love for her, had recognized this, and in all respects treated her as his equal" (1:3:20). One of the principal characters in *The Small House at Allington.*

DALE, COL. ORLANDO. Bernard Dale's father, who had married Lady Fanny de Guest and lived at Torquay. ". . . an effete, invalid, listless couple, pretty well dead to all the world beyond the region of the Torquay card-tables" (1:2:12). *Allington* 2, 12, 20, 26, 32-33

DALE, PHILIP. The younger brother of Christopher Dale, and father of Bell and Lily. A government land surveyor who died early, leaving his family only £150 per year. *Allington* 2

D'ALMAVIVAS, MARQUIS. A wealthy Spanish nobleman with a taste for rich and picturesque clothing, who was mistaken by John Pomfret for a bullfighter. *John Bull*

DALRYMPLE, CONWAY. In his youth a poor, struggling artist, and a friend of Johnny Eames. But he ". . . had pushed himself into high fashion . . . [and] the rich English world was beginning to pelt him with gilt sugarplums" (1:24:204). He married the wealthy Clara Van Siever, whose portrait he had painted. Appears frequently in *The Last Chronicle of Barset.*

DALY, MR. J. An attorney in Tuam, employed by Barry Lynch in an attempt to obtain the property left by his father to his sister Anty. ". . . a clever, though not over-scrupulous practitioner" (1:7: 165). *Kellys* 7-9, 17-20, 23, 34

DALY, KATE. Harry Heathcote's sister-in-law, who lived with the family in the bush at Gangoil. She fell in love with Giles Medlicot, their nearest neighbor, whom Harry regarded as his bitter enemy. Not until Medlicot proved his friendship by standing with Heathcote against the Brownbie gang did Kate and Giles admit their love for each other. One of the principal characters in *Harry Heathcote of Gangoil.*

DALY, TOM ("Black Daly"). MFH of the Galway Hounds in County Galway, and a fierce enemy of the Landleaguers because they prevented hunting out of spite to the "gentry." "Black Daly was a man quite as dark as his sobriquet described him. He was tall, but very thin and bony, and seemed not to have an ounce of flesh about his face or body. He had large, black whiskers, —coarse and jet black,—which did not quite meet beneath his chin. . . . He had great dark eyes in his head, deep down, so that they seemed to glitter at you out of caverns. And above them were great bushy eyebrows, every hair of which seemed to be black, and harsh, and hard. . . . For him fox-hunting—fox-hunting for others—was the work of his life" (1:9:154-55, 62). *Land.* 9-11, 20, 23, 46

DAMER, MR. An Englishman traveling in Egypt with his wife, two energetic sons and a charming daughter. *Unprotected*

DAMER, FANNY. One of the party who climbed the Pyramids, where she received and accepted a proposal of marriage from Jefferson Ingram, a young American. *Unprotected*

"DANDY" and "FLIRT." Lady Glencora Palliser's horses, which she drove when she was at Matching Priory. *Can You* 22

D'ARCY, MRS. A friend of Ada and Edith Jones, with whom they stayed when they went to the Galway ball. *Land.* 25

DAUBENY, MR. A Conservative representing East Barsetshire, a friend of the Duke of Omnium, and at one time Prime Minister. Some commentators find in him a resemblance to Disraeli. Most prominent in *Phineas Redux* and *The Prime Minister*; and appears frequently in *Phineas Finn.*

DAVIS, MR. A London moneylender to whom John Caldigate became heavily indebted, causing a serious breach between John and his father. *Caldigate* 1-4

DAVIS, MRS. The landlady at the Cat and Whistle, who tried to persuade Charley Tudor to marry Norah Geraghty. *Clerks* 20, 27-28, 31

DAVIS, JULIA. A friend of Marian Leslie, who demanded suitors with more spirit than Marian's lover Maurice Cummins seemed to have, and remonstrated with her friend for becoming engaged to him. *Sarah*

DAWKINS, SABRINA. An English spinster who prided herself on her ability to travel alone about the world, but who attached herself to organized parties whenever it served her purpose. Principal character in *An Unprotected Female at the Pyramids.*

DEANS STAPLE. A house belonging to the Marquis of Stapledean, near Hurst Staple, Hampshire. *Bertrams* 3

DE BARON, MR. Father of Adelaide Houghton, a friend and neighbor of the Marquis of Brotherton. *Popenjoy* 4, 23, 31, 33, 50-53, 62

DE BARON, ADELAIDE. *See* Houghton, Mrs. Adelaide (de Baron)

DE BARON, CAPT. JACK. Cousin of Adelaide Houghton, and an admiring and devoted friend to Lady Mary Germain. An impecunious young guardsman, much sought-after in society, in particular by Augusta Mildmay, who eventually captured him. "He was about the middle height, light-haired, broad-shouldered, with a pleasant smiling mouth, and well-formed nose; but above all, he had about him that pleasure-loving look, that appearance of taking things jauntily, and of enjoying life . . ." (1:12:165-66). One of the principal characters in *Is He Popenjoy?*.

DE COURCY, LADY ALEXANDRINA. *See* Crosbie, Lady Alexandrina (de Courcy)

DE COURCY, LADY AMELIA. *See* Gazebee, Lady Amelia (de Courcy)

DE COURCY, EARL. The head of the De Courcy family, and brother of Lady Arabella Gresham. "He was a man who had been much given to royal visitings and attendances, to parties in the Highlands, to . . . prolongations of the London season . . . and to various other absences from home. . . . But of late gout, lumbago, and perhaps also some diminution in his powers of making himself generally agreeable, had reconciled him to domestic duties. . . . The Earl was one of those men who could not endure to live otherwise than expensively, and yet was made miserable by every recurring expense" (*Allington* 1:17:162; 1:26:263). Most prominent in *The Small House at Allington*; briefly in *Thorne* 16

DE COURCY, The HON. GEORGE. The second son. ". . . having been a spendthrift all his life, he had now [since his marriage] become strictly parsimonious. Having reached the discreet age of forty, he had at last learned that beggary was objectionable; and he, therefor, devoted every energy of his mind to save shillings and pence. . . . Though possessed of an income, he would take no steps towards possessing himself of a house. He hung by the paternal mansion, either in town or country; drank the paternal wines, rode the paternal horses, and had even contrived to obtain his wife's dresses from the maternal milliner" (*Allington* 1:17:163). Most prominent in *The Small House at Allington*; briefly in *Barchester* 37, 42; *Thorne* 16, 18; and *Last Chron.* 8

DE COURCY, The HON. MRS. GEORGE. Married for her £30,000. "Very young she was not,—having reached some years of her life in advance of thirty. The lady herself was not beautiful, or clever, or of imposing manners—nor was she of high birth. But neither was she ugly, nor unbearably stupid. Her manners were, at any rate, innocent; and as to her birth,—seeing that, from the first, she was not supposed to have had any,—no disappointment was felt. Her father had been a coal merchant" (1:17:162-63). *Allington* 17, 23, 26

DE COURCY, The HON. JOHN. ". . . the third son had as yet taken to himself no wife, and as he had not hitherto made himself conspicuously useful in any special walk of life, his family were beginning to regard him as a burden. Having no income of his own to save, he had not copied his brother's virtue of parsimony; and . . . had made himself so generally troublesome to his father, that he had been on more than one occasion threatened with expulsion from the family roof" (*Allington* 1:17: 163). Most prominent in *The Small House at Allington*; briefly in *Barchester* 37; and *Thorne* 4-5

DE COURCY, LADY MARGARETTA. "The Lady Margaretta was her mother's favorite, and she was like her mother in all things,—except that her mother had been a beauty. The world called her proud, disdainful, and even insolent; but the world was not aware that in all that she did she was acting in accordance with a principle which had called for much self-abnegation. She had considered it her duty to be a De Courcy and an earl's daughter at all times; and consequently she had sacrificed to her idea of duty all popularity, adulation, and such admiration as would have been awarded to her as a well-dressed, tall, fashionable, and by no means stupid young woman" (*Allington* 1:17:165). Most prominent in *The Small House at Allington*; briefly in *Barchester* 37; and *Thorne* 6

DE COURCY, COUNTESS ROSINA. Wife of the Earl. A scheming, heartless woman, intent on forwarding the interests of her large and impecunious family, no matter at whose expense. Most prominent in *The Small House at Allington* and *Dr. Thorne*; briefly in *Barchester* 37

DE COURCY, LADY ROSINA. "The Lady Rosina was very religious, and I do not know that she was conspicuous in any other way" (*Allington* 1:17: 165). Lady Rosina never married, and as the family fortunes waned, she ". . . lived alone in a little cottage outside the old park palings, and still held fast within her bosom all the old pride of the De Courcys. . . . She was a tall, thin, shrivelled-up old woman . . . very melancholy, and sometimes very cross" (*Prime Min.* 1:20:322; 2:7:112). Most prominent in *The Small House at Allington*; briefly, as a guest at the Ullathorne sports, in *Barchester Towers* 37; and, as a guest at Omnium and at Matching Priory, in *Prime Min.* 20-21, 27, 42

DE COURCY FAMILY. "The De Courcys had never been plain. There was too much hauteur, too much pride, we may perhaps even fairly say, too much nobility in their gait and manners, and even in their faces, to allow of their being considered plain; but they were not a race nurtured by Venus or Apollo. They were tall and thin, with high cheek-bones, high foreheads, and large, dignified, cold eyes. The De Courcy girls had all good hair; and, as they also possessed easy manners and powers of talking, they managed to pass in the world for beauties, till they were absorbed in the matrimonial market, and the world at large cared no longer whether they were beauties or not" (*Thorne* 1:1:11-12).

DE GUEST, LADY JULIA. Sister of Lord De Guest, whose household she managed at Guestwick Manor. "She was a tedious, dull, virtuous old woman, who gave herself infinite credit for having remained all her days in the home of her youth, probably forgetting, in her present advanced years, that her temptations to leave it had not been strong or numerous" (*Allington* 1:12: 122). Most prominent in *The Small House at Allington* and *The Last Chronicle of Barset.*

DE GUEST, THEODORE, EARL. Brother-in-law and neighbor of Christopher Dale. Johnny Eames saved him from an attack by a bull, and became a great favorite with him, receiving a substantial legacy in his will.

". . . an unmarried nobleman, who devoted himself chiefly to the breeding of cattle. . . . He was a short, stumpy man, with red cheeks and a round face; who was usually to be seen till dinner-time dressed in a very old shooting coat, with breeches, gaiters, and very thick shoes. . . . There was not much of nobility in his appearance; but they greatly mistook Lord de Guest who conceived that on that account his pride of place was not dear to his soul. His peerage dated back to the time of King John, and there were but three lords in England whose patents had been conferred before his own" (1:12:120-21).

One of the principal characters in *The Small House at Allington.*

DEEPBELL, LADY. A friend of the Wanless family, who exchanged gossip between the Hall and the village. *Dugdale*

DELABARBE DE L'EMPEREUR, M. The Frenchman who bored Katie Woodward at the flower show. In retaliation she danced him to exhaustion at Mrs. Val's ball. *Clerks* 25-26

DELABORDEAU, M. A Frenchman connected in an official capacity with the Suez Canal, whom Miss Dawkins tried to inveigle into an invitation to join his party going to Jerusalem. *Unprotected*

D'ELBÉE, GENERAL (real person). The Vendean soldier chosen as commander-in-chief after the death of Cathelineau. Wounded at Cholet, and soon after shot by the Republicans. *Vendée* 7, 9-11

DEMIJOHN, CLARA. Niece of Mrs. Jemima, with whom she lived, who devoted her leisure to the affairs of the Rodens, the Fays and their guests. She became engaged successively to Daniel Tribbledale, Samuel Crocker and again to Tribbledale, whom she finally married. Appears frequently in *Marion Fay.*

DEMIJOHN, MRS. JEMIMA. One of the gossips of Paradise Row. *Fay* 5-6, 15, 29, 55, 57

DEMOLINES, LADY. "Her husband had been a physician in Paris, and had been knighted in consequence of some benefit supposed to have been done to some French scion of royalty" (1:24:207-8). Appears frequently in *The Last Chronicle of Barset.*

DEMOLINES, MADALINA. An admirer of Johnny Eames, from whose advances, with an eye to matrimony, Johnny extricated himself with difficulty and the aid of a London bobby. Married Peter Bangles. ". . . though she was hardly to be called beautiful, was at any rate remarkable. She had large, dark, well-shaped eyes, and very dark hair, which she wore tangled about in an extraordinary manner, and she had an expressive face,—a face made expressive by the owner's will. Such power of expression is often attained by dint of labour,—though it never reaches to the expression of anything in particular. She was almost sufficiently good-looking to be justified in considering herself to be a beauty" (1:24:208). One of the principal characters in *The Last Chronicle of Barset.*

Caricatured as Anastasia Fitzapplejohn in the burlesque *Never, Never,—Never, Never.*

DENOT, ADOLPHE. A school friend of Henri Larochejaquelin, and a constant visitor at Durbellière, where he came to love Agatha, Henri's sister. Rejected by her, he joined the Republicans and led them against the chateau in an effort to seize her. Half mad with jealousy and pride he disguised himself, rejoined the Royalists, and as the "Mad Captain" became the leader of "La Petite Vendée" in Brittany, and was killed at Laval.

". . . he had beautifully white teeth, an almost feminine mouth, a straight Grecian nose, and delicately small hands and feet; but he was vain of his person, and ostentatious; fond of dress and of jewellery. He was, moreover, suspicious of neglect, and vindictive when neglected; querulous of others, and intolerant of reproof himself; exigeant among men, and more than politely flattering among women. . . . Those who knew him least . . . liked him best" (1:1:11-12).

One of the principal characters in *La Vendée.*

DERBY. Lord Silverbridge and Major Tifto entered their horse "Prime Minister," which came in second, losing them some £2,000. Gerald Palliser, who attended the Derby without permission of his tutor at Cambridge, was sent down because of it. *Duke* 17

DESMOND, CLARA, Dowager Countess of Desmond. Mother of Lady Clara and Patrick. She had married while very young for position, and had gained a title of which she was very proud, a huge estate, with no money to sustain it, and a great deal of unhappiness. She fell in love with Owen Fitzgerald, only to discover that he was in love with her daughter. One of the principal characters in *Castle Richmond.*

DESMOND, LADY CLARA. Although burdened with an unhappy love affair and suffering under her mother's disapproval, she worked with her neighbors the Fitzgeralds for the relief of the peasants during the awful famine of 1846-47. When Herbert Fitzgerald was cleared of the taint of illegitimacy, she married him. Heroine of *Castle Richmond.*

DESMOND, PATRICK, Earl of Desmond. A schoolboy at Eton, who made Owen Fitzgerald his hero although he disapproved of his wish to marry Lady Clara. *Castle Rich.* 1, 5, 11, 29, 31, 36, 38

DESMOND COURT. The huge, ungainly, poverty-stricken residence of Lady Desmond, her son the young Earl, and her daughter Lady Clara. Described in *Castle Richmond* 1

DE TERRIER, LORD. The Tory Prime Minister who succeeded Lord Brock and was succeeded by William Mildmay. *Framley* 23, 25, 29; *Finn* 1, 7, 9, 12, 29, 35

DEVONSHIRE.

Bragg's End Cottage, Cawston. Home of Rachel Ray. *Rachel*

Creamclotted Hall. Home of Squire Crowdy. *Framley*

Sir Francis Geraldine's country estate. *Kept Dark*

Heavitree. Home of Mrs. French and her daughters. *He Knew*

Heavybed House. Estate adjoining Creamclotted Hall. *Framley*

Nuncombe Putney. Where Mrs. Stanbury and her daughters lived. *He Knew*

Oxney Colne. Where the Rev. Mr. Woolsworthy and his daughter Patience lived. *Parson*

DICKENS, CHARLES (real person). It has been suggested that Charles Dickens was the prototype of Mr. Popular Sentiment. *Warden* 15

DID HE STEAL IT? A Comedy in Three Acts. London, privately printed, 1869. 64p.

Notes. A play based on that part of *The Last Chronicle of Barset* having to do with the accusation against Mr. Crawley of having stolen a check. There are some changes in the names and relationships of the characters, but the plot is the same. Major Grantly is represented by Captain Oakley, Mrs. Proudie by Mrs. Goshawk and Mrs. Arabin by Mrs. Lofty. The play was privately printed, and but two copies are known to have survived.

Cast of Characters:

Crawley, Josiah. . . . A schoolmaster at Silverbridge

Crawley, Mrs. . . . His wife

Crawley, Grace. . . . His daughter
Goshawk, Mr. . . . Magistrate at Silverbridge, and director of the school
Goshawk, Mrs. . . . His wife
Hoggett, Dan. . . . Brickmaker at Hogglestock, who cashed the check
Hoggett, Mrs. . . . His wife
Lofty, Mrs. . . . Benevolent old lady of Silverbridge
Oakley, Captain. . . . Son of Mrs. Goshawk, in love with Grace Cawley
Thrumble, Caleb. . . . Schoolmaster who tried to replace Mr. Crawley
Toogood, Mr. . . . Cousin to Mrs. Crawley, a London attorney
Mick Stringer, Clerk; John, Waiter } at The Dragon of Wantly, Silverbridge
Ostler
Policeman
Schoolchildren

DIDON, ELISE. Marie Melmotte's French maid, who assisted in making plans for Marie's elopement with Sir Felix Carbury, and was, in fact, the only one who got on the boat for New York. *Way We Live* 23-25, 41, 49-50, 53

DIE, NEVERSAYE. ". . . the rich, quiet, hard-working old Chancery barrister" (1:16:182). George Bertram began his reading of the law with him. *Bertrams* 12-16

Herbert Fitzgerald went to London to read law under his guidance. *Castle Rich.* 35, 39, 41-42

Consulted as to the legality of Sir Roger Scatcherd's will. *Thorne* 46

DILLSBOROUGH. A small English town, in and about which the action of *The American Senator* takes place. The Bush Inn was the center of its social life, and it was there Senator Gotobed stayed while investigating Goarly's poisoning of the foxes. Mr. Runciman was the innkeeper. The town is also mentioned briefly in *Ayala* 23-24

DILLSBOROUGH CLUB. A group of townspeople who met every Saturday evening at the Bush Inn. *Amer. Sen.* 3-5, 19

"DISABILITIES." A woman's-rights institute, presided over by Miss Mildmay, for the control of which a battle was waged between the Baroness Banmann and Dr. Olivia Q. Fleabody. Frequently mentioned in *Is He Popenjoy?*.

DISRAELI, BENJAMIN (real person). Mentioned in *Ralph the Heir*: "[Squire Newton was] . . . a thorough-going Tory, who, much as he loved England and Hampshire and Newton Priory, feared that they were all going to the dogs because of Mr. Disraeli and household suffrage" (1:11:193). Some critics identify Daubeny with Disraeli.

DOBBES, REGINALD. A friend of Lord Popplecourt, who shared with him the shooting at Crummie-Toddie. ". . . a man of about forty, strong, active, well-made, about five feet ten in height, with broad shoulders and greatly developed legs. He was not a handsome man, having a protrusive nose, high cheek-bones, and long upper-lip; but there was a manliness about his face which redeemed it. Sport was the business of his life, and he thoroughly despised all who were not sportsmen . . ." (2:12:135-136). *Duke* 38, 42

DOBBS, MONTGOMERIE. Adolphus Crosbie's special friend, and best man at his wedding. *Allington* 5, 45, 56

DOCIMER, IMOGENE. In love with her cousin Frank Houston, whom she thought it impossible to marry because they had no fortune. After Frank tried unsuccessfully to marry Gertrude Tringle, Imogene welcomed him back, and they agreed to live in comparative poverty. *Ayala* 14, 18, 28, 38, 41-42, 59-60, 64

DOCIMER, MUDBURY. Imogene's brother, who disapproved of her mar-

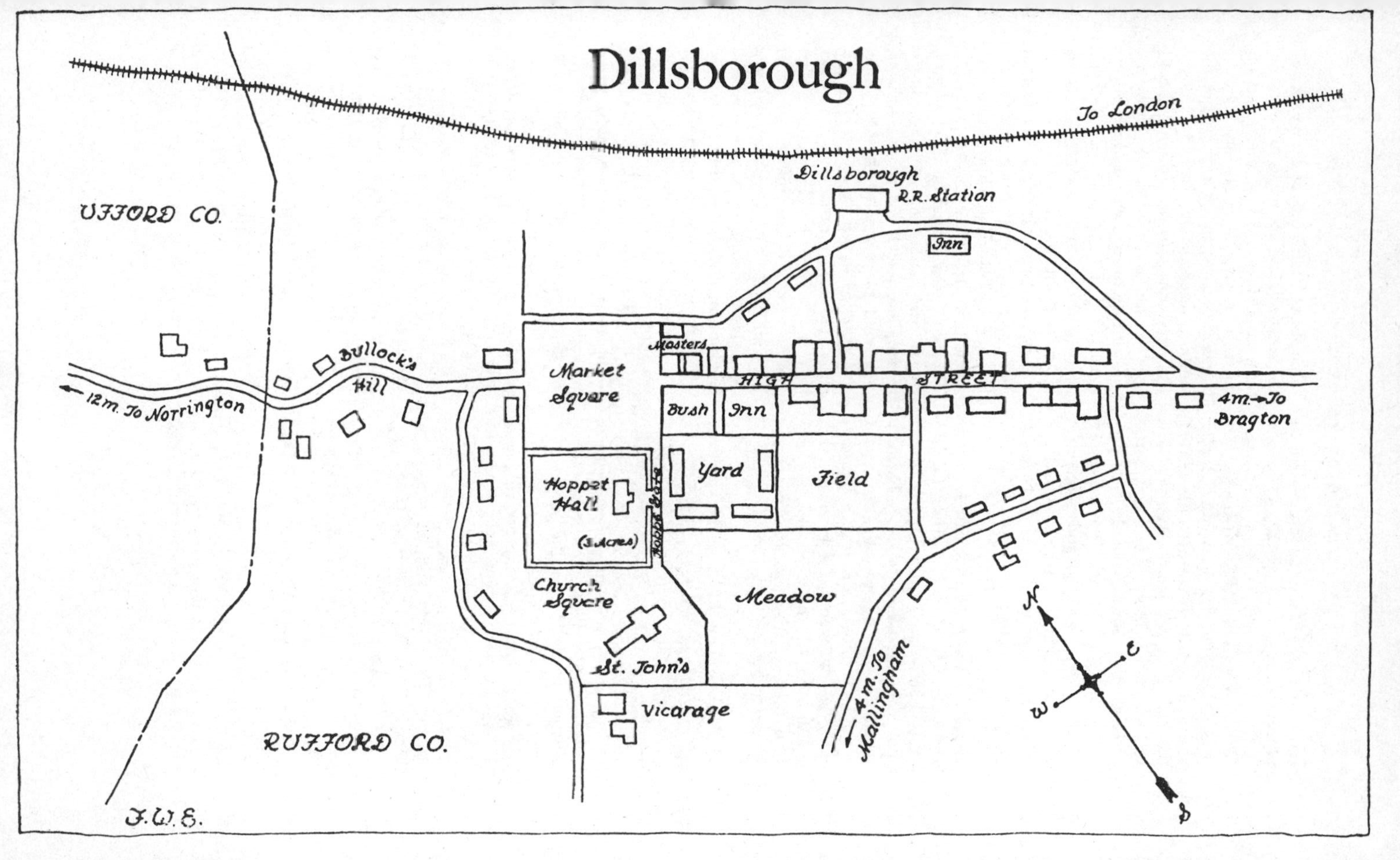
Dillsborough
To London
Dillsborough
R.R. Station
Inn
UFFORD CO.
Masters
Bullock's
Hill
12m. To Norrington
Market
Square
HIGH
STREET
Bush
Inn
4m. To
Bragton
Yard
Field
Hoppet
Hall
(3 Acres)
Hobbs Gate
Church
Square
Meadow
St. John's
Vicarage
4m. To
Mallingham
N
E
W
S
RUFFORD CO.
F.W.S.

riage to Frank Houston and tried to prevent it. *Ayala* 28, 38, 42, 59-60

DOCKWRATH, MRS. MIRIAM (Usbeck). Daughter of Jonathan Usbeck, and wife of Samuel Dockwrath. Under the codicil of Sir Joseph Mason's will she received £2000. "Hers was a nature in which softness would ever prevail;—softness, and that tenderness of heart, always leaning, and sometimes almost crouching, of which a mild eye is the outward sign" (1:1:9). *Orley* 1, 5, 7, 12, 32, 42-43

DOCKWRATH, SAMUEL. A shyster lawyer in Hamworth, married to Miriam Usbeck, and, until Lucius Mason took over the whole of Orley Farm, a tenant. As son-in-law of the old lawyer who had drawn Sir Joseph Mason's will, he discovered the evidence that made necessary the second Orley Farm trial. One of the principal characters in *Orley Farm.*

DOCTOR THORNE. A Novel. London, Chapman and Hall, 1858. 3v.

AUTHOR'S COMMENT. "The plot . . . is good, and I am led therefore to suppose that a good plot,—which, to my feeling, is the most insignificant part of a tale,—is that which will most raise it or most condemn it in the public judgment."—*Autobiography*, 1:7:169.

"Those who don't approve of a middle-aged country doctor as a hero, may take the heir of Greshamsbury in his place, and call the book, if it so please them, 'The loves and adventures of Francis Newbold Gresham the younger'" (*Thorne* 1:1:11).

NOTES. "There are . . . fire-and-thunder Trollopians who will die for Doctor Thorne. By not a few it is considered the best Trollope of them all."—Walpole, p. 52.

PLOT. When young Frank Gresham came of age, the once-prosperous Greshamsbury estate had, by mismanagement, become greatly reduced in value. Boxall Hill, one of the glories of the property, had been sold to Sir Roger Scatcherd, who also held mortgages on the rest of the estate. It was evident that Frank must marry money and his mother, sister of the Earl de Courcy and very conscious of her rank, would hear of nothing else. Frank, however, was already in love with Mary Thorne, a niece of Dr. Thorne, his father's friend and the family doctor—a man of family but with no fortune.

It was known only to the doctor that Mary was the niece of the wealthy Sir Roger, the illegitimate child of his only sister, and that her father was Dr. Thorne's scapegrace brother Henry. Roger Scatcherd, then a village stonemason, had killed his sister's seducer, and while in prison for the crime, she had married a former sweetheart and emigrated to America, telling her brother that the child had died. Dr. Thorne adopted the infant, educated her and finally took her into his home as a loved daughter, where she had been intimate with the Gresham family.

After serving his prison term Roger became a contractor, made a large fortune and for some conspicuous service to the Empire was knighted. Dr. Thorne had remained on good terms with him, trying vainly to restrain the constant drinking that was slowly killing him. After a particularly violent attack of delirium tremens, Sir Roger asked the Doctor to be trustee for his fortune, explaining that his son Louis would inherit and after him the oldest child of his sister in America. The doctor was thus forced to reveal Mary Thorne's identity, whereupon Sir Roger wished to arrange a marriage between his two heirs. Dr. Thorne was appalled, as Louis Scatcherd was notoriously following in his father's footsteps, and in fact outlived him only by a few months.

Mary's large fortune soon dissipated the cloud hanging over her because of her birth, and she was welcomed into the clan by all the Greshams and the

De Courcys, and the family property was once more placed on a firm foundation.

DR. WORTLE'S SCHOOL. London, Chapman and Hall, 1881. 2v. Originally published in *Blackwood's Magazine*, May-Dec. 1880.

Notes. ". . . contains a last addition to the long portrait gallery—a pedagogue in holy orders, in whom, to judge by his temperament, the artist must have taken an autobiographical interest."—Escott, p. 302.

Plot. The Rev. Mr. Peacocke, after a brilliant record at Trinity, became vice-president of a college in St. Louis, Missouri. While there he befriended the deserted wife of Ferdinand Lefroy, and after having verified, as he thought, a report of the man's death, married the widow. Soon after Lefroy returned, made himself known to them, but immediately disappeared again. Unable to trace him, the Peacockes left St. Louis and went to England. There they obtained positions in Dr. Wortle's school where they became very popular, Mrs. Peacocke as house-mother for the smaller boys, and Mr. Peacocke as an inspiring teacher.

Stimulated by Mrs. Stantiloup, a woman who had been worsted by Dr. Wortle in a suit involving school fees, rumors arose that the past of the Peacockes would not bear investigation. The Bishop interfered and Dr. Wortle made inquiry of his teacher, whose story was sympathetically received.

The same day Robert Lefroy, Ferdinand's brother, appeared at the school in an attempt at blackmail, but, finding that the story he had to tell was already known, admitted that his brother had since died. To obtain proof of this statement Mr. Peacocke induced Lefroy to accompany him to San Francisco, where he located Ferdinand's grave. On his return, Dr. Wortle performed another marriage ceremony, and the gossip gradually died down.

The love story of Mary Wortle and the young Lord Carstairs is incidental to the main theme.

DOCTORS in Trollope's works. Trollope's doctors are not an outstanding lot. It may be that his own rugged health brought him into such rare contact with them that his interest in their profession had never been awakened. His best doctor is, of course, Doctor Thorne, but little is said of his ability in the sickroom. Dr. Fillgrave at the deathbed of Sir Roger Scatcherd gives a good account of himself, and the august presence of Sir Omicron Pie adds dignity to the last moments of many of the notables.

Blake, Dr. *Macdermots*
Bold, John, Sr. *Warden*
Broderick, Sir William. *Scarborough*
Bumpwell, Dr. *Barchester*
Century, Dr. *Thorne*
Colligan, Dr. *Kellys*
Crofts, Dr. James. *Allington*
Dugdale, Dr. *Dugdale*
Easyman, Dr. *Thorne, Framley*
Fillgrave, Dr. *Warden, Barchester, Thorne, Last Chron.*
Finn, Dr. Malachi. *Finn, Redux*
MacNuffery, Dr. *Fixed*
Merton, Dr. *Scarborough*
Mewnew, Sir Lamda. *Barchester*
Nupper, Dr. *Amer. Sen.*
Pie, Sir Omicron. *Bertrams, Barchester, Thorne, Redux, Allington*
Powell, Dr. *Cousin*
Pullbody, Dr. *Popenjoy*
Rerechild, Dr. *Barchester, Thorne*
Robarts, Dr. *Framley*
Sawyer, Dr. *Popenjoy*
Shand, Dr. *Caldigate*
Thorne, Dr. Thomas. *Thorne, Last Chron.*

DOLAN, CORNEY. One of the outlaw distillers of potheen at Drumleesh, to whose home Thady Macdermot fled after his murder of Myles Ussher. *Macdermots* 9, 12, 22-23, 25, 33

DOLAN, WIDOW. An intimate acquaintance of Terry Lax, to whose house he escaped after murdering Florian Jones. *Land.* 39

DONELLAN, CAPTAIN. A friend and frequent guest of Owen Fitzgerald at Hap House. *Castle Rich.* 14, 23-24, 30

DORCAS SOCIETY. Founded by Mrs. Prime as an outlet for her managing ability. Rachel Ray's failure to attend was a continual source of antagonism between the two sisters. *Rachel* 1

DORMER, AYALA. Daughter of the artist Egbert Dormer and niece of Lady Tringle and Reginald Dosett. After the death of her parents she lived first with the wealthy Tringles, and then with the Dosetts in comparative poverty. Her love affairs, first with Tom Tringle, then with Captain Batsby, and finally with Colonel Stubbs, form the pattern of the story.

"Ayala the romantic; Ayala the poetic! . . . Her long dark black locks . . . were already known as the loveliest locks in London. She sang as though Nature had intended her to be a singing-bird . . . and flatterers had already begun to say that she was born to be the one great female artist of the world. Her hands, her feet, her figure were perfect. Though she was as yet but nineteen, London had already begun to talk of Ayala Dormer" (1:1:6-7).

Heroine of *Ayala's Angel.*

DORMER, EGBERT. An artist, who died leaving his two daughters Ayala and Lucy utterly dependent on his deceased wife's sister and brother, Lady Tringle and Reginald Dosett. *Ayala* 1

DORMER, LUCY. The older daughter of Egbert Dormer, who lived, as a dependent, first in the home of her uncle Reginald Dosett, and then with her aunt, Lady Tringle. She married a sculptor, Isadore Hamel. One of the principal characters in *Ayala's Angel.*

DORSETSHIRE.

CUSTINS. Lady Cantrip's country place, where she acted as duenna to Lady Mary Palliser. *Duke*

SCROOPE MANOR. Estate of the old Earl of Scroope. *Eye*

DOSETT, MRS. MARGARET. The very worthy but stodgy and parsimonious aunt of Lucy and Ayala Dormer, who gave them a home, one after the other, when their father died. One of the principal characters in *Ayala's Angel.*

DOSETT, REGINALD. Brother of Lady Tringle, and uncle of Ayala and Lucy Dormer, who was a clerk at the Admiralty, and willingly shared his small income with his impoverished nieces. One of the principal characters in *Ayala's Angel.*

DOVE, THOMAS. The learned counsel employed by Mr. Camperdown to give an opinion in the case of the Eustace diamonds. Mr. Dove's opinion was written for Trollope by Charles Merewether. "He was a thin man, over fifty years of age, very full of scorn and wrath, impatient of a fool, and thinking most men to be fools; afraid of nothing on earth,—and, so his enemies said, of nothing elsewhere; eaten up by conceit; fond of law, but fonder, perhaps, of dominion; soft as milk to those who acknowledged his power, but a tyrant to all who contested it; conscientious, thoughtful, sarcastic, bright-witted, and labourious" (1:25:328-29). *Eustace* 23-25, 28, 61, 72, 78

DOWNING (club). *See* London

DOWNING STREET. *See* London

DRAGON (pub). *See* Baslehurst

DRAGON OF WANTLY. *See* Barchester

DRESDEN. Where Lady Laura Kennedy and her father Lord Brentford lived after Lady Laura had left her husband. *Redux* 11-12

Where George Western went when he left his wife, and where his sister Lady Grant followed him to effect a reconciliation. *Kept Dark* 18, 21

DRIBBLE, The REV. ABRAHAM. "A Low-Church scoundrel," who became Bishop of Rochester. A caricature of Mr. Slope in the burlesque *Never, Never,—Never, Never.*

DROUGHT, SIR ORLANDO. A prominent Conservative in Parliament, who held various high positions in the Cabinet. He bitterly opposed the leadership of the Duke of Omnium, and resigned in the hope that it would break up the Coalition. Most prominent in *The Prime Minister*; briefly in *Redux* 35, 63; and *Way We Live* 69, 83

DRUMBARROW. A parish near Castle Richmond, of which the Rev. Aeneas Townsend was rector, and the Rev. Bernard McCarthy was priest. The two men hated each other bitterly, but they were brought together through the Relief Committee work during the famine. *Castle Rich.* 10

DRUMCALLER. A small place near Glenbogie, Scotland, owned by Colonel Stubbs. *Ayala* 18-20

DRUMLEESH. The region near Ballycloran, largely given over to the illegal distilling of potheen, where Corney Dolan lived. *Macdermots* 22

DRUMMOND, LORD. Although in the Coalition government under the Duke of Omnium's leadership, he failed to uphold the Duke's policies, and was much offended when he was not named a Knight of the Garter. On the Duke's withdrawal from politics, Lord Drummond became Prime Minister. Most prominent in *The Prime Minister*; briefly in *Redux* 9; *Duke* 21-22, 71, 78; and, as a guest at Mistletoe, in *Amer. Sen.* 46, 76-77, 80

DRUMSNA. A village in County Leitrim near Ballycloran, where Trollope was living when he conceived the plot for *The Macdermots of Ballycloran.*

DRY and STICKATIT. The lawyers in London who had charge of the affairs of George Bertram, Sr. *Bertrams* 12, 45-46

DUBLIN. Dot Blake and Lord Ballindine stayed at Morrison's Hotel in Dublin during the trial of Daniel O'Connell. *Kellys* 3

TRINITY COLLEGE. Phineas Finn was a graduate (*Finn*); the Rev. Mr. Maguire had been a student there (*Mackenzie*).

DU BOUNG, MR. The local brewer in Silverbridge, who contested the seat for Silverbridge in opposition to Arthur Fletcher. *Prime Min.* 34

He withdrew his name when Lord Silverbridge stood for the borough. *Duke* 14

DUCHESS OF EDINBURGH INN. *See* Holloway

DUFFER, MRS. A gossip of Paradise Row. *Fay* 5, 15, 17, 29, 39, 42, 46

DUGDALE, DR. A country doctor at Beetham, father of Alice and of seven younger children. One of the principal characters in *Alice Dugdale.*

DUGDALE, ALICE. The eldest daughter of the Beetham country doctor, who married John Rossiter, her childhood sweetheart, despite the plans of Lady Wanless to snare him for her daughter Lady Georgiana. "She had a sweet countenance, rather brown, with good eyes . . . far, far away the prettiest girl in that part of the world" (1:11-12). Heroine of *Alice Dugdale.*

DUKE'S CHILDREN, The. A Novel. London, Chapman and Hall, 1880. 3v. Originally published in *All The Year Round,* Oct. 4, 1879-July 24, 1880.

NOTES. The social education of the Duke, begun by Lady Glencora, is continued by their children.

PLOT. Between the close of *The Prime Minister* and the opening of *The Duke's Children,* the Duchess of Omnium died, leaving to the Duke the care of his three children. The eldest, Lord Silverbridge, had been sent down from Oxford as a result of a certain amount of red paint applied to the front of the Dean's house; the second son, Lord Gerald Palliser, was doing indifferently well at Cambridge; Lady Mary Palliser, the only daughter, was determined on what seemed to her father an unsuitable marriage.

Before the story opens, while the family were in Italy, young Frank Tregear, a friend of Lord Silverbridge, had joined them, and with the Duchess' consent had become engaged to Lady Mary. Of this the Duke knew nothing, until, through the insistence of Mrs. Finn, Lady Mary's chaperone, Frank asked for her hand. The Duke was enraged at the temerity of this young man who, without place, position or money, should dare to look so high. The engagement was declared impossible and the young suitor was forbidden to see or communicate with Lady Mary. The daughter conceded her father's authority but made it quite clear that she still considered herself bound by her promise to Frank.

Meanwhile Lord Silverbridge became a partner with a certain Major Tifto in the ownership of a race horse called "Prime Minister," which failed to win the Leger, as a result of Tifto's treachery, and with a loss to Silverbridge of £70,000. The Duke paid the debt on his son's promise to forsake the turf and devote himself to his duties as MP from the family borough. He urged an early marriage, thinking it would steady his son. At about this time a beautiful and talented American girl, Isabel Boncassen, had come to London with her parents and had been received into the best society. Lord Silverbridge met her and fell deeply in love. Although the Duke was attracted to her charm and beauty, and had a sincere respect for her scholarly father, he was strongly opposed to the marriage of the heir to a dukedom and the granddaughter of an American laboringman. Like Lady Mary, Lord Silverbridge had something of the self-will and tenacity of purpose of their mother, and would not be denied. It was not long before his son's insistence and Isabel's charm had vanquished the Duke's prejudice, and when Frank Tregear secured a seat in Parliament he sanctioned both marriages.

DUMBELLO, GRISELDA (Grantly), LADY. *See* Hartletop, Griselda (Grantly), Marchioness of

DUMBELLO, GUSTAVUS, LORD. *See* Hartletop, Gustavus, Marquis of

DUNMORE, Ireland. Where Mrs. Kelly had her inn, and the Lynch family their large house on the edge of the town. ". . . a dirty, ragged little town, standing in a very poor part of the country" (1:4:86-87). The setting for much of the action in *The Kellys and the O'Kellys.*

DUNN, AARON. A young civil engineer, who boarded with Mrs. Bell in Saratoga Springs, N.Y., fell in love with her daughter Susan and married her despite family opposition. Hero of *The Courtship of Susan Bell.*

DUNN, ONESIPHORUS ("Siph"). A friend of Mrs. Thorne, who was delegated by her to be Lily Dale's escort on her rides in Rotten Row. "He was an Irishman, living on the best of everything in the world, with apparently no fortune of his own, and certainly never earning anything. Everybody liked him, and it was admitted on all sides that there was no safer friend in the world. . . . He did not borrow money, and he did not encroach. He did like being asked out to dinner, and he did think that they to whom he gave the light of his countenance in town owed him the return of a week's run in the country" (2:10:97-98). *Last Chron.* 53-54, 59

DUNRIPPLE PARK. The seat of Sir Gregory Marrable, in Worcestershire, which eventually came to Walter Marrable. *Vicar* 44, 59

DUNSTABLE, EMILY. A young cousin of Mrs. Thorne of Chaldicotes, whose wealthy connections caused Mrs. Grantly to hope that she would marry Major Henry Grantly. She became a dear friend of Lily Dale, and married Lily's cousin Bernard. *Last Chron.* 2, 14, 45, 52-53, 59, 76

DUNSTABLE, MARTHA. *See* Thorne, Mrs. Martha (Dunstable)

DUPLAY, ELEANOR. Affianced to Robespierre, but distrusted by him after she pled for mercy for the Vendeans. *Vendée* 23

DUPLAY, SIMON. A French cabinet-maker, in whose home in Paris Robespierre lived. *Vendée* 22

DURBELLIÈRE, CHATEAU OF. The estate of the Larochejaquelin family near St. Florent. Captured by Santerre, retaken by the Royalists, but finally abandoned when the family fled to Chatillon. Described in chapter 3. The setting for much of *La Vendée.*

DURHAM.

SCARROWBY. One of Sir Harry Hotspur's estates. *Hotspur*

TANKERVILLE. The borough represented in Parliament by Phineas Finn. *Redux*

DURTON LODGE. Mr. Western's home in Berkshire. The setting for much of *Kept in the Dark.*

EAMES, MRS. A widow living in Guestwick, whose husband, an unsuccessful farmer, had been an intimate friend of Squire Dale. The Squire was guardian of the two children, Johnny and Mary. *Allington* 4, 9, 13, 52

EAMES, JOHNNY. Johnny Eames has much in common with the young Trollope; living meagerly on a clerkship of £80 a year, and in his loneliness and discouragement getting into all sorts of scrapes, borrowing money from the Jews and narrowly escaping marriage with a barmaid. Johnny's hopeless love for Lily Dale was the guiding light of his life. By saving the life of Lord de Guest he came to be a favorite at Guestwick, and at the old Lord's death received a substantial legacy. He was a cousin of Grace Crawley, and when Mr. Crawley was accused of stealing Mr. Soames' check, he brought Mrs. Arabin back from Italy to clear up the mystery. Prominent in *The Small House at Allington* and *The Last Chronicle of Barset.*

Caricatured as John Thomas in the burlesque *Never, Never,—Never, Never.*

EAMES, MARY. Johnny's sister, and a close friend of Lily and Bell Dale. *Allington* 4, 9, 52

EARDHAM, LADY. Sir George's wife, whom Ralph Newton characterized as "the old harridan." *Ralph* 52, 55-56

EARDHAM, AUGUSTA ("Gus"). Daughter of Sir George Eardham of

Brayboro Park. A dowerless but otherwise eligible girl, who, through the machinations of her managing mother, married Ralph, the heir, and became mistress of Newton Priory. *Ralph* 52, 55-56

EARDHAM, SIR GEORGE. Father of a large family, including three marriageable but dowerless daughters, Emily, Augusta and Josephine. ". . . a stout, plethoric gentleman, with a short temper and many troubles. . . . Sir George suffered much from gout, and had obtained from the ill-temper which his pangs produced a mastery over his daughters which some fathers might have envied" (3:17:297, 302). *Ralph* 52, 55-56

EARLYBIRD, EARL OF. Recommended by the Duke of Omnium for the Garter, despite almost universal objections, particularly vocal from Lord Drummond, who had hoped to get it. "For nearly half a century he had devoted himself to the improvement of the labouring classes, especially in reference to their abodes and education. . . . He was a man very simple in his tastes. . . . He had therefore been able to do munificent things with moderate means. . . . He was a fat, bald-headed old man, who was always pulling his spectacles on and off, nearly blind, very awkward, and altogether indifferent to appearance. Probably he had no more idea of the Garter in his own mind than he had of a Cardinal's hat" (4:4:63-64). *Prime Min.* 64

EAST BARSETSHIRE. *See* Barsetshire, East

EASYMAN, DR. Miss Dunstable's personal physician, who traveled about with her. Since she was never ill, and he was always ill, she took excellent care of him. *Thorne* 16; *Framley* 7-8, 29

EATON SQUARE. *See* London

EBNER, CASPAR. The elderly and wealthy owner of the Black Eagle Inn at Gossau, Austria, who was in love with Katerina Kester. When she cut off and sold her hair to help her lover repay a debt, without her knowledge he bought it, and gave it to her as a wedding present. One of the principal characters in *Katchen's Caprices.*

EBURY STREET. *See* London

ECHANBROIGNES. The town in La Vendée where Michael Stein and his family lived, and to which Madame and Marie de Lescure fled after the burning of Clisson. *Vendée* 6, 20

EDGEHILL HUNT. The hunt twelve miles from Roebury in Oxfordshire, where both George Vavasor and Burgo Fitzgerald hunted. *Can You* 17

EFFINGHAM, VIOLET. *See* Chiltern, Violet (Effingham), Lady

EGHAM. The members of the Runnymede Hunt met at their headquarters in Egham, the inn called the Bobtailed Fox, to dismiss their MFH, Major Tifto. *Duke* 57

EGYPT. The setting for *An Unprotected Female at the Pyramids.*

EIDERDOWN AND STOGPINGUM. A neighboring parish to Plumstead, held, along with Crabtree Canonicorum, by the Rev. Dr. Vesey Stanhope. *Barchester* 9

ELDON (club). *See* London

ELECTION SCENES in Trollope's works. "Very early in life, . . . when I was utterly impecunious and beginning to fall grievously into debt, I was asked by an uncle of mine . . . what destination I should like best for my future life. . . . I replied that I should like to be a Member of Parliament."—*Autobiography*, 2:16:127.

It was not until Trollope was fifty-three that he found leisure to contest a borough, but in 1868, just after his return from the United States, he stood for Beverley. His failure to win the election was not all loss, for in novel after novel he drew on the remembrance of those miserable days of canvassing, to bring out our sympathy for Sir Thomas Underwood, Arthur Fletcher and Phineas Finn in their struggles for a seat.

Cornbury, Butler. *Rachel* 17, 24
Finn, Phineas. *Finn* 27, 32; *Redux* 4, 71
Fletcher, Arthur, and Ferdinand Lopez. *Prime Min.* 29-34
Melmotte, Augustus. *Way We Live* 63-64
Scatcherd, Sir Roger, and Gustavus Moffat. *Thorne* 17, 22
Scott, Undecimus. *Clerks* 8, 24, 29
Silverbridge, Lord. *Duke* 14
Tregear, Frank. *Duke* 55
Underwood, Sir Thomas, and Ontario Moggs. *Ralph* 29, 39, 44
Vavasor, George. *Can You* 44

ELLISON, MRS. A gossip in Exeter, "who lived only four miles from Nuncombe, and kept a pony carriage," primarily to aid her in gathering news. She was particularly detested by Aunt Stanbury, who declared that she had "the bitterest tongue in Devonshire and the falsest." *He Knew* 15

EMBANKMENT THEATRE. *See* London

EMILIUS, The REV. JOSEPH. A Bohemian Jew, who had become a popular preacher in London and moved on the fringe of smart society. He came into Lizzie Eustace's range when all her suitors were withdrawing because of the scandal connected with the theft of her diamonds. Fully aware of the benefit to be derived from Lizzie's fortune, he induced her to marry him. Within the year she had left him, willing to accede to his demand of half her fortune as the price of his absence. Mr. Bonteen attempted to prove that there was a former wife in Prague, and shortly after was found murdered in the streets. Phineas Finn was accused of the murder but was acquitted, and, although suspicion was directed toward Mr. Emilius, the evidence was insufficient to prove the crime. He was, however, convicted of bigamy and sentenced to a prison term.

"He was among the most eloquent of London preachers, and was reputed by some to have reached such a standard of pulpit-oratory, as to have had no equal within the memory of living hearers. In regard to his reading it was acknowledged that no one since Mrs. Siddons had touched him. . . . He had come up quite suddenly . . . and had made church-going quite a pleasant occupation to Lizzie Eustace" (*Eustace* 1:36:123-24).

Most prominent in *The Eustace Diamonds* and *Phineas Redux*.

ENNIS. The small town in County Clare in which Fred Neville's company was located. Frequently mentioned in *An Eye for an Eye*.

ERLE, BARRINGTON. Cousin of Lady Laura Standish, to whom he introduced Phineas Finn. He was for many years private secretary to William Mildmay, the Prime Minister, and could conceive no rewarding life outside the parliamentary circle. Appears frequently in *Phineas Finn, Phineas Redux* and *The Prime Minister*; briefly in *Eustace* 17, 47-48, 54, 80; and *Duke* 52

ESSEX.

George Bertram, Sr., lived at Hadley in Essex. *Bertrams*

POLLINGTON. Home of Dick Shand's parents. *Caldigate*

ETON. Dr. Wortle's school prepared for Eton. *Wortle* 1

STUDENTS.

Ballindine, Lord. *Kellys*
Desmond, Patrick. *Castle Rich.*
Germain, Lord George. *Popenjoy*
Lynch, Barry. *Kellys*
Popplecourt, Lord. *Duke*
Scarborough, Mountjoy and Augustus. *Scarborough*
Scatcherd, Louis. *Thorne*
Silverbridge, Lord. *Duke*
Stanhope, Ethelbert. *Barchester*
Tregear, Frank. *Duke*
Tringle, Tom. *Ayala*

EUPHEMIA. A beautiful fairy-tale princess, who lived in a castle, protected by guards with poisoned arrows. When the Lord of Mountfidget came wooing, she saved his life by applying an antidote to the wound made by one of her retainers' arrows. Heroine of *The Gentle Euphemia.*

EUSTACE, BISHOP. The Bishop of Bobsborough, and uncle of Sir Florian Eustace. *Eustace* 2, 10-11

EUSTACE, FLORIAN. Son of Sir Florian and Lady Lizzie, who was born after his father's death. Seldom appears, but frequently mentioned in *The Eustace Diamonds.*

EUSTACE, SIR FLORIAN. A wealthy young baronet, whom Lady Linlithgow selected as a husband for her penniless niece Lizzie Greystock. Cleverly aided by Lizzie, they won the gamble, although they knew that he was dying, and within a year he was dead. Even before that, he had ample proof of the sort of girl he had married, but by his will she received a generous competence. In addition to that she claimed the family diamonds as a gift. Her fight to keep them is the center of the plot of *The Eustace Diamonds.*

". . . a young man about eight-and-twenty, very handsome, of immense wealth, quite unencumbered, moving in the best circles, popular, so far prudent that he never risked his fortune on the turf or in gambling-houses, with a reputation of a gallant soldier, and a most devoted lover" (1:1:7).

Appears in *The Eustace Diamonds* only in chapter 1, but is mentioned briefly throughout the novel.

EUSTACE, JOHN. Sir Florian's brother and, until the birth of Sir Florian's son, his heir. He was disposed to be much more lenient with Lizzie's claim to the heirloom diamonds than the family lawyer. Appears frequently in *The Eustace Diamonds.*

EUSTACE, LIZZIE (Greystock), LADY. A young adventuress, who trapped Sir Florian Eustace into marriage, knowing that he would soon die and leave her rich and independent. Her claim to the family diamonds brought her into conflict with lawyers, suitors and thieves, but she was determined to keep them. Her later attempts at a brilliant marriage were ill-fated. Frank Greystock knew her too well to risk it; Lord Fawn, frightened by her notoriety, withdrew, although he sorely needed her money; Lord George Carruthers evaded the issue; and she was left at last to the charlatan Emilius. But even the failure of her marriage to Mr. Emilius did not entirely daunt her, and when she disposed of him, it was rumored that she was about to marry Lord George.

"It must be understood, in the first place, that she was very lovely. . . . She was small, but taller than she looked to be, for her form was perfectly symmetrical. Her feet and hands might have been taken as models by a sculptor. Her figure was lithe, and soft, and slim, and slender. . . . And her voice would have suited the stage. . . . Her face was oval. . . . Her hair, which was nearly black . . . she wore bound tight round her perfect forehead, with one long love-lock hanging over her shoulder. . . . Her teeth were without flaw or blemish, even, small, white, and delicate. . . . Her nose was small, but struck many as the prettiest feature of her face. . . . Her eyes, in which she herself thought that the lustre of her beauty lay, were blue and clear, bright as cerulean waters" (*Eustace* 1:2:23-25).

Most prominent in *The Eustace Diamonds*; appears also in *Redux* 45-47, 59, 72, 80; and *Prime Min.* 9, 47, 54

EUSTACE DIAMONDS, The. London, Chapman and Hall, 1873. 3v. Originally published in *The Fortnightly Review*, July 1872-Feb. 1, 1873.

AUTHOR'S COMMENT. ". . . achieved the success which it certainly did attain, not as a love story, but as a record of a cunning little woman of pseudo-fashion, to whom, in her cunning, there came a series of adventures, unpleasant enough in themselves, but pleasant to the reader."—*Autobiography*, 2:19:196.

NOTES. ". . . Disraeli did not consume much contemporary fiction. . . . But soon after the appearance of *The Eustace Diamonds*, meeting Trollope at Lord Stanhope's dinner-table, the great man said to our novelist, 'I have long known, Mr. Trollope, your churchmen and churchwomen; may I congratulate you on the same happy lightness of touch in the portrait of your new adventuress?' "—Escott, p. 280.

PLOT. Lizzie Eustace was the very beautiful, superficially clever and completely selfish daughter of an admiral who was no credit whatever to the British Navy. Her wiles were sufficient to induce the wealthy Sir Florian Eustace to marry her, but within a few months he was dead, leaving her possessed of a life interest in the Scotch property, Portray Castle, and an income of £4000. There was also a diamond necklace, valued at £10,000, which she claimed had been given to her earlier by Sir Florian. Mr. Camperdown, the Eustace family lawyer, asserted with much energy that the jewels were an heirloom and could not be disposed of in the casual manner described by Lizzie, but she refused to give them up.

After a few months of widowhood, she began to search for another husband. Her first choice was Frank Greystock, her cousin, an MP and a rising barrister. Although badly in need of money, he did not rise to her bait as he was engaged to Lucy Morris. Her second candidate was Lord Fawn, an undersecretary in the India Office, who thought that her income would compensate for the fact that he did not love her. He proposed and was accepted, but when he learned about the Eustace diamond scandal he tried to withdraw.

Returning to London from Portray Castle, her hotel room at Carlisle was entered and the safe in which she was known to carry the diamonds was stolen. When the police arrived she did not tell them that the jewels were still in her possession. Lord George Carruthers, whom she had thought might be the "Corsair of her Byronic dreams," and who was a member of her party, was suspected of being in league with the thieves. The Eustace diamonds became the talk of the town, the gossip concerning them even reaching the old Duke of Omnium. Frank Greystock believed Lizzie's story that the jewels had been stolen and defended her against those who proclaimed it to be a clever ruse to retain them. Soon after, there was a second robbery from her London house and this time the jewels finally disappeared, although Lizzie still pretended they had been taken at Carlisle. One of the thieves and the jeweler who had acted as fence were convicted and given prison terms. When Lord George learned the truth he threw Lizzie over, as did Lord Fawn. Frank Greystock had had enough of her and married Lucy, whom he had continued to love despite some philandering with Lizzie. She went back to Portray Castle and shortly after married Mr. Emilius, a reformed

Jew who had become a popular preacher in London.

EVANS, GREGORY. The owner and editor of the "Carmarthen Herald," who, by publishing a series of articles attacking Henry Jones, forced him to sue the paper, thus bringing him into court for questioning. *Cousin* 17, 22

"EVENING PULPIT." Edited by Ferdinand Alf, who later opposed Augustus Melmotte for the Westminster seat in Parliament. " 'The Evening Pulpit' was supposed to give daily to its readers all that had been said and done up to two o'clock in the day by all the leading people in the metropolis, and to prophesy with wonderful accuracy what would be the sayings and doings of the twelve following hours. This was effected with an air of wonderful omniscience, and not unfrequently with an ignorance hardly surpassed by its arrogance" (1:1:5). *Way We Live* 1, 11, 35, 44, 54

EVERSCREECH, The REV. MR. The rector of the church at Hampton that the Woodwards attended. *Clerks* 5

"EVERYBODY'S BUSINESS." A London gossip sheet, which hinted that Dr. Wortle was too friendly with Mrs. Peacocke. *Wortle* 14, 17

EXETER. The setting for many of the scenes in *Kept in the Dark* and *He Knew He Was Right.*

Dr. Robarts, father of Mark and Lucy, was a physician in Exeter. *Framley* 10

Rachel Ray's parents lived in Exeter when they were first married. *Rachel* 1

The inns were the Railway Inn, where Hugh Stanbury stayed when not invited to his aunt's house in the Close, and the Nag's Head, a low place where Aunt Stanbury assumed that Hugh would choose to stay. *He Knew* 12

EYE FOR AN EYE, An. London, Chapman and Hall, 1879. 2v. Originally published in *The Whitehall Review*, Aug. 24, 1878-Feb. 1, 1879.

Notes. ". . . describes the struggle in the mind of a young Englishman of family between the claims of tradition and of personal comfort and those of moral obligation toward the Irish girl who has become his mistress."—Sadleir, p. 394.

Plot. Fred Neville, heir of the Earl of Scroope and a lieutenant of cavalry stationed in Ireland, was a self-indulgent young man, too weak to follow his own best impulses. The Earl wanted him to marry the eminently suitable Sophia Mellerby, but he had already fallen in love with Kate O'Hara, a young girl living in the vicinity of his barracks. She and her mother had been deserted by Kate's scapegrace father, who had served a prison term for swindling and had fled to France to escape punishment for other crimes. Kate was sweet and beautiful, and her distracted mother saw in Fred Neville a means of lifting her daughter from her present poverty. Trusting in Fred's intent to marry her, Kate found that she was bearing his child. When he refused to marry her, giving the feeble excuse of a promise given his uncle that he would not marry a Catholic girl, Kate's maddened mother pushed him over a cliff and he was killed. She was adjudged insane and confined in an asylum. Kate's child died and she joined her dishonored father in France, where they lived on the bounty of Fred's brother, who had succeeded to the title.

FADDLE, SAMUEL. A friend of Tom Tringle, and a fellow member in the Mountaineers Club. Against his better judgment he carried Tom's challenge for a duel to Colonel Stubbs. *Ayala* 32, 35

FAIRSTAIRS, CHARLOTTE, FANNY and JOE. Mrs. Greenow's protégées at Yarmouth. Through her management Mr. Cheesacre was induced to propose to Charlotte. *Can You* 8-9, 20, 39-40, 65, 77

FAMINE YEARS in Ireland, 1846-47. Descriptions of the famine sufferers runs like an undercurrent throughout all of *Castle Richmond.*

FARAGON, MADAME. The owner of the Hôtel de la Poste, in Colmar, who turned over its management to her young relative George Voss. *Granpère* 3, 10, 14, 18

FATHER GILES OF BALLYMOY. In *Lotta Schmidt and Other Stories*, 1867. Originally published in *The Argosy*, May 1866.

AUTHOR'S COMMENT. "I will not swear to every detail . . . but the main purport . . . is true."—*Autobiography*, 1:4:84.

NOTES. Using the nom de plume of Archibald Green, Trollope relates several stories of his own adventures.

PLOT. Archibald Green, sleeping in a squalid inn at Ballymoy, was awakened by someone entering his room and preparing to go to bed. He threw the intruder down the stairs, badly bruising him, only to find that the man was the village priest, who had generously allowed the stranded stranger to share his own room. Father Giles quickly recovered and the two men became good friends.

FATHER JOHN. *See* McGrath, The Rev. John

FAWCETT FAMILY. They were rather above the Tappitts in social standing in Baslehurst, but, nevertheless, attended the Tappitt ball. "The Fawcetts were a large family living in the centre of Baslehurst, in which there were four daughters, all noted for dancing, and noted also for being the merriest, nicest, and most popular girls in Devonshire. There was a fat good-natured mother, and a thin good-natured father who had once been a banker in Exeter. Everybody desired to know the Fawcetts" (1:6:113). *Rachel* 6-7

FAWN, LADY. Mother of Lord Fawn, with one married daughter, Mrs. Clara Hittaway, and seven unmarried—Augusta, Amelia, Georgiana, Diana, Lydia, Cecilia, Nina. A friend and patron of Lucy Morris. One of the principal characters in *The Eustace Diamonds.*

FAWN, FREDERICK, VISCOUNT. A dull and timid nobleman, desperately in need of money, who held several small posts in the government with no distinction whatever. He was decoyed by Lizzie Eustace into a proposal of marriage, but withdrew, not without much unpleasantness. He tried successively to marry Violet Effingham and Madame Goesler, but, since he had nothing to offer but his title, they did not accept him. At the trial of Phineas Finn for the murder of Mr. Bonteen, he gave such confused and inaccurate testimony that Phineas was almost convicted. Shaken by the possible results of his words, he retired to the country, where he married "a pretty mincing girl" of his mother's choosing. Most prominent in *The Eustace Diamonds* and *Phineas Redux*; briefly in *Finn* 40-41, 53; and *Prime Min.* 6

FAWN COURT. The Fawn estate in Richmond, where Lucy Morris was governess to the two youngest of Lady Fawn's seven daughters. The setting for many of the scenes in *The Eustace Diamonds.*

FAY, MARION. Daughter of the Quaker Zachary Fay, and loved by Lord Hampstead. She refused to marry him as she foresaw her early death. Heroine of *Marion Fay.*

FAY, ZACHARY. The senior clerk of Pogson and Littlebird, commission agents in the City, and regarded by his neighbors in Paradise Row as a wealthy man. One of the principal characters in *Marion Fay.*

FENTON'S HOTEL. *See* London

FENWICK, The REV. FRANK. The Vicar of Bullhampton, ". . . a tall, fair-haired man, already becoming somewhat bald on the top of his head, with bright eyes, and the slightest possible amount of whiskers, and a look about his nose and mouth which seems to imply that he could be severe if he were not so thoroughly good-humoured" (1:5-6). Principal character in *The Vicar of Bullhampton.*

FENWICK, MRS. JANET (Balfour). The charming wife of the Vicar of Bullhampton, and close friend of Harry Gilmore and Mary Lowther. "Mrs. Fenwick is as good a specimen of an English country parson's wife as you shall meet in a county,—gay, good-looking, fond of the society around her, with a little dash of fun, knowing in blankets and corduroys and coals and tea; knowing also as to beer and gin and tobacco; acquainted with every man and woman in the parish; thinking her husband to be quite as good as the squire in regard to position, and to be infinitely superior to the squire, or any other man in the world, in regard to his personal self; a handsome, pleasant, well-dressed lady, who has no nonsense about her" (1:6). One of the principal characters in *The Vicar of Bullhampton.*

FETTER LANE. *See* London

FIASCO, MAJOR. A member of the General Committee, in which office Adolphus Crosbie worked. ". . . a discontented, broken-hearted, silent man, who had been sent to the General Committee Office some few years before because he was not wanted anywhere else" (1:28:286). *Allington* 28, 48

FIELD, NORA. An English girl engaged to marry a wealthy American, who sympathized so deeply with the poor weavers out of work because of the cotton famine that, to aid them, she gave all the money she had planned to spend for her trousseau. Heroine of *The Widow's Mite.*

FIELDING, The REV. EDWARD. The Rector of Humbleton, a parish near Clavering, who married Harry Clavering's sister Mary. Of minor importance, but frequently mentioned in *The Claverings.*

FILLGRAVE, DR. A doctor at Barchester, always in a feud with Dr. Thorne of Greshamsbury.

". . . he was five feet five; and he had a little round abdominal protuberance, which an inch and a half added to the heels of his boots hardly enabled him to carry off as well as he himself would have wished. . . . There was, however, a personal dignity in his demeanour, a propriety in his gait, and an air of authority in his gestures which should prohibit one from stigmatising those efforts at altitude as a failure. . . . If his legs were short, his face was not. . . . His hair was gray, not grizzled, nor white, but properly gray; and stood up straight from off his temples on each side with an unbending determination of purpose. His whiskers, which were of an admirable shape, coming down and turning gracefully at the angle of his jaw, were gray also, but somewhat darker than his hair. . . . His eyes were not brilliant, but were very effective, and well under command. . . . His nose was long, and well pronounced, and his chin, also, was sufficiently prominent; but the great feature of his face was his mouth. The amount of secret medical knowledge of which he could give assurance by the pressure of those lips was truly wonderful. By his lips, also, he could be most exquisitely courteous, or most sternly forbidding" (*Thorne* 1:12: 243-45).

Most prominent in *Doctor Thorne* 10, 12, 24, 30-31, 37, 40, 43; briefly in *Barchester* 31, 33; and *Last Chron.* 66-67, 81

FINESPUN, MR. The Chancellor of the Exchequer before Plantagenet Palliser. The Duke of St. Bungay described him: "I admire his character and his genius, but I think him the most dangerous man in England as a statesman. He has high principles,—the very highest; but they are so high as to be out of sight to ordinary eyes. They are too exalted to be of any use for everyday purposes. . . . He has no instinct in politics, but reaches his conclusions by philosophical deduction." *Can You* 59, 80

FINN, DR. MALACHI. Father of Phineas Finn and five daughters, of whom Mathilda and Barbara are the only ones named. A successful doctor in County Clare, who financed his son through his first years in London, although not entirely sympathizing with him in his choice of a lifework. Died in the interim between *Phineas Finn* and *Phineas Redux*. *Finn* 1, 16, 35, 65-66

FINN, MRS. MARIE (Goesler). The widow of a wealthy Viennese banker, Max Goesler, who made such a place for herself in London society that an invitation to her small house in Park Lane became a coveted honor. Gifted with brains, charm and fortune, she had many suitors: the old Duke of Omnium sought her, first as mistress and then as his Duchess; Lord Fawn and Maurice Maule tried to marry her; and finally Phineas Finn, whom she eventually married.

"She was a woman probably something over thirty years of age. She had thick black hair, which she wore in curls,—unlike anybody else in the world,—in curls which hung down low beneath her face. . . . Her eyes were large, of a dark blue colour, and very bright. . . . Her forehead was broad and somewhat low. Her nose was not classically beautiful, being broader at the nostrils than beauty required, and, moreover, not perfectly straight in its line. Her lips were thin. . . . Her chin was well formed, and divided by a dimple which gave to her face a softness of grace which would otherwise have been much missed. But perhaps her great beauty was in the brilliant clearness of her dark complexion. . . . She was somewhat tall, though by no means tall to a fault, and was so thin as to be almost meagre in her proportions" (*Finn* 2:40:23).

Most prominent in *Phineas Finn* and *Phineas Redux*; also an important character in *The Prime Minister* and *The Duke's Children*; and briefly in *Eustace* 17, 47, 54, 64, 80

FINN, PHINEAS. On graduating from Trinity, Phineas Finn went to London to read law. His great friend Laurence Fitzgibbon, who was in Parliament, persuaded him to seek a seat and, on his election to represent Loughshane, introduced him to London society. His first influential friend and political adviser was Lady Laura Standish, with whom he promptly fell in love. Marriage was impossible as neither had property, and she married Robert Kennedy, while he turned for sympathy to the wealthy and beautiful Violet Effingham. After fighting a duel with Lord Chiltern because of her, and refusing to vote with his party on the matter of tenant right, he was forced to resign his seat. Madame Goesler, who had long been interested in him, wished to finance him in gaining another seat, and, when he refused, offered to marry him. Phineas considered himself bound to a childhood sweetheart, and returning to Ireland he married her. *Finn*

After the death of his young wife,

Phineas returned to London to resume his parliamentary career. He was returned from Tankerville, and served the government at various times, as Junior Lord of the Treasury, Undersecretary for the Colonies, Chancellor of the Duchy of Lancaster, Secretary for the Colonies, Chief Secretary for Ireland and First Lord of the Admiralty. In his political life he made a bitter enemy of Mr. Bonteen, and when, following a violent disagreement at the Club, Mr. Bonteen was found murdered, Phineas was accused of the crime. A long, bitter trial followed, but, with evidence secured by Madame Goesler, Phineas was acquitted. Soon after he and Madame Goesler were married. *Redux*

". . . six feet high, and very handsome, with bright blue eyes, and brown wavy hair, and light silken beard" (*Finn* 1:6:50).

Most prominent in *Phineas Finn* and *Phineas Redux*; also an important character in *The Prime Minister* and *The Duke's Children.*

FINNEY, MR. A Barchester attorney, who induced John Bold to interfere in the management of Hiram's Hospital. He was also an attorney for Louis Scatcherd. *Warden* 2, 7, 10, 20; *Barchester* 10; *Thorne* 19, 37, 41

FISHER, MR. Joseph Cradell's friend, who was consulted about his quarrel with Mr. Lupex. *Allington* 10

FISKER, HAMILTON K. The promoter of the South Central Pacific and Mexican Railway, and senior partner in the firm of Fisker, Montague and Montague. After the collapse of the London branch of the firm, managed by Augustus Melmotte, he married Marie Melmotte. ". . . a shining little man,—perhaps about forty years of age, with a well-twisted moustache, greasy brown hair . . . insignificant in appearance. He was gorgeously dressed, with a silk waistcoat and chains, and he carried a little stick. . . . He was troubled by no shyness, by no scruples, and by no fears. His mind was not capacious, but such as it was it was his own, and he knew how to use it" (1:9:55). One of the principal characters in *The Way We Live Now.*

FISKER, MONTAGUE and MONTAGUE. The firm in which Paul Montague had invested all his money, and in which he was junior partner. The main business of the firm was the promotion of a fictitious railroad—the South Central Pacific and Mexican—with headquarters in San Francisco, and a London branch of which Augustus Melmotte was the head. Frequently mentioned in *The Way We Live Now.*

FITZALLEN, ALBERT. The Peckham apothecary who married Mary Snow. ". . . a pale-faced, light-haired youth, with an incipient moustache" (2:17:129). *Orley* 54, 57

FITZAPPLEJOHN, ANASTASIA. She remotely resembles Madalina Demolines, who claimed to be engaged to Johnny Eames. In the burlesque *Never, Never,—Never, Never.*

FITZGERALD, BURGO. Nephew of Lady Monk, and Lady Glencora's first lover. After her marriage he continued to make love to her, and she, persuading herself that her husband would be better off without her, almost agreed to elope with him. Purposeless, and without funds, he wandered about Europe from one gambling place to another, until Plantagenet Palliser found him and arranged for a monthly stipend so long as he lived in a "certain small German town . . . in which there was no public gambling-table."

". . . a terribly handsome man about town, who had spent every shilling that anybody would give him, who was very fond of brandy, who was known, but not trusted, at Newmarket, who was said to be deep in every vice . . ." (*Allington* 2:25:265).

". . . a young man born in the purple of the English aristocracy. He was related to half the dukes in the kingdom, and had three countesses for his aunts. . . . He was one of those young men with dark hair and blue eyes,—who wear no beard, and are certainly among the handsomest of God's creatures" (*Can You* 1:18:141-42).

Prominent in *Can You Forgive Her?*; and briefly in *Allington* 55

FITZGERALD, EMMELINE and MARY. Daughters of Sir Thomas, and the closest friends of Lady Clara Desmond. They appear throughout *Castle Richmond.*

FITZGERALD, HERBERT. The heir of Sir Thomas, the question of whose succession to the title forms the main plot of *Castle Richmond.* An Oxford graduate, eager to fit himself for his place in the country, he organized soup kitchens for the famine sufferers, and built a mill to grind corn for them. After the cloud on his name was cleared away, he married Lady Clara Desmond.

"He was not handsome, as was his cousin Owen; not tall and stalwart and godlike in his proportions. . . . He was smaller and darker than his cousin; but his eyes were bright and full of good-humour. He was clean looking and clean made; pleasant and courteous in all his habits; attached to books in a moderate, easy way, but no bookworm; he had a gentle affection for bindings and titlepages . . ." (1:5:81).

One of the principal characters in *Castle Richmond.*

FITZGERALD, LETTY. Sister of Sir Thomas, living with the family at Castle Richmond. A militant Protestant, and a foe of both the Catholics and the Puseyites. "She was short and dapper in person; not ugly, excepting that her nose was long, and had a little bump or excrescence at the end of it. She always wore a bonnet, even at meal times. . . . She was not illnatured; but so strongly prejudiced on many points as to be equally disagreeable as though she were so" (1:5:95). Of minor importance, but appears throughout *Castle Richmond.*

FITZGERALD, MARY (Wainwright), LADY. Daughter of a poor clergyman in Dorsetshire, whose early marriage to an unscrupulous profligate forms the key to the story of *Castle Richmond.* After her husband had absconded and was reported dead, she married Sir Thomas Fitzgerald.

"They who remembered her in those days told wondrous tales of her surprising loveliness;—how men from London would come down to see her in the parish church; how she was talked of as the Dorsetshire Venus. . . ." In later life, "Her hair was gray, and her eyes sunken, and her lips thin and bloodless; but yet never shall I see her equal for pure feminine beauty, for form and outline, for passionless grace, and sweet, gentle, womanly softness" (1:5:92, 94).

Principal character in *Castle Richmond.*

FITZGERALD, OWEN. The owner of Hap House in County Cork, near Castle Richmond. He loved Lady Clara Desmond and considered himself engaged to her, notwithstanding the opposition of Lady Desmond, who was herself in love with him. "He was a very handsome man—tall, being somewhat over six feet in height—athletic, almost more than in proportion—with short, light, chestnut-tinted hair, blue eyes, and a mouth perfect as that of Phoebus. He was clever, too, though perhaps not educated as carefully as might have been: his speech was usually rapid, hearty, and short, and not seldom caustic and pointed" (1:2:15). One of the principal characters in *Castle Richmond.*

FITZGERALD, SIR THOMAS. The wealthy owner of Castle Richmond, whose marriage to Mary Wainwright was later challenged as illegal by the return of the man who claimed to be her first husband. Almost ruined by the demands made upon him by Mollet, he was at last forced to accept the situation, but the disgrace killed him. Only after his death was it found that Mollet had been married when he went through the ceremony with Mary Wainwright, and that it was that marriage, not Sir Thomas', that was illegal. One of the principal characters in *Castle Richmond.*

FITZGIBBON, MISS ASPASIA. An older sister of Laurence Fitzgibbon, who held the purse strings. She did, however, pay the "little bill" that Phineas Finn had unwisely endorsed for her brother. "She was an old maid, over forty, very plain, who, having reconciled herself to the fact that she was an old maid, chose to take advantage of such poor privileges as the position gave her. . . . She was greatly devoted to her brother Laurence,—so devoted that there was nothing she would not do for him, short of lending him money" (1: 5:33). *Finn* 5, 22, 31

FITZGIBBON, The HON. LAURENCE. Son of Lord Claddaugh, and one of Phineas Finn's best friends. A charming Irishman, who had been in Parliament for his father's borough for fifteen years and persuaded Phineas that there was no life comparable to it. He held various secondary posts in the government: Junior Lord of the Treasury and Undersecretary for the Colonies. Appears frequently in *Phineas Finn* and *Phineas Redux*; briefly in *Prime Min.* 13; and *Eustace* 17

FITZ HOWARD, LORD JAMES. The youngest son of the Duke of St. Bungay. A private secretary to Sir Raffle Buffle in the Income Tax Office, a position later held by Johnny Eames. *Allington* 46, 51-52, 59; *Finn* 8

FITZWARREN, LADY. A guest of the Lovels at Yoxham, who upheld the rector in his refusal to recognize the validity of the Countess of Lovel's title, or the legitimacy of Lady Anna. *Anna* 19, 28-29, 48

FIXED PERIOD, The. A Novel. London, Blackwood and Sons, 1882. 2v. Originally published in *Blackwood's Magazine*, Oct. 1881-March 1882.

PLOT. On an imaginary island near Australia over which the English had renounced their sovereignty, a government had been established, one of whose leading principles was the doctrine of the "Fixed Period." This law sought to solve the problem of old age, by "depositing" all inhabitants at the age of sixty-seven in a "college" where they would be comfortably housed until, at some time before their next birthday, there would be euthanasia. The protagonist of the plan was President Neverbend whose best friend, Gabriel Crasweller, was the first on the list to be "deposited." As the fatal day drew near, Mr. Crasweller's enthusiasm for the doctrine decreased, but because of his respect for law and the fervent arguments of its supporters, he was forced to agree. On the road to the college, the carriage was halted by a mob that informed the President that a British man-of-war, bearing a pressing invitation to the new state to resume its allegiance, was in the harbor with a heavy gun trained on the capital. The citizens, already roused to rebellion against the fixed period law, admitted the cogency of the big gun, and without hesitation accepted the new British Governor. President Neverbend returned to England, and the vexatious law was soon repealed.

FLANNELLY, JOE. The builder of the house at Ballycloran and holder of the mortgage. He attempted to introduce his daughter into the landlord-class by marrying her to Larry Macdermot and, failing in this, became Larry's bitter enemy, intent on his ruin. Does not appear, but is mentioned frequently in *The Macdermots of Ballycloran.*

FLANNELLY, SALLY. *See* Keegan, Mrs. Sally (Flannelly)

FLATFLEECE. A confederate of Herr Vossmer at the Beargarden Club. He bought up all the I O U's of the club members and pressed for immediate payment. He is sometimes referred to as "Fleeceflat." *Way We Live* 69

FLEABODY, OLIVIA Q. A Vermont spinster, a Ph.D., and an ardent advocate and lecturer on women's rights, who contended with the Baroness Banmann for the control of the "Disabilities." *Popenjoy* 17, 27, 33, 60

FLEECEFLAT. *See* Flatfleece

FLETCHER, MR. The butcher at Silverbridge to whom Mr. Crawley paid the check he was accused of stealing. *Last Chron.* 12

FLETCHER, MRS. The benevolent matriarch of the Herefordshire Fletchers, who was anxious that Emily Wharton should marry her younger son Arthur. A distant relative of the De Courcy family. ". . . a magnificently aristocratic and high-minded old lady, with snow-white hair, and lace worth fifty guineas a yard" (1:15:238). *Prime Min.* 15-16, 69-71

FLETCHER, ARTHUR. A neighbor of the Wharton family in Herefordshire, who had loved Emily Wharton since childhood. When she married Ferdinand Lopez he was greatly distressed, knowing the man's reputation and fearing the inevitable suffering Emily must endure. Persuaded by his friend Frank Gresham to contest Silverbridge, he found himself opposed by Lopez, and tried vainly to withdraw. Lopez was defeated and shortly after committed suicide. After a lapse of some time Arthur renewed his suit, and he and Emily were married.

". . . the very pearl of the Fletcher tribe. Though a younger brother, he had a very pleasant little fortune of his own. Though born to comfortable circumstances, he had worked so hard in his younger days as to have already made for himself a name at the bar. He was a fair-haired, handsome fellow, with sharp, eager eyes, with an aquiline nose and just that shape of mouth and chin which . . . [are] regarded as characteristic of good blood. He was rather thin, about five feet ten in height, and had the character of being one of the best horsemen in the county. . . . He looked like one of those happy sons of the gods who are born to success" (1:15:236).

One of the principal characters in *The Prime Minister.*

FLETCHER, JOHN. Brother of Arthur, and husband of Sir Alured Wharton's daughter Sarah. ". . . He was warm-hearted, sharp-witted, and, though perhaps a little self-opinionated, considered throughout the country to be one of the most prudent in it" (1:16:267). *Prime Min.* 15-17, 33, 36, 69-70

FLICK, MR. The junior partner of the firm of Norton and Flick, who was employed in the service of the young Earl Lovel. He proposed a compromise providing for the marriage of the young Earl and Lady Anna that would settle the rival claims. Appears frequently in *Lady Anna.*

FLORENCE, Italy. Part of the action in *He Knew He Was Right* is located in Florence.

FOLKING. A parish of Utterden, the estate of Daniel Caldigate near Cambridge, and the setting for much of *John Caldigate.*

FOLLEVILLE, ABBÉ DE. (real person). *See* Agra, Bishop of

FOLLIOTT, MRS. One of the family whose relatives married both into the Amedroz and the Aylmer families. A cousin of Mrs. Winterfield, but hostile to her low-church views. *Belton* 10

FOOKS, CAPTAIN. A loyal sporting friend of Ralph, the heir. *Ralph* 8-9, 21, 42, 46, 52, 56

FOOLSCAP, MARGIN and VELLUM. Law stationers in Carey Street, the employers of Mr. Bunce, Phineas Finn's landlord. *Finn* 7

FORREST, MR. The manager of the Barchester bank at which Mark Robarts borrowed money to pay Mr. Sowerby for his horse. *Framley* 12, 19, 21, 33, 42, 44

FORREST, RALPH. A passenger aboard the "Serrapique," sailing for Panama, who became the confidant of Emily Viner, and tried to persuade her to return to England rather than marry a man she did not love. On their arrival he had the unpleasant task of telling her that the man had died and of helping her arrange her return trip to England. One of the principal characters in *The Journey to Panama.*

FORREST, SERGEANT. A sergeant of the Colonial Police, called in to apprehend Nokes and the Brownbies after their attempt to burn Harry Heathcote's sheep ranch. ". . . a graduate of Oxford, the son of an English clergyman, who, having his way to make in the world, had thought that an early fortune would be found in the colonies. He had come out, had failed, had suffered some very hard things, and now, at the age of thirty-five, enjoyed life thoroughly as a sergeant of the colonial police" (11:278). *Heathcote* 11

FORRESTER, KATTIE. The fiancée of the Rev. Mr. Blake. *Old Man* 9, 12-17, 23

FORSTER, MR. The Earl of Brentford's lawyer. *Redux* 32, 38, 52

FORSTER, ADA. A young orphan, an heiress and a beauty, who went to live with a distant relative in Kentucky just before the Civil War. Although she sympathized with the Union cause, she fell in love with Tom Reckenthorpe, a general in the Confederate Army, and, when he returned from the war, married him. Heroine of *The Two Generals.*

FOTHERGILL, MR. The land agent for the old Duke of Omnium, and a great friend of Nathaniel Sowerby. After the old Duke's death, his indifference to the noble sport of fox-hunting resulted in his dismissal, at the instance of Lord Chiltern, then M F H of the Brake Hounds.

"He enacted two altogether different persons on occasions which were altogether different. Generally speaking, with the world at large, he was a jolly, rollicking, popular man, fond of eating and drinking, known to be devoted to the Duke's interest, and supposed to be somewhat unscrupulous, or at any rate hard, where they were concerned; but in other respects a good-natured fellow" (*Framley* 2:11:216).

Most prominent in *Framley Parsonage* and *Phineas Redux*; briefly in *Allington* 43, 55; and *Last Chron.* 8, 10

FOWLER'S HOTEL. *See* London

FRAMLEY CHURCH. The church of which Mark Robarts was vicar. "It was but a mean, ugly building, having been erected about a hundred years since, when all churches then built were made to be mean and ugly; nor was it large enough for the congregation, some of whom were thus driven to the dissenting chapels. . . . It was, therefore, a matter near to Lady Lufton's heart to see a new church built . . ." (*Framley* 1:2:21).

FRAMLEY COURT. The "residence for life" of Lady Lufton. "The house was a low building of two stories, built at different periods, and devoid of all pretensions of any style of architecture; but the rooms, though not lofty, were warm and comfortable, and the gardens were trim and neat beyond all others in the county. Indeed, it was for its gardens only that Framley Court was celebrated" (*Framley* 1:2:20). Briefly throughout *Framley Parsonage*; and in *Last Chron.* 9-10, 17, 19

FRAMLEY CROSS. A village in East Barsetshire near Lady Lufton's estate. The inn was the Lufton Arms. *Framley* 2

FRAMLEY MILL. Halfway between Hogglestock Parsonage and Barchester. When Mr. Crawley was summoned by Bishop Proudie to the Palace, Mrs. Crawley arranged with Farmer Mangle to pretend that he had an errand at the Mill, so that he could give Mr. Proudie a lift that far along his journey. *Last Chron.* 17

FRAMLEY PARSONAGE. London, Smith, Elder and Co., 1861. 3v. Originally published in *The Cornhill Magazine,* Jan. 1860-April 1861.

AUTHOR'S COMMENT. "The story was thoroughly English. There was a little fox-hunting and a little tuft-hunting, some Christian virtue and some Christian cant. There was no heroism and no villainy. There was much Church, but more love-making."—*Autobiography*, 1:8:191.

NOTES. ". . . nothing is out of place in *Framley Parsonage.* Harold Smith's politics, Sowerby's rascalities, the social pleasures of the Chaldicotes set, the dinner-party of the Duke of Omnium, belong to the central themes as truly as the diseases and penury of the Crawleys or the ointment of Lebanon of Miss Dunstable."—Walpole, p. 56.

PLOT. The Rev. Mark Robarts, a college friend of his neighbor Lord Lufton, was as a young man presented with the comfortable living of Framley by his friend's mother Lady Lufton, and soon married her protegée Fanny Monsell. Robarts, a genial, easy-going young clergyman, became acquainted with Nathaniel Sowerby of Chaldicotes, the old Duke of Omnium's M P from West Barsetshire. Although Mark knew that Sowerby was a gambler and a blackleg with whom Lord Lufton had already had unfortunate financial dealings, he accepted an invitation to Chaldicotes and to dinner at Gatherum Castle, the old Duke's seat. While there, flattered by the attention shown him, he was induced to sign a note for £400, and later, when it became due, another for £500. The notes were soon in the hands of the Jews, but Sowerby made no attempt to pay them, placating Mark by securing for him a prebendal stall at Barchester Cathedral.

The old Duke, who held the mortgages on the Chaldicotes property, pressed for payment, and Sowerby made a half-hearted and ineffectual attempt to marry the wealthy patent-medicine heiress Martha Dunstable, as a means of extricating himself from his complicated financial difficulties. Miss Dunstable refused, but did buy up the mortgages, and after her marriage to Doctor Thorne made Chaldicotes her home.

After the death of Mark Robarts' father, his young sister Lucy went to live at the parsonage, where she was cordially welcomed by Lady Lufton until it became apparent that Lord Lufton was attracted to her. Lady Lufton's dearest plan was that her son should

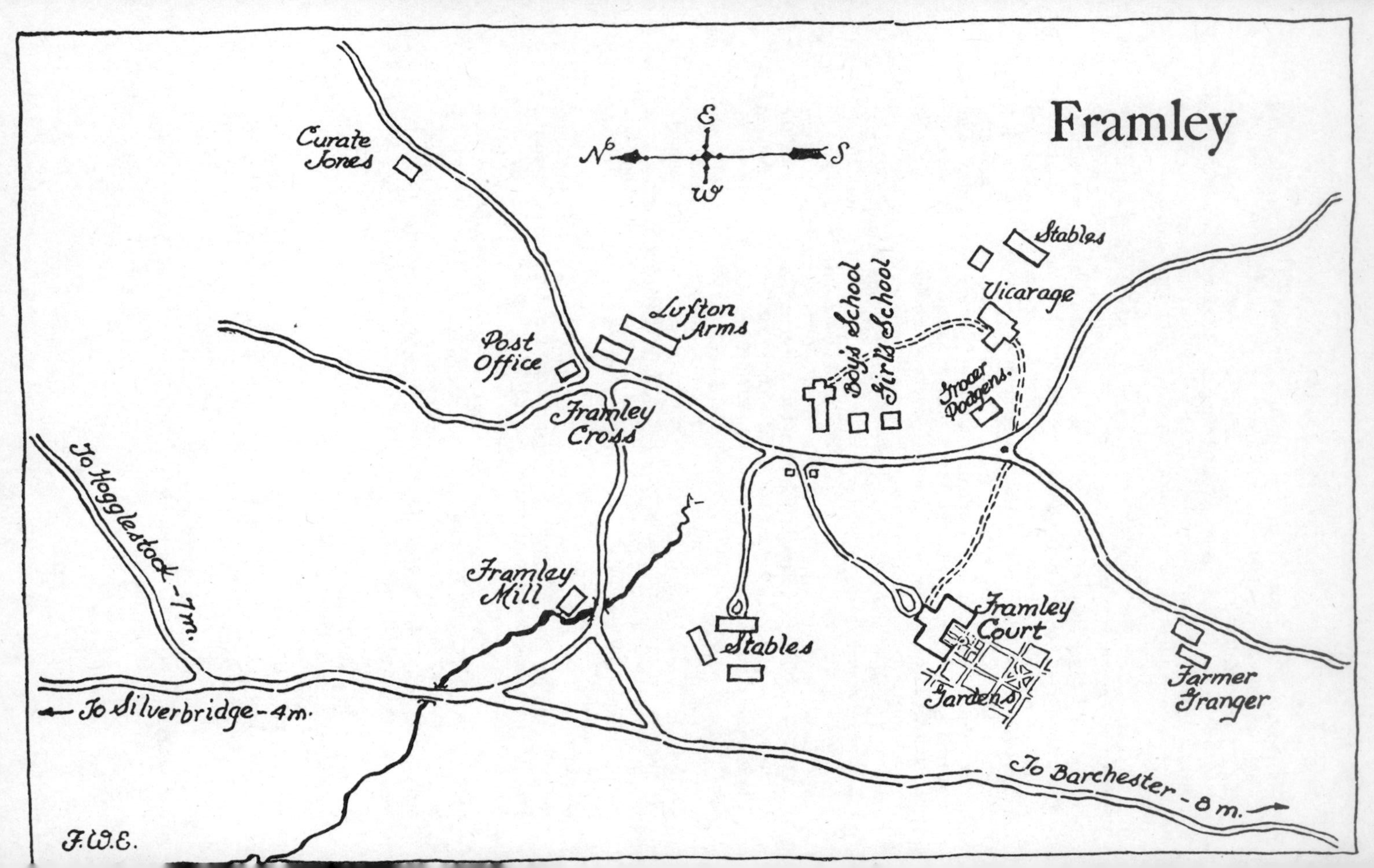
Framley
E
N
S
W
Curate Jones
Post Office
Lufton Arms
Framley Cross
Boy's School
Girl's School
Grocer Podgens.
Vicarage
Stables
Framley Mill
Stables
Framley Court
Gardens
Farmer Granger
To Hogglestock - 7m.
To Silverbridge - 4m.
To Barchester - 8 m.
F.W.E.

marry the stately Griselda Grantly, but the young lord refused and Griselda soon married the stupid but highly placed Lord Dumbello. When Lord Lufton proposed to Lucy she would not accept him, knowing that such a marriage would be displeasing to her brother's patroness, and declared that she would marry him only when Lady Lufton herself requested it.

The resourcefulness and unselfishness with which she nursed Mrs. Crawley, wife of a neighboring clergyman, through a serious illness completely won Lady Lufton's admiration, and she drove over to Hogglestock to ask Lucy to marry her son. Mark, meantime, had been bedeviled by the moneylenders on account of the Sowerby notes, and it was only when the bailiffs were at the parsonage door, ready to take his belongings, that Lord Lufton bought up the notes and saved his friend from disgrace.

FREEBORN, The REV. MR. The rector at Plumplington, who assisted Emily Greenmantle and Polly Peppercorn in obtaining parental consent to their marriages. One of the principal characters in *Two Heroines of Plumplington.*

FRENCH FAMILY. Consisting of a spiritless mother; Camilla, who for a time enjoyed the distinction of an engagement with the Rev. Mr. Gibson; and Arabella, who engineered a quarrel between the two lovers and snared the prize for herself. Appear frequently in *He Knew He Was Right.*

FRENCH REVOLUTION. *La Vendée,* Trollope's only historical novel, is based on the Royalist revolt in the province of La Vendée.

FREW, FREDERIC F. A wealthy American from Philadelphia, who married Nora Field. One of the principal characters in *The Widow's Mite.*

FROHMANN, FRAU. The proprietor of the Peacock, an inn in the Tyrol. Her fight to avoid changing her prices to match rising costs is the plot of *Why Frau Frohmann Raised Her Prices.*

FROHMANN, AMALIA ("Malchen"). The pretty and progressive daughter of Frau Frohmann, who was engaged to Fritz Schlessen and feared that the continued loss of money at the inn would affect the amount of her dowry. One of the principal characters in *Why Frau Frohmann Raised Her Prices.*

FROHMANN, PETER. Son of Frau Frohmann, in charge of the out-of-doors work of the inn. He was conservative like his mother, and hated the idea of any change. He was, unlike her, somewhat stupid, but even he came to realize that there was a definite connection between hotel prices and the cost of produce. One of the principal characters in *Why Frau Frohmann Raised Her Prices.*

FRUMMAGE, MRS. A shopkeeper in Allington, who ". . . sells ribbons, and toys, and soap, and straw bonnets, with many other things too long to mention." *Allington* 1

FULHAM. The location of Popham Villa, the home of Sir Thomas Underwood and his daughters, Patience and Clarissa, and the setting for much of *Ralph the Heir.*

Home of John Grey and his daughter Dorothy. *Scarborough* 16

FULL MOON (pub). *See* London

FURNIVAL, MRS. KITTY. Wife of Thomas Furnival, bitterly jealous of her husband's supposed attachment to Lady Mason. ". . . a stout, solid woman, sensible on most points, but better adapted, perhaps, to the life in Keppel Street than that to which she had now been promoted. . . . Her eye was still round, and her cheek red, and her bust full,—there had certainly been no falling off there . . . but the bloom of her charm had passed away, and she was now a solid, stout, motherly woman, not bright in converse but by no means deficient in mother-wit" (1:10:79). Appears frequently in *Orley Farm.*

FURNIVAL, SOPHIA. Daughter of Thomas Furnival. An intelligent, clever girl, very much alive to her own interests, who was engaged briefly to Lucius Mason. "She was a handsome, tall girl, with expressive grey eyes and dark-brown hair" (1:10:80). Appears frequently in *Orley Farm.*

FURNIVAL, THOMAS. A London barrister, and M P for the Essex Marshes. He was a sincere friend of Lady Mason, and appeared for her in both trials. "He was nearly six feet high, and stood forth prominently, with square, broad shoulders, and a large body. His head also was large; his forehead was high, and marked strongly by signs of intellect; his nose was long and straight, his eyes were very grey, and capable to an extraordinary degree both of direct severity and of concealed sarcasm" (1:10:75-76). One of the principal characters of *Orley Farm.*

GABERLUNZIE, LORD. Father of the eleven Scotts, whose home was Cauld-Kale Castle, Aberdeenshire, Scotland. Without wealth to launch his sons in public life, he used great skill in manipulating events so that those indebted to him politically were under some pressure to forward his sons' ambitions. The two sons most prominent in *The Three Clerks* are Undy and Val Scott. *Clerks* 8, 29

GAGER, MR. A young detective from Scotland Yard, whose theory of a double robbery in the Eustace diamond case was opposed by Detective Bunfit. In proving his case he fell in love with and married Patience Crabstick, whose story vindicated his theories. *Eustace* 49-52, 57-58, 78

GALWAY HOUNDS. Tom Daly was MFH. *Land.* 9

GANGOIL. Harry Heathcote's sheep ranch in Queensland. The setting for *Harry Heathcote of Gangoil.*

GARIBALDI (real person). Carlo Pepé was one of Garibaldi's officers in the war with Austria in 1866. *Last Aust.*

GARNETT, MR. A jeweler who at one time had the care of the Eustace diamonds. *Eustace* 5, 11, 14, 16, 24, 26

GARROW, MAJOR. A retired officer of the Engineers, who, with his wife, daughter and two lively sons, lived at Thwaite Hall near Penrith in Westmoreland. One of the principal characters in *The Mistletoe Bough.*

GARROW, ELIZABETH. The only daughter of Major Garrow, who broke her engagement to Godfrey Holmes because she convinced herself that her love was too absorbing, and that by denying it she would be true to her higher nature. ". . . a very good girl, but it might almost be a question whether she was not altogether too good. She had learned, or thought that she had learned, that most girls are vapid, silly, and useless—given chiefly to pleasure-seeking and a hankering after lovers; and she had resolved that she would not be such a one. Industry, self-denial, and a religious purpose in life, were the tasks which she set herself" (1:13-14). Heroine of *The Mistletoe Bough.*

GATHERUM CASTLE. The Duke of Omnium's seat in West Barsetshire. "The castle was a new building of white stone, lately erected at an enormous cost by one of the first architects of the day. It was an immense pile, and seemed to cover ground enough for a moderate-sized town. But, nevertheless, report said that, when it was completed, the noble owner found that he had no rooms to live in; and that, on this account, when disposed to study his own comfort, he resided in a house of perhaps the tenth the size, built by his grandfather in another county" (*Thorne* 2:5:88). Mentioned in all of the Parliamentary series, but particularly in *The Prime Minister,* when it was used by the Duchess for her great political house-parties; also in *Framley Parsonage* and *Doctor Thorne.*

GAUNTLET, ADELA. Daughter of the Vicar of West Putford, friend of Caroline Waddington, and in love with Arthur Wilkinson, whom she finally married. Appears frequently in *The Bertrams.*

GAUNTLET, PENELOPE. The maiden aunt of Adela, living at Littlebath. *Bertrams* 25, 32, 42

GAZEBEE, LADY AMELIA (de Courcy). After persuading her cousin Augusta Gresham that to marry Mr. Gazebee would be beneath her dignity "as a matter of family consideration," Lady Amelia herself married him. Most prominent in *The Small House at Allington*; briefly in *Barchester* 37; and *Thorne* 38

GAZEBEE, MORTIMER. After the dismissal of Mr. Umbleby from the management of the Greshamsbury estate, Mr. Gazebee, junior partner in the firm Gumption, Gazebee and Gazebee, "the sharp gentleman from London, reigned over the diminished rent-roll." Augusta Gresham thought that she was in love with him. He became M P for Barchester and active in the management of the De Courcy interests. ". . . a very elegant young man. . . . He was rather bald . . . but he had a really remarkable pair of jet-black whiskers. . . . He had also dark eyes, and a beaked nose, what may be called a distinguished mouth, and was always dressed in fashionable attire" (*Thorne* 3:4:58). Most prominent in *Doctor Thorne* and *The Small House at Allington*; briefly in *Last Chron.* 43-44

GAZY, WILLIAM. One of the bedesmen at Hiram's Hospital. *Warden*

GEESE. A debating club, of which George Robinson was an important member. *Struggles* 17-18

GENET, CHAPEL OF. In their flight from Clisson, Madame and Marie de Lescure took refuge there and found Father Jerome in hiding. *Vendée* 25

GENTLE EUPHEMIA. In *The Fortnightly Review*, May 1866.

Plot. A pseudo-medieval tale in which the Lord of Mountfidget, hearing of the beauty of the gentle Euphemia, repaired to the Castle of Grandnostrel to assure himself of the truth of her reputed charms. He drove before him a herd of beeves and swine that he hoped to exchange for olives and fruit for which the neighborhood was famous. On the way the herd was attacked by the rinderpest and, by the command of the Queen, was slaughtered and buried ten fathoms deep. Arriving empty-handed at the Castle, the noble Lord was attacked by the guards and wounded in the neck by a poisoned arrow. From her oriel window the gentle Euphemia saw him fall and, hastening to him, applied an antidote made by the Sage Alasco that saved his life.

GEORGE AND DRAGON (inn). *See* Barchester

GEORGE AND VULTURE (inn). *See* Silverbridge

GEORGE WALKER AT SUEZ. In *Tales of All Countries*, Second Series,

1863. Originally published in *Public Opinion*, Dec. 28, 1861.

PLOT. George Walker, in Egypt for his health, went to Suez for a week's sight-seeing and while there was mistaken for an important dignitary named Sir George Walker, whose approaching visit was expected. To his surprise he was invited by a local Arab chieftain to go on an elaborately planned excursion to see the Well of Moses. The morning they were to start the distinguished official arrived, and George was unceremoniously left behind. Nothing daunted, he obtained a dragoman and made the expedition alone.

GERAGHTY, NORAH. A pretty Irish barmaid at the Cat and Whistle, who fell in love with Charley Tudor. After failing to induce him to marry her, she accepted Mr. Peppermint, a widower with two children. "Her face was her fortune, and her fortune she knew was deteriorating from day to day" (2:11: 237). *Clerks* 17, 19-20, 27-28, 30-31

In his early London days, Trollope had a similar entanglement.

GERALDINE, SIR FRANCIS. A callous and intemperate baronet, who engaged himself to Cecilia Holt to prevent his cousin from succeeding to the title. Cecilia soon sensed his true purpose and broke the engagement, deeply wounding his pride. Later, when Cecilia married George Western, Sir Francis, with the malicious aid of Francesca Altifiorla, brought about an estrangement between them. He narrowly escaped an engagement with the conspirator. One of the principal characters in *Kept in the Dark*.

GERALDINE, CAPT. WALTER. Cousin of Sir Francis. He married Miss Tremenhere, who had been the fiancée of George Western. *Kept Dark* 4, 6, 8

GERMAIN, LADY ALICE. *See* Holdenough, Lady Alice (Germain)

GERMAIN, LADY AMELIA. The youngest of the three sisters of the Marquis of Brotherton, and an echo of her sister Lady Sarah. "Ritual, indeed, was the one point of interest in Lady Amelia's life" (1:3:35). One of the principal characters in *Is He Popenjoy?*.

GERMAIN, LADY GEORGE (Mary Lovelace). Daughter of Dean Lovelace of Brotherton, wife of Lord George (later Marquis of Brotherton), and mother of the real Lord Popenjoy. Dominated by a jealous husband and three pious spinster sisters-in-law. "She was a sweet, innocent, lady-like, high-spirited, joyous creature . . . clever, well-educated, very pretty, with a nice sparkling way . . . and her father's heiress" (1:1: 13; 1:2:21). Heroine of *Is He Popenjoy?*.

GERMAIN, LORD GEORGE. The younger brother of the Marquis of Brotherton, who married Mary Lovelace, eventually succeeded to the title and became the father of the real Lord Popenjoy.

"He was a tall, handsome dark-browed man, silent generally, and almost gloomy, looking, as such men do, as though he were always revolving deep things in his mind, but revolving in truth things not very deep—how far the money would go, and whether it would be possible to get a new pair of carriage-horses for his mother. Birth and culture had given to him a look of intellect greater than he possessed. . . . He was simple, conscientious, absolutely truthful, full of prejudices, and weak-minded" (1:1:9).

One of the principal characters in *Is He Popenjoy?*.

GERMAIN, LADY SARAH. The eldest and most intelligent of the three spinster sisters of the Marquis of Brotherton, and the only one of the family with courage to oppose him. "She knew every poor woman on the estate, and had a finger in the making of almost every petticoat worn. . . . She was doctor and surgeon to the poor people. . . . But she was harsh-looking, had a harsh voice, and was dictatorial" (1:2:34). One of the principal characters in *Is He Popenjoy?*.

GERMAIN, LADY SUSANNA. The second of the three Germain sisters, noted alike for her piety and her spitefulness. A thorn in the flesh to her young sister-in-law Lady Mary, whom she attempted to guide so that she might be acceptable to the family. One of the principal characters in *Is He Popenjoy?*.

GIBLET, LORD. Son of Lord Gosling, who was inveigled by the matchmaking Mrs. Montacute Jones into a marriage with Olivia Green. *Popenjoy* 38, 50-51, 55-58

GIBSON, The REV. THOMAS. The Rector of St. Peter's-cum-Pumpkin, near Exeter, and a minor canon at the Cathedral. His love affairs are described at great length and provide the comic highlights in *He Knew He Was Right*. "He was a nice-looking man enough, with sandy hair, and a head rather bald, with thin lips, and a narrow nose. . . . He had a house and an income, and all Exeter had long decided that he was a man who would certainly marry. . . . He was fair game, and unless he surrendered himself to be bagged before long, would subject himself to just and loud complaint" (1:30:233-34). One of the principal characters in *He Knew He Was Right*.

GIGGS, SIR RICKETTY. A famous London lawyer, consulted as to the legality of Sir Roger Scatcherd's will. *Thorne* 46

He also acted on a case with Sir Henry Harcourt. *Bertrams* 12

GILES, FATHER (of Ballymoy). The priest who generously allowed the innkeeper at Ballymoy to lodge a stranded guest in his room. When he entered at night, the guest mistook him for a marauder and threw him downstairs, severely injuring him. When the situation was explained the two became good friends. Principal character in *Father Giles of Ballymoy*.

GILES, FATHER (of Headford). The parish priest at Headford, where he had been for forty years. Not in sympathy with the Landleaguers, nor with his curate Father Brosnan, who was hand in glove with them. *Land*. 2, 4

GILES, MR. The steward at Ongar Park, whose good will Lady Ongar failed to win. *Claverings* 12

GILLIFLOWER, The REV. GABRIEL. Arthur Wilkinson's spineless curate, who took over his duties while Arthur was in Cairo and pleased Mrs. Wilkinson by his meek acceptance of her domination. *Bertrams* 42

GILMORE, HARRY. The Squire of Bullhampton, a warm friend of the Vicar and his wife, and an unsuccessful suitor of Mary Lowther. ". . . a man somewhat over thirty . . . who had done fairly well at Harrow and at Oxford . . . a man with a good heart, and a pure mind, generous, desirous of being just, somewhat sparing of that which is his own, never desirous of that which is another's. He is good-looking, though, perhaps, somewhat ordinary in appearance; tall, strong, with dark-brown hair, and dark-brown whiskers, with small, quick grey eyes, and teeth which are almost too white and too perfect for a man" (1:4). One of the principal characters in *The Vicar of Bullhampton*.

GITEMTHRUET, MR. Alaric Tudor's attorney in his trial for embezzlement. *Clerks* 40-41

GLADSTONE, WILLIAM EWART (real person). "Daubeny is an interesting sketch, though not an intimate one of Disraeli, and the same is true of Gresham for Gladstone."—Nichols, pp. 29-30.

GLADSTONOPOLIS. The capital of Britannula, the setting for *The Fixed Period.*

GLASCOCK, The HON. CHARLES. *See* Peterborough, Lord

GLEDD, OPHELIA. A popular society girl in Boston, who had at the same time an American and an English suitor, both as typical of their country as Trollope could make them. She accepted the Englishman, not without misgivings as to her reception in English society. Heroine of *Miss Ophelia Gledd.*

GLENBOGIE. The summer home of Sir Thomas Tringle, in Scotland. *Ayala* 4-6, 18

GLOMAX, CAPTAIN. The Master of the Hounds for the URU, who was succeeded by Sir Harry Albury but continued to ride with them. *Ayala* 49-51, 56; *Amer. Sen.* 9-11, 48, 52, 64, 73, 80

GLOUCESTER SQUARE. *See* London

GLOUCESTERSHIRE.

CURRY HALL. Country home of Mrs. Montacute Jones. *Popenjoy*

LORING. Where Mary Lowther lived. *Vicar*

GOARLY, DAN. A small farmer in the neighborhood of Bragton Hall, who was implicated in the poisoning of foxes. He was befriended by the American Senator, greatly to the disgust of the members of the hunt club. Appears frequently in *The American Senator.*

GOAT AND COMPASSES. *See* London

GOESLER, MME. MAX. *See* Finn, Mrs. Marie (Goesler)

GOFFE, MR. The attorney for the Countess of Lovel in her suit to establish her right to the title and the estate. Appears frequently in *Lady Anna.*

GOGRAM, MR. ". . . an attorney who lived at Penrith, and who was never summoned to Vavasor Hall unless the Squire had something to say about his will" (2:13:98). *Can You* 53, 55, 57

GOLDEN LION. A rival inn near Frau Frohmann's Peacock that had higher rates, with no lessening in its trade. *Frohmann*

GOLDEN LION OF GRANPÈRE, The. The hotel owned by Michel Voss. The setting for *The Golden Lion of Granpère.*

GOLDEN LION OF GRANPÈRE, The. London, Tinsley Brothers, 1872. Originally published in *Good Words*, Jan.-Aug. 1872.

NOTES. ". . . not only Trollope's very best shorter book, but one of the most charming idylls in English literature. . . . It has all the colour and richness and cohesion of something done irresistibly."—Walpole, Introduction to the Everyman ed., London, Dent, 1904.

PLOT. The Lion d'Or, only hotel in a small town in Lorraine, was owned by Michel Voss. His son George lived with him, as did his second wife and her niece Marie Bromar. Marie was a vigorous, attractive and intelligent young woman, devoted to her uncle and most efficient in the work at the inn. It was inevitable that she and George should fall in love, but Michel, feeling that each could make a more advantageous marriage, stubbornly refused his consent to their engagement. George angrily left home to take charge of an inn in Colmar, where he remained for a year without communicating with his family. Marie, feeling that she was forsaken and urged by her uncle, became engaged to Adrian Urmand, a prosperous linen buyer from Basle who was often at the inn. When the news of the engagement reached George he set out immediately for Granpère, where his father, overjoyed at his return, consented to his marriage to Marie.

"GOLDFINDER." The ship on which John Caldigate and Dick Shand voyaged to New South Wales. *Caldigate* 5-8

GOLIGHTLY, MR. One of the defense lawyers in Phineas Finn's trial for the murder of Mr. Bonteen. ". . . that subtle, courageous, eloquent and painstaking youth" (2:7:139). *Redux* 57

GOLIGHTLY, CLEMENTINA. *See* Jaquêtanàpe, Mrs. Clementina (Golightly)

GONDIN, M. LE CURÉ. The Roman Catholic priest at Granpère, who tried to convince Marie Bromar that her engagement to Adrian Urmand was as binding as a marriage. The name is sometimes spelled "Goudin." *Granpère* 1-2, 6, 13, 16, 19, 21

GOODALL, MR. Mrs. Ray's agent at Exeter, who handled all her small property and sold her cottages to Luke Rowan. *Rachel* 21

GOOSE AND GRIDIRION. The meeting place of "The Geese," a London debating club. *Struggles* 17-18

GORDELOUP, SOPHIE. Sister of Count Pateroff, who followed Lady Ongar from Florence to England and sponged on her. "A little, dry, bright woman she was, with quick eyes, and thin lips, and small nose, and mean forehead, and scanty hair drawn back quite tightly from her face and head; very dry, but still almost pretty with her quickness and her brightness" (1:13:163).

". . . the power of *The Claverings* lies in atmosphere rather than in character. Sophie Gordeloup *is* the atmosphere—she brings it with her, the meanness and shabbiness and malice, the impudence and cheek and impertinence, the pluck and the self-reliance and the sangfroid, the humour and cynicism and general disbelief in any of the human virtues. . . . She is one of Trollope's three best wicked women."—Walpole, pp. 132-33.

One of the principal characters in *The Claverings.*

GORDON, JOHN. In love with Mary Lawrie, he went to the diamond mines in South Africa, hoping to make a fortune and return to marry her. His fortune gained, he returned to find Mary engaged to marry Mr. Whittlestaff, an elderly friend of her father who had befriended her after his death. She had told Mr. Whittlestaff of her love for John, and after some hesitation he released her from her engagement and she married her young suitor. ". . . his short black hair, his bright pleasant eyes, his masterful mouth, his dark complexion, and broad, handsome, manly shoulders" (1:6:109). One of the principal characters in *An Old Man's Love.*

GORLACH, MR. A wealthy English merchant in Peru, engaged to marry Emily Viner. He died shortly before her boat arrived, leaving her a small competence with which she returned to England. Does not appear in person, but is an important element in the plot of *The Journey to Panama.*

GORSE HALL. The cottage used as a hunting lodge by Lord Hampstead, in Northumberland. *Fay* 2, 17, 22, 38-39, 42, 46

GORTNACLOUGH. The village near Castle Richmond where the Fitzgeralds set up a soup kitchen for the relief of the famine sufferers. *Castle Rich.* 7-10, 17-18, 25, 33

GOSHAWK, MR. A magistrate in Silverbridge, who was managing director of the school of which Mr. Crawley was the headmaster. At his wife's instigation he decided that Mr. Crawley was not fit to teach the children and attempted to oust him. The characterization follows closely that of Bishop Proudie in *The Last Chronicle of Barset.* One of the principal figures in *Did He Steal It?*.

GOSHAWK, MRS. Wife of the magistrate; vindictive and a gossip-monger, whose enmity for Mr. Crawley resulted in an attempt to dismiss him from the school. The characterization suggests Mrs. Proudie in *The Last Chronicle of Barset.* One of the principal figures in *Did He Steal It?*.

GOSSAU, Austria. The background for *Katchen's Caprices.* There were two inns, the Golden Lamb, owned by Josef Kester, and the Black Eagle, owned by Caspar Ebner.

GOTOBED, ELIAS. An American Senator, visiting England to study the government and people at close range. He was very critical of English habits and customs and free in his comments on them. A rather conventional picture of an American seen through English eyes. ". . . a person of an imposing appearance, tall and thin, with a long nose and a look of great acuteness" (*Amer. Sen.* 1:16:165). Most prominent in *The American Senator*; briefly, as the American Ambassador to the Court of St. James, in *Duke* 70

GOWER STREET. *See* London

GOWRAN, ANDY. The steward and manager of the estate at Portray, Lizzie Eustace's house in Scotland. ". . . an honest, domineering, hard-working, intelligent Scotchman, who had been brought up to love the Eustaces, and who hated his present mistress with all his heart. He did not leave her service, having an idea in his mind that it was now the great duty of his life to save Portray from her ravages" (*Eustace* 1: 22:296). Most prominent in *The Eustace Diamonds* 22-24, 26, 31, 59-63, 76; briefly in *Redux* 45

GRAHAM, FELIX. One of the London lawyers at the second Orley Farm trial, an intelligent and high-minded young man, but disinclined to run in harness with the other lawyers. After an amusing attempt to educate and "mold" Mary Snow to be his wife, he ended by marrying Madeline Staveley. ". . . by no means a handsome man. He was tall and thin, and his face had been slightly marked with the small-pox. He stooped in his gait as he walked, and was often awkward with his hands and legs. But he was full of enthusiasm . . . and when he talked on subjects which were near his heart there was a radiance about him" (1:18:139). One of the principal characters in *Orley Farm.*

GRAHAM, LUCY. A telegraph girl, who generously took the responsibility of caring for her roommate who had become ill and had been sent to the seashore. Heroine of *The Telegraph Girl.*

GRANDNOSTREL, COUNT. Father of the Gentle Euphemia. *Euphemia*

GRANGER, MRS. Wife of a Framley farmer, who had a daughter of the same age as Grace Crowley. *Framley* 36

GRANGER, The REV. MR. The Rector of Plumstock parish in Cheshire, and head of the Relief Committee to aid weavers who had been thrown out of work by the cotton famine. He had a wife, Molly, and two sons, Bob and Charley. One of the principal characters in *The Widow's Mite.*

GRANPÈRE. A village in Lorraine, the setting for *The Golden Lion of Granpère.*

GRANT, LADY BERTHA. The widowed sister of George Western, whose intervention in the misunderstanding between him and his wife resulted in their reconciliation. *Kept Dark* 8, 15-22

GRANTLY, BISHOP. The gentle Bishop of Barchester, whose son, the Archdeacon, hoped to succeed him. He was a close friend of Mr. Harding, and their oldest children had married. After his death, told with great sympathy in the opening pages of *Barchester Towers*, Mr. Proudie became Bishop. ". . . he was a bland and a kind old man, opposed by every feeling to authoritative demonstrations and episcopal ostentation" (3:44). *Warden* 1-3, 8-9, 19-20

GRANTLY, CHARLES JAMES. The eldest son of the Archdeacon, described in his youth as ". . . an exact and careful boy; he never committed himself; he well knew how much was expected from the eldest son of the Archdeacon of Barchester, and was therefore mindful not to mix too freely with other boys. He had not the great talents of his younger brothers, but he exceeded them in judgment and propriety of demeanour" (*Warden* 8:117). In his middle age, again described as ". . . a busy, stirring, eloquent London preacher, who got churches built, and was heard of far and wide as a rising man, who had married a certain Lady Anne, and who was already mentioned as a candidate for high places" (*Last Chron.* 1:22: 185). *Warden* 8, 12; *Barchester* 53; *Last Chron.* 22, 81, 83

GRANTLY, EDITH. Major Henry Grantly's daughter. *Last Chron.* 2-3, 14, 22, 36, 49

GRANTLY, FLORINDA. One of the Archdeacon's daughters, in *The Warden* spoken of as the elder, but later as the younger. Her death is noted in *The Small House at Allington. Warden* 8, 12; *Barchester* 5, 20, 53; *Allington* 55

GRANTLY, GRISELDA. *See* Hartletop, Griselda (Grantly), Marchioness of

GRANTLY, HENRY. The favorite son of the Archdeacon. After service as a major in India, where he received the Victoria Cross, and after the death of his wife, he retired with his daughter Edith to Cosby Lodge, near Plumstead. There he fell in love with Grace Crawley and, overcoming the objections of the Archdeacon, married her. Most prominent in *The Last Chronicle of Barset*; briefly, as a boy, in *Warden* 8, 12; and *Barchester* 53

In *Did He Steal It?*, represented by Captain Charles Oakley, the son of Mrs. Goshawk. His part in the play, however, is identical with that in the scenes dealing with the check Mr. Crawley is supposed to have stolen in *The Last Chronicle of Barset.*

GRANTLY, SAMUEL. The third son of the Archdeacon. ". . . dear little Soapy, as he was familiarly called, was as engaging a child as ever fond mother petted. He was soft and gentle in his manners, and attractive in his speech; the tone of his voice was melody, and every action was a grace; unlike his brothers he was courteous to all, he was affable to the lowly, and meek even to the very scullery maid. He was a boy of great promise, minding his books and delighting the hearts of his masters" (*Warden* 8:119). After a brief appearance in *Warden* 8, 12, and *Barchester* 53, no further mention of him is made. In *The Last Chronicle of Barset* the Archdeacon speaks of his "two" sons.

GRANTLY, MRS. SUSAN (Harding). The elder daughter of Mr. Harding, and wife of the Archdeacon. Most prominent in *The Warden* and *Barchester Towers*; also appears frequently in *Doctor Thorne, Framley Parsonage* and *The Last Chronicle of Barset.*

GRANTLY, REV. THEOPHILUS. The intrepid Archdeacon of Barchester and Rector of Plumstead Episcopi. He was the son of Bishop Grantly and hoped vainly to follow his father as Bishop of the diocese. ". . . he looked like an ecclesiastical statue . . . as a fitting impersonation of the church militant here on earth; his shovel hat, large, new, and well-pronounced, a churchman's hat in every inch, declared the profession as plainly as does the Quaker's broad brim; his heavy eyebrow, large, open eyes, and full mouth and chin expressed the solidity of his order; the broad chest, amply covered with fine cloth, told how well to do was his estate; one hand ensconced within his pocket, evinced the practical hold which our mother church keeps on her temporal possessions; and the other, loose for action, was ready to fight if need be for her defence; and, below these, the decorous breeches and neat black gaiters showing so admirably that well-turned leg, betokened the decency, the outward beauty, and grace of our church establishment" (*Warden* 5:76-77).

". . . for whom I confess that I have all a parent's fond affection."—*Autobiography*, 1:5:124. .

"There is no finer moment in all fiction, more deserving or less appreciated, than that at the opening of *Barchester Towers,* when the beloved Grantly, Bishop of Barchester, lies dying in his palace. His son, the Archdeacon, meditates upon the realization that if his aged father passes away in the lifetime of the expiring Ministry, the present Prime Minister will select him to succeed his father; if not, another will take his place. For a moment worldly motives claim him and he almost wishes that his father might be taken. But for a moment, then his own piety and love for his father prevail, and in his sorrow he falls upon his knee in prayer, asking forgiveness and that his father may be spared to him, even a few days more. He is; the Ministry fails and a new Prime Minister appoints Proudie, not Grantly!"—Nichols, p.43.

Most prominent in *The Warden, Barchester Towers* and *The Last Chronicle of Barset*; appears frequently in *Framley Parsonage* and *Doctor Thorne.*

GRANTLY FAMILY. It is suggested that the three boys were named for contemporary bishops: Charles James Blomfield, Bishop of London; Henry Phillpotts, Bishop of Exeter; and Samuel Wilberforce, Bishop of Oxford, who was disrespectfully known as "Soapy Sam." Of the two girls, "the elder, Florinda, bore the name of the Archbishop of York's wife, whose godchild she was; and the younger had been christened Grizzel, after a sister of the Archbishop of Canterbury" (*Warden* 8:117).

GRASCOUR, M. A member of the Belgian Foreign Office, who fell in love with Florence Mountjoy while she was living at the British Legation in Brussels. *Scarborough* 14, 45-47, 64

GRASSLOUGH, LORD. A member of the Beargarden Club, and a rejected suitor for the hand of Marie Melmotte. He was a man who had ". . . no income of his own, who was ugly, vicious, ill-tempered, and without any power of recommending himself to a girl" (*Way We Live* 1:6:22). Most prominent in *The Way We Live Now*; briefly, as an acquaintance of Lord Silverbridge, in *Duke* 6, 17

GRAY. *See also* Grey

GRAY, MR. George Western's outspoken legal adviser, who attempted to heal the breach between him and his wife. *Kept Dark* 13-15

GRAYBODY, MR. The curator of the Fixed Period "college." *Fixed* 6-7

GRAY'S INN. *See* London

GRAY'S INN COFFEE-HOUSE. *See* London

GREAT BROAD STREET. *See* London

GREAT HOUSE AT ALLINGTON. The home of Christopher Dale. "... the house itself was very graceful. It had been built in the days of the early Stuarts, in that style of architecture to which we give the name of the Tudors. On its front it showed three pointed roofs, or gables ... and between each gable a thin, tall chimney stood, the two chimneys thus raising themselves just above the three peaks. ... I think that the beauty of the house depended much on those two chimneys; on them, and on the mullioned windows with which the front of the house was closely filled ..." (*Allington* 1:1:5). Frequently mentioned throughout *The Small House at Allington.*

GREAT MARLBOROUGH STREET. *See* London

GREAT ST. HELEN'S STREET. *See* London

GREAT WESTERN RAILWAY HOTEL. *See* London

GREEN, CAPTAIN. A sporting man with no visible means of support, who persuaded Major Tifto to lame the horse "Prime Minister," belonging to Lord Silverbridge, so that it would lose the race, and the £70,000 Lord Silverbridge had bet on it. *Duke* 36, 43-44, 75

GREEN, The REV. ADOLPHUS. The curate at Groby, near Joseph Mason's home. *Orley* 23

GREEN, MRS. ADOLPHUS. Wife of the curate at Groby, who taught music to Joseph Mason's daughters, and was paid with a damaged set of metal furniture that Mrs. Mason had bought for the purpose from Mr. Kantwise. *Orley* 23

GREEN, ARCHIBALD. A fictitious character used by Trollope to tell several of his tales. In *Father Giles of Ballymoy*, he was the guest at the inn who threw the village priest down the stairs, not knowing that he was occupying the priest's room as a courtesy. In *The O'Conors of Castle Conor* he tells the story of the young man who lacked dancing pumps and forced the unwilling butler to exchange his run-down slippers for the hunting boots of the guest. In *Miss Ophelia Gledd*, he is the visiting Englishman to whom the American girl confides her fears that she would not be considered a "lady" in English society.

GREEN, MRS. BESSIE. Wife of a minor canon at Exeter, and a colorless and somewhat spiteful friend of Cecilia Holt. *Kept Dark* 1, 20

GREEN, MR. and MRS. CONNOP. Distant relatives of Lady Augustus Trefoil, and her unwilling hosts when more advantageous invitations were not forthcoming. Described by Arabella as "... nasty, hard, unpleasant people. They have lots of money ... and nothing else." *Amer. Sen.* 41, 44, 49, 61-62, 66

GREEN, JOSEPH. A London attorney in Lincoln's Inn, who was both friend and adviser to Will Belton. He also managed the affairs of Mr. Amedroz. *Belton* 14, 20, 28, 31

GREEN, MOUNSER. A member of the Foreign Office staff, who was appointed Ambassador to Patagonia. On the death of John Morton, he married Arabella Trefoil. "... a handsome man

. . . about six feet high . . . a distinguished clerk . . . and distinguished also in various ways, being one of the fashionable men about town, a great adept at private theatricals, remarkable as a billiard player at his club, and a contributor to various magazines" (2: 1:1). *Amer. Sen.* 28, 51, 65-67, 75-76

GREEN, OLIVIA. Daughter of Mrs. Patmore Green, and a friend of Mrs. Montacute Jones, who married her off to Lord Giblet. *Popenjoy* 37, 50, 55-56

GREEN, MRS. PATMORE. Mother of Olivia, and a relative of the Germain family. *Popenjoy* 34, 50, 59

GREEN STREET. *See* London

GREENACRE, FARMER. One of the churchwardens at St. Ewold's, and a prosperous farmer in East Barsetshire. *Barchester* 23, 35, 39

GREENACRE, HENRY. Son of Farmer Greenacre, and one of Miss Thorne's helpers at the Ullathorne sports. In an effort to make the riding at the quintain a success he most ingloriously fell from his horse. *Barchester* 35

GREENE, MR. An English gentleman traveling in Italy, with his daughter and second wife, who carried all his money in currency in one of his boxes. How it was lost and found again forms the plot of *The Man Who Kept His Money in a Box.*

GREENE, MRS. An attractive but shallow young Irishwoman, whose jewels were kept with her husband's money in one of their boxes. When it was lost she was suspicious of Mr. Robinson, who had made himself very attentive to her stepdaughter, and accused him of stealing the box. *Money*

GREENE, SOPHONISBA. Daughter of Mr. Greene by his first wife, and not at all fond of the second. *Money*

GREENMANTLE, MR. The manager of a bank in Plumplington, whose ideas of his social importance almost wrecked his daughter's happiness. One of the principal characters in *Two Heroines of Plumplington.*

GREENMANTLE, EMILY. The banker's daughter, in love with Philip Hughes, her father's clerk. One of the heroines in *Two Heroines of Plumplington.*

GREENOW, MRS. ARABELLA. Aunt of Alice, George and Kate Vavasor. She had married an old man when she was twenty-four and, when he died shortly after, was left with a fortune of £40,000. Although her grief for him was uncontrolled, she was not too discouraging to her suitors, and married Captain Bellfield. ". . . a buxom widow, who with her eyes open chooses the most scampish of two selfish suitors, because he is better looking."—*Autobiography*, 1: 10: 240. One of the principal characters in *Can You Forgive Her?.*

In *The Noble Jilt*, represented by Madame Brudo.

GREENWOOD, MR. The tenant on the Old Farm of the Orley Farm property, a matter of about three hundred acres, who was ". . . regarded by all the Orley people as an institution on the property" (1:1:6). *Orley* 1, 2, 14

GREENWOOD, The REV. THOMAS. The officious chaplain and private secretary of the Marquis of Kingsbury, who conspired with the Marchioness against her stepchildren and so enraged the Marquis that he was dismissed with a small pension. One of the principal characters in *Marion Fay.*

GREGG'S HOTEL. *See* London

GREGORY. MISS AMALIA. The elderly sister of the Rev. Joshua Gregory, living in Avranches. Bessy Pryor was sent to live with her when she refused to abandon her intention to marry Philip Launay. *Launay*

GREGORY, The REV. JOSHUA. The Rector of Launay, whose daughters were Bessy Pryor's friends, and whose sister was Bessy's hostess during her banishment from England. *Launay*

GREISSE, EDMOND. A servant at the Lion d'Or. *Granpère* 2-3, 5-6

GRENDALL, LORD ALFRED. One of the dummy directors in the railroad company promoted by Augustus Melmotte, for whom he acted as private secretary. A brother of the Duchess of Stevenage. "Playing whist was Lord Alfred's only accomplishment, and almost the only occupation of his life" (1:4:24). Appears frequently in *The Way We Live Now.*

GRENDALL, MILES. Son of Lord Alfred, and a henchman of Melmotte's, making himself useful both at the office and as a social secretary. Appears frequently in *The Way We Live Now.*

GRESHAM, MR. (Prime Minister). A member of the family of Greshams of Greshamsbury. Some commentators imply that Trollope drew his portrait of Mr. Gresham from Mr. Gladstone. "Said to be the greatest orator in Europe . . . a man with no feelings for the past, void of historical association, hardly with memories,—living altogether for the future which he is anxious to fashion anew out of the vigour of his own brain" (*Finn* 1:29:243). Most prominent in *Phineas Finn* and *Phineas Redux*; briefly in *Prime Min.* 6; and *Eustace* 54-55

GRESHAM, LADY ARABELLA (de Courcy). Sister of the Earl de Courcy, a fact she never let her children forget. A selfish, managing woman, intent on arranging successful marriages for her son Frank and his nine dowerless sisters. One of the principal characters in *Doctor Thorne.*

GRESHAM, AUGUSTA. At one time engaged to Mr. Moffat, who broke the engagement, hoping to marry Martha Dunstable. Her cousin Lady Amelia de Courcy persuaded her that her next suitor was beneath her station in life, although she later married him herself.

Most prominent in *Doctor Thorne*; briefly, as a bridesmaid at Lady Alexandrina de Courcy's wedding, in *Allington* 45

GRESHAM, BEATRICE. *See* Oriel, Beatrice (Gresham)

GRESHAM, FRANCIS NEWBOLD. Son of John Newbold Gresham, whom he followed in representing East Barsetshire in Parliament, though with no great distinction. He married Lady Arabella de Courcy and retired to Greshamsbury, where he lived under the domination of his wife and utterly subdued by the decline of the family fortunes. One of the principal characters in *Doctor Thorne.*

GRESHAM, FRANCIS NEWBOLD, the younger ("Frank"). The heir of the heavily encumbered Greshamsbury estate. By his mother Lady Arabella, and her De Courcy relatives, he was considered to be bound to rehabilitate the family fortunes by a wealthy marriage. His love for Mary Thorne very greatly distressed his family until she was discovered to be the heiress of the great Scatcherd property.

"The Greshams from time immemorial had all been handsome. They were broad-browed, blue-eyed, fair-haired, born with dimples in their chins, and that pleasant, aristocratic, dangerous curl of the upper lip, which can equally express good-humour or scorn.

Young Frank was every inch a Gresham" (*Thorne* 1:1:11).

Hero of *Doctor Thorne*; and prominent in *Framley Parsonage*. Briefly in *Last Chron.* 33, 47; and *Prime Min.* 20, 33-34, 36

GRESHAM, HARRY. "Son of the Greshams of Greshamsbury," who Mr. Greenmantle hoped would become the husband of his daughter. Harry may have been the son of Mary and Frank. *Plumplington*

GRESHAM, JOHN NEWBOLD. M P for Barsetshire in his time. Grandfather of Frank. *Thorne* 1

GRESHAM, MRS. MARY (Thorne). The illegitimate daughter of Thomas Thorne and Mary Scatcherd, adopted in her infancy and educated by Doctor Thorne. Her love for Frank Gresham seemed hopeless until it became known that she was the heiress of the Scatcherd fortune.

"... in Mary Thorne is embodied the true essence of the Trollope heroine. This heroine in her purest form is no tremendous beauty; certainly no minx. She is of small stature and of retiring mode; her woman's strength and her woman's tenderness come forth to meet the crises of her life, but for the rest she lives obscure and quietly dutiful. . . . She is Trollope's most complete creation of the normal English girl . . . the loveliest of all his lovely heroines."—Sadleir, pp. 376, 384.

"Of her personal appearance it certainly is my business as an author to say something. She is my heroine, and, as such, must necessarily be very beautiful; but, in truth, her mind and inner qualities are more clearly distinct to my brain than her outward form and features. I know that she was far from being tall, and far from being showy; that her feet and hands were small and delicate; that her eyes were bright when looked at, but not gleaming so as to make their brilliancy palpably visible to all around her; her hair was dark brown, and worn very plainly brushed from her forehead; her lips were thin, and her mouth, perhaps, in general inexpressive, but when she was eager in conversation it would show itself to be animated with curves of wondrous energy; and, quiet as she was in manner, sober and demure as was her usual settled appearance, she could talk, when the fit came on her, with an energy which in truth surprised those who did not know her; ay and sometimes those who did" (*Thorne* 1:3:71).

Heroine of *Doctor Thorne*; and is also prominent in *Framley Parsonage.*

GRESHAMSBURY. A small village in East Barsetshire, fifteen miles from Barchester and at the gates of the Gresham estate. Frequently mentioned in *Doctor Thorne.*

GRESHAMSBURY PARK. "... a fine old English gentleman's seat . . . built in the richest, perhaps we should rather say in the purest, style of Tudor architecture. . . . The gardens . . . have been celebrated for two centuries and any Gresham who would have altered them would have been considered to have destroyed one of the well-known landmarks of the family" (1:1:15-16). The setting for most of the action in *Doctor Thorne.*

GRESLEY, LORD ALFRED. Sir Harry Hotspur's choice as a husband for his daughter Emily. He was eminently suitable, an M P and a minor government official, but Emily had already fallen in love with her worthless cousin, and refused Lord Alfred. *Hotspur* 1-4, 6-8

GRESLEY, MARY. A charming young girl, in whom the Editor became interested to the point of trying to teach her

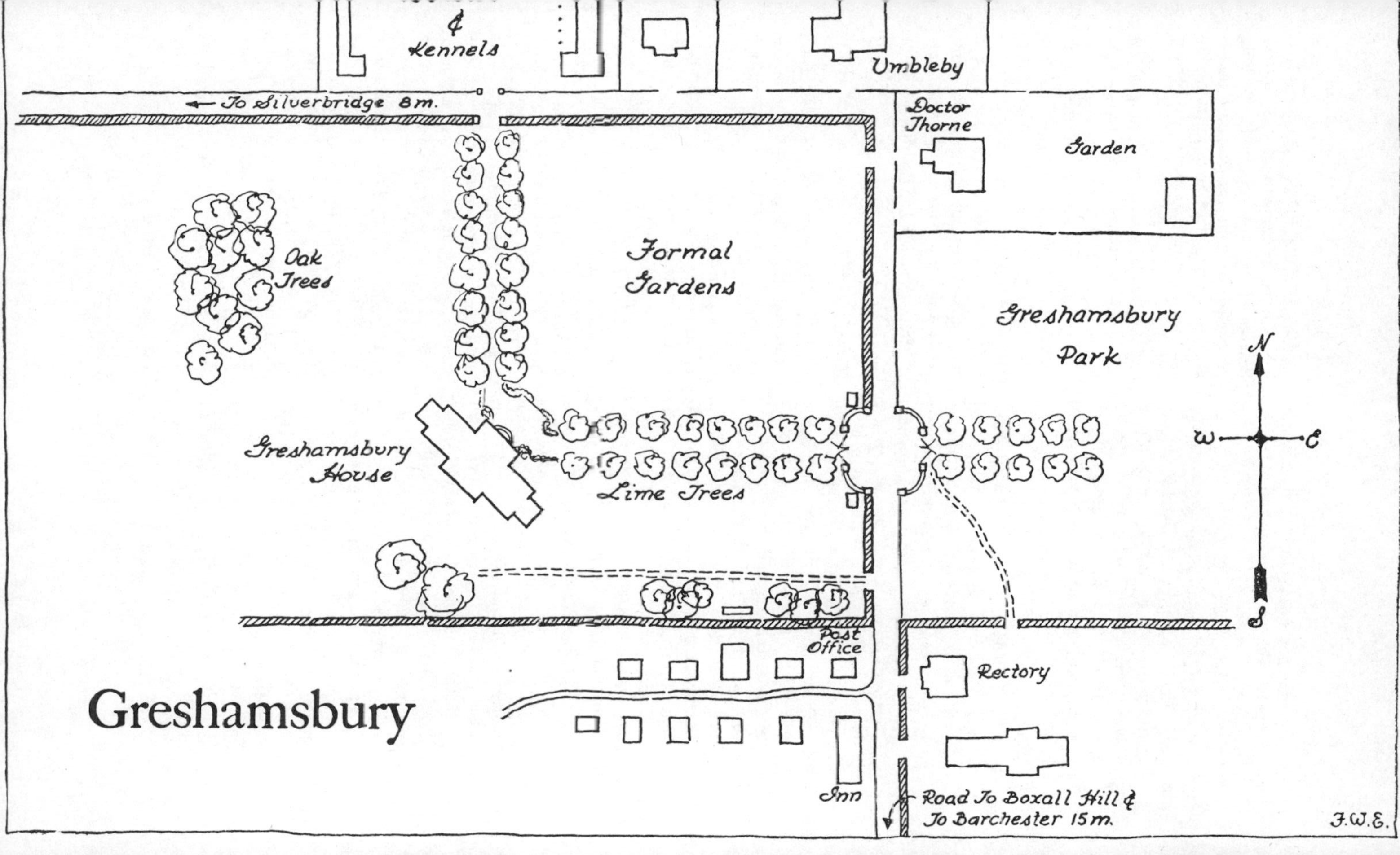
& Kennels
Umbleby
To Silverbridge 8 m.
Doctor Thorne
Garden
Oak Trees
Formal Gardens
Greshamsbury Park
N
W
E
S
Greshamsbury House
Lime Trees
Post Office
Rectory
Greshamsbury
Inn
Road To Boxall Hill & To Barchester 15 m.
F.W.E.

to write her stories so that they would be acceptable for his magazine. Heroine of *Mary Gresley*.

GREX. The country seat of Lord Grex, in Westmoreland, very shabby and out of repair, but in beautiful country. It was never visited by Lord Grex or his son Lord Percival, but greatly loved and often used by Lady Mabel. *Duke* 37

GREX, EARL. Father of Lady Mabel and of the unscrupulous gambler, Lord Percival. A widower, with a house in Belgrave Square. "A nobleman of very ancient family . . . better known at Newmarket and the Beaufort,—where he spent a large part of his life in playing whist,—than in the House of Lords. He was a grey-haired, handsome, worn-out old man, who through a long life of pleasure had greatly impaired a fortune which, for an earl, had never been magnificent, and who now strove hard, but not always successfully, to remedy that evil by gambling" (1:9:110). *Duke* 9, 19-20, 77

GREX, LADY MABEL. A cousin of Frank Tregear, with whom she was in love. Since they were both poor, they agreed to part and to seek advantageous marriages. Frank soon courted Lady Mary Palliser and won her love. Lady Mabel half-heartedly schemed to marry Lord Silverbridge, but not until he was engaged to Isabel Boncassen did she really exert her wiles to capture him. It was then too late, and she retired to the gloomy country house at Grex, an embittered woman. One of the principal characters appearing in *The Duke's Children*.

GREY, ADOLPHUS. *See* Kilcullen, Lord

GREY, DOROTHY. Daughter of John Grey, the London attorney for the Scarboroughs, who kept house for him, counseled him in his business affairs and was so happy in his companionship that she refused to marry his partner Mr. Barry and leave him.

"She had bright eyes, somewhat far apart, and well-made, wholesome, regular features. Her nose was large, and her mouth was large; but they were singularly intelligent, and full of humour when she was pleased in conversation. As to her hair, she was too indifferent to enable one to say that it was attractive; but it was smoothed twice a day . . . and always very clean. Indeed, for cleanliness from head to foot she was a model" (1:16:225-26). Appears frequently in *Mr. Scarborough's Family*.

GREY, JOHN. The attorney for John Scarborough, but not entirely in his confidence, as the story of the two marriages to the same wife, and its reason, was unknown to him. After the death of his client, he turned over the business of the estate to his partner and retired. Appears frequently in *Mr. Scarborough's Family*.

GREY, JOHN. Alice Vavasor's successful suitor. Through Alice he came to know Plantagenet Palliser, and represented the Duke of Omnium's pocket-borough of Silverbridge in Parliament, until he was sent on an important diplomatic misson to Persia. ". . . a man of high character, of good though moderate means; he was, too, well educated, of good birth, a gentleman, and a man of talent. . . . He was tall and very handsome, with brown hair, and bright blue eyes, and a mouth like a god" (*Can You* 1:2:11; 1:11:85). Most prominent in *Can You Forgive Her?*; also briefly in *Eustace* 47; *Finn* 40; *Prime Min.* 21

In *The Noble Jilt*, represented by Count Upsel.

GREY, The REV. OPTIMUS. ". . . a very excellent young clergyman in the diocese," who married one of Bishop Proudie's daughters (probably Augusta). *Framley* 7

GREY, LADY SELINA. The only daughter of Lord Cashel. "She had a most exaggerated conception of her own station and dignity, and of what was due to her, and expected from her. . . . She was plain, red-headed, and in no ways attractive. . . . But she was true, industrious, and charitable. . . . She truly loved her family, and tried hard to love her neighbours, in which [she] would have succeeded but for the immeasurable height from which she looked down upon them. . . . The specific gravity of Lady Selina could not be calculated. It was beyond the power of figures, even in algebraic denominations, to describe her moral weight" (1:11:242; 3:1:6). *Kellys* 11-14, 23-31, 36-39

GREY ABBEY. Lord Cashel's estate, near Kilcullen, eight miles from The Curraugh. The setting for part of *The Kellys and the O'Kellys*, and described in chapter 11.

GREYSTOCK, ADMIRAL. Lizzie Eustace's father, ". . . a man who liked whist, wine,—and wickedness in general . . . and whose ambition it was to live every day of his life up to the end of it. . . . The Admiral died greatly in debt" (1:1:1-2). *Eustace* 1

GREYSTOCK, DEAN. Brother of the Admiral, father of Frank and two charming daughters, who was Dean of the Cathedral of Bobsborough and who offered Lizzie Eustace a home after her father's death. Lizzie refused it, wishing for a wider scope for her peculiar talents. *Eustace* 2-3, 16, 30, 46

GREYSTOCK, MRS. "Frank's mother was, as we are so wont to say of many women, the best woman in the world. She was unselfish, affectionate, charitable, and thoroughly feminine. But she did think that her son Frank, with all his advantages,—good looks, cleverness, general popularity, and seat in Parliament,—might just as well marry an heiress as a little girl without twopence in the world" (2:30:40). Appears frequently in *The Eustace Diamonds.*

GREYSTOCK, ELLINOR. Frank's sister, who was a dear friend of Lucy Morris, and who feared the influence of Lizzie Eustace on her favorite brother. *Eustace* 2, 30

GREYSTOCK, FRANK. Son of Dean Greystock, and an M P for Bobsborough. Needing money, he played with the idea of marrying his cousin Lizzie Eustace although he was engaged to Lucy Morris. "He was a good-looking, but not a strikingly handsome man; thin, of moderate height, with sharp grey eyes, a face clean shorn with the exception of a small whisker, with wiry, strong dark hair, which was already beginning to show a tinge of gray. . . . He was quick, ready-witted, self-reliant, and not over scrupulous in the outward things of the world. He was desirous of doing his duty to others, but he was specially desirous that others should do their duty to him" (1:4:47). One of the principal characters in *The Eustace Diamonds.*

GREYSTOCK, LIZZIE. *See* Eustace, Lizzie (Greystock), Lady

GRIFFENBOTTOM, MR. The Tory representative of Percycross in Parliament, who campaigned to hold his seat with Sir Thomas Underwood as his running mate. ". . . a heavy, hale man, over sixty, somewhat inclined to be corpulent, with a red face, and a look of assured independence about him which nothing could quell or diminish.

. . . He could boast neither birth, nor talent, nor wit" (2:6:104). *Ralph* 20, 25-26, 29, 37, 39-40, 44, 51

GRIFFITH, JOHN. A tenant at Llanfeare, where his wife was housekeeper for Indefer Jones. He was at first friendly to Henry Jones, believing him to be the heir, but was finally convinced that Henry was concealing the will that would disinherit him. *Cousin* 5-10, 12-15, 17, 19, 22-24

GRIGGS, ADOLPHUS. A guest at Mrs. Tappitt's party, where he paid some attention to Rachel Ray. ". . . a man very terrible in his vulgarity, loud, rampant, conspicuous with villainous jewellery, and odious with the worst abominations of perfumery. . . . Of all men he was the most unconscious of his own defects. He had once shown some symptoms of admiration for Cherry [Tappitt], by whom he was hated with an intensity of dislike that had amounted to a passion" (1:6:115). *Rachel* 6

GRIMES, MRS. Wife of John Grimes, landlord of the inn. She believed in Julius Mackenzie, and pitied him for his domestic difficulties so much that she gave up her bedroom so that he might have a quiet place in which to work. One of the principal characters in *The Spotted Dog.*

GRIMES, JACOB. The proprietor of the public house, the Handsome Man, which, in George Vavasor's first election, served as his headquarters. *Can You* 12-13, 35, 41, 44, 46, 60

GRIMES, JOHN. The landlord of, and one of the principal characters in, *The Spotted Dog.*

GROBY PARK. The Yorkshire home of Joseph Mason, seven miles from Leeds. *Orley* 7-8, 81

GROGRAM, LADY. One of Mrs. Stantiloup's friends, whom she persuaded to join in her campaign against Dr. Wortle. *Wortle* 12

GROGRAM, SIR GREGORY. Attorney-General at the time of Phineas Finn's trial for the murder of Mr. Bonteen, he led the case for the prosecution. He was later Lord Chancellor under Mr. Gresham. *Redux* 32, 44, 57, 61-67, 74; *Prime Min.* 7, 12, 41

GROSCHUT, The REV. JOSEPH. A converted Jew, who became chaplain to the Bishop of Brotherton. He was a bitter and voluble enemy of Dean Lovelace, but was eventually banished from the Cathedral to a vicarage at Pugsby because of conduct unbefitting a clergyman with Farmer Hawkins' daughter. *Popenjoy* 4, 9-10, 14, 44, 49, 52-57

GROSVENOR PLACE. *See* London

GROWLER, MRS. Harry Heathcote's housekeeper at Gangoil. *Heathcote* 1, 8, 12

GRUMPY, MR. Mr. Grumpy, his wife and daughter Angela were traveling companions of Emily Viner in *The Journey to Panama.*

GRUNDLE, ABRAHAM. A young Britannulan, who aspired to marry Eva Crasweller and strongly supported the Fixed Period law in the hope of an early control of the Crasweller property. ". . . a good-looking young man, with black hair and bright eyes, and a remarkably handsome moustache" (1:2:42). *Fixed* 2-6, 8, 10

GRUNDLE and GRABBE. Wool merchants in Britannula, in whose business Gabriel Crasweller had a large interest. *Fixed* 3

GUADALQUIVIR. The Spanish river on which John Pomfret traveled in going down to Seville. *John Bull*

GUATEMALA. Ferdinand Lopez planned to become manager of a mine in Guatemala, and to compel his estranged wife Emily to go with him. *Prime Min.* 49, 53-55, 58

GUESTWICK. The market town nearest to Allington, where Johnny Eames's mother and her children lived. The inn was the Magpie. *Allington* 1

GUESTWICK MANOR. The seat of Lord and Lady de Guest. Mentioned frequently in *The Small House at Allington.*

GUMPTION, GAZEBEE, and GAZEBEE of Mount Street, London. ". . . a house that never defiled itself with any other business than the agency business, and that in the very highest line. They drew out leases, and managed property both for the Duke of Omnium and Lord de Courcy" (*Thorne* 3:4:56-57). *Thorne* 34, 45; *Framley* 8, 27, 32, 42

GUNLIFFE, BARTY. He attempted to gather seaweed from the cove that Mahala Tringlos considered as her own domain. She threatened him, saying that she hoped he would be drowned. When he did slip into a whirlpool, at the risk of her own life she rescued him, and in deep thankfulness found that she loved him. Hero of *Malachi's Cove.*

GUNLIFFE, FARMER. A small farmer near Malachi's Cove, who accused Mahala Tringlos of murdering his son. *Malachi*

GUNNER, CAPTAIN. A friend of Major Poultney, with whom he was entertained at one of the great Gatherum Castle house parties. *Prime Min.* 20, 28, 48

GURNEY and MALCOLMSON. The firm name used by Mr. Tyrrwhit, the moneylender. *Scarborough*

GUSHING, MISS. A determined old maid, making her home with the Umblebys. By strict attendance at church services and a show of great piety she hoped to interest the Rev. Caleb Oriel in herself, but when he became engaged to Beatrice Gresham, she became an independent Methodist and married a preacher of that sect. *Thorne* 32, 47

GWYNNE, DR. The Master of Lazarus, and a power in Oxford. Through his friendship with Archdeacon Grantly and Mr. Arabin, the deanship of the Barchester Cathedral was offered to Mr. Harding in the face of a strong party behind the candidacy of Mr. Slope. *Barchester* 1, 14, 20, 34, 43, 47, 52

HADLEY. The home of George Bertram, Sr., near London. *Bertrams* 5, 37

HALL, ABRAHAM. An engineer living in the same boardinghouse with two telegraph girls. He came to love Lucy Graham for her self-sacrifice in helping her friend Sophie Wilson when she became ill, and when he was promoted to a responsible position outside London, he persuaded Lucy to marry him. One of the principal characters in *The Telegraph Girl.*

HALL, SQUIRE. The squire of Little Alresford, in Hampshire, a neighbor and friend of Mr. Whittlestaffe. He was the father of four daughters, Miss Hall, Augusta, Mary and Evelina, ". . . varying up from thirty to thirty-five. They were fair-haired, healthy young women, with good common-sense." *Old Man* 12-15, 17

HALLAM, JACK. A member of the committee that planned to publish a magazine called "The Panjandrum." *Panjandrum*

HALLAM HALL. The home of George Wade, where he entertained his sister and brother-in-law, Mr. and

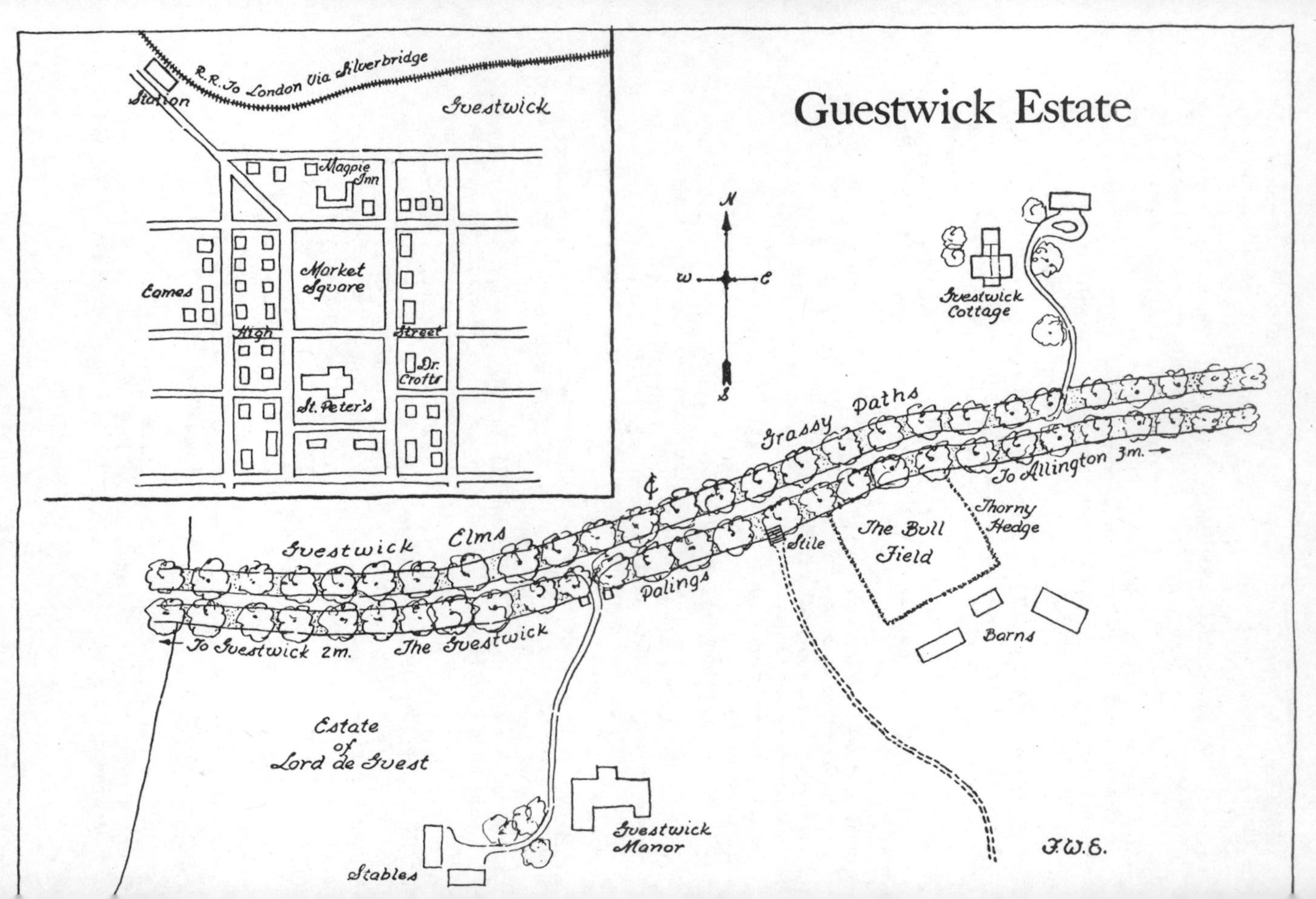
Guestwick Estate
R.R. To London Via Silverbridge
Station
Guestwick
Magpie Inn
Eames
Market Square
High
Street
Dr. Crofts
St. Peter's
N
W
E
S
Guestwick Cottage
Grassy Paths
To Allington 3m.
Thorny Hedge
The Bull Field
Stile
Guestwick Elms
Palings
Barns
To Guestwick 2m.
The Guestwick
Estate of Lord de Guest
Guestwick Manor
Stables
F.W.E.

Mrs. Wilfred Horton, for Christmas. The setting for *Not If I Know It.*

HAMEL, ISADORE. A young English sculptor, who had been brought up in Rome by a disreputable but artistically successful sculptor father. When he fell in love with Lucy Dormer, he was too proud to accept help from Lucy's uncle Sir Thomas Tringle, so they could marry. Sir Thomas, however, provided a generous dot for Lucy that made their marriage possible. *Ayala* 4, 6, 17-20, 33-34, 53, 63

HAMERSHAM. The assize town nearest to Allington. *Allington* 1

HAMILTON, BARON. The judge who presided at Thady Macdermot's trial for the murder of Miles Ussher at Carrick-on-Shannon. *Macdermots* 29-32

HAMPSHIRE.

CROKER'S HALL. Mr. Whittlestaff's home. *Old Man*

DEAN'S STAPLE. Property of the Marquis of Stapledean. *Bertrams*

HURST STAPLE. Home of the Wilkinsons. *Bertrams*

MARYGOLD. Home of Connop Green, host to Arabella Trefoil and her mother. *Amer. Sen.*

NEWTON PRIORY. Estate of Ralph Newton, the heir. *Ralph*

HAMPSTEAD, LORD. The courtesy title of John Trafford, eldest son of the Marquis of Kingsbury. He was a close friend of George Roden, although he considered George presumptuous in wishing to marry his sister Lady Frances. His love for Marion Fay, daughter of a Quaker clerk in the City, ended unhappily, as Marion refused to marry him, knowing she was soon to die. One of the principal characters in *Marion Fay.*

HAMPTON. The home of Mrs. Woodward and her three daughters, Gertrude, Linda and Katie. The setting for most of *The Three Clerks.*

HAMPTON PRIVETS. The home of Harry Gilmore, at Bullhampton in Wiltshire, a mile and a half from the vicarage. *Vicar* 51

HAMWORTH. The nearest town to Orley Farm, about twenty-five miles from London. Mentioned frequently in *Orley Farm.*

HAMWORTH HUNT. Young Peregrine Orme was an enthusiastic member of the Hamworth Hunt. *Orley* 3, 19, 28-29

HANDCOCK, HARRY. A tepid and unsuccessful suitor for Margaret Mackenzie in her youth. *Mackenzie* 1, 8, 11-12, 14

HANDICAP LODGE. The home of Walter Blake, near the Curragh racetrack, where Lord Ballindine was frequently entertained. *Kellys* 10, 15

HANDSOME MAN (pub). *See* London

HANDY, ABEL. One of the bedesmen of Hiram's Hospital, who had been a stonemason in Barchester and had broken his thigh in a fall from the scaffolding while employed about the Cathedral. *Warden*

HAP HOUSE. The home of Owen Fitzgerald, about four miles from Castle Richmond in County Cork. It is repeatedly mentioned in *Castle Richmond*, and described in chapter 1.

HAPHAZARD, SIR ABRAHAM. The great London lawyer and Attorney-General whom Mr. Harding consulted in the Hiram's Hospital case. "Sir Abraham was a man of wit, and sparkled among the brightest. . . . Indeed he always sparkled . . . coruscations flew from him; glittering sparkles, as from hot steel; but no heat; no cold heart was ever cheered by warmth from him, no unhappy soul ever dropped a portion of its burden at his door" (17: 273). *Warden* 5, 7-9, 16-18

He was consulted as to the legality of Sir Roger Scatcherd's will. *Thorne* 46

HARCOURT, CAROLINE (Waddington), LADY. Granddaughter of George Bertram, Sr., though not acknowledged by him in her youth. She was brought up by her aunt Miss Baker in Littlebath, and on a journey with her to the Holy Land met George Bertram, with whom she fell in love. Refusing to marry him because of his inadequate income, she finally married Sir Henry Harcourt, who almost immediately commanded her to obtain money from her grandfather to support an extravagant ménage in London. She refused, came to hate him, and returned to live in seclusion with her grandfather. After her husband's suicide, Caroline and George were reconciled, and finally married.

". . . a Juno rather than a Venus. She was tall. . . . Her head stood nobly on her shoulders, giving to her bust that ease and grace of which sculptors are so fond. . . . Her hair was very dark—not black, but the darkest shade of brown, and was worn in simple rolls on the side of her face. It was very long and very glossy, soft as the richest silk, and gifted apparently with a delightful aptitude to keep itself in order. . . . She had the forehead of a Juno; white, broad, and straight. . . . Her mouth had all the richness of youth, and the full enticing curves and ruby colour of Anglo-Saxon beauty. . . . The contour of her face was admirable: nothing could exceed in beauty the lines of her cheeks or the shape and softness of her chin" (1:9:90-91).

Heroine of *The Bertrams.*

HARCOURT, SIR HENRY. An Oxford friend of George Bertram, who became a successful barrister, an M P from Battersea Hamlets and Solicitor-General. After George broke with Caroline Waddington, Sir Henry married her, thinking that she was her grandfather's heir. He set up an elaborate establishment in London and ran into debt on his expectations. Although almost forcing George to renew his acquaintance with his wife, he became jealous, and Caroline left him. When the government fell and he was out of office, disappointed in his career and crippled by debt, he killed himself. One of the principal characters in *The Bertrams.*

HARDING, ELEANOR. *See* Arabin, Mrs. Eleanor (Harding)

HARDING, The REV. SEPTIMUS. The Warden of Hiram's Hospital, who resigned when convinced that he was receiving more money than he was entitled to, and became Rector of the little church of St. Cuthbert's.

"Mr. Harding is a small man, now verging on sixty years, but bearing few signs of age; his hair is rather grizzled, though not grey; his eye is very mild, but clear and bright, though the double glasses which are held swinging from his hand, unless when fixed upon his nose, show that time has told upon his sight; his hands are delicately white, and both hands and feet are small; he always wears a black frock coat, black knee-breeches, and black gaiters, and somewhat scandalises some of his more hyper-clerical brethren by a black neck-handcherchief" (*Warden* 1:9-10).

"Mr. Harding holds the Barchester novels together. . . . With every aspect of the Barchester life he has been brought into contact, from the rough bullying worldliness of his son-in-law, the dominating autocracy of his bishop's wife, the bigoted aristocracy of De Courcy Castle, to the child companionship of his granddaughter Posy and the haughty tinsel splendour of Adolphus Crosbie. . . . He is Trollope's grandest gentleman."—Walpole, pp. 45-46.

Most prominent in *The Warden* and *Barchester Towers*, but appears in each of the six novels of the Barchester series.

HARDING, SUSAN. *See* Grantly, Mrs. Susan (Harding)

"HARDING'S CHURCH MUSIC." The title of the Rev. Septimus Harding's privately printed book of sacred music. *Warden* 16

A second edition is suggested. *Barchester* 2

HARDLINES, SIR GREGORY. The chief clerk in the Weights and Measures Office, where his proposals for a system of examinations for Civil Service secured for him the position of Chief Commissioner of the Board of Civil Service Examination. Trollope never lost an opportunity to ridicule these examinations, which he remembered as a bugbear of his youth. The character is admitted by Trollope to be patterned after Sir Charles Trevelyan. Appears frequently in *The Three Clerks.*

HARDY, MR. One of the counsel for the young Earl Lovel. "A keener, honester, more enlightened lawyer . . . did not wear silk at that moment" (1:5:56). Appears frequently in *Lady Anna.*

HARFORD, The REV. MR. The elderly Rector of Baslehurst, who had grown rather sour with age, had become a violent Tory, and whose "hatred of Mr. Prong was the strongest passion of [his] heart at the present moment" (2:3:50). *Rachel* 4, 18

HARKAWAY, MR. MFH of the Cumberlow Green Hunt. *Scarborough* 28-29

HARLEY STREET. *See* London

HARRINGTON HALL. The home of Lord and Lady Chiltern, in the fox-hunting country. When Phineas Finn returned to London after the death of his wife, he and Madame Goesler met at Harrington Hall and renewed their friendship. Adelaide Palliser and Gerard Maule became engaged there. Often mentioned in *Phineas Redux* and *The Duke's Children.*

HARROW STUDENTS.
- Amedroz, Charles. *Belton*
- Caldigate, John. *Caldigate*
- Gilmore, Harry. *Vicar*
- Gresham, Frank. *Thorne*
- Hampstead, Lord. *Fay*
- Lovel, two sons of the Rev. Charles Lovel. *Anna*
- Lufton, Lord. *Framley*
- Orme, Peregrine. *Orley*
- Robarts, Mark. *Framley*
- Stanbury, Hugh. *He Knew*

HARRY HEATHCOTE OF GANGOIL. A tale of Australian bush life. London, Sampson Low, 1874. Originally published in *The Graphic*, Christmas number, Dec. 25, 1873.

AUTHOR'S COMMENT. "I was not loath to describe the troubles to which my son had been subjected, by the mingled accidents of heat and bad neighbours, on his station in the bush." —*Autobiography*, 2:20:214.

PLOT. A young Englishman, Harry Heathcote, had leased 120,000 acres of bush from the Australian government, on which he ran 30,000 sheep. With him at Gangoil lived his wife, two small sons and his sister-in-law Kate Daly. Giles Medlicot was his nearest neighbor, but the two men had not become friends. Medlicot had purchased land that lay between Gangoil and the river for a sugar plantation and had erected a sugar-mill. The loss of the river frontage was a serious matter to Heathcote and he considered its acquisition by his neighbor a personal affront. This was the more unfortunate as Kate Daly and Medlicot had already fallen in love. Heathcote, high-tempered and imperious, had made many enemies, not only of some of his own workers whom he had discharged, but also of his lawless neighbors, the Brownbies, a father and six sons, whose cattle range bordered on Gangoil. In December when the bush was very dry and fires frequent, the Brownbies, joined by two of Harry's discharged sheepmen since employed by Medlicot, attempted to burn out the entire range. Heathcote and his men spent day and night in the saddle and were later joined by Medlicot—who helped him control the fires, and to win in a pitched battle with the Brownbie gang.

HART, MR. A London tailor of the firm of Hart and Jacobs, who desired to be M P for Baslehurst, and contested the election with Butler Cornbury. *Ray* 17, 24

HART, ABRAHAM. A Jewish money-lender, who held a good deal of George Hotspur's paper. *Hotspur* 8, 10, 15, 18-19, 21, 23

HART, SAMUEL. A Jewish money-lender, who held a great part of Captain Scarborough's obligations. Appears frequently in *Mr. Scarborough's Family.*

HARTER and BENJAMIN. London jewelers of questionable honesty, with whom Lizzie Eustace had had dealings in her youth, and who were proven to have been implicated in the theft of the Eustace diamonds. Mr. Benjamin, the junior member of the firm, was tried and sentenced to a term of imprisonment. "That there was nothing 'too hot or too heavy' for Messrs. Harter and Benjamin was quite a creed with the police of the West end of London" (2:48:287). Appear frequently in *The Eustace Diamonds.*

HARTLEBURY. The seat of the Marquis of Hartletop, in Shropshire. It is sometimes spoken of as "Hartletop Priory." Mentioned frequently in *The Small House at Allington, Framley Parsonage* and *The Last Chronicle of Barset.*

HARTLEPOD, MR. The manager of the mining company in Guatemala that Ferdinand Lopez hoped to represent. *Prime Min.* 53, 58

HARTLETOP, DOWAGER MARCHIONESS OF. Mother of Lord Dumbello, and one of the few intimate women friends of the old Duke of Omnium. She engaged in an effort to dislodge Madame Goesler from London society when the Duke seemed to prefer her company, and was not, in consequence, in favor with Lady Glencora Palliser's set. When the old Duke was dying, she journeyed out to Matching Priory to see him, claiming a friendship of forty years, but Lady Glencora refused her. Most prominent in *Phineas Redux*; briefly, as a "worldly" woman of whom Lady Lufton disapproved, in *Framley* 16-17, 23, 28-31. She is named as one of a dinner party at the Pallisers in *Finn* 57; and briefly in *Allington* 2, 12, 43

HARTLETOP, GRISELDA (Grantly), MARCHIONESS OF. Daughter of Archdeacon Grantly of Barchester. Her mother and Lady Lufton desired to marry her to Lord Lufton, but she married, instead, Lord Dumbello, who later became the Marquis of Hartletop. Plantagenet Palliser once made tentative love to her.

"She was decidedly a beauty, but somewhat statuesque in her loveliness. Her forehead was high and white, but perhaps too like marble to gratify the taste of those who are fond of flesh and blood. Her eyes were large and exquisitely formed, but they seldom showed much emotion. She, indeed, was impassive herself, and betrayed but little of her feeling. Her nose was nearly Grecian, not coming absolutely in a straight line from her forehead, but doing so nearly enough to be considered classical. Her mouth, too, was very fine—artists, at least, said so, and connoisseurs in beauty. . . . The exquisite symmetry of her cheek and chin and lower face no man could deny. Her hair was light, and being always dressed with considerable care, did not detract from her appearance; but it lacked that richness which gives such luxuriance to feminine loveliness. She was tall and slight and very graceful in her movements" (*Framley* 1:11:219-20).

Mentioned briefly in *The Warden* as the younger daughter, but Florinda disappears from the later books and Griselda is called the only daughter. She is pictured as "a slim, pale retiring girl . . . who gave promise of much beauty" in *Barchester Towers*; as "without peer the best dressed woman in London . . . and then she was so beautiful. Her smile was loveliness itself . . . a miracle of a woman," in *Can You Forgive Her?*; in *The Small House at Allington*, "she contributed nothing to society but her cold, hard beauty, her gait, and her dress." In *Miss Mackenzie*, she is noted briefly as one of the patronesses at the Negro Soldiers' Orphan Bazaar; and as having "a little Lord Dumbello of her own," in *The Last Chronicle of Barset*.

Appears frequently in *Framley Parsonage* and *The Small House at Allington*; briefly, in *Warden* 8, 12; *Barchester* 5, 10, 14, 20, 53; *Can You* 49-50; *Finn* 40; *Last Chron.* 2, 49; and *Mackenzie* 27

HARTLETOP, GUSTAVUS, MARQUIS OF. ". . . than whom no English nobleman was more puissant, if broad acres, many castles, high title, and stars and ribbons are any sign of puissance" (*Last Chron.* 1:2:131).

"It satisfied his ambition to be led about as the senior lacquey in his wife's train. He believed himself to be a great man because the world fought for his wife's presence; and considered himself to be distinguished even among the eldest sons of marquises, by the greatness reflected from the parson's daughter whom he had married" (*Allington* 1:17:167).

Most prominent in *The Small House at Allington* and *Framley Parsonage*; briefly in *Last Chron.* 2, 49

HARTLETOP PRIORY. *See* Hartlebury

HATFIELD, DUKE OF. The British Minister of the Crown Colonies who ordered President Neverbend to return from Britannula because of the Fixed Period law. *Fixed* 9

HATHERLY, SIR FREDERICK. ". . . had one of the finest fortunes in England, for a commoner." He changed the "Resurgam" that his father had chosen for his monument to "Requiescat in pace." *Thorne* 4

HAUTBOY, LORD. The eldest son of Lord Persiflage. *Fay* 11-13, 16, 18, 39-40, 42, 46

HAUTBOY CASTLE. The country estate of Lord and Lady Persiflage, in Westmoreland. *Fay* 12, 18-19, 26, 50

HAUTEVILLE, LADY AMALDINA. The eldest daughter of Lord Persiflage, who succeeded in marrying the Marquis of Llwddythlw, in spite of his many duties as eldest son of the Duke of Merioneth. She was very condescending to her cousin Lady Frances Trafford, who had the misfortune to be in love with a Post Office clerk. ". . . as beautiful in colour, shape, and proportion as wax could make a Venus" (1:12:157). Appears frequently in *Marion Fay*.

HE KNEW HE WAS RIGHT. London, Strahan and Co., 1869. 2v.

AUTHOR'S COMMENT. "I do not know that in any literary effort I ever fell more completely short of my own intention than in this story. . . . I look upon the story as being nearly altogether bad."—*Autobiography*, 2:17:166.

NOTES. ". . . a long and detailed study of the gradual falling into madness of a suspicious husband. From obstinate egoism to proud and dangerous reserve, from reserve to desolate monomania, Trevelyan travels with tragic certainty. The final stages of his mental and moral dilapidation have a wild affliction unusual in the controlled world of Trollope characters. . . . the pathological study . . . is at once the book's main theme and its importance in the chronology of Trollope's work."—Sadleir, p. 393.

"One could indeed read this book with profit for the sole purpose of discovering how Englishmen behaved in the 1860s."—Christopher LaFarge, "I Know He Was Right," *Saturday Review of Literature*, Jan. 27, 1940, pp. 12-14.

PLOT. Louis Trevelyan on a visit to the Mandarin Islands fell in love with Emily Rowley, daughter of the Governor. After their marriage they returned to England, taking with them Nora Rowley, a young sister of the bride. As "master in his own house" Trevelyan forbade Emily to receive her father's old friend Colonel Osborne, who had a reputation in London as a philanderer. The Colonel persisted in his attentions, and the young husband became madly jealous. Emily indignantly resented her husband's continued outbursts of distrust and finally, taking their small son, left him. Knowing that he was right, he decided that Emily was unworthy to care for their child and, after making careful plans, succeeded in abducting him. He fled to Italy where, brooding on his misfortunes, he went completely mad. Emily followed him and he was eventually induced to return to England where he soon died.

One of Trevelyan's oldest friends was Hugh Stanbury, who had decided on a career as a newspaper man in London, greatly to the outspoken dismay of his old Aunt Stanbury, who had paid his college bills and expected great things of him. Hugh and Nora Rowley were thrown much together during the sad day of the Trevelyans' troubles, and although Nora was courted by the wealthy Charles Glascock and could have looked forward to a future as Lady Peterborough, she chose to marry for love.

Life in the Cathedral Close with Aunt Stanbury fell to the lot of Hugh's pretty sister Dorothy, and the story of her life and loves forms a happy contrast to the gloom of the principal plot.

HEADFORD. A village in County Galway near Castle Morony, where Father Giles and Father Brosnan lived. *Land.* 2-4

HEARN, MRS. The widow of a former vicar, who lived in one of Squire Dale's houses in the village. *Allington* 1, 9

HEATHCOTE, HARRY. An imperious and hot-tempered Englishman, owner of a large sheep ranch at Gangoil in Queensland. "He was a tall well-made young fellow, with fair hair and a good-humoured smile, but ever carrying in his countenance marks of what his enemies called pigheadedness, his acquaintances obstinacy, and those who loved him, firmness" (1:7). Hero of *Harry Heathcote of Gangoil.*

HEATHCOTE, MRS. MARY (Daly). Harry's wife, and mother of two small sons. One of the principal characters in *Harry Heathcote of Gangoil.*

HEAVITREE. The home of Mrs. French and her two daughters, Arabella and Camilla, in Exeter. *He Knew* 35

HEAVYBED HOUSE. When Squire Crowdy brought his sister-in-law Jane Robarts to Creamclotted Hall, he planned to marry her to a neighboring squire whose home was at Heavybed House. *Framley* 10

HEINE, ERNEST. The junior partner in the firm of "The House of Heine," and father of Isa, Agnes and young Hatto. *Heine*

HEINE, HATTO. The senior partner in the Heine firm, a crotchety old bachelor living in the suburbs of Munich. One of the principal characters in *The House of Heine Brothers in Munich.*

HEINE, ISA. The beautiful daughter of Ernest Heine, who fell in love with their English clerk, Herbert Onslow. Although Herbert was eventually to become a member of the firm, he became increasingly restless as the promotion failed to materialize. Isa braved her formidable Uncle Hatto, and with great tact induced him to accept Herbert as a partner at once, so that they could marry. Heroine of *The House of Heine Brothers in Munich.*

HEINE BROTHERS. A small banking firm in Munich. *Heine*

HEIRLOOMS. Mr. Dove's opinion that the Eustace diamonds were not heirlooms was written for Trollope by Charles Merewether.

HEISE, FANNY. *See* Bogen, Mrs. Fanny (Heise)

HEISE, JACOB. Father of Fanny, who believed that all children had a right to a happy, carefree life. *Linda* 2, 7

HENDON HALL. The suburban residence of Lord Hampstead, where he entertained Marion Fay and her father. *Fay* 1, 5, 10-12, 20

HENNIKER'S HOTEL. *See* Nobble, New South Wales

HEREFORD. The home of Isabel Broderick's parents and of her suitor, William Owen. *Cousin* 1-2, 11, 16, 23

HEREFORDSHIRE.

LONGBARNS. Home of the Fletchers. *Prime Min.*

MAULE ABBEY. Country seat of Maurice Maule, practically in ruins. *Redux*

WHARTON HALL. Seat of Sir Alured Wharton. *Prime Min.*

HERRIOT, ARTHUR. A friend of Frank Greystock, who accompanied Frank to Portray Castle. *Eustace* 23-24, 26, 56

HERTFORD STREET. *See* London

HERTFORDSHIRE.

BUSTON. Owned by Peter Prosper. *Scarborough*

HUNTINGTON. Home of the Thoroughbung brewing family. *Scarborough*

MARMADUKE LODGE. Matilda Thoroughbung's home. *Scarborough*

TRETTON PARK. Mr. Scarborough's estate. *Scarborough*

HESTERWELL SISTERS. ". . . the two Miss Hesterwells, of Hesterwell Park, the younger of whom boldly declared her purpose of civilizing the savage [Rev. Mr. Oriel] . . ." *Thorne* 32

HIPPESLEY, DEAN. The Dean of Exeter Cathedral, brother-in-law to Sir Francis Geraldine. *Kept Dark* 1, 3, 6, 9, 16, 20

HIPPESLEY, MAUDE. *See* Thorne, Mrs. Maude (Hippesley)

HIRAM, JOHN. A woolstapler in Barchester, who died in 1434, leaving his estate to found an almshouse, later known as Hiram's Hospital, for "twelve superannuated woolcarders, all of whom should have been born and bred and spent their days in Barchester" (1:3). *Warden* 1

HIRAM'S HOSPITAL. The Hiram's Hospital case, an important theme in *The Warden*, is based on the actual case of St. Cross at Winchester, which was in the courts in the 1850's. The wardens were successively Mr. Harding and Mr. Quiverful.

"It stands on the banks of the little river. . . . The London road crosses the river by a pretty one-arched bridge, and, looking from this bridge, the stranger will see the windows of the old men's rooms, each pair of windows separated by a small buttress. . . . The entrance to the hospital is from the London road, and is made through a ponderous gateway under a heavy stone arch . . . greatly conducive to the good appearance of Hiram's charity" (*Warden* 1:8-9).

Most important in *The Warden* and *Barchester Towers*; briefly in *Allington* 16; and *Last Chron.* 49, 67, 81

HITTAWAY, MRS. CLARA. Lady Fawn's eldest daughter, vigorously opposed to her brother's marriage to Lizzie Eustace. *Eustace* 9, 11, 32, 56, 59-60, 67

HITTAWAY, ORLANDO. Husband of Clara, and brother-in-law of Lord Fawn. Although Chairman of the Board of Civil Appeals, his chief interest lay in collecting and retailing to Lord Fawn's worried family the gossip about Lizzie Eustace. Appears frequently in *The Eustace Diamonds*.

HOFF, HERR. An Innsbruck butcher, who refused to lower his prices for Frau Frohmann so that she could keep down her rates at the inn. *Frohmann*

HOGGETT, MRS. Wife of Giles, crippled with rheumatism. *Last Chron.* 69

Appears also in the play *Did He Steal It?*.

HOGGETT, GILES. An old brickmaker at Hoggle End, who counseled Mr. Crawley, when he was in despair on being accused of stealing a check, ". . . there ain't nowt a man can't bear if he'll only be dogged. . . . It's dogged as does it. It ain't thinking about it" (2:18:188). *Last Chron.* 61, 69

In *Did He Steal It?*, represented by Dan Hoggett.

HOGGLE END. A community of brickmakers in the Rev. Mr. Crawley's parish. *Last Chron.* 12

HOGGLESTOCK PARISH. The Rev. Mr. Crawley's impoverished parish in the northern extremity of East Barsetshire, inhabited mostly by brickmakers, small farmers and field laborers. Mentioned frequently in *Framley Parsonage* and *The Last Chronicle of Barset*.

HOLDENOUGH, CANON. A member of the Brotherton Cathedral chapter, who married Lady Alice Germain. ". . . a most unexceptional clergyman, rather high, leaning toward the high and dry, very dignified, and quite as big a man in Brotherton as the Dean himself" (1:3:35). *Popenjoy* 1, 3-4, 6, 10, 22, 44, 52-53

HOLDENOUGH, LADY ALICE (Germain). The only married sister of the Marquis of Brotherton and, in her sisters' eyes, inclined to be worldly. Appears frequently in *Is He Popenjoy?*.

HOLLOWAY. A suburb of London. The inn was the Duchess of Edinburgh, at the top of Paradise Row, where lived the Rodens, the Fays and several families of gossiping neighbors. *Fay*.

HOLLYCOMBE, JACK. A malt salesman living in Barchester, who was in love with Polly Peppercorn. One of the principal characters in *Two Heroines of Plumplington*.

HOLMES, GODFREY. A rising young banker of Liverpool, at one time ward of Major Garrow. Elizabeth Garrow broke her engagement to him because of her warped idea that love should not flow along smoothly with no admixture of pain. When Godfrey understood her unconscious reason, he convinced her that she was wrong, and they were married. Hero of *The Mistletoe Bough*.

HOLMES, ISABELLA. Godfrey's sister, a guest at Thwaite Hall for the Christmas holidays. *Mistletoe*

HOLT, MRS. Cecilia Holt's mother, who bitterly resented George Western's treatment of her daughter. One of the principal characters in *Kept in the Dark*.

HOLT, CECILIA. *See* Western, Mrs. Cecilia (Holt)

HOLT, RALPH. A tenant at Twopenny Farm, part of the Folking estate, and a warm and loyal friend to John Caldigate. *Caldigate* 3, 23, 27, 30

HONEYBUN, MR. A legal friend of Sir John Jorum. *Caldigate* 53

HONYMAN, MR. Mr. Tappitt's lawyer at Baslehurst, whose caution frequently infuriated his client, but whose common sense was always vindicated. *Rachel* 10, 17, 22, 24, 27-28

HOOK COURT. *See* London

HOPKINS. The gardener at both the Great and the Small houses at Allington. "One of the best gardeners in fiction."—Walpole, p. 62. *Allington* 53-54, 57-58, 60

HOPKINS, MRS. The housekeeper at Bragton Hall. *Amer. Sen.* 6, 8, 15, 53, 57-58, 64

HOPPEN, HERR VON. The Burgomaster of Bruges, who aspired to the hand and fortune of Madame Brudo, with no success. One of the principal characters in *The Noble Jilt*.

In *Can You Forgive Her?*, represented by Samuel Cheesacre.

HOPPET HALL. Inherited by Reginald Morton (3rd) from his grandfather, and the object of years of litigation between Reginald and John (3rd), who considered himself heir of all his grandfather's estates. *Amer. Sen.* 1-2, 5

HORNE, The REV. AUGUSTUS. An effervescent clergyman traveling in Belgium, who wagered his friend that he could wear the trousers of the Dutch General Chassé that they found in his old quarters. While the clergyman was in another room, a group of women tourists came in and snipped souvenirs from the clergyman's own trousers, thinking they were the General's. The difficulty of finding another pair of trousers, and the trip back to Brussels with the clergyman clad in red plush knee-breeches, are incidents in *Relics of General Chassé*.

HORNS, The. A ". . . pretty little villa down in Richmond . . . with all its gardens, conservatories, lawns, shrubberies, paddocks, boat-houses, and boats," which was given to Lady Glencora as a wedding present by the old Duke of Omnium. It was Lady Glencora's favorite home, and she was often there. Frequently mentioned in *Phineas Finn, The Small House at Allington, The Prime Minister, Can You Forgive Her?* and *The Duke's Children*.

HORSBALL, MR. The manager of the Moonbeam, the pub at Barnfield, headquarters of the B B Hunt. *Ralph* 8, 17, 21, 27, 35-37, 43

HORTON, MRS. MARY (Wade). Wife of Wilfred Horton, and sister of George Wade. One of the principal characters in *Not If I Know It.*

HORTON, WILFRED. Owing to a misunderstanding about the nature of a paper he asked his brother-in-law to sign for him, the two men were in an angry mood when they went to hear the Christmas sermon. It affected them so strongly that each was anxious to placate the other, the difficulty was explained, and they became reconciled. One of the principal characters in *Not If I Know It.*

HOSKINS, HANNIBAL. The discarded American suitor in *Miss Ophelia Gledd.*

HOTSPUR, LADY ELIZABETH. Sir Harry Hotspur's wife, a colorless buffer between her strong-willed husband and her equally determined daughter. One of the principal characters in *Sir Harry Hotspur.*

HOTSPUR, EMILY. Having fallen in love with her scapegrace cousin George Hotspur, she refused to believe the proofs of his villainy and remained faithful to him until her death. ". . . very like her Father . . . the same arch in her eyebrows . . . the same well-formed nose . . . the same short lip, and small mouth, and delicate dimpled chin. . . . Her hair, which was very plentiful, was light in colour, but by no means flaxen. Her complexion was as clear as the finest porcelain; but there were ever roses in her cheeks, for she was strong by nature, and her health was perfect. She was somewhat short of stature . . . and her feet and hands and ears were small and delicate" (2:22). Heroine of *Sir Harry Hotspur of Humblethwaite.*

HOTSPUR, GEORGE. A totally unprincipled but charming young man, who made love to his cousin Emily, hoping to unite the title that would come to him with the property that was to go to her. Although he won Emily's love and broke her heart, she refused to marry him, and he married the mistress who had been supporting him. One of the principal characters in *Sir Harry Hotspur.*

HOTSPUR, SIR HARRY. When Sir Harry Hotspur's only son died, the title reverted to a worthless nephew, George, though all the property was to go to Emily Hotspur, the only daughter. George made love to Emily, but Sir Harry had his daughter's promise not to marry without his consent, and he refused to allow the marriage.

"He was a handsome man . . . with grey hair, bright, keen eyes, and arched eyebrows, with a well-cut eagle nose, and a small mouth, and a short dimpled chin. . . . He was a proud man, with but few intimacies,—with a few dear friendships which were the solace of his life. . . . never assuming aught, deferring much to others outwardly, and showing his pride chiefly by a certain impalpable *noli me tangere*, which just sufficed to make itself felt and obeyed" (1:2-3).

One of the principal characters in *Sir Harry Hotspur.*

HOUGHTON, MRS. ADELAIDE (de Baron). The worldly and flirtatious daughter of a distant relative of the Germain family, loved by Lord George Germain. She refused to marry him, and took Jeffrey Houghton "for an income." After George's marriage to Mary Lovelace, she succeeded in bedeviling him into a series of most embarrassing situations that he was too weak to avoid, but too loyal to Mary to enjoy. One of the principal characters in *Is He Popenjoy?*.

HOUGHTON, HETTA. The wealthy unmarried sister of Jeffrey, who lived in London. *Popenjoy* 12-13, 16

HOUGHTON, JEFFREY. The elderly husband of Adelaide. ". . . very rich, almost old enough to be the girl's father, and a great gambler. But he had a house in Berkeley Square, kept a stud of horses in Northamptonshire, and was much thought of at Newmarket" (1:1:12). *Popenjoy* 1, 4, 7-9, 12-13, 16, 18, 27, 47, 50

HOUSE OF HEINE BROTHERS IN MUNICH, The. In *Tales of All Countries*, Second Series, 1863. Originally published in *Public Opinion*, Literary Supplement, Nov. 16, 23, 1861.

PLOT. Isa Heine, daughter of the junior partner of Heine Brothers, bankers in Munich, fell in love with their young English clerk Herbert Onslow. Herbert's father had promised him a partnership in the firm, and since his income made marriage impossible before this should be obtained, his apprenticeship seemed endless to the impatient lover. Although Isa would have been content to wait, she sympathized with his restlessness and courageously approached her formidable Uncle Hatto, senior member of the firm and a crotchety old bachelor, to ask that Herbert be given a partnership at once so that they might marry. Uncle Hatto was inclined to stand on the letter of the agreement, but Isa's pleading persuaded him and Herbert was given the promotion.

HOUSTON, FRANK. A suitor, purely mercenary, for the hand of Gertrude Tringle, who disengaged himself on learning that she was to have no dowry and married his first love, Imogene Docimer. *Ayala* 14, 18, 28-30, 37-38, 41-42, 59-60

HOUSTON, ROSINA. The elderly and romantic aunt of Frank Houston, whose generosity made it possible for him to marry Imogene Docimer. *Ayala* 60

HUBBLES and GREASE. A London firm doing business at Houndsditch, who were the employers of Mr. Moulder and Mr. Kenneby. *Orley* 6, 42

HUGHES, PHILIP. A cashier in Mr. Greenmantle's bank, in love with his daughter. One of the heroes in *Two Heroines of Plumplington*.

HUMBLETHWAITE HALL. The home of Sir Harry Hotspur, in Cumberland. The setting for *Sir Harry Hotspur of Humblethwaite Hall*, described in great detail in chapter 3.

HUNDLEWICK HALL. The home of Maurice Archer, five miles from Kirkby Cottage, in Yorkshire. *Kirkby*

HUNTER, MR. Capt. Yorke Clayton's bodyguard, wounded by the Landleaguers. Appears frequently in *The Landleaguers*.

HUNTER, MR and MRS. A bridal couple whom George Bertram met in Jerusalem, and at Miss Todd's party in the Valley of Jehoshaphat. ". . . a somewhat fashionable couple, who were both got up with considerable attention as to Oriental costume." *Bertrams* 7-11

HUNTING SCENES in Trollope's works. Not all Trollope lovers are in sympathy with his long and frequent detailed descriptions of riding with the hounds, but no one in English fiction has done them better. His sense of inferiority, which had grown during his unhappy schooldays and his wasted years at uncongenial tasks at the Post Office, was first dispelled by his participation in the sport of hunting, which gave him at the same time full employment for his abounding energy and the joy of companionship he had always craved. There are few scenes in all the novels more dramatically written than the account of Black Daly's war with the Landleaguers to preserve for the "gentry" the continuance of their sport.

BB Hunt. *Ralph* 31
Braeside Harriers. *Fay* 39-40
Brake Hunt. *Redux* 16
Brotherton Hounds. *Popenjoy* 7-8
Cumberlow Green Hunt. *Scarborough* 28-29
Dunhallow Hunt. *Castle Rich.*
Edgehill Hunt. *Can You* 17
Galway Hounds. *Land.* 9
Hamworth Hunt. *Orley* 28-29
Kelly's Court Hounds. *Kellys* 21-22
Rufford and Ufford Hunt Club. *Ayala* 23-24
Rufford United Hunt Club. *Amer. Sen.* 9-11, 22-23
Runnymede Hunt. *Duke* 62-63

The following hunting scenes also appear, without the name of the club:
From Portray Castle in Scotland. *Eustace* 37-41
The MFH was Thomas O'Conor. *O'Conors*
Lord Chiltern hunted with two unnamed clubs from the Willingford Bull. *Finn* 24

HURST STAPLE. A parish in Hampshire in the gift of the Marquis of Stapledean, which was held by the Rev. Arthur Wilkinson, and later by his son Arthur. *Bertrams* 1, 15-16, 25-27

HURTLE, MRS. WINIFRED. An American widow with a lurid past, to whom Paul Montague was for a time engaged and from whom he found it very hard to separate himself. "She was very dark,—a dark brunette,—with large round blue eyes. . . . Her silken hair, almost black, hung in a thousand curls all round her head and neck. Her cheeks and lips and neck were full. . . . Her nose also was full. . . . Her mouth was large, and she rarely showed her teeth. Her chin was full, marked by a large dimple. . . . Her bust was full and beautifully shaped; but she invariably dressed as though she were oblivious . . . of her own charms. . . . She was certainly a most beautiful woman and she knew it" (1:26:162). One of the principal characters in *The Way We Live Now.*

HYTESBURY. An assize town near Bullhampton, where Sam Battle was imprisoned as the suspected murderer of Farmer Trumbull, and where the trial was held. *Vicar* 14-15

INCHARROW. Sir Walter Mackenzie's home, in Rossshire, Scotland. *Mackenzie* 26

INGRAM, JEFFERSON. A young American, making the grand tour, who found himself in Egypt in the party of Mr. Damer and his family. He and Fanny Damer became engaged at the top of the Great Pyramid. Hero of *An Unprotected Female at the Pyramids.*

INNSBRUCK. The nearest town to Frau Frohmann's Peacock Inn, in the Brunnenthal Valley. *Frohmann*

INTERNAL NAVIGATION OFFICE. The very badly run government bureau in which Charley Tudor worked. The clerks were generally known as "Infernal navvies." Mentioned frequently in *The Three Clerks.*

IRELAND. Trollope began his writing career in Ireland, while engaged in work for the postal authorities, and used that country for the setting of his first and second novels, *The Macdermots of Ballycloran* and *The Kellys and the O'Kellys.* Later he added *Castle Richmond* and *An Eye for an Eye,* and at the time of his death was working on his unfinished novel with an Irish theme, *The Landleaguers.* Two short stories also have this background, *Father Giles of Ballymoy* and *The O'Conors of Castle Conor.*

COUNTY CAVEN. Represented in Parliament by Gerald O'Mahoney. *Land.*

COUNTY CLARE. The setting for *An Eye for an Eye*

CASTLE QUIN. Seat of the Earl of Kilfenora. *Eye*

CASTLEMORRIS. The estate of the Earl of Tulla. *Finn*

KILLALOE. Dr. Malachi Finn's home. *Finn*

COUNTY CORK. The setting for *Castle Richmond.*

COUNTY GALWAY. The setting for *Father Giles of Ballymoy*, much of *The Landleaguers* and *The Kellys and the O'Kellys.*

BALLYTOWNGAL. Home of Sir Nicholas Bodkin. *Land.*

CARNLOUGH. Where Thomas Blake lived. *Land.*

CASTLE MORONY. Home of Philip Jones. *Land.*

COUNTY KILDARE.

GREY ABBEY. Where Fanny Wyndham lived with her uncle and guardian, Lord Cashel. *Kellys*

COUNTY LEITRIM. The setting for *The Macdermots of Ballycloran*

COUNTY MAYO.

CASTLE CONOR. Home of Thomas O'Conor. *O'Conors*

TONEROE. Martin Kelly's farm, which he held under Lord Ballindine. *Kellys*

COUNTY ROSCOMMON.

KELLY'S COURT. Home of Lord Ballindine. *Kellys*

IS HE POPENJOY? London, Chapman and Hall, 1878. 3v. Originally published in *All the Year Round*, Oct. 13, 1877-July 13, 1878.

NOTES. *"Is He Popenjoy?* will survive for the Dean of Brotherton—a Trollope dignitary of the first water; for his gay, loving, whimsical daughter; for her husband Lord George Germain, with his excessive sense of duty and inadequate sense of humour; for her aristocratic sisters-in-law, shrouding in ill-nature and good works the emptiness of their lives and purses; for the feminist lecturer Baroness Banmann; for the society siren and society matchmaker; and for the ill-tempered, dissolute marquis, on the legitimacy of whose son turns the whole mechanism of the story."—Sadleir, p. 397.

PLOT. The Marquis of Brotherton, after spending most of his life in Italy, returned to England, bringing with him an Italian woman whom he said was his wife, and a small child whom he asserted was his heir Lord Popenjoy. The Dowager Marchioness with her three daughters and son Lord George Germain were summarily ordered out of the family estate Manor Cross, so that it could be made ready for the Marquis' use.

Lord George had married Mary Lovelace, daughter of the Dean of Brotherton Cathedral, and at the Dean's instigation made inquiry in Italy as to the legitimacy of the child. The resulting information did not prove conclusive, but soon after the child's mother returned to Italy with him, where he died, making the question an academic one. In a short while the Marquis also died and the title went to Lord George, whose newborn son became the real Lord Popenjoy.

ISCHEL, Austria. Where Mr. and Mrs. Finn met the Duke of Omnium and his daughter Lady Mary Palliser. *Duke* 41

ISLINGTON. The district in London in which Winifred Hurtle lived. *Way We Live*

Where Samuel Crocker took a house, expecting to marry Clara Demijohn. *Fay*

ITALY. Florence and Siena provide a background for several chapters in *He Knew He Was Right.*

Lake Como is the setting for *The Man Who Kept His Money in a Box.*

The Rev. Dr. Vesey Stanhope lived with his family in Italy before being recalled to his duties in Barchester, and returned there after Mr. Slope's influence in Cathedral matters ended. *Barchester*

"JACK." A hunter loaned by Lord Rufford to Arabella Trefoil while she was his guest. Although he told her, "When I am going to be married, he will be the first present I shall make her," and later, "Jack must be yours now. . . . he is your horse," she failed to make use of these admissions in her efforts to force him to marry her. The oversight must be laid to Trollope, for Arabella was not the girl to forget anything so much to her advantage. *Amer. Sen.* 22, 66

JACK, MISS SARAH. A wealthy spinster, who successfully managed an engagement between the two young people she loved best, Maurice Cummings and Marian Leslie. Principal character in *Miss Sarah Jack of Spanish Town, Jamaica.*

JACKO. An otherwise nameless boy, who wandered into Gangoil from no one knew where and was hired by Heathcote. ". . . a rough-looking lad, about sixteen years of age . . . unwashed, uncombed, and with that wild look which falls upon those who wander about the Australian plains, living a nomad life" (1:29). *Heathcote* 1-3, 8-10

JACOBI, RUTH. The orphaned granddaughter of Stephen Trendellsohn, living with him in the Jewish quarter in Prague. A friend of both Nina Balatka and Rebecca Loth. *Nina* 1, 4, 6-7, 11, 13

"JAEL AND SISERA." A painting by Conway Dalrymple of Clara Van Siever. *Last Chron.* 38, 51, 60, 64, 84

JAMAICA. The setting for *Miss Sarah Jack of Spanish Town.*

JAQUÊTANÀPE, MRS. CLEMENTINA (Golightly). She had a fortune of £20,000, a passion for dancing, and little else. Alaric Tudor was one of the trustees of her fortune, and urged Charley Tudor to marry her. Charley was not interested, and Clementina married Victoire Jaquêtanàpe.

". . . in the common parlance of a large portion of mankind, 'a doosed fine gal.' She stood five feet six, and stood very well, on very good legs, but with rather large feet. She was as straight as a grenadier. . . . Waltzes and polkas suited her admirably; for she was gifted with excellent lungs and perfect powers of breathing; and she had not much delight in prolonged conversation. . . . We have said nothing about the face of the beauteous Clementina, and indeed nothing can be said about it. . . . You might look at her for four hours consecutively on a Monday evening, and yet on Tuesday you would not know her" (2:1:7-8).

Appears frequently in *The Three Clerks.*

JAQUÊTANÀPE, VICTOIRE. A fortune-hunter who married Clementina Golightly. "The happy Victoire was dressed up to his eyes. That, perhaps, is not saying much, for he was only a few feet high; but what he wanted in quantity he fully made up in quality. He was a well-made, shining, jaunty little Frenchman, who seemed to be perfectly at ease with himself, and all the world. He had the smallest little pair of moustaches imaginable, the smallest little imperial, the smallest possible pair of boots, and the smallest possible pair of gloves" (2:9:185). *Clerks* 17, 25-27, 29

JAWSTOCK, JEREMIAH. A member of the Runnymede Hunt, who led the attack against Major Tifto and deprived him of his position as MFH. *Duke* 57-58

JAY, MR. and MRS. Daughter and son-in-law of Jacob Brattle, the miller at Bullhampton. Prosperous, but ungenerous to Carry Brattle in her disgrace. *Vicar* 6, 15, 19, 41, 46

JEANNETTE. The maid of Mrs. Greenow, and an expert in assisting her mistress in her affairs of the heart. *Can You* 7-8, 19, 39-40, 47

In *The Noble Jilt*, represented by the maid to Madame Brudo.

JELLYBAG STREET. *See* London

"JEMIMA." A wild horse belonging to Sir John Purefoy, on which Major Caneback was riding at the Rufford Hunt when he was killed. *Amer. Sen.* 22

JENNINGS, The REV. MR. A minor canon at Exeter Cathedral, in attendance on Miss Stanbury during her illness. *He Knew* 54

JERMYN STREET. *See* London

JERNINGHAM, MR. The head of the section of the Post Office in which George Roden worked. *Fay* 7, 12, 23, 30, 46, 49, 57, 61, 64

JEROME, FATHER. The curé of St. Laud's, and one of the soldiers in the Vendean revolt. ". . . a tall, well-made, brawny man; his face was not exactly handsome, but it was bold and intellectual; his eye was bright and clear, and his forehead high and open—he was a man of immense muscular power and capable of great physical exertion—he was above forty-five years of age but still apparently in the prime of his strength" (1:3:88-89). One of the principal characters in *La Vendée.*

JEROME, FATHER. Nina Balatka's father confessor, who endeavored to save her soul by preventing her marriage with the Jew Anton Trendellsohn. *Nina* 2-3, 5, 13

JERUSALEM. Where George Bertram met his father. *Bertrams* 6-10

JOBBLES, The REV. MR. One of the examining board of Civil Service, who resigned in opposition to Sir Gregory Hardlines. On his resignation Alaric Tudor was promoted to the position. "Mr. Jobbles was created for the conducting of examinations" (1:11:239). *Clerks* 11, 27, 31

JOCKEY CLUB. *See* London

"JOHN BRIGHT." The British warship that brought the order for the deposition of President Neverbend of Britannula and carried him back to England. *Fixed* 2, 8

JOHN BULL ON THE GUADALQUIVIR. In *Tales of All Countries* [First Series], 1861. Originally published in *Cassell's Illustrated Family Paper*, Nov. 17, 24, 1860.

NOTES. In speaking of the story, Trollope confessed to a friend that the adventure had been one of his own.

PLOT. John Pomfret, traveling down the Guadalquivir in Spain on his way to propose to Marie Daguilar, met the gaudily dressed Marquis d'Almavivas on the boat, and mistook him for a bullfighter. Assuming that such an ignorant fellow knew no English, John examined his costume minutely, even twisting off one of the buttons, and commented volubly to his companion on the improvidence of spending money so dangerously earned on personal adornment. Arriving at his destination, he was greatly embarrassed, on receiving an invitation to a splendid entertainment, to find that his host was the man he had treated so rudely.

JOHN CALDIGATE. London, Chapman and Hall, 1879. 3v. Originally published in *Blackwood's Magazine*, April 1878-June 1879.

NOTES. "... the plot is one of his most interesting, ingenious, elaborate, and unexpected. The pages about the Civil Service make an instructive contrast with those of twenty years before in *The Three Clerks*."—Walpole, p. 138.

PLOT. After taking his degree at Cambridge, John Caldigate found himself, in consequence of certain amusements at Newmarket and elsewhere, heavily indebted to a moneylender, Davis, and with no means to meet his obligation. His father Daniel Caldigate, disgusted with his extravagance and folly, arranged through his banker friend Nicholas Bolton for the sale by his son of the reversion of the estate and for a mortgage to clear his debts. At Mr. Bolton's home where John went to sign the papers, he met, briefly, Bolton's young daughter Hester, and fell in love with her. With his college friend Dick Shand, he went out to New South Wales to try his fortune in goldmining. On the long voyage out he met Euphemia Smith, an adventuress, and was trapped into a quasi-engagement. The two young men had the good fortune to locate a paying mine and worked together until Dick, who had been drinking heavily, disappeared. John, in his loneliness, foolishly renewed his attentions to Euphemia Smith, and for a time they lived together.

After John had acquired a considerable property he sold his mine and returned to England, where he was reconciled with his father and married Hester Bolton. Soon after the birth of his son, Euphemia Smith and Tim Crinkett, a former partner to whom he had sold his interest in the mine, followed him to England to blackmail him into a repayment of £20,000. They alleged that the mine was worked out; that he had married Mrs. Smith in New South Wales; and that his marriage to Hester Bolton was bigamous. He recognized that there was a moral though not a legal claim for the return of part of the purchase price of the mine, but was advised against buying them off. In the course of the trial, however, he very foolishly did so, and when this became known, opinion ran against him. He was convicted and sentenced to two years' imprisonment. The evidence against him rested largely on an envelope posted in Sydney, addressed by him to Mrs. Smith as Mrs. Caldigate. A postal clerk succeeded in proving that the postmark on the envelope was a forgery, and that the stamp was not issued until after the date of the postmark. At this fortunate moment Dick Shand returned and by his testimony proved that there had been no marriage. An appeal was made to the Home Office, and John received the Queen's pardon.

JOHNSON, MR., of Manchester. A fictitious merchant invented by Robinson, the junior partner of Brown, Jones and Robinson, as publicity for his firm. *Struggles* 11

JOHNSON, THOMAS. John Pomfret's traveling companion on the Guadalquivir. *John Bull*

JOLLY BLACKBIRD (inn). *See* London

JONES, MISS. The Rev. Evan Jones's meek daughter, who was invited to dine at Framley once every three months. *Framley* 2

JONES, MR. An Englishman traveling alone in Palestine, who allowed himself to be duped into taking with him a girl masquerading as a young man. Principal character in *A Ride Across Palestine.*

JONES, MR. A haberdasher's clerk, who married Sarah Jane Brown and persuaded her father to put his fortune in a haberdashery business. He became one of the partners and, when the firm failed, retired with most of the scanty capital. One of the principal characters in *The Struggles of Brown, Jones and Robinson.*

JONES, MR. A Hytesbury lawyer, who defended Sam Battle at his trial for the murder of Farmer Townsend. *Vicar* 15, 19, 49

JONES, MR. The London landlord who helped eject George Vavasor after he had attempted to kill Mr. Grey. *Can You* 52

JONES, MR., MRS. and MISS. In Jerusalem at the time of George Bertram's visit. Mr. Jones "was steadily engaged in antiquarian researches, being minded to bring out to the world some startling new theory as to certain points in Bible chronology and topography. He always went about the city with a trowel and a big set of tablets . . ." (1:9:89). *Bertrams* 8-9

JONES, MRS. A valued servant and friend of Lady Fitzgerald since her girlhood. *Castle Rich.* 9-10, 13-14, 19-23, 25, 29, 33

JONES, ADA. Philip Jones's eldest daughter, a recognized beauty. ". . . tall, fair-haired, and very lovely. It was admitted in County Galway that among the Galway lasses no girl exceeded Ada Jones in brightness of beauty. She was sweet-tempered also, and gracious as she was lovely" (1:1:7). Trollope calls her "one of the three heroines" of *The Landleaguers.*

JONES, CHARLES BURNABY. Waking in a Paris hotel with a badly blistered chest, he discovered that a mustard plaster had been placed on it during the night. Mrs. Brown confessed that she had mistaken him for her husband, who had a bad cold. Greatly to everyone's surprise, they later met at Thompson Hall where they were all to spend Christmas, and Mr. Jones was introduced as the fiancé of Mrs. Brown's sister Jane Thompson. One of the principal characters in *Christmas at Thompson Hall.*

JONES, EDITH. The younger daughter of Philip Jones, who considered herself so plain, in comparison with her beautiful sister, that she mistook Captain Clayton's love as for Ada. No amount of argument on her part made him change his mind.

"She was dark, and small of stature, not ungraceful in her movements, or awkward in her person. She was black-haired . . . and almost swarthy in her complexion, and there was a squareness about her chin which robbed her face of much of its feminine softness. But her eyes were very bright, and when she would laugh . . . her face would be brightened up with fun, good-humour, or wit, in a manner which enabled no one to call her plain" (1:1:8).

One of the "three heroines" of *The Landleaguers.*

JONES, The REV. EVAN. The curate of Framley Church for many years, "and though he was personally disliked by Lady Lufton, as being Low Church in his principles and unsightly in his appearance, nevertheless, she would not urge his removal" (1:2:23). *Framley* 2, 5, 8-9

JONES, FLORIAN. The ten-year-old son of Philip Jones, whose conversion to Catholicism gave him a feeling that he must stand by his Catholic friends even at the expense of his own father. On breaking his vow to protect Pat Carroll and other Landleaguers, and giving evidence against them, he was shot and killed by one of their number. "He was small of his age, but clever and sharp, and, since his mother's death, had been his father's darling. He was beautiful to look at" (1:1:9). One of the principal characters in *The Landleaguers.*

JONES, FRANK. The eldest son of Philip Jones, whose engagement to Rachel O'Mahony, the opera singer, was broken after the Landleaguers ruined the family fortune, as he would not consent to live on her earnings. When Rachel lost her voice the engagement was renewed. One of the principal characters in *The Landleaguers.*

JONES, HENRY. The heir of Indefer Jones, who discovered between the pages of a book of sermons a later will leaving the property to his cousin Isabel Broderick. Lacking courage to destroy it, he buried himself in the library, and so woke the suspicions of the household. When the will was found he returned to London. One of the principal characters in *Cousin Henry.*

JONES, INDEFER. A landed proprietor of Llanfeare, in Carmarthenshire, Wales. As he was without a child, his choice of an heir forms the plot of *Cousin Henry.*

JONES, MARY FLOOD. The young Irish girl whom Phineas Finn married, and who died in childbirth. ". . . a little girl about twenty years of age, with the softest hair in the world, of a colour varying between brown and auburn . . . and she was as pretty as ever she could be. She was one of those girls, so common in Ireland, whom men with tastes that way given, feel inclined to take up and devour on the spur of the moment; and when she liked her lion, she had a look about her which seemed to ask to be devoured . . ." (1:2:17). *Finn* 2, 16, 35, 50, 65-66, 69, 76

JONES, MRS. MONTACUTE. A good-natured old lady, who loved to give large parties and entertain reluctant but eligible young men at her country house in the interest of unreluctant young women friends. A confidante and champion of Mary Germain. ". . . a stout-built but very short old lady, with gray hair curled in precise rolls down her face, with streaky cheeks, giving her a look of extreme good health, and very bright gray eyes. She was always admirably dressed. . . . She was very old . . . very enthusiastic, particularly in reference to her friends; very fond of gaiety, and very charitable" (*Popenjoy* 2:9:118-19). Most prominent in *Is He Popenjoy?*; briefly in *Duke* 28, 39-40, 42

JONES, PHILIP. The owner of the Ballintubber and Morony estates in County Galway, whose treatment at the hands of the Landleaguers is the basis of the novel of that name.

JONES, SEPTIMUS. A friend and toady of Augustus Scarborough. *Scarborough* 7-9, 19-21, 37, 53, 63

JORAM, JACKY (probably the same as Sir John Jorum). Mr. Toogood tried to persuade Mr. Crawley to allow him to brief Jacky Joram as barrister, and said of him, ". . . as well known at Westminster as the Speaker, and more thought of at Guildhall and the Old Bailey than the Lord Mayor" (p. 12). *Did He*

The barrister in the case of the Percycross petition. *Ralph* 44

JORUM, SIR JOHN. The barrister who defended John Caldigate in his bigamy case, and was active in securing his pardon. *Caldigate* 40-43, 47-55, 57, 64

JOSEPHINE DE MONTMORENCI. In *An Editor's Tales*, 1870. Originally published in *Saint Paul's Magazine*, Dec. 1869.

Plot. The Editor received a peremptory demand from a young woman who signed herself "Josephine de Montmorenci" that he publish her story in his magazine. Amused by the letter, he requested her to call. She proved to be a charming young woman who confessed that she had used an assumed name, which she considered more distinguished than her own, Mrs. Puffle, and that the novel was not hers but had been written by her sister-in-law Maryanne Puffle.

JOURNEY TO PANAMA, The. In *Lotta Schmidt and Other Stories*, 1867. Originally published in *The Victoria Regia*; a volume of original contributions in poetry and prose, edited by Adelaide A. Proctor. London, Emily Faithfull and Co., 1861.

NOTES. ". . . which tale stands high among Trollope's short stories, being not only the most courageously 'unfinished' of them all, but also . . . the most vital to an understanding of his full-length work."—Sadleir, p. 185-86.

PLOT. On the voyage out to Panama Emily Viner confided to a casual acquaintance, Ralph Forrest, that she had, as a young woman, engaged herself to Mr. Gorlach more as insurance against spinsterhood than for love. He had gone out to Central America to make his fortune, and for years only the most desultory communication had passed between them. Middle-aged and about to become a charge on unwilling relatives, she had staked her last funds on a ticket to Panama to marry him. Forrest tried to persuade her to return to England rather than risk the inevitable unhappiness of such a marriage, and, on her confession that she could not pay for her return passage, offered to pay it for her. She refused, but on arriving at Panama learned that Mr. Gorlach had died on his way to meet her, leaving her a small legacy, with which she returned to England.

JUDD STREET. *See* London

JUNIPER, RICHARD. A horse-trainer at Newmarket, who had loaned money to Captain Scarborough. He was a suitor for the hand of Amelia Carroll until he found that her dowry lacked £50 of the figure he required. *Scarborough* 34-36, 55, 60, 62

"JUPITER." A London newspaper, sometimes called the "Daily Jupiter," used by Trollope as a pseudonym for "The Times." It is mentioned repeatedly in *The Warden, Barchester Towers, The Small House at Allington, Framley Parsonage*; and incidentally in *The Bertrams* and *The Struggles of Brown, Jones and Robinson*.

KANTURK. A town in County Cork, not far from Castle Richmond, where a Union workhouse was established to help care for the famine sufferers. *Castle Rich.* 18

KANTURK HOTEL. *See* Cork

KANTWISE, MR. A commercial traveler in hardware, particularly in steel furniture. He was a friend of Mr. Moulder, and one of the "commercial gentlemen" who made the Bull Inn at Leeds their headquarters. "He looked as though a skin rather too small for the purpose had been drawn over his head and face, so that his forehead and cheeks and chin were tight and shiny. His eyes were small and green, always moving about in his head. . . . It was not that he did not look you in the face, but he always looked at you with a sidelong glance . . . so that sometimes he would prefer to have his antagonist almost behind his shoulder. . . . His nose seemed to have been compressed almost into nothing by that skin-squeezing operation. . . . it possessed length without breadth. . . . the hair . . . stood up erect all around to the height of two inches. . . . it was very red" (1:6:40). *Orley* 6, 8-9, 16, 24, 61, 77

KATCHEN'S CAPRICES. In *Harper's Weekly*, Dec. 22, 29, 1866; Jan. 5, 12, 1867.

PLOT. Katrina Kester, daughter of the

Golden Lamb innkeeper at Gassau, Upper Austria, was loved by Fritz Rosenheim, but, as he was only a courier, Katrina's father hoped that she would marry the rich Caspar Ebner, landlord of the flourishing Black Eagle Inn on the other side of the lake. Katrina was torn between a desire to obey her father and her own unacknowledged love for Fritz. However, when Fritz was accused of stealing a valuable box intrusted to his care by his employers, Katrina cut off and sold her beautiful golden hair to help him repay the loss. When the thief was discovered, Fritz and Katrina were married, receiving as a wedding gift from Caspar Ebner the long braid of Katrina's hair.

KEEGAN, HYACINTH. The agent and son-in-law of Joe Flannelly, whose ambition to dispossess the Macdermots from Ballycloran is one of the main themes of *The Macdermots of Ballycloran*.

"He was a hardworking man. . . . he was a plausible man, a good flatterer, not deficient in that sort of sharpness which made him a successful attorney in a small provincial town. . . . Principle had never stood much in his way. . . . In appearance he was a large, burly man, gradually growing corpulent, with a soft, oily face, on which there was generally a smile. . . . it concealed the malice, treachery and selfishness which his face so plainly bore without it. His eyes were light, large and bright. . . . his mouth was very large, and his lip heavy, and he carried a huge pair of brick coloured whiskers. His dress was somewhat dandified" (1:10:239-44).

One of the principal characters in *The Macdermots of Ballycloran*.

KEEGAN, MRS. SALLY (Flannelly). Offered by her father to Larry Macdermot, so that she might marry a "rale gintleman." When Larry refused, she married Hyacinth Keegan, who, "if he had not the same advantages as Larry in birth and blood, had compensation for his inferiority, in cash and comforts" (1:3:23). *Macdermots* 3, 19

KELLY, JACK. A poor, half-witted vagrant. "He was a dirty, barefooted, unshorn, ragged ruffian, who ate potatoes in the kitchen of the Court, and had never done a day's work in his life. Such as he was, however, he was presented to Captain O'Kelly, as 'his honor the masther's fool'" (1:2:33-34). *Kellys* 2, 7

KELLY, JANE. The youngest Kelly daughter, who was greatly interested in a young neighbor, John Nolan. *Kellys* 6-8, 17-19, 25, 40

KELLY, MARTIN. A tenant farmer of Lord Ballindine, and a distant relative. Not unaware of Anty Lynch's fortune, he planned to marry her, but eventually did so for love. "He was a good-looking young fellow, about twenty-five years of age, with that mixture of cunning and frankness in his bright eye, which is so common among those of his class in Ireland" (1:1:7-8). One of the principal characters in *The Kellys and the O'Kellys*.

KELLY, MRS. MARY. An inn- and shopkeeper at Dunmore, and mother of John, Martin, Meg and Jane. A fiery-tempered but good-hearted woman who, though aiding Anty Lynch to escape from her brother, complained bitterly at all the trouble it caused her. One of the principal characters in *The Kellys and the O'Kellys*.

KELLY, MEG. Sister of Martin, and devoted to Anty Lynch in her illness. *Kellys* 6-8, 17-19, 40

KELLY SERVANTS.

SALLY. ". . . an antiquated female . . . who was more devoted to her teapot than ever was bacchanalian to his glass" (1:1:10). *Kellys* 1, 6, 27

KATE. "Poor Kate was very ugly. Her hair had that appearance of having been dressed by the turkey-cock. . . . her mouth extended nearly from ear to ear; her neck and throat, which always were nearly bare, presented no feminine charms to view, and her short coarse petticoat showed her red legs nearly to the knee . . ." (1:1:11-12). *Kellys* 1, 6, 19, 27

KELLYS AND THE O'KELLYS, The; *or* Landlords and Tenants. A tale of Irish Life. London, Colburn, 1848. 3v.

AUTHOR'S COMMENT. ". . . a good Irish story, much inferior to *The Macdermots* as to plot, but superior in the mode of telling."—*Autobiography*, 1:4: 101.

NOTES. "Lord Ballindine and Fanny Wyndham, the hero and heroine, who have been estranged before the story begins, do not meet again until the middle of the next to the last chapter,—and their only recorded conversation is the two exclamations there set down:— "My own Fanny!—once more my own!" "Oh, Frank! dear Frank!"— Irwin, pp. 24-25.

PLOT. Francis O'Kelly, Lord Ballindine, had as near neighbors, distant relations and tenants, Mrs. Kelly and her son Martin. Another neighbor was Barry Lynch, whose father had filched from the Ballindine estate a considerable fortune, which he left in equal portions to his worthless son Barry and to his daughter Anty. Barry attempted to force Anty into an asylum, declaring her to be mentally unfit to manage her fortune, and, failing this, tried to murder her. She fled to the Kellys, where Martin, not unmindful of her wealth, planned to marry her. Before he made this sordid proposal, he fell in love with her—and she with him.

Lord Ballindine had been engaged to Fanny Wyndham, a wealthy heiress whose guardian Lord Cashel tried to marry her to his dissipated son Lord Kilcullen. His plan failed, and the lovers were reunited. Lord Kilcullen, crippled by debt, escaped from his creditors by going to Boulogne, where Barry Lynch was soon compelled to follow him.

KELLY'S COURT. The seat of the O'Kellys, represented by Lord Ballindine, and the setting for many of the scenes in *The Kellys and the O'Kellys*.

KELLY'S COURT HOUNDS. The hunt club with which Lord Ballindine rode. *Kellys* 21-22

KENNEBY, JOHN. An honest moron, who testified as a witness to the signing of Sir Joseph Mason's will at both trials of the Orley Farm case. In his early life he had been in love with Miriam Usbeck, but later was persuaded by his sister Mrs. Moulder to marry Mrs. Smiley and her brickyard. *Orley* 1, 7, 24-26, 42-43, 61, 67, 71, 77

KENNEDY, LADY LAURA (Standish). Daughter of the Earl of Brentford and sister of Lord Chiltern. Greatly interested in politics, she maintained a distinguished salon in London. When Phineas Finn came out of Ireland to try for a career in Parliament, she became interested in him and undertook to advise and aid him in his ambition. She soon fell in love with him, but refused to marry him as her fortune had been spent in the payment of her brother's debts, and he had none. Her ambition led her to marry Robert Kennedy, a wealthy landowner in Scotland and an MP, but her life with him was desperately unhappy and she left him, retiring to Dresden with her father. After her husband's death she returned to England, hoping at last to marry Phineas Finn, but on his marriage to Madame Goesler she became an embittered and tragic recluse.

"She was in fact about five feet seven in height, and she carried her height well. There was something of nobility in her gait, and she seemed thus to be taller than her inches. Her hair was in truth red,—of a deep thorough redness. . . . Her face was very fair, though it lacked that softness which we all love in women. Her eyes, which were large and bright, and very clear, never seemed to quail, never rose and sunk or showed themselves to be afraid of their own power. . . . Her nose was perfectly cut, but was rather large. . . . Her mouth also was large, but was full of expression, and her teeth were perfect. Her complexion was very brilliant . . ." (*Finn* 1:4:29).

". . . the best character in *Phineas Finn* and its sequel *Phineas Redux*."—*Autobiography*, 2:17:164.

KENNEDY, ROBERT. A wealthy but morose and self-centered man, representing a Scotch group of boroughs in Parliament. Although Lady Laura Standish was in love with Phineas Finn when she married Mr. Kennedy, she felt that her social and political ambitions could best be served as his wife. She soon found him so despotic and unreasonable that she returned to her father. Believing that Phineas Finn was responsible for his wife's action, he quarreled with and tried to murder him. He was taken back to Loughlinter where he became quite mad, and soon died.

"Mr. Kennedy was a man who had very little temptation to do anything wrong. He was possessed of over a million and a half of money . . . a magnificent place in Perthshire . . . a house in London, and a stud of horses in Leicestershire" (*Finn* 1:5:36).

One of the principal characters in *Phineas Finn* and *Phineas Redux*.

KENTUCKY. The setting for *The Two Generals*.

KEPPEL STREET. *See* London

KEPT IN THE DARK. A Novel. London, Chatto and Windus, 1882. 2v. Originally published in *Good Words*, May-Dec. 1882.

NOTES. "It is a study of a morbid obsession. . . . Nevertheless it reads agreeably and ranks among the brief studies in individual psychology . . . as a book which must be read to be realized, and which, when read, will be found to offer genuine, if conventional, Trollope to such as seek him."—Sadleir, p. 396.

PLOT. Cecilia Holt of Exeter became engaged to Sir Francis Geraldine, but soon discovered her mistake and jilted him. A year later in Rome, she fell in love with George Western and promised to marry him. He confided to her the story of a previous engagement, but her own experience had been so nearly identical, and his bitterness so great against a girl who would jilt a lover, that she could not return his confidence. Even after their marriage the occasion did not arise when she could speak of it without seeming to give the matter undue importance. Sir Francis and a meddling gossip of Exeter contrived to make this earlier engagement of Cecilia's known to her husband, and he was furiously angry at having been kept in the dark. He brooded over his wife's duplicity until he lost all sense of proportion and finally deserted her. She returned to her old home in Exeter, too proud to plead for forgiveness and feeling she had not been at fault. In this she was supported by her sister-in-law Lady Grant, who was devoted to her brother, understood his nature and was able to bring about a reconciliation.

KERRYCULLION. Where the Landleaguers killed a whole family because the old mother, who had seen one of her neighbors stoned to death for no reason, had dared to voice her indignation. *Land.* 47

KESTER, JOSEF. Father of Katrina, and landlord of the Golden Lamb. One of the principal characters in *Katchen's Caprices.*

KESTER, KATRINA. Daughter of an Austrian innkeeper, who cut off and sold her beautiful golden hair to help her lover repay his employers for a box he was accused of stealing. ". . . as fresh and fair and rounded as a Hebe . . . a blonde, peach-like skin, large, limpid light-blue eyes, and an enormous wealth of fair hair. This hair was splendid from its silken quality and great quantity . . . fell down straight to her knees in a silken mass" (*Harper's Weekly,* Dec. 22, 1866, p. 810). Heroine of *Katchen's Caprices.*

KESWICK. A town ten miles from Lovel Grange, where the Countess Lovel lived with her daughter Lady Anna while trying to prove her right to the title and her daughter's legitimacy. The setting for much of *Lady Anna.*

"KESWICK POET," The. An unnamed friend of the Thwaites, father and son, whom Daniel consulted about his love affairs, and who advised him to give up his hope of marrying Lady Anna. *Anna* 26

KILCULLEN, ADOLPHUS, LORD. Son of Lord Cashel, who tried, with his father's aid, to marry Fanny Wyndham and use her fortune to defray his gambling debts. *Kellys* 13, 15, 26, 28-33

KILFENORA, EARL OF. Father of Lady Mary Quin, who lived at Quin Castle, near Liscannor, County Clare. *Eye* 2, 5

KILFENORA, LORD. Defeated George Vavasor for the seat representing Chelsea in the Commons. At the death of his father, the Marquis of Bunratty, he was moved up to the House of Lords, leaving George to contest the seat with Mr. Travers for only part of a session. *Can You* 12-13, 41

KILLALOE. The home of the Finn family, in County Clare, Ireland. *Finn* 1, 16, 35, 65-66

KILLANCODLEM. Mrs. Montacute Jones's place in Scotland, where her matchmaking capabilities were aided by the romantic scenery. *Duke* 39, 42; *Popenjoy* 50-51, 55

KILMACRENNY. A small town near the home of Mrs. O'Hara and her daughter Kate. *Eye*

KIMBERLEY DIAMOND MINES. Where John Gordon made his fortune. *Old Man* 18

KING'S HEAD (pub). *See* Baslehurst

KINGSBURY, MARQUIS OF. Father of Lady Frances Trafford and Lord Hampstead, and of three small sons by a second marriage. Driven to his bed by the machinations of his wife and his chaplain, he finally forced his wife to confess her indiscretion and, when the chaplain was pensioned off, again became master of his own house. One of the principal characters in *Marion Fay.*

KINGSBURY, CLARA, MARCHIONESS OF. The second wife of the Marquis, bitterly envious of the two older children, Lady Frances and Lord Hampstead, who stood in the way of her own three sons. Her schemes to alienate her husband's affection from them, made with the resident chaplain, almost brought her to disaster. "If words would not serve her occasion at the moment, her countenance would do so,—and if not that, her absence. She could be very eloquent with silence, and strike an adversary dumb by the way in which she would leave a room. She was a tall, handsome woman, with a sublime gait. To be every inch an aristocrat . . . was the object of her life" (1:3:30). One of the principal characters in *Marion Fay*.

KINGSBURY CRESCENT. *See* London

KINGSBURY HOUSE. The Park Lane residence of the Marquis of Kingsbury. *Fay* 1

KIRKBY CLIFFE, Yorkshire. The setting for *Christmas Day at Kirkby Cottage*.

KIRWAN, PAT. Pat and his vindictive wife kept the inn at Ballymoy. *Father Giles*

KNOWL, MRS. The housekeeper at Launay, who assumed the duty of being Bessy Pryor's jailor and escorted her to Avranches. *Launay*

KNOX, MR. The much-harassed man of business for the Marquis of Brotherton. Appears frequently in *Is He Popenjoy?*.

KÖNIGSGRAAF. A schloss in Saxony owned by the Marquis of Kingsbury, to which Lady Frances Trafford was sent in an effort to break off her engagement to George Roden. *Fay* 4, 9

KÖNIGSTEIN. A fortress in the Saxon Alps to which Lady Laura Kennedy took Phineas Finn during his visit to her in Dresden. *Redux* 12

KRAPP, SUSE. An old peasant woman, who tried to persuade Frau Frohmann to pay the market price for her produce, rather than force the valley people to take their goods to Innsbruck. *Frohmann*

LACORDAIRE, M. A French tailor in Le Puy, who planned an expedition to a neighboring estate, the chateau of Prince Polignac, for Mrs. Thompson and her daughters, and while there proposed to Mrs. Thompson. *Chateau*

LADY ANNA. London, Chapman and Hall, 1874. 2v. Originally published in *The Fortnightly Review*, April 1873-April 1874.

AUTHOR'S COMMENT. "In it a young girl, who is really a lady of high rank and great wealth, though in her youth she enjoyed none of the privileges of wealth or rank, marries a tailor who has been good to her, and whom she had loved when she was poor and neglected."—*Autobiography*, 2:19:200.

NOTES. Trollope's readers censured him severely for allowing his heroine to marry the tailor rather than the young Lord Lovel, but Trollope says: "If I had not told my story well, there would have been no feeling in favour of the young lord."—*Autobiography*, 2:19:200-1.

PLOT. The disreputable but wealthy old Lord Lovel married Josephine Murray, but later disowned her and her daughter, claiming that he had another wife at the time of their marriage. Without funds, but befriended by a tailor who had become interested in the case, his wife sued him for bigamy, and although he was acquitted, a cloud was left on her right to the title. The old Earl returned to Italy and for twenty years the tailor supported the wife and her daughter Anna. Returning to England with a new mistress, Lord Lovel soon died, leaving his entire estate to the woman. The heir to the title claimed the estate, and attempted to prove by law that the Italian mistress had no right to it, and that the Countess had no right to her title. The courts upheld his contention as to the estate, but the case was so complicated by the claim of yet another woman calling herself the first wife that clear proof seemed impossible to obtain. Lawyers were sent to Italy, and were convinced that the woman was a fraud, but the story was too old to be proven conclusively. As a compromise, they suggested that the young Earl and Lady Anna should marry. The Earl agreed and, after meeting Anna, offered not only his hand, but his heart.

Anna, however, had already promised herself to Daniel Thwaite, son of the tailor. Lady Lovel, despite her obligation, was indignant at this misalliance, but not even virtual imprisonment by her mother was enough to shake Lady Anna's determination to keep her word. Finally, in desperation, the Countess invited Daniel to a conference and when he appeared tried to murder him. He was only slightly injured, but she was afraid to oppose their marriage further. When the courts awarded the fortune to Lady Anna, she deeded a large part of her wealth to the young Earl, and with the remainder she and her husband emigrated to Sydney.

LADY OF LAUNAY, The. N. Y., Harper, 1878. Also published in *Why Frau Frohmann Raised Her Prices and Other Stories*, 1882.

PLOT. Mrs. Miles, the wealthy owner of Launay, confused her dominating will with a sense of duty. Her favorite son, Philip, had taken the family name of Launay and was to inherit the property. She planned to marry him to a distant cousin who owned another large family estate, and thus consolidate the two properties. Philip, however, wished to marry his mother's foster daughter Bessy Pryor, but Mrs. Miles angrily refused to have her plans disrupted, and banished Bessy to Normandy. Philip soon followed, and Mrs. Miles, deprived of the companionship of the two people she loved best, capitulated and called them home.

LAKE COMO, Italy. The setting for *The Man Who Kept His Money in a Box.*

LAMBTON ARMS (inn). *See* Tankerville

LANDLEAGUERS, The. London, Chatto and Windus, 1883. 3v. Originally published in *Life: A Weekly Journal of Society, Literature, the Fine Arts and Finance*, Nov. 16, 1882-Oct. 4, 1883.

NOTES. More of a tract on the agrarian troubles in Ireland in 1879-81, than a novel. It was unfinished at the time of Trollope's death, as only 49 of the 60 chapters had been completed. "Sad accounts of wretched actuality, in which characterization is submerged in floods of almost literal fact."—Sadleir, p. 144.

PLOT. Philip Jones of Castle Marony, an extensive estate in County Galway, incurred the enmity of Pat Carroll, a tenant and a Landleaguer, who incited his friends to refuse to pay their rent and finally to flood and ruin a large field. Florian Jones, the ten-year-old son, was a witness to the deed, but he had recently become a Catholic and had given a solemn oath to Father Brosnan that he would not identify the culprits. Others who knew the facts were too terrified to tell what they knew. The only hope of obtaining legal redress was through Florian's testimony, and he was finally persuaded to reveal what he had seen. Pat's brother Terry was also induced to testify against the Landleaguers. Pat was brought to trial, but on the way to the court Florian was shot and killed, and Terry was murdered in the courtroom.

Frank Jones, the eldest son, was engaged to Rachel O'Mahony, an Irish-American girl who had achieved a great success in London as an opera singer; but he would not marry her because of the poverty that had overtaken the family as a result of the depredations of the Landleaguers. She became engaged to Lord Castlewell, a wealthy patron of Covent Garden who had helped her materially in her career, but when she lost her voice she broke her engagement to him, and returned to Frank.

The two daughters of the family, Ada and Edith, saw a great deal of Captain

Clayton—a vigorous opponent of the Landleaguers, who was often at Castle Marony. Ada was beautiful and charming and Edith, though she loved the Captain dearly, was sure he must love her sister, and unselfishly contrived to throw them together. When he was shot from ambush by the outlaws and brought to the Castle, the two girls nursed him, and it was soon apparent that the Captain's love was for Edith.

LANGHAM HOTEL. *See* London

LAROCHEJAQUELIN. Trollope's account of the part this family played in the Vendean insurrection is substantially accurate, though Agatha is his own creation. The correct spelling of the name seems to be "de la Rochejaquelein," although authorities differ.

LAROCHEJAQUELIN, AGATHA DE. Sister of Henri, and cousin of Charles and Marie de Lescure. She was loved by Adolphe Denot, a friend of Henri, and when she refused his hand, he joined the Republicans and led them back to her home in an attempt to abduct her. She was also loved by the peasant-general Cathelineau, who was brought back to be nursed by her when mortally wounded.

"Her complexion was clear and bright, her forehead was white, and the colour in her cheeks, when she had colour there, was that of the clearest carnation. . . . her figure was exquisitely perfect, and her gait was that of a queen. She was the Rose of Poitou—the beauty and queen of the whole district. She was all but worshipped by the peasantry around her; if they admired her beauty much, they much more strongly appreciated her virtues" (1:3: 69-70).

One of the principal characters in *La Vendée*.

LAROCHEJAQUELIN, HENRI DE (real person). The heir to extensive property in Poitou, whose home was the Chateau of Durbellière. Cousin of Charles and Marie de Lescure, and in love with Marie, whom he married. After the battle of Cholet, he was made Commander-in-Chief of the Vendean forces, which he led until they were defeated and he was killed.

". . . not quite twenty years of age. . . . Without being absolutely handsome . . . was of a very prepossessing appearance. He was tall and robust, well made, and active. . . . his eyes were bright, and of a clear blue colour; his hair was light, and his upper lip could already boast that ornament which the then age, and his own position made allowable" (1:1:8-9).

One of the principal characters in *La Vendée*.

LAROCHEJAQUELIN, LOUIS DE (real person). The younger brother of Henri, in England at the time of the Vendean rebellion, who became the second husband of Mme. Victorine de Lescure. *Vendée* 34

LAROCHEJAQUELIN, MARQUIS DE. Father of Agatha, Henri and Louis, who was crippled at the time of the Vendean uprising, and unable to engage in it except by his advice, his bounty and his authority. One of the principal characters in *La Vendée*.

LARRON, MAM'SELLE. The French governess at Greshamsbury, who accused one of the servants of stealing a locket, highly valued by Augusta Gresham. Mary Thorne took the part of the servant, the daughter of a neighboring farmer, and it was discovered that the locket was in Mam'selle Larron's possession. *Thorne* 3, 7

LAST AUSTRIAN WHO LEFT VENICE, The. In *Lotta Schmidt and Other Stories*, 1867. Originally published in *Good Words*, Jan. 1867.

PLOT. In the last year of the Austrian

occupation of Venice, Captain Von Vincke fell in love with Nina Pepé, sister of Carlo Pepé, a young Italian advocate with whom he had become friendly. Carlo, who had secretly joined Garibaldi's forces, was furious when he discovered that Nina had given her heart to an enemy of her country, and exacted a promise from his sister that she would not marry so long as the Austrians held Venice. When Venice was ceded to Italy, and still the Captain did not return, Nina set out alone to find him. After many trials she discovered him, wounded, in a hospital at Verona, and nursed him back to health. Since the Austrians had left Venice her brother withdrew his opposition, and they were married.

LAST CHRONICLE OF BARSET, The. London, Smith, Elder and Co., 1867. 2v.

AUTHOR'S COMMENT. "I regard this as the best novel I have written. I was never quite satisfied with the development of the plot, which consisted in the loss of a cheque, of a charge made against a clergyman for stealing it, and of absolute uncertainty on the part of the clergyman himself as to the manner in which the cheque found its way into his hands. . . . I have never been capable of constructing with complete success the intricacies of a plot that required to be unravelled."—*Autobiography*, 2:15: 106-7.

PLOT. Congeries of tales of Barsetshire: of Mr. Soames's check, which Mr. Crawley was accused of stealing; of Major Grantly's love for Grace Crawley, which so displeased the Archdeacon; of Johnny Eames and his unsuccessful suit for the hand of Lily Dale; of the affairs of the Dobbs Broughtons and Mrs. Van Siever; of the painting of "Jael and Sisera"; and finally the distressful story of how Mrs. Proudie met defeat at the hands of Mr. Crawley and Dr. Tempest, and died, freeing the poor Bishop from his thralldom.

LAUNAY. A large property in Somersetshire belonging to Mrs. Miles, which she planned to leave to her second son, Philip. *Launay*

LAUNAY, PHILIP. Mrs. Miles's second son, who had assumed his mother's family name, as he was to inherit the Launay estate. He refused to marry a distant cousin in order to add to the family property, and at length persuaded his mother to consent to his marriage with Bessy Pryor. Hero of *The Lady of Launay.*

LAURIER, JOHANN. The Swiss courier who cleared Fritz Rosenheim from the charge of stealing a box he had been commissioned to deliver. When Katrina Kester sold her hair to raise money for Fritz's defense, Johann managed the sale. One of the principal characters in *Katchen's Caprices.*

LAVAL. The town in Brittany to which the Vendeans retired, and where they won a victory against the Republicans. Headquarters of "La Petite Vendée," led by the "Mad Captain" Adolphe Denot. *Vendée* 29-32

LAWRIE, MARY. An orphan befriended and loved by Mr. Whittlestaff, who wished to marry her. The day after she had given her promise, John Gordon, whom she had loved for years, returned from South Africa with a fortune made in the diamond mines. Mr. Whittlestaff released Mary from her engagement, and she and John were married. Heroine of *An Old Man's Love.*

LAWYERS in Trollope's works. Trollope loved his lawyers, and, although he frequently allowed them to play fast and loose with English law, they were individuals he delighted to portray. He followed them to their dingy offices and even to court, not contenting himself, as he did with his Members of Parliament, with confining himself to their social life.

Mr. Chaffanbrass is the most famous of them all, but there are others not so well-known who deserve mention: John Grey, long-suffering attorney for the rascally Mr. Scarborough; Gregory Masters, who conducted the affairs of the Mortons as though they were his own; Samuel Camperdown, determined that the Eustace diamonds should not be allowed to go to Lizzie; Thomas Toogood, rebuffed and insulted by Mr. Crawley, but determined to befriend him; Sir Thomas Furnival, who almost lost a wife because of his defense of Lady Mason. Even the rogues were dear to him and their cunning carefully chronicled, some of the most memorable scenes having to do with the machinations of Hyacinth Keegan, Samuel Dockwrath, the unspeakable Moylan and Dolly Longestaffe's shyster lawyer, Squercum.

AUGSBURG, Germany. Bogen, Max. *Linda*

BARCHESTER.
- Apjohn, Mr. *Thorne*
- Curling, Mr. *Framley*
- Finney, Mr. *Warden, Thorne*

BASLEHURST.
- Honyman, Mr. *Rachel*
- Sharpit and Longfite. *Rachel*

BUNTINGFORD. Soames and Simpson. *Scarborough*

CAMBRIDGE.
- Bolton, Robert. *Caldigate*
- Bramber, Mr. Justice. *Caldigate*
- Seely, Mr. *Caldigate*

CARMARTHEN, Wales. Apjohn, Nicholas. *Cousin*

CARRICK, Ireland. Keegan, Hyacinth. *Macdermots*

DILLSBOROUGH.
- Bearside, Mr. *Amer. Sen.*
- Masters, Gregory. *Amer. Sen.*

DUBLIN.
- Allewinde, Mr. *Macdermots*
- O'Laugher, Mr. *Macdermots*
- O'Malley, Mr. *Macdermots*

DUNMORE, Ireland. Moylan, Mr. *Kellys*

ENNIS, Ireland. Crowe, Mr. *Eye*

EXETER. Goodall, Mr. *Rachel*

GRESHAMSBURY. Umbleby, Yates. *Thorne*

HAMWORTH.
- Dockwrath, Samuel. *Orley*
- Usbeck, Jonathan. *Orley*

HEREFORD. Broderick, Mr. *Cousin*

HYTESBURY.
- Charleys, Sir Thomas. *Vicar*
- Jones, Mr. *Vicar*

INNSBRUCK, Austria. Schlessen, Fritz. *Frohmann*

LIVERPOOL. Ramsbottom, Mr. *Way We Live*

LONDON.
- Aram, Solomon. *Orley*
- Badger and Blister. *Brumby*
- Balsam, Mr. *Cousin*
- Barry, Mr. *Scarborough*
- Battle, Mr. *Popenjoy*
- Bideawhile, Mr. *See* Slow and Bideawhile
- Birdblott, Serjeant. *Redux*
- Block and Curling. *Vicar*
- Bluestone, Serjeant. *Anna*
- Boanerges, Lord. *Framley, Orley*
- Boltby, John. *Hotspur*
- Bolton, William. *Caldigate*
- Boothby, Messrs. *Vicar*
- Burnaby, Serjeant. *Ralph*
- Camperdown, John. *Redux, Eustace*
- Camperdown, Samuel. *Eustace*
- Carey, Mr. *Ralph*
- Chaffanbrass, Mr. *Orley, Redux, Clerks*
- Cheekey, John. *Cousin*
- Cox and Cummins. *Warden*
- Cunningham, Mr. *Fay*
- Crumbie, Judge. *Ralph*
- Die, Neversaye. *Beltons, Barchester, Castle Rich.*
- Dove, Thomas. *Eustace*
- Dry and Stickatit. *Bertrams*
- Flick, Mr. *Anna*
- Forster, Mr. *Redux*
- Furnival, Sir Thomas. *Orley*
- Gazebee, Mortimer. *Thorne*

Giggs, Sir Ricketty. *Beltons, Barchester*
Gitemthruet, Mr. *Clerks*
Goffe, Mr. *Anna*
Golightly, Mr. *Redux*
Graham, Felix. *Orley*
Gray, Mr. *Kept Dark*
Green, Joseph. *Belton*
Grey, John. *Scarborough*
Haphazard, Sir Abraham. *Warden, Barchester*
Harcourt, Sir Henry. *Bertrams*
Hardy, Mr. *Anna*
Honeybun, Mr. *Caldigate*
Joram, Jacky. *Did He, Ralph*
Jorum, Sir John. *Caldigate*
Leatherham, Sir Richard. *Orley*
Low, Mr. *Finn*
Mainsail, Mr. *Anna*
Maltby, Baron. *Orley*
Mowbray and Mopus. *Eustace*
Norton and Flick. *Anna*
Patterson, Sir William. *Anna*
Potter, Mr. *Framley*
Prendergast, Mr. *Cousin*
Quickenham, Richard. *Vicar*
Romer, Mr. *Thorne*
Round, Mr. *Can You*
Round and Crook. *Orley*
Scruby, Mr. *Can You*
Slope, Sir Simon. *Redux*
Slow and Bideawhile. *Thorne, Mackenzie, Framley, Way We Live*
Snow, Mr. *Redux*
Squercum, Mr. *Way We Live*
Staveley, Judge. *Orley*
Steelyard, Mr. *Orley*
Stickatit, George. *See* Dry and Stickatit
Stokes, Mr. *Popenjoy*
Tombe, Mr. *Can You*
Toogood, Thomas. *Did He, Last Chron.*
Underwood, Sir Thomas. *Ralph*
Walker, Mr. *Prime Min.*
Wharton, Abel. *Prime Min.*
Wickerby, Mr. *Redux*
Younglad, Mr. *Clerks*

PERIVALE. Palmer, Mr. *Belton*
PENRITH. Grogam, Mr. *Can You*
SILVERBRIDGE.
Walker, George. *Last Chron.*
Winthrop, Zachary. *Last Chron.*
TUAM, Ireland. Daly, Mr. *Kellys*

LAX, TERRY. The ringleader of the Landleaguers, who was called the "Man with the Mask." He was definitely connected with many of the murders committed and was back of most of the disturbances throughout southern Ireland. *Land.* '16, 21, 31, 39

LEADHAM and LOITER. Lady Carbury's publishers. *Way We Live* 1, 11, 89

LEATHERHAM, SIR RICHARD. The Solicitor-General, and leading counsel for the prosecution of Lady Mason at the second trial of the Orley Farm case. *Orley* 64, 68, 70-72, 75

LECHELLE, GENERAL. The Republican commander at Laval, who shot himself when his army was defeated. *Vendée* 31

LEEDS. The Bull Inn in Leeds was the scene of the meeting between Mr. Dockwrath, Mr. Moulder, Mr. Kantwise and the other "commercial gentlemen." *Orley* 6, 8-9

LEFROY, FERDINAND. Mrs. Peacocke's first husband, a scoundrel who was believed to be dead, but who reappeared soon after his wife had married again. Having shown himself to her so that she could never be happy in her second marriage, but not wishing her for himself, he again disappeared, and shortly after died in San Francisco. *Wortle* 3, 7, 10, 18, 21-22

LEFROY, ROBERT. Ferdinand's brother, who attempted to blackmail Mr. Peacocke by publishing his story at Dr. Wortle's school and in the village. He was paid to accompany Mr. Peacocke to San Francisco to secure proof of his brother's death. *Wortle* 3, 6-8, 10, 18, 21

LEGER. The race in which Lord Silverbridge lost £70,000, betting on his own horse "Prime Minister." Major Tifto, enraged at the snubs inflicted on him by his partner, drove a nail into the horse's foot. *Duke* 43-44

LEGG and LOOSEFIT. Hosiery dealers patronized by Brown, Jones and Robinson. *Struggles* 10

LE GROS, MR. The impresario who engaged Rachel O'Mahony to sing at Covent Garden. *Land.* 17-18, 26

LEIPZIG, UNIVERSITY OF. Ethelbert Stanhope was a student there for two years. *Barchester* 9

LE PUY. The setting for *The Chateau of Prince Polignac.*

LESCURE, CHARLES DE (real person). A wealthy landowner living at Clisson, in the province of Poitou. Leader of the Royalist party in La Vendée and for a time its Commander-in-Chief. He was wounded at the battle of Saumur, and recovered only to be mortally wounded at Cholet. ". . . a married man, about twenty-seven years of age, of grave and studious habits, but nevertheless of an active temperament . . . his strongest passion was the love of his fellow-creatures; his pure heart had glowed, at an early age, with unutterable longings for the benefits promised to the human race by the school of philosophy from which the revolution originated" (1:1:6). One of the principal characters in *La Vendée.*

LESCURE, MARIE DE. Sister of Charles, and cousin of Henri Larochejaquelin, whom she married. "Marie had dark hair, nearly black, very dark eyes, and a beautiful rich complexion; her skin was dark, but never sallow; her colour was not bright, but always clear and transparent; her hair curled naturally round her head, and the heavy curls fell upon her neck and shoulders; she was rather under the middle height, but the symmetry of her figure was so perfect, that no one would have called her too short. She had high animal spirits, and was always happy and good humoured . . ." (1:3:68). One of the principal characters in *La Vendée.*

LESCURE, MME. VICTORINE DE (real person). Wife of Charles, who, after his death, married Louis Larochejaquelin, younger brother of Henri. Although she published her memoirs, there is no indication that Trollope used them in his novel. In Mrs. Maxwell Scott's *Life of Madame de la Rochejaquelein*, the name is consistently spelled as in her title. Her full name was Marie Louise Victorine de Donnissan, Marquise de la Rochejaquelein. One of the principal characters in *La Vendée.*

LESLIE, MARIAN. Niece of Miss Sarah Jack, and the object of Maurice Cummings' affections. Heroine of *Miss Sarah Jack of Spanish Town, Jamaica.*

LE SMYRGER, PENELOPE. A spinster of fifty years, owner of 135 acres of land in the Oxney Colne parish in Devonshire, which she intended to leave to her young friend Patience Woolsworthy. Aunt of Capt. John Broughton. One of the principal characters in *The Parson's Daughter of Oxney Colne.*

LEVY, MR. George Vavasor's clerk, who was sent to Alice to demand additional money for election expenses. *Can You* 60

LIESE. Josef Kester's servant, who stole the box for which Fritz Rosenheim was accused. *Katchen*

LIMEHOUSE THAMES BRIDGE COMPANY. Promoted by Undy Scott, who persuaded Alaric Tudor to use money belonging to his ward in heavy buying of its stock. *Clerks* 24, 29, 31-32, 34, 38, 39, 41

LINCOLN'S INN. *See* London

LINCOLNSHIRE. The location of Mistletoe, seat of the Duke of Mayfair, where the American Senator was entertained. *Amer. Sen.*

LINDA TRESSEL. Edinburgh and London, William Blackwood and Sons, 1868. Originally published in *Blackwood's Magazine*, Oct. 1867-May 1868.

AUTHOR'S COMMENT. "There was more of romance proper than had been usual with me. And I made an attempt at local colouring, at descriptions of scenes and places."—*Autobiography*, 2: 11:13.

NOTES. Published anonymously, and with little success.

PLOT. Linda Tressel, a young girl in Nuremberg, lived with her aunt Frau Staubach, a religious fanatic who thought that all young girls were inclined to think too much of worldly things. To provide a stabilizing effect she arranged a marriage for her niece with old Peter Steinmarc, who had an eye on Linda's property. Linda disliked him intensely and had, moreover, fallen in love with Ludovic Valcarm, a young man of her own age, and Peter's cousin. Ludovic's political views were displeasing to the police, and when Linda ran away with him to Augsburg, he was arrested as they stepped from the train. Frau Staubach followed them and took Linda back to Nuremberg, where her elderly suitor repudiated her.

LINLITHGOW, PENELOPE, LADY (also "Susanna"). Lizzie Eustace's aunt, with whom she lived in London after her father's death, and who engineered Lizzie's marriage to Sir Florian.

". . . worldly, stingy, ill-tempered, selfish, and mean. . . . She would tell any number of lies to carry a point. . . . It was said of her that she cheated at cards. In backbiting no venomous old woman between Bond Street and Park Lane could beat her,—or, more wonderful still, no venomous old man at the clubs. . . . The old woman was not tall; —but her face was long, and at the same time large, square at the chin and square, at the forehead, and gave her almost an appearance of height. Her nose was very prominent, not beaked, but straight and strong, and broad at the bridge, and of a dark-red colour. Her eyes were sharp and grey. Her mouth was large, and over it there was almost beard enough for a young man's moustache. Her chin was firm, and large, and solid. Her hair was still brown, and was only just grizzled in parts" (1:6:74-75).

One of the principal characters in *The Eustace Diamonds.*

LION D'OR. The inn in which centers most of the action of *The Golden Lion of Granpère.*

LIQUORPOND STREET. *See* London

LISCANNOR. A town in County Clare, near Ennis, where Fred Neville was stationed. Frequently mentioned in *An Eye for an Eye.*

"LITERARY CHRONICLE." A periodical edited by Alfred Booker, in which Lady Carbury published some of her work. *Way We Live* 1

LITTLE ALRESFORD. The home of Mr. Hall and his daughters. Frequently mentioned in *An Old Man's Love.*

LITTLE CHRISTCHURCH. The home of Gabriel Crasweller and his daughter Eva, in Britannula, about six miles from Gladstonopolis. *Fixed* 2

LITTLE TANKARD YARD. *See* London

LITTLEBATH. Trollope's pseudonym for Bath. Miss Baker and Miss Todd lived at the Paragon in Littlebath, and it was there that Sir Lionel Bertram retired when his official duties were over. Penelope Gauntlet, the maiden aunt of Adela, also lived there, and when George Bertram visited Caroline Waddington, he made the Plough his headquarters. *Bertrams*

Miss Mackenzie moved to the Paragon, Littlebath, when she inherited her fortune. *Mackenzie*

LIVERPOOL. Mr. Ramsbottom was a lawyer living in Liverpool. *Way We Live*

Home of Godfrey Holmes. *Mistletoe*

LLANFEARE. An estate in Carmarthenshire, Wales, owned by Indefer Jones; the scene of much of *Cousin Henry.*

LLWDDYTHLW, MARQUIS OF. The eldest son of the Duke of Merioneth, and a hard-working MP, who took his duties so seriously that he found it almost impossible to find time to marry Lady Amaldina Hauteville. *Fay* 12, 19, 26, 39-40, 46, 50, 52, 60

LOFTY, MRS. In the play *Did He Steal It?*, Mrs. Lofty has the part played by Mrs. Arabin in the matter of the check that she gave to Mr. Crawley, and which he was accused of stealing, as told in *The Last Chronicle of Barset.*

LOMBARD STREET. *See* London

LONDON. Trollope knew his London, and even a superficial study of the names of his streets gives an outline of the London of his day. What could have been more fitting than Carleton Terrace as the residence of the Duke of Omnium; or Park Lane as the location of Madame Goesler's house, to which an invitation was accounted an honor? Where could the Spotted Dog pub have been, if not on Liquorpond Street, and could there have been a better choice than Grosvenor Place for Augustus Melmotte to establish himself? It would be incredible that the Gazebees should live anywhere but in St. John's Wood, or for Tom Towers to live in any place but the Temple.

ABCHURCH STREET. Location of Augustus Melmotte's office. *Way We Live*

ACROBATS (club). Louis Trevelyan, Colonel Osborne and Sir Marmaduke Rowley were members. *He Knew*

ACTIVE SERVICE (club). Major Poultney and Captain Gunner were members. *Prime Min.*

ADAM STREET, near the Adelphi. Address of Beilby and Burton, engineers. *Claverings*

ARUNDEL STREET. Margaret Mackenzie's girlhood home, to which she returned when she lost her fortune. *Mackenzie*

BAKER STREET. The Rowleys stayed at Gregg's Hotel, on Baker Street. *He Knew*

Home of Mr. and Mrs. Low. *Redux*

Mr. Slope's church. *Barchester*

BANKS OF JORDAN (pub). Frequented by Mr. M'Ruen. *Clerks*

BAYSWATER ROAD. Adolphus Crosbie had an apartment there after his marriage to Lady Alexandrina de Courcy. *Allington*

BEARGARDEN (club). A sporting club, among whose members were Sir Felix Carbury, Dolly Longestaffe, Lord Grasslough, Lord Nidderdale and other members of the dummy railroad board. *Way We Live*

Lord Silverbridge and Major Tifto were members. *Duke*

BEAUFORT (club). Bernard Dale and Adolphus Crosbie were members. *Allington*

Lord Grex spent most of his time playing whist there. *Duke*

Harry Clavering's club. *Claverings*

BEDFORD ROW. Office of Round and Crook, attorneys. *Orley*

BEDFORD SQUARE. Serjeant Bluestone's home, where Lady Anna took refuge after being disowned by her mother. *Anna*

BELGRAVE SQUARE. Town house of Lord Grex. *Duke*

BERKELEY SQUARE. Where Lady Baldock had a house. *Finn*

Sir Hugh Clavering's town house. *Claverings*

Residence of the Houghtons. *Popenjoy*

Mrs. Roby, aunt of Emily Wharton, lived there. *Prime Min.*

BISHOPSGATE. Magenta House, the haberdashery owned by Brown, Jones and Robinson. *Struggles*

BLOOMSBURY SQUARE. Where Harry Clavering stayed when in London. *Claverings*

Sir Thomas Fitzgerald's attorney, Mr. Prendergast, lived there. *Castle Rich.*

BLUE POSTS. The restaurant where Count Pateroff gave Harry Clavering a dinner. *Claverings*

BOLTON STREET. After the death of her husband, Lady Ongar had lodgings there. *Claverings*

BOND STREET. Where Ralph the Heir had rooms. *Ralph*

BOW STREET POLICE COURT. Alaric Tudor was examined there after his arrest for embezzlement. *Clerks*

Phineas Finn was questioned there before being taken to Newgate. *Redux*

BROMPTON ROAD. Location of the Handsome Man pub. *Can You*

BROOK STREET. London home of the Marchesa Baldoni, where Ayala Dormer met Colonel Stubbs. *Ayala*

Where the Boncassens had a house. *Duke*

Home of Lady Linlithgow. *Eustace*

BROOKS'S (club). Considered by Phineas Finn to be the most select club in London. Phineas and Laurence Fitzgibbon were members. *Finn, Redux*

BROWN'S HOTEL. Where Rachel O'Mahony and her father lived for a time. *Land.*

BRUTON STREET. Town house of Sir Harry Hotspur. *Hotspur*

Residence of the Longestaffes. *Way We Live*

Lady Lufton's London house. *Framley*

Bishop Proudie's London house. *Barchester*

BURTON CRESCENT. Mrs. Roper's boardinghouse, where Johnny Eames lived. *Allington*

CARLTON CLUB. Lord George Germain was a member. *Popenjoy*

CARLTON GARDENS. Location of Altringham House, home of the Earl of Altringham. *Hotspur*

CARLTON TERRACE. Town house of the Duke of Omnium. *Prime Min., Redux, Duke*

CAT AND WHISTLE (pub). Where Charley Tudor spent many evenings in the company of Nora Geraghty, the barmaid. *Clerks*

CAVENDISH SQUARE. Town house of the Marquis of Brotherton. *Popenjoy*

Sir Walter Mackenzie lived there. *Mackenzie*

CECIL STREET. Rachel Mahony and her father had lodgings. *Land.*

Where George Vavasor had rooms. *Can You*

CHAPTER HOTEL AND COFFEE HOUSE. Where Mr. Harding stayed when in London. *Warden*

CHESHIRE CHEESE. Where Ontario Moggs made a reputation at the debating club. *Ralph*

CHISWICK GARDENS. Scene of the flower show patronized by Mrs. Val Scott and her guests. *Clerks*

CONDUIT STREET. Location of Tailor Neefit's shop. *Ralph*

COVENT GARDEN. Where Rachel O'-Mahony met with sudden and marked operatic success. *Land.*

CRANBOURN HOUSE. The London house of Miss Dunstable, disrespectfully known as "Ointment Hall." *Thorne*

CURZON STREET. Louis Trevelyan's home. *He Knew*

DOWNING (club). Alaric Tudor and Undy Scott were both members, and both expelled after Alaric's trial. *Clerks*

DOWNING STREET. The Prime Minister's official residence, where Mr. Monk held an important Cabinet meeting. *Finn*

EATON SQUARE. Sir Henry Harcourt's house. *Bertrams*

EBURY STREET. Home of the Val Scotts. *Clerks*

ELDON (club). An old law club to which Abel Wharton belonged. *Prime Min.*

EMBANKMENT THEATRE. Owned by Mahomet Moss, where Rachel O'Mahony first sang. *Land.*

FENTON'S HOTEL. Senator Gotobed's headquarters on his first visit to London. *Amer. Sen.*

FETTER LANE. Office of Dolly Longestaffe's lawyer, Mr. Squercum. *Way We Live*

Where Quintus Slide had his office. *Finn*

FOWLER'S HOTEL. Where Phineas Finn lived when he returned to London after the death of his wife. *Redux*

FULL MOON. Pub near St. Diddulph's rectory, from which Bozzle spied on Mrs. Trevelyan. *He Knew*

GLOUCESTER SQUARE. Lady Monk's town house, from which Burgo Fitzgerald planned to elope with Lady Glencora. *Can You*

Bishop Proudie took a house for the season there, and Mrs. Proudie entertained at a "conversazione." *Framley*

GOAT AND COMPASSES. In Cromwell's time named "God Encompasseth Us." Used by the Tozers to meet their clients. *Framley*

GOWER STREET. Home of Tom Mackenzie. *Mackenzie*

GRAY'S INN. Thomas Toogood was a member. *Last Chron.*

GRAY'S INN COFFEE-HOUSE. Where Frank Gresham stayed. *Thorne*

GREAT BROAD STREET. The office of Pogson and Littlebird, employers of Marion Fay's father. *Fay*

GREAT MARLBOROUGH STREET. Where Phineas Finn had lodgings in the home of Mr. Bunce. *Finn, Redux*

George Vavasor's attorney, Mr. Scruby, had his office there. *Can You*

GREAT ST. HELEN'S STREET. Home of Mr. Moulder. *Orley*

GREAT WESTERN RAILWAY HOTEL. Clara Amedroz stayed there on her way to and from Aylmer Castle. *Belton*

Where Johnny Eames lived after he left Mrs. Roper's boardinghouse. *Allington*

GREEN STREET. The Mildmays' London house. *Popenjoy*

Mr. and Mrs. Harold Smith had a house there, near Park Lane. *Framley*

GREGG'S HOTEL. On their return from the Mandarin Islands, the Rowleys lived there. *He Knew*

GROSVENOR PLACE. Town house of Mrs. Montacute Jones. *Duke, Popenjoy*

Augustus Melmotte bought a large house there. *Way We Live*

Where Lady Laura Standish lived after her marriage to Mr. Kennedy. *Finn*

Location of the Marquis of Trowbridge's town house. *Vicar*

HANDSOME MAN (pub). Headquarters of George Vavasor when he contested Chelsea. *Can You*

HARLEY STREET. Home of William Bolton. *Caldigate*

Thomas Furnival's home. *Orley*

HERTFORD STREET. Lizzie Eustace and Mrs. Carbuncle took a house there. *Eustace*

HOOK COURT. Office of Broughton and Musselboro. *Last Chron.*

JELLYBAG STREET, near Edgeware Road. Where Mr. Emelius lived after he left the Meager home. *Redux*

JERMYN STREET. Location of Fowler's Hotel. *Redux*; Pawkins's (hotel) *Allington*

JOCKEY CLUB. Lord Lufton and Nathaniel Sowerby were members. *Framley*

JOLLY BLACKBIRD (inn). Where Abel Wharton invited Arthur Fletcher to dinner. *Prime Min.*

JUDD STREET. Mr. Kennedy tried to murder Phineas Finn at Macpherson's Hotel on Judd Street. *Redux*

KEPPEL STREET. Lady Anna and the Countess Lovel lived there for a time. *Anna*

KINGSBURY CRESCENT. Home of Reginald Dosett, where he gave a home to Ayala and Lucy Dormer. *Ayala*

LANGHAM HOTEL. The Boncassens lived there until they found a house. *Duke*

LINCOLN'S INN. Messrs. Boothby, lawyers for the Marquis of Trowbridge, had offices there. *Vicar*

Where Cox and Cummins had their quarters. *Warden*

Neversaye Die had offices in the Stone Building. *Belton, Barchester, Castle Rich.*

Mr. Furnival had chambers in Old Square. *Orley*

Joseph Green, Will Belton's attorney and friend, lived there. *Belton*

Location of John Grey's office, attorney for Mr. Scarborough. *Scarborough*

Sir Abraham Haphazard had chambers there. *Warden, Thorne*

Mr. Low had chambers in Old Square. *Finn, Redux*

Abel Wharton's office was in the Stone Building. *Prime Min.*

LIQUORPOND STREET. Location of the Spotted Dog pub. *Spotted*

LITTLE TANKARD YARD. ". . . a dingy little court near the Bank of England," where Sexty Parker carried on his shady business. *Prime Min.*

LOMBARD STREET. Office of Sir Thomas Tringle, where suitors came and went, asking for the hand (and dowry) of his daughters and nieces. *Ayala*

MACPHERSON'S. The hotel in which Mr. Kennedy attacked Phineas Finn. *Redux*

MAGENTA HOUSE. The haberdashery shop of Brown, Jones and Robinson. *Struggles*

MANCHESTER SQUARE. Home of Abel Wharton and his daughter Emily. *Prime Min.*

MARYLEBONE ROAD. Location of the "Disabilities" institute. *Popenjoy*

MIDDLE TEMPLE. Where George Bertram had chambers. *Bertrams*

Augustus Staveley was a member of Middle Temple. *Orley*

MILE END BOROUGH. Represented in Parliament by Mr. Nogo. *Clerks*

MOUNT STREET. Captain Aylmer had lodgings there. *Belton*

Adolphus Crosbie had rooms, "elegant in all their belongings." *Allington*

Lizzie Eustace had a house there at one time. *Eustace*

Madame Gordeloup's rooms were in Mount Street. *Claverings*

Town house of Archdeacon Grantly of Barchester. *Framley*

Gumption, Gazebee and Gazebee's offices. *Thorne, Framley*

MOUNTAINEERS (club). Tom Tringle and Samuel Faddle were members. *Ayala*

MUNSTER COURT. Where Dean Lovelace took a house for Lady Mary and Lord George Germain. *Popenjoy*

NEW BURLINGTON STREET. Where George Vavasor lived while selling mining stock. *Can You*

NEWGATE PRISON. Where Phineas Finn was held during his trial for the murder of Mr. Bonteen. *Redux*

NIMROD CLUB. Richard Roby was a member. *Prime Min.*

NORTHUMBERLAND STREET. Home of the Meager family, with whom Mr. Emilius lived at the time of Mr. Bonteen's murder. *Redux*

OLD BAILEY CRIMINAL COURT. Where Alaric Tudor was tried for embezzlement. *Clerks*

Phineas Finn was tried there for the murder of Mr. Bonteen. *Redux*

ONSLOW CRESCENT. Home of Theodore Burton, where Harry Clavering was a constant visitor. *Claverings*

PANDEMONIUM (club). Lord Hauteboy was a member. *Fay*

PARK LANE. Home of Madame Goesler. *Finn, Redux, Prime Min.*

Town house of the Marquis of Kingsbury. *Fay*

Plantagenet Palliser's town house. *Can You*

PARKER'S HOTEL. A deserted hotel from which Louis Trevelyan abducted his son. *He Knew*

PAWKINS'S (hotel), in Jermyn Street. Where Lord De Guest stayed because he considered it "thoroughly old fashioned." *Allington*

PECKHAM. Where Mary Stone lived. *Orley*

PICCADILLY. Lord Mistletoe, a cousin of Arabella Trefoil, lived there. *Scarborough*

John Scarborough lived at the Albany, a fashionable Piccadilly apartment house. *Scarborough*

PORCHESTER GARDENS. Home of Lady Desmolines. *Last Chron.*

PORTMAN SQUARE. Home of the Earl of Brentford, where Lady Laura Standish maintained a salon before her marriage. *Finn*

The De Courcys' London house was there. *Allington*

Where Violet Effingham lived before her marriage to Lord Chiltern. *Finn*

The Greshams' town house was there. *Thorne*

PROGRESS (club). Everett Wharton and Ferdinand Lopez were members. *Prime Min.*

QUARTPOT ALLEY, near Fleet Street. Where the "People's Banner" was published. *Finn*

QUEEN ANNE STREET. Alice Vavasor and her father shared a house there. *Can You*

QUEEN'S GATE. Location of Sir Thomas Tringle's town house. *Ayala*

RAG (club). Archie Clavering and Captain Boodle were members. *Claverings*

REFORM CLUB. Phineas Finn was a member. *Finn*

ST. JAMES HALL. Where Senator Gotobed gave his lecture on English institutions. *Amer. Sen.*

ST. JAMES'S PLACE. Where Mr. Bonteen lived. *Redux*

ST. JAMES'S STREET. George Hotspur had lodgings there. *Hotspur*

ST. JOHN'S WOOD. The Gazebees lived at the Albert Villa. *Allington*

SCUMBERG'S HOTEL. Scene of the quarrel between Dean Lovelace and the Marquis of Brotherton. *Popenjoy*

SEBRIGHT'S (club). Bernard Dale and Adolphus Crosbie were members. *Allington*

SOMERSET HOUSE. Where Walter Mackenzie worked as a clerk. *Mackenzie*

SOUTH AUDLEY STREET. Offices of Gumption and Gazebee, and used by Mr. Fothergill when in London on business for the Duke of Omnium. *Framley*

SOUTHAMPTON BUILDINGS. Sir Thomas Underwood had offices there. *Ralph*

SPINNEY LANE, St. Botolph's in the East. Where Mary Swan, the unacknowledged wife of Matthew Mollett, lived. *Castle Rich.*

SPOTTED DOG (pub). The inn where Julius Mackenzie worked on the manuscript that his wife later burned. *Spotted*

SUFFOLK STREET. Where John Grey had his lodgings, and where George Vavasor tried to kill him. *Can You*

TAVISTOCK SQUARE. Home of the Toogoods. *Last Chron.*

TEMPLE, The. Frank Greystock had chambers there. *Eustace*

Where Tom Towers lived. *Warden*

UNIVERSE (club). A political club, whose members included Phineas Finn, Mr. Bonteen, Lord Fawn, Laurence Fitzgibbon, Barrington Erle, Mr. Bouncer and Joshua Monk. *Redux*

WALBECK STREET. Where Lady Carbury had a modest house. *Way We Live*

WARWICK SQUARE. Home of the Hittaways. *Eustace*

WESTBOURNE TERRACE. After his marriage to Gertrude Woodward, Alaric Tudor took a house in Albany Row. *Clerks*

WYNDHAM STREET, New Road. Where Lady Anna and her mother lived before their right to the title had been established. *Anna*

LONGBARNS. The Fletcher estate, not far from Wharton Hall in Herefordshire. Mentioned frequently in *The Prime Minister.*

LONGESTAFFE, ADOLPHUS. The Squire of Caversham in Suffolk, supposed to be wealthy, but in fact hard-pressed for money. Because of this he became involved with Augustus Melmotte, furthered his social ambitions and finally agreed to sell him one of his country houses. ". . . a tall, heavy man, about fifty, with hair and whiskers carefully dyed, whose clothes were made with great care, though they always seemed to fit him too tightly, and who thought very much of his personal appearance. . . . He was intensely proud of his position in life, thinking himself to be immensely superior to all those who earned their bread" (1:13:77-78). Appears frequently in *The Way We Live Now.*

LONGESTAFFE, ADOLPHUS, JR. ("Dolly"). A good-natured but moronic member of the Beargarden Club, and a friend of Lord Silverbridge. He tried unsuccessfully to marry Isabel Boncassen. Urged by his family to court Marie Melmotte for her money, he admitted that he was too indolent to make the effort. Most prominent in *The Way We Live Now*; briefly in *Duke* 32-33, 47, 69-70. (Longstaff in *Duke*)

LONGESTAFFE, GEORGIANA. A shopworn beauty, ill-tempered over her failure to find a rich husband, and finally driven by her determination to secure wealth to engage herself to an elderly Jewish banker. When she found that he had lost a great deal of money through his connections with Augustus Melmotte, and could not provide her a London house, she threw him over and as a last resort married a country curate. One of the principal characters in *The Way We Live Now.*

LONGESTAFFE, LADY POMONA. The scheming and greedy mother of Dolly, Sophia and Georgiana. Appears often in *The Way We Live Now.*

LONGESTAFFE, SOPHIA. The elder daughter of the family, who, failing in the London marriage market, settled for a stodgy, brainless country squire, George Whitstable. Appears frequently in *The Way We Live Now.*

LONGROYSTON. The country seat of the Duke of St. Bungay, ". . . at which whig hospitality had been dispensed with a lavish hand for two centuries." *Redux* 13. Briefly mentioned in most of the Parliamentary novels.

LONGSTOP, SIR LORDS. A member of the British cricket team playing in Britannula. *Fixed* 5, 7

LONGSWORD, MAJOR. Jonas Brown's second in his duel with Counsellor Webb. *Macdermots* 19, 26

LOOKALOFT, MR., and Family. A tenant farmer at Ullathorne, whose wife and three daughters had such social ambition that their behavior at the Ullathorne sports caused much excitement among the jealous neighboring farmers. *Barchester* 35-36, 39

LOPEZ, MRS. EMILY (Wharton). The only daughter of Abel Wharton, and the unhappy and disillusioned wife of Ferdinand Lopez. After her husband's suicide she married Arthur Fletcher, a childhood sweetheart. "Emily Wharton was a tall, fair girl, with grey eyes, rather exceeding the average proportions as well as height of women. Her features were regular and handsome, and her form was perfect; but it was by her manner and her voice that she conquered, rather than by her beauty,—by those gifts and by a clearness of intellect joined with that feminine sweetness which has its most frequent foundation in self-denial" (1:5:68). Heroine of *The Prime Minister.*

LOPEZ, FERDINAND. An adventurer, who married Emily Wharton in spite of parental opposition and tried to force her to obtain money from her father for his own use. He contested the Silverbridge borough against Arthur Fletcher, thinking that he had the backing of the Duchess of Omnium, but was defeated. Having lost the respect of his acquaintances, and being utterly without money, he tried to go to Guatemala to manage a mining property. When that failed, he threw himself before a train and was killed.

"It was known of him that he had been at a good English school. . . . at the age of seventeen, he had been sent to a German university, and at the age of twenty-one had appeared in London, in a stockbroker's office, where he was soon known as an accomplished linguist, and as a very clever fellow. . . . He was certainly a handsome man,—his beauty being of a sort which men are apt to deny and women to admit lavishly. He was nearly six feet tall, very dark, and very thin, with regular, well-cut features. . . . His hair was cut short, and he wore no beard beyond an absolutely black moustache. His teeth were perfect in form and whiteness. . . . he was essentially one of those men who are always, in the inner workings of their minds, defending themselves and attacking others" (1:1:5-8).

One of the principal characters in *The Prime Minister.*

LORING. The home, in Gloucestershire, of Mary Lowther, who lived with her aunt Miss Marrable. The Rev. John Marrable was the rector at Loring. The inn was the Bull, where Harry Gilmore stayed. *Vicar* 2, 8

LORRAINE. The setting for *The Golden Lion of Granpère.*

LOTH, REBECCA. A Jewish girl, who was brought up to consider herself the future wife of Anton Trendellsohn. She befriended Nina Balatka, and saved her life. "Rebecca Loth was dark, with large dark-blue eyes and jet black tresses, which spoke out loud to the beholder of their own loveliness. . . . she stood like a queen; strong on her limbs, wanting no support, somewhat hard withal, with a repellent beauty that seemed to disdain while it courted admiration" (1:7:181). *Nina* 7, 10-13, 15-16

LOTTA SCHMIDT. In *Lotta Schmidt and Other Stories*, 1867. Originally published in *The Argosy*, July 1866.

Plot. Two young Viennese shopgirls, Lotta Schmidt and Marie Weber, on their way home from their work stopped at the Volksgarten to hear an elderly violinist, one of Lotta's admirers, conduct the orchestra. A younger suitor joined them and made cruel comments on the artist's appearance, his musicianship and his advanced age. Lotta resented it keenly, and that night, at a ball at which the younger lover danced too often with her rival, Lotta accepted Herr Crippel.

LOUGH CARRIB. A large tract of land on this lake was flooded by discontented tenants of Philip Jones, and the act formed the beginning of the violence in County Galway. *Land.*

LOUGHLINTER. The country estate in Scotland belonging to Mr. Kennedy. *Finn* 14-15, 31-32, 51; *Redux* 10, 52, 70

LOUGHSHANE. The Irish borough in County Galway that returned Phineas Finn to Parliament. *Finn* 1-2, 50

LOUGHTON. Lord Brentford's pocket-borough, which returned Phineas Finn to Parliament after he lost his seat for Loughshane. *Finn* 27, 32

LOUISIANA. Three of the characters in *Dr. Wortle's School* were born in Louisiana: Ferdinand and Robert Lefroy and Ella Beaufort, who later married in turn Ferdinand Lefroy and Henry Peacocke. *Wortle* 39

LOVEL, COUNTESS. Josephine Murray, a poor but beautiful and ambitious girl of "the real Murrays," who, knowing the reputation of the old Earl Lovel, married him for the title. Within a few months he informed her that he had earlier married in Italy, and that she was not legally his wife. The account of her attempt to prove the legitimacy of her daughter Anna and to clear her own name forms the plot of *Lady Anna.*

LOVEL, EARL ("The old Earl"). A disreputable peer, who married Josephine Murray and later, after their daughter was born, claimed that the marriage was void, since he had a wife living in Italy. *Anna* 1

LOVEL, LADY ANNA. Known as Anna Murray when her legitimacy was denied by her father, the old Earl Lovel. In her poverty she fell in love with Daniel Thwaite, only son of the tailor who befriended and supported her and her mother. Upon being recognized as Lady Anna and an heiress, she refused to repudiate him. Heroine of *Lady Anna.*

LOVEL, The REV. CHARLES. Uncle of the young Earl Lovel, who was loud in his denunciation of the Countess and her daughter Lady Anna. Father of two boys at Harrow and one small daughter, Minnie. "The parson, though a popular man, was not strong-minded. He was passionate, loud, generous, affectionate and indiscreet" (1:5:61-62). Appears frequently in *Lady Anna.*

LOVEL, FREDERICK ("The young Earl"). Nephew of the old Earl, who succeeded to the title. He fell in love with Lady Anna, but she refused to marry him as she loved Daniel Thwaite, the tailor. However, since he had no money to keep up the dignity of the name, she divided her fortune with him. ". . . a gay-hearted, kindly young man . . . fair-haired, well-made . . . looking like a sailor and every inch a gentleman" (1:5:61). One of the principal characters in *Lady Anna.*

LOVEL, MRS. JANE. Wife of the Rev. Charles Lovel, who entertained Lady Anna, learned to love her and forwarded with all her skill the love affair between the young Earl Lovel and Anna. *Anna* 6, 11, 13-19, 29

LOVEL, JULIA. Sister of the Rev. Charles Lovel, living with him at Yoxham. ". . . of all the Lovels . . . the wisest and most strong-minded" (1:5:61). *Anna* 5-6, 13-19

LOVEL, MINNIE. The young daughter of the Rev. Charles Lovel, who loved Lady Anna dearly, and was her bridesmaid when she married Daniel Thwaite. *Anna* 13, 15-17, 19

LOVEL GRANGE. The seat of Earl Lovel, ten miles from Keswick in Cumberland, where Lady Lovel retired after the marriage of Lady Anna. *Anna* 48

LOVELACE, The REV. HENRY. Dean of Brotherton Cathedral, and father of Mary. His ambition for his daughter was the basis of his challenge to the legitimacy of the son of the Marquis of Brotherton. ". . . a man of very humble origin, with none of what we commonly call Church interest, with nothing to recommend him but a handsome person, moderate education, and a quick intellect, he had married a lady with a considerable fortune, whose family had bought for him a living. Here he preached himself into fame" (1:1:3-4). One of the principal characters in *Is He Popenjoy?*.

LOVELACE, MARY. *See* Germain, Lady George (Mary Lovelace)

LOW, MR. Phineas Finn's oldest London friend, with whom he read law for three years before deciding to try for a seat in Parliament. Mr. Low advised strongly against it, feeling that Phineas should master his profession and make his fortune before attempting it, as he himself had planned to do. Later Mr. Low became MP for North Broughton. *Finn* 5, 7, 35, 44, 63; *Redux* 6, 23, 27-28, 49, 54-55, 68

LOW, MRS. GEORGIANA. Outspoken in her criticism of Phineas Finn's parliamentary ambitions, and derisive of his social success. *Finn*, 5, 7, 35, 44, 63; *Redux*, 6, 23, 68

LOWESTOFFE. A seaside resort visited by Mrs. Hurtle and Paul Montague. *Way We Live* 42, 46-47, 51, 76, 84

LOWND, ISABEL. In love with Maurice Archer, but deeply hurt at his seeming cynicism in regard to Christmas. Hearing of his generosity to his tenants, and placated by his explanation that it was the observance and not the spirit of Christmas that bored him, she forgave him. "She was tall, active, fair, the very picture of feminine health, with bright gray eyes, a perfectly beautiful nose . . . a mouth by no means delicately small, but eager, eloquent, and full of spirit, a well-formed short chin, with a dimple, and light brown hair, which was worn plainly smoothed over her brows, and fell in short curls behind her head" (p. 3). Heroine of *Christmas Day at Kirkby Cottage.*

LOWND, The REV. JOHN. The Rector of Kirkby Cliffe Church, father of Isabel and her younger sister, Mabel. One of the principal characters in *Christmas Day at Kirkby Cottage.*

LOWTHER, MARY. An intimate friend of the Vicar of Bullhampton and his wife. Her love affairs with their neighbor Harry Gilmore and her cousin Walter Marrable form the secondary plot of *The Vicar of Bullhampton.*

"She was a tall girl, with dark brown hair, which she wore fastened in a knot at the back of her head, after the simplest fashion. Her eyes were large and grey, and full of lustre. . . . If you judged her face by any rules of beauty, you would say that it was too thin, but feeling its influence with sympathy, you could never wish it to be changed. . . . Her movements . . . had a grace about them which touched men and women alike. It was the very poetry of motion; but its chief beauty consisted in this, that it was what it was by no effort of her own" (1:7-8).

Heroine of *The Vicar of Bullhampton.*

LOWTHER ARMS (inn). *See* Shap

LUFTON, LADY. A widowed peeress, an avowed enemy of the old Duke of Omnium, and a patroness of Mark Robarts. Her ambition for her only son led her to desire his marriage with the beautiful Griselda Grantly, but Griselda was looking for a more splendid match, and Lord Lufton loved Lucy Robarts. Lady Lufton objected to her son's love for Lucy, but when she came to love her herself, she asked her to honor the family by joining it. Most prominent in *Framley Parsonage*; appears frequently in *The Last Chronicle of Barset.*

LUFTON, LUDOVIC, LORD. The close friend and eventually brother-in-law of Mark Robarts. "... a fine, bright-looking young man ... there was in his countenance a thorough appearance of good-humour and sweet temper" (*Framley* 1:9:186-87). Most prominent in *Framley Parsonage*; appears frequently in *The Last Chronicle of Barset.*

LUFTON PARK. ". . . an ancient ramshackle place . . . family residence of the Lufton family," in Oxfordshire. *Framley* 5

LUIGI, CATARINA, MARCHESA D'. The reputed wife of the Marquis of Brotherton, and mother of the son whose right to the title of Lord Popenjoy was questioned. *Popenjoy* 6, 13, 18, 32, 36, 47-48

LUPEX, MRS. MARIA. An untidy, overdressed woman, formerly an actress, who lived with her shoddy husband at Mrs. Roper's boardinghouse, where she flirted with the young men behind her husband's back. "I should simply mislead a confiding reader if I were to tell him that Mrs. Lupex was an amiable woman" (1:10:95). *Allington* 4, 10-11, 29, 36, 41, 47

LUPEX, ORSON. One of the boarders at Mrs. Roper's boardinghouse, who became jealous of Mr. Cradell's attentions to his wife. A scene-painter, with definite ideas about the drama. *Allington* 4, 10-11, 36, 41, 47

LUPTON, MR. A friend of Lord Silverbridge, both in Parliament and at the races. He advised him in the matter of Major Tifto and the horse "Prime Minister." *Duke* 16-17, 32, 43-44, 75

LUXA, LOTTA. A servant and confidante of Madame Zamenoy. It was she who hid the deed in Nina Balatka's desk, which caused Anton Trendellsohn to think Nina was false to him. *Nina* 1-5, 7, 12

LYNCH, ANASTASIA ("Anty"). A pathetic figure, dominated in turn by two ruthless men. After her father tried in vain to induce her to become a nun, and her brother to murder her for her share of the estate, she took refuge with Mrs. Kelly the innkeeper. Martin Kelly schemed to marry her for her money, but her sweetness and helplessness won his heart, and their marriage was for love, not fortune.

". . . in all Ireland, there was not a more single-hearted, simple-minded young woman. I do not use the word simple, as foolish; for, though uneducated, she was not foolish. But she was unaffected, honest, humble, and true, entertaining a very lowly idea of her own value, and unelated by her newly-acquired wealth" (1:4:78).

One of the two heroines of *The Kellys and the O'Kellys.*

LYNCH, BARRY. Brother of Anty, and one of Trollope's best villains. He was educated at Eton along with Lord Ballindine. Scheming to secure his sister's fortune for himself, he plotted to murder her, and when she was befriended by the Kelly family, his hate was concentrated on them. He was finally driven from Ireland, and went to the Continent. One of the principal characters in *The Kellys and the O'Kellys.*

LYNCH, SIMEON ("Sim"). Father of Anty and Barry. As agent of Captain O'Kelly, he had succeeded in converting a large share of the estate into a fortune for himself. In a fit of anger with his son, he left half the estate to his daughter. Barry's efforts to obtain his sister's share provides the plot of *The Kellys and the O'Kellys.*

M'BUFFER, MR. The representative in Parliament of Tillietudlum for thirteen years, who was violently hated by Undy

Scott, his opponent for the post. *Clerks* 24, 29

McCARTHY, The REV. BERNARD. The parish priest of Drumbarrow, who was "a most uncompromising foe" of the Rev. Mr. Townsend, his Protestant colleague. Appears frequently in *Castle Richmond.*

MacCLUSKIE, LADY GLENCORA. *See* Omnium, Duchess of

McCOCKERELL, MR. A successful butter-dealer in Smithfield, who left a substantial fortune to his wife which was lost by her second husband, Mr. Brown, in his haberdashery shop. *Struggles* 2

McCOLLOP, CAPTAIN. Dick Ross's successor as toady to Sir Francis Geraldine. *Kept Dark* 23

MACDERMOT, EUPHEMIA ("Feemy"). A tragic figure of strong will combined with ignorance and an aversion to any guidance. Seduced by Myles Ussher, she died in childbirth during her brother Thady's trial for the murder of her lover.

". . . one of the finest of all Trollope's heroines . . . moreover, had something that none of the later heroines possess, a certain poetry and tragic inevitability." —Walpole, p. 27.

"She was a tall, dark girl, with that bold, upright, well-poised figure, which is so peculiarly Irish. She walked as if all the blood of the old Irish princes was in her veins. . . . had large, bright brown eyes, and long, soft, shining dark hair . . . and she had a well-formed nose, as all coming of old families have; and a bright olive complexion" (1:2:17).

Heroine of *The Macdermots of Ballycloran.*

MACDERMOT, LAWRENCE ("Larry"). The owner of the dilapidated, heavily mortgaged estate of Ballycloran in County Leitrim, where he lived with his two children, Feemy and Thady. "He was only about fifty; but a total want of energy, joined to a kind of despairing apathy, had rendered him by this time little better than an idiot" (1:6:105-6). One of the principal characters in *The Macdermots of Ballycloran.*

MACDERMOT, THADY. Son of Larry, who, as his father's agent, spent his days trying to collect rents from a peasantry too poor to pay them. Thinking that Myles Ussher was forcing Feemy to elope with him, Thady killed him, and was hanged for it. "Had he been brought up to anything, he would have done it; he was more energetic [than his father], and felt the degradation of his position: he felt that his family was sinking lower and lower daily; but as he knew not what to do, he only became more gloomy and tyrannical" (1:2:16). One of the principal characters in *The Macdermots of Ballycloran.*

MACDERMOT, CAPT. TOM. A revenue officer at Ballymoy, who protected Archibald Green from the wrath of the villagers after Archibald had thrown their priest down the stairs at the inn. *Father Giles*

MACDERMOT SERVANTS.

BIDDY. Feemy Macdermot's confidante and adviser, and her accomplice in eloping with Myles Ussher. *Macdermots* 12-13, 15, 18, 20-21, 29

KATTY. Stupid, overworked and sullen. *Macdermots* 10, 21

MACDERMOTS OF BALLYCLORAN, The. London, Newby, 1847. 3v.

AUTHOR'S COMMENT. "As to the plot itself, I do not know that I ever made one so good,—or, at any rate, one so susceptible of pathos. . . . *The Macdermots* is a good novel, and worth reading by anyone who wishes to understand what Irish life was before the potato disease, the famine, and the Encumbered Estates Bill."—*Autobiography*, 1:4:94.

NOTES. Trollope's first novel, suggested to him by the ruins of an estate near Drumsna, County Leitrim.

"*The Macdermots* is almost in the first flight of Trollope. . . . The story is of the simplest, but broadens, as every story ought to do, into the full bounds of its environment. . . . The characters are all revealed by natural and lively dialogue, and every character has his work to do in the development of the central theme."—Walpole, pp. 25, 27-28.

PLOT. In a pretentious but half-ruined house in County Leitrim called "Ballycloran" lived Larry Macdermot, senile at fifty; Thady, his well-meaning but ignorant son, who acted as his father's agent; and a daughter, Feemy. She considered herself engaged to Captain Ussher, a police officer charged with the detection and destruction of the illegal potheen stills scattered throughout the neighboring mountains, and who was, quite naturally, hated by the local peasants.

Ballycloran had been built by Joe Flannelly of Carrick who, as his bills had never been paid, held a mortgage on the estate. His son-in-law Hyacinth Keegan, an attorney who aspired to become a country gentleman by acquiring the property, threatened to evict the Macdermots and swore to make beggars of the whole family. The tenants hated him almost as much as they did Ussher.

Joe Reynolds, leader of a gang of potheen distillers, plotted to kill Ussher and tried in vain to persuade Thady to join them, but Thady's confidential servant Pat Brady had become Hyacinth Keegan's spy and stool-pigeon, and succeeded in involving him in the conspiracy. Thady distrusted Ussher thoroughly but was unable to prevent his frequent visits to Feemy, although he suspected that Ussher did not intend to marry his sister. When the Captain was given a promotion that would take him out of the county, Feemy confessed that she was bearing his child and begged him to marry her. He claimed that was impossible, but arranged to take her with him. By chance Thady surprised them as they were departing and, believing that Feemy was being abducted against her will, struck Ussher and killed him. He was tried, convicted of murder and hanged. During the trial Feemy died and their father became completely insane.

McDONNEL, MAJOR. The steward at the Carrick races, and Counsellor Webb's second in his duel with Jonas Brown. *Macdermots* 17, 26

M'GABBERY, MR. A young tourist at Miss Todd's picnic in the Valley of Jehoshaphat, who fell in love with Caroline Waddington, whom he bored to tears. *Bertrams* 6, 8-9, 16

McGOVERY, DENIS. The blacksmith at Drumsna, who jilted Betsy Cane because the cow, the major part of her dowry, proved not to be with calf. He married Mary Brady, who brought with her "two small pigs, a thrifle of change," as well as a new pair of sheets. "A hard-working ill-favoured, saving man" (1:5:77). *Macdermots* 5, 12-14, 30

McGOVERY, MRS. MARY (Brady). A friend of Feemy Macdermot and later nurse to Larry. ". . . a very tall woman . . . with a plain, though good-humoured looking face, over which her coarse hair was divided on the left temple; she had long ungainly limbs, and was very awkward in the use of them" (1:8:171). *Macdermots* 5, 8, 12-13, 24, 27, 31-32

McGRATH, The REV. JOHN. Known to all his parishioners as Father John. The priest of the parish of Drumsna, which included Ballycloran. "He had been . . . educated in France; he had been at college at St. Omer, and afterwards at Paris, and had officiated as a curé there; he had consequently seen more of French manners and society than usually falls to the lot of Irish theological students. . . . a man of good family . . . He possessed also very considerable talents, and much more than ordinary acquirements; great natural *bonhommie*, and perpetual good temper. . . . But his appearance was anything but dignified; he was very short, and very fat, and had little or no appearance of neck; his face, however, was very intelligent, he had bright, small black eyes, a fine, high forehead, very white teeth, and short, thick, curling, dark hair" (1:5:66, 71). One of the principal characters in *The Macdermots of Ballycloran*.

McGREW, PETER. Mr. Jones's butler, a complaining but loyal servant who remained at Castle Morony despite the threats of the Landleaguers and their boycott of the estate. Appears frequently in *The Landleaguers*.

McHUGH, MRS. A close friend of Miss Stanbury, at Exeter. Appears frequently in *He Knew He Was Right*.

MACKENZIE, MRS. CLARA. A cousin of Margaret Mackenzie, and daughter-in-law of Sir Walter, who prodded John Ball into renewing his proposal of marriage to Margaret and setting the day for the ceremony. *Mackenzie* 26-27, 29

MACKENZIE, JULIUS. A highly educated and well-born man, reduced to poverty by his own and his wife's drunkenness, who attempted to redeem himself through the help of the Editor. A valuable manuscript on which he was at work was partially destroyed by his wife, and he committed suicide. Principal character in *The Spotted Dog*.

MACKENZIE, MARGARET. A tired, unattractive spinster, who, after spending her youth in nursing a complaining father and later a selfish brother, came into a small fortune. Her money made her the recipient of various offers of marriage: from the Rev. Mr. Maguire, who wished to establish himself in an independent church; from Samuel Rubb, whose business was in need of capital; and from her elderly cousin John, who needed money to maintain his family of nine children. She refused them all, but when John was proven to be the rightful heir of the fortune, he persuaded her to marry him. Heroine of *Miss Mackenzie*.

MACKENZIE, MRS. SARAH. Margaret Mackenzie's sister-in-law, wife of Thomas, a narrow-minded and vindictive woman, furious at receiving no portion of Margaret's fortune and ungrateful for such assistance as was offered her. One of the principal characters in *Miss Mackenzie*.

MACKENZIE, SUSANNA. Margaret Mackenzie's niece, whom she undertook to educate at a private school in Littlebath. *Mackenzie* 2-3, 5, 8-16, 19, 23

MACKENZIE, THOMAS. One of the brothers to whom Jonathan Ball had left his fortune. Margaret's older brother. He had disgraced the family by going into business in the firm of Rubb and Mackenzie. He was not a successful businessman, and died leaving his wife Sarah and seven children with no means of support. *Mackenzie* 1, 3, 6, 8, 10, 14-15

MACKENZIE, WALTER. Margaret's younger brother, a Somerset House clerk. Jonathan Ball had left Walter half his fortune, which on his death went to Margaret. *Mackenzie* 7, 16

MACKENZIE, WALTER. Sir Walter's son, whose wife befriended Margaret and arranged for her marriage to

John Ball from her home in Cavendish Square. *Mackenzie* 26

MACKENZIE, SIR WALTER. Margaret's cousin, who lived at Incharrow, in Scotland. *Mackenzie* 26

McKEON, MRS. Wife of Tony, and mother of Louey and Lyddy. She befriended Feemy Macdermot despite her fear that Feemy was not frank with her as to her affair with Myles Ussher. One of the principal characters in *The Macdermots of Ballycloran.*

McKEON, TONY. A farmer in the neighborhood of Ballycloran, who believed firmly in Thady Macdermot's innocence, and with Father John worked ceaselessly for his acquittal. "He was something between forty-five and fifty, about six feet two high, with a good-humoured red face; he was inclined to be corpulent . . . was a great eater, and a very great drinker; it is said that he could put any man in Connaught under the table, and carry himself to bed sober" (2:3:68). One of the principal characters in *The Macdermots of Ballycloran.*

MACKINNON, CONRAD. A successful American writer living in Rome with his wife, the center of a brilliant group of American and British artists. *Talboys*

MACKINTOSH, MAJOR. The Chief of the London police, who induced Lizzie Eustace to tell the truth about the diamonds. *Eustace* 47-49, 51-54, 57, 63, 74, 78

Also mentioned in connection with Mr. Bonteen's murder. *Redux* 28, 47

MACLEOD, LADY. The widow of Sir Archibald Macleod, with whom Alice Vavasor lived in her youth. She was a pathetic hanger-on of the wealthy and titled members of her family, and tried to teach Alice reverence for them. *Can You* 1-3, 5, 11, 14-15, 22, 82

MACMULL, LADY JULIA. "Lady Julia had been a terrible flirt and greatly given to waltzing with a German count, with whom she had since gone off." Lord Dumbello had been engaged to her "three seasons back," but, in view of the affair with the German count, had jilted her. *Framley* 45

MACNUFFERY, DR. The physician for the British cricket team when it went to Britannula. *Fixed* 5

MACNULTY, JULIA. The paid companion of Lizzie Eustace, who was much attracted by Mr. Emilius, and thought he was in love with her. *Eustace* 5-13, 21-26, 31, 76

MACPHERSON'S, in Judd Street. *See* London

M'RUEN, JABESH. The first of Trollope's moneylenders, who "was in the habit of relieving the distresses of such impoverished young gentlemen as Charley Tudor; and though he did this with every assurance of philantropic regard . . . Mr. M'Ruen's young friends seldom contrived to hold their heads well up over the world's waters. . . . He was a little man with thin gray hair, which stood upright from his narrow head—what his age might have been it was impossible to guess; he was wizened, and dry, and gray . . . as keen in all his senses as though years could never tell against him" (2:1:19; 2:2:25-26). *Clerks* 17-21, 24, 28

MAGENTA HOUSE. *See* London

MAGGOTT, MICK. A miner, who worked with John Caldigate and Dick Shand on their first claim and taught them all they knew about gold-mining. *Caldigate* 10-12

MAGRUIN, MR. A moneylender with whom both Burgo Fitzgerald and George Vavasor had unfortunate dealings. *Can You* 29-30

MAGUIRE, The REV. JEREMIAH. The curate to Mr. Stumfold in Littlebath, eager to marry Margaret Mackenzie for her money, with which he hoped to establish himself in an independent church. When he learned that she was to marry her cousin and had lost her money, he imagined that it had been unlawfully taken from her, and that her marriage was arranged to prevent detection. He wrote a series of articles in the "Christian Examiner" of Littlebath denouncing the scheme under the thinly veiled title "The Lion and the Lamb." Since the arrangement was entirely legal, and Margaret and John were really in love, his intervention came to nothing, and he was glad to marry Miss Colza, who had a small competence, and fade from the scene.

". . . the possessor of a good figure, of a fine head of jet black hair, of a perfect set of white teeth, of whiskers which were also black and very fine . . . and of the most terrible squint in his right eye which ever disfigured a face that in all other respects was fitted for an Apollo" (1:4:72).

One of the principal characters in *Miss Mackenzie.*

MAHOUD AL ACKBAR. The Arab chieftain who invited George Walker to an excursion to see the Well of Moses, thinking him to be Sir George Walker, a visiting diplomat whom he wished to honor. *Walker*

MAINSAIL, MR. The junior counsel for the Countess Lovel. *Anna* 7, 30

MAINWARING, The REV. MR. The Rector of St. John's at Dillsborough, and a fellow student at Christchurch of the Duke of Mayfair. Very fond of dining out, and quite willing that his curate should attend to his churchly duties. *Amer. Sen.* 13, 42

MALACHI, FATHER. The Catholic priest in Ballintubber, not in sympathy with the Landleaguers. *Land.* 2-4

MALACHI'S COVE. In *Lotta Schmidt and Other Stories*, 1867. Originally published in *Good Words*, Dec. 1864.

Plot. Mahala Tringlos gathered seaweed in a cove on the coast of Cornwall, and supported her aged and crippled grandfather by selling it as fertilizer. She lived a desolate life of the hardest physical labor, hewing a poor path down the cliff side, and harnessing herself like an animal to drag back the heavy weed. The son of a neighboring farmer trenched on her preserves, and with his greater strength and the aid of a pony was able to scoff at the amount of her daily harvest. Mahala was wildly angry and declared that she hoped he would drown. Working one day near her, he fell into a whirlpool from which she rescued him at the risk of her own life. His peril aroused in her the first tenderness she had ever known and, her anger having disappeared, she found that she loved him.

MALTBY, BARON. The judge at the second Orley Farm trial. *Orley* 64, 68

MAN WHO KEPT HIS MONEY IN A BOX, The. In *Tales of All Countries*, Second Series, 1863. Originally published in *Public Opinion*, Literary Supplement, Nov. 2, 9, 1861.

Plot. Mr. Greene, a wealthy Englishman on a European holiday with his family, carried his money and his wife's jewels in one of their many boxes. On transferring from the boat on Lake Como to their hotel, the box was lost. Since he spoke no Italian, he asked Mr. Robinson, one of their traveling companions whose linguistic ability had already been of service, if he would search for it. Mr. Robinson, who was somewhat enamored of the daughter, agreed and traveled up and down the lake, but with no success. A few days later when his own boxes were brought down for his departure, greatly to his embarrassment the missing box was among them. Although Mr. Greene did not audibly express his suspicion, it was evident by his manner that he believed Mr. Robinson had planned to rob him.

MANCHESTER. The home of Fred Pickering, which he left to try his fortune in London, but to which he returned, penitent, to become an attorney's clerk. *Adventures*

MANCHESTER SQUARE. *See* London

MANDARIN ISLANDS. The colony of which Sir Marmaduke Rowley was the governor. Mentioned frequently in *He Knew He Was Right.*

MANOR CROSS. The home of the Marquis of Brotherton, where his mother, the Dowager Marchioness, and his brother and sisters lived in his absence, and from which they were ejected when he returned to England. The setting for much of *Is He Popenjoy?.*

MANYLODES, MR. The promoter of the tin mine "Wheal Mary Jane" who, with Undy Scott, bribed Alaric Tudor with cheap shares to write a glowing report on the mine. *Clerks* 9-10, 34

MARIGNY, BERNARD DE (real person). One of the few professonal soldiers in the Vendean revolt. *Vendée* 11

MARION FAY. London, Chapman and Hall, 1882. 3v. Originally published simultaneously in *The Graphic*, Dec. 3, 1881-June 3, 1882, and in *The Illustrated Sydney News.*

Notes. One of the thinnest and least satisfactory of the novels, relieved only by the abortive conspiracy of Lady Kingsbury and the Chaplain.

Plot. The Marquis of Kingsbury and his second wife were highly indignant at the behavior of the Marquis' two older children, Lord Hampstead and Lady Frances Trafford, both of whom were determined to marry beneath their rank. The Marchioness, jealous for the future of her own three small sons, intrigued with the unscrupulous family chaplain Mr. Greenwood to deepen the breach between the father and his older children, and even came to hope for the death of Lord Hampstead so that her oldest son would succeed to the title.

Lord Hampstead had fallen in love with Marion Fay, only living daughter of an old Quaker who worked as a clerk in the City, whose wife and other children had all died of consumption. Although Marion loved Lord Hampstead she refused to marry him, foreseeing her early death, which soon occurred. Lady Frances had engaged herself to George Roden, a postal clerk and a friend of her brother, a young man who claimed neither birth nor fortune. He knew that his mother had been unhappily married but she had never told him of her early life. However, when she was summoned to Italy, it became necessary for her to explain that his father had been the Duca di Crinola, who had abandoned them in George's infancy, that the father was now dead and the title was his. He refused the honor, but the knowledge that he was of noble birth served to change the attitude of Lady Frances' parents toward him, and when he was appointed to a responsible position in the Foreign Office all objection to their marriage was removed.

MARLBRO' SCHOOL (Marlborough). Dean Arabin sent his godson Bob Crawley to Marlbro' to prepare for Cambridge. *Last Chron.* 1

MARMADUKE LODGE. The home of Matilda Thoroughbung, in Hertfordshire. *Scarborough* 26

MARRABLE, COLONEL. The scapegrace brother of Sir Gregory, and father of Walter, from whom he embezzled his entire estate. "He was a thin, old man, who wore padded coats, and painted his beard and his eyebrows, and had false teeth, and who, in spite of chronic absence of means, always was possessed of clothes apparently just new from the hands of a West End tailor. . . . He was good-tempered, sprightly in conversation, and had not a scruple in the world" (33:208). *Vicar* 13, 16, 33, 44-45

MARRABLE, GREGORY (4th). The invalid son of Sir Gregory, an antiquarian of some note, "the projector of a new theory about Stonehenge. . . ." On his death the property went to Walter Marrable. "He was very tall and thin, narrow in the chest, and so round in the shoulders as to appear to be almost hump-backed. He was so short-sighted as to be nearly blind, and was quite bald. He carried his head so forward that it looked as though it was going to fall off. He shambled with his legs, which seemed never to be strong enough to carry him from one room to another . . . " (44:282-83). *Vicar* 44, 54, 58-59

MARRABLE, SIR GREGORY (3rd). Uncle of Walter, who became his heir on the death of Sir Gregory's son. His seat was at Dunripple Park, Worcestershire. "The baronet was old and disposed to regard himself as entitled to all the indulgences of infirmity. He rose late, took but little exercise, and got through his day with the assistance of his steward, his novel, and occasionally of his doctor. He slept a good deal, and was never tired of talking of himself" (44:282). Appears frequently in *The Vicar of Bullhampton.*

MARRABLE, The REV. JOHN. Brother of Sir Gregory Marrable, and uncle of Walter. Rector of St. Peters, Lowtown, in Loring. ". . . a kindly-hearted, good, sincere old man,—not very bright, indeed, nor particularly fitted for preaching the gospel, but he was much liked . . ." (13:75). Appears frequently in *The Vicar of Bullhampton.*

MARRABLE, SARAH. Mary Lowther's aunt, with whom she lived in Loring. "As to Miss Marrable herself nobody could doubt that she was a lady; she looked it every inch. There were not, indeed, many inches of her, for she was one of the smallest, daintiest, little old women that ever was seen. But now, at seventy, she was very pretty, quite a woman to look at with pleasure. Her feet and hands were exquisitely made, and she was very proud of them. She wore her own grey hair of which she showed very little, but that little was always exquisitely nice. Her caps were the perfection of caps. Her green eyes were bright and sharp, and seemed to say that she knew very well how to take care of herself. Her mouth, and nose, and chin were all well-formed, small, shapely, and concise . . ." (9:56). Appears frequently in *The Vicar of Bullhampton.*

MARRABLE, CAPT. WALTER. Son of Colonel Marrable, and nephew of Sir Gregory from whom he inherited his estate. Home on leave from India, he met his cousin Mary Lowther, fell in love with and eventually married her.

"He had served in India, and the naturally dark colour of his face had thus become very swarthy. His black hair curled round his head, but the curls on his brow were becoming very thin, as though age were already telling on them. . . . His eyebrows were thick and heavy, and his eyes seemed to be black. . . . He wore no beard beyond a heavy black moustache, which quite covered his upper lip. His nose was long and straight, his mouth large, and his chin square. . . . he lacked two full inches of the normal six feet. He was broad across the chest, strong on his legs" (13: 77-78).

One of the principal characters in *The Vicar of Bullhampton.*

MARSHAM, MRS. A girlhood friend of Plantagenet Palliser's mother, whom he thought would be a good duenna for his young wife, Lady Glencora. Lady Glencora detested her, and indignantly protested to her husband when she found herself spied upon. Mrs. Marsham married Mr. Bott. ". . . had many good points. She was poor, and bore her poverty without complaint. She was connected by blood and friendship with people rich and titled; but she paid to none of them egregious respect on account of their wealth or titles. . . . She was a little woman, with small sharp eyes, with a permanent colour in her face, and two short, crisp, grey curls at each side of her face; always well dressed, always in good health . . . altogether incapable of fatigue" (2:3: 19-21). *Can You* 42-43, 48-50, 58, 62, 79

MARTOCK, MR. Sir Joseph Mason's London partner, whose deed, dissolving the partnership, was brought by Mr. Torrington to the second Orley Farm trial. *Orley* 68

MARTY, FATHER. The parish priest at Kilmacrenny, the only friend and confidant of Mrs. O'Hara and her daughter Kate. He was in part responsible for the friendship between Kate and Fred Neville, and insistent on their marriage. "But justice for Ireland in the guise of wealthy English husbands for pretty Irish girls he desired with all his heart. He was true to his own faith, to the backbone, but he entertained no prejudice against a good looking Protestant youth when a fortunate marriage was in question" (1:7:12). One of the principal characters in *An Eye for an Eye.*

MARY GRESLEY. In *An Editor's Tales,* 1870. Originally published in *Saint Paul's Magazine,* Nov. 1869.

PLOT. A charming young girl with literary ambition but no ability took her stories to the Editor, telling him that she was engaged to an invalid curate, and that it was necessary for her to support them both by her pen. The sympathetic Editor endeavored to teach her to write, but with small success. The dying curate was emphatic in his disapproval of novels and pledged Mary to give up her attempt to write them.

MARYGOLD. The home of the Connop Greens, in Hampshire, where Arabella Trefoil and her mother were entertained. *Amer. Sen.* 61-62

MARYLEBONE, MARQUIS OF. The leader of the British cricket team that went to Britannula. *Fixed* 4-5, 7

MARYLEBONE ROAD. *See* London

MASON, MRS. DIANA. Wife of Joseph, and mother of three daughters, Diana, Creusa and Penelope. "She was a little woman with long eyes, and regular eyelashes, with a straight nose, and thin lips and regular teeth. . . . She had been a beauty; but if it had been her lot to be known in history, it was not as a beauty she would have been famous. Parsimony was her great virtue and saving her strong point" (1:7:50). *Orley* 7-8, 23

MASON, JOSEPH, of Groby Park. The heir of Sir Joseph, but not content that Orley Farm should be left to his stepbrother Lucius. His greed resulted in his accusation that the codicil of his father's will had been forged, and brought about the two trials. He had two sons: John, at Cambridge, and

Joseph, in the army; and three unhappy and undernourished daughters, victims of their mother's parsimony. "His mind and heart were equally harsh and hard and inflexible. He was a man who considered that it behoved him as a man to resent all injuries, and to have his pound of flesh in all cases" (1:7:49). One of the principal characters in *Orley Farm*.

MASON, SIR JOSEPH. A wealthy London merchant, owner of Groby Park and of Orley Farm, where he lived. His son Joseph and three daughters of his first marriage were much displeased at his marriage to Mary Johnson, and enraged when a son, Lucius, was born. Since he failed to provide for this youngest son in his will, the child's mother forged a codicil, leaving the small property at Orley Farm to Lucius. *Orley* 1-2, 5

MASON, LUCIUS. The only son of Lady Mason, for whose sake she forged the codicil to her husband's will leaving Orley Farm to him. He was educated at private schools and in Germany, returning home to introduce scientific farming. Honest, but opinionated and self-willed, he returned Orley Farm to his older brother Joseph Mason when he learned that his father had not left it to him. An unsuccessful suitor of Sophia Furnival. ". . . a handsome, well-mannered lad, tall and comely to the eye, with soft brown whiskers sprouting on his cheek, well grounded in Greek, Latin and Euclid, grounded also in French and Italian . . ." (1:2:16). One of the principal characters in *Orley Farm*.

MASON, MARY (Johnson), LADY. The second wife of Sir Joseph, and mother of Lucius. "In person she was tall and comely. . . . Her forehead was high . . . and gave evidence of considerable mental faculties. . . . Her eyes were large and well formed, but somewhat cold. Her nose was long and regular. Her mouth also was very regular, and her teeth perfectly beautiful; but her lips were straight and thin. . . . The quietness and repose of her manner suited her years and her position; age had given fullness to her tall form; and the habitual sadness of her countenance was fair in accordance with her condition and character" (1:2:14-15). Principal character in *Orley Farm*.

MASON and MARTOCK. The firm whose deed, dissolving their partnership, was a major factor in the second Orley Farm trial. *Orley* 7, 24-25, 53, 61, 75

MASTERS, MRS. The shrewish second wife of Gregory, who resented the presence of Mary in her household. Appears frequently in *The American Senator*.

MASTERS, GREGORY. An attorney at Dillsborough, whose main business in life was managing the Morton property. Father of Mary, Dolly and Kate. "He was a round-faced, clean-shorn man, with straggling grey hair, who always wore black clothes and a white cravat" (1:4:36). Appears frequently in *The American Senator*.

MASTERS, KATE. *See* Twentyman, Mrs. Kate (Masters)

MASTERS, MARY. Daughter of Gregory Masters and his first wife, who for many years lived, almost as a daughter, with Lady Ushant at Bragton Hall, where she grew up in the companionship of Reginald Morton. When she returned to her father's home, her stepmother attempted to force her to marry Larry Twentyman, who was deeply in love with her. Mary had fallen in love with Reginald and, although the match seemed above her station, she eventually married him. Heroine of *The American Senator*.

MATCHING PRIORY. A beautiful country place in Yorkshire, the old Duke of Omnium's favorite home, which he gave to Plantagenet Palliser as a wedding gift. Often mentioned in the novels of the Parliamentary series.

MAULE, GERARD. A useless young man, with only money enough to live a meager life, made up of hunting, visiting complaisant friends and mooning over Adelaide Palliser's refusal to marry him. He accused Adelaide of thinking him ". . . a poor creature, generally half asleep, shallow-pated, slow-blooded, ignorant, useless and unambitious" (*Redux* 1:7:60). Since neither of them had any money, it was impossible for them to marry until Madame Goesler settled on Adelaide the fortune that the old Duke of Omnium had left her. Most prominent in *Phineas Redux*; briefly in *Duke* 62-63

MAULE, MAURICE, of Maule Abbey. Father of Gerard Maule, a widower who attempted unsuccessfully to marry Mme. Max Goesler. As a young man, "He proposed to himself the life of an idle man with a moderate income,—a life which should be luxurious, refined, and graceful, but to which should be attached the burden of no necessary occupation. . . . He became an idler, a man of luxury, and then a spendthrift. . . . He was a slight, bright-eyed, grey-haired, good-looking man, who had once been very handsome . . ." (1:21:170-72). *Redux* 3, 7, 15-16, 18-19, 21, 42-43, 69

MAULE ABBEY. The dilapidated country estate of Maurice Maule, in Herefordshire. *Redux* 18, 21

MAYFAIR, DUCHESS OF. Her chief characteristic seemed to be a violent dislike for her husband's niece Arabella Trefoil. Appears frequently in *The American Senator.*

MAYFAIR, DUKE OF. Brother of Lord Augustus Trefoil, and uncle of Arabella. He had been a classmate at Christchurch of the Rev. Mr. Mainwaring. ". . . a hospitable, easy man who was very fond of his dinner and performed his duties well; but could never be touched by any sentiment. . . . He was a grey-haired comely man of sixty, with a large body and a wonderful appetite" (2:9:89). Appears frequently in *The American Senator.*

MEAGER FAMILY. The lodging-house keepers who lived opposite the Marylebone workhouse. After Lizzie Eustace left Mr. Emilius, he lodged with them, and it was their testimony that turned the suspicion of the police from him to Phineas Finn, in the murder of Mr. Bonteen. *Redux* 56

MEALYUS, YOSEF. *See* Emilius, Joseph

MEDLICOT, MRS. Giles Medlicot's mother, who went out to Queensland from England to keep house for him. "She was a handsome old woman, with grey hair, seventy years of age, with wrinkled face, and a toothless mouth, but with bright eyes, and with no signs of the infirmity of age" (3:66). *Heathcote* 3, 7, 11-12

MEDLICOT, GILES. A bachelor Englishman, who went out to Queensland to make his fortune as a sugar grower. His purchase of land earlier leased to Harry Heathcote by the government stirred up enmity between the two men, but they became friends when Medlicot joined forces with Heathcote to put out the fires that threatened to destroy the sheep ranch. He married Kate Daly, Heathcote's sister-in-law. One of the principal characters in *Harry Heathcote of Gangoil.*

MEHAN, MRS. The keeper of a whiskey shop at Mohill, where Mary

Brady and Denis McGovery were married. *Macdermots* 8, 12-13

MELBOURNE. Where John Caldigate and Dick Shand landed from the "Goldfinder," and from which they made their way inland, in search of gold. *Caldigate* 8

MELLERBY, SOPHIA. A wealthy young granddaughter of a duke, whom Lady Scroope desired Fred Neville, her husband's heir, to marry. Fred's brother Jack fell in love with her, and after Fred's death they were married. ". . . a tall, graceful, well-formed girl, showing her high blood in every line of her face . . . the Mellerbys had been Mellerbys from the time of King John, and had been living on the same spot for at least four centuries. . . . She was fair, with a somewhat thin, oval face, with dark eyes, and an almost perfect Grecian nose. Her mouth was small, and her chin delicately formed. . . . Her education had been as good as England could afford, and her intellect had been sufficient to enable her to make use of it" (1:3:51-52). *Eye* 2-4, 8-10, 18-20, 24

MELMOTTE, MADAME. A Bohemian Jewess, who strove valiantly, but with no success, to assist in her husband's ambitious social plans, and to aid in securing an advantageous marriage for his daughter Marie. She feared and hated her husband, and soon after his suicide married his confidential clerk, with whom she emigrated to America.

"She was fat and fair . . . but she had the Jewish nose and the Jewish contraction of the eyes. . . . There was certainly very little . . . to recommend her, unless it was a readiness to spend money on any object that might be suggested to her by her new acquaintances. It sometimes seemed that she had a commission from her husband to give away presents to any who would accept them" (1:4:21).

One of the principal characters in *The Way We Live Now.*

MELMOTTE, AUGUSTUS. A financial plunger, for a long time considered by all London to be a "great financier." He entertained royalty and was elected to represent Westminster in Parliament. His house of cards about to fall, on the eve of his prosecution for forgery, he committed suicide.

". . . a large man, with bushy whiskers and rough thick hair, with heavy eyebrows, and a wonderful look of power about his mouth and chin. This was so strong as to redeem his face from vulgarity. . . . He looked as though he were purse-proud and a bully" (1:4:21).

"Melmotte is a figure of dominating size . . . something bigger than anything he has said or done . . . a kind of symbolic figure. . . . In sober fact he is a dirty, bullying, greedy, ignorant charlatan, who tumbles swiftly to absolute ruin."—Walpole, p. 166.

". . . a grotesque and nauseating monstrosity, he personified the commercial corruptions of the time with all their brutalizing effects upon character, as in private, so in public life."—Escott, p. 297.

Principal character in *The Way We Live Now.*

MELMOTTE, MARIE. The illegitimate daughter of Augustus Melmotte, who was offered by her father to the highest bidder, socially speaking—he to furnish a dot sufficient to make the match desirable. Various impoverished noblemen entered the lists, but she selected the most worthless of them all, Sir Felix Carbury. After she had stolen money from her father for their elopement, Sir Felix gambled it away. After her father's death she married the adventurer Hamilton Fisker and went with him to America. "She was not beautiful, she was not clever, and she was not a saint. . . . She was a little thing, hardly over twenty years of age" (1:4:22). One of the principal characters in *The Way We Live Now.*

MÈRE BAUCHE, La. In *Tales of All Countries* [First Series], 1861.

PLOT. La Mère Bauche, an autocratic innkeeper in the Eastern Pyrenees, was excessively ambitious for her only son's future. She had adopted an orphan girl, Marie Calvert, and brought her up as a daughter of the house until she learned that her son also loved the girl. The marriage would have made impossible her dreams for Adolphe's success in life, and she sent him away for a year's travel, planning to marry Marie to an elderly habitué of the inn, Theodore Campan. Before leaving, Adolphe required a promise from Marie that she would be true to him, but at the end of the year he returned and weakly submitted to his mother. Marie, brokenhearted, allowed the marriage to her elderly suitor to take place, and when she disappeared after the ceremony, Adolphe found her dead at the foot of the cliffs from which she had plunged.

MEREDITH, SIR GEORGE. Son-in-law of Lady Lufton. *Framley* 5

MEREDITH, JUSTINIA, LADY. Daughter of Lady Lufton, and a dear friend of Mrs. Robarts. *Framley* 5

MEREWETHER, CHARLES (real person). "The legal opinion as to the heirlooms [in *The Eustace Diamonds*] . . . was written for me by Charles Merewether."—*Autobiography*, 1:6:155n.

MERIONETH, DUKE OF. Father of the Marquis of Llwddythlw, ". . . one of those half-dozen happy noblemen . . . reported to be the richest man in England" (1:12:158). *Fay* 12, 19, 26, 60

MERLE PARK. The suburban home of Sir Thomas Tringle, in Sussex. *Ayala* 47

MERTON, DR. The resident doctor at Tretton Park. Appears frequently in *Mr. Scarborough's Family*.

MEWNEW, SIR LAMDA. A famous London physician, called to Barchester for consultation in the illness of Bishop Grantly. *Barchester* 1

MICKEWA. Senator Gotobed represented the fictitious state of Mickewa in the Congress of the United States. *Amer. Sen.* 8, 10-11, 29, 41

MIDDLE TEMPLE. *See* London

MIDDLE WASH. The great dike that bisected Folking, John Caldigate's home, ". . . so sluggish, so straight, so ugly, and so deep, as to impress the mind of a stranger with the ideas of suicide" (1:1:4). *Caldigate* 1

MIDDLESEX. Where Sir John Ball's home, The Cedars, was located. *Mackenzie*

MIDLOTHIAN, COUNTESS OF. For value received by impoverished members of her family, she attended the Melmotte ball, where her presence gave it social importance. *Way We Live* 4

MIDLOTHIAN, MARGARET, LADY. One of Alice Vavasor's wealthy relatives, who most officiously and persistently interfered in Alice's love affairs. When Alice was taken up by Lady Glencora and her marriage to Mr. Grey was planned to take place at Matching Priory, Lady Margaret showed her forgiveness to her erring niece by allowing her daughters Lady Jane and Lady Mary to be in the wedding party. Appears frequently in *Can You Forgive Her?*.

MILBOROUGH, DOWAGER COUNTESS OF. The old family friend of Louis Trevelyan, who warned him of Colonel Osborne's attentions to his wife, and advised taking her to Naples. She later befriended Nora Rowley. Appears frequently in *He Knew He Was Right*.

MILDMAY, MR. Augusta's father, ". . . a gray-haired old gentleman, rather short and rather fat" (1:12:162-63). *Popenjoy* 12, 15, 18, 20, 53, 58

MILDMAY, AUGUSTA ("Gus"). In love with, and determined to marry, the reluctant Jack de Baron. When the Marquis of Brotherton left him a fortune, Jack's last hope of escape vanished and he was led to the altar. "She was certainly handsome, but she carried with her that wearied air of being nearly worn out by the toil of searching for a husband" (1:12:163). Appears frequently in *Is He Popenjoy?*.

MILDMAY, JULIA ("Aunt Ju"). One of the backers of the "Disabilities." She was responsible for inviting Baroness Banmann to lecture in London. *Popenjoy* 15-18, 27, 30, 33, 50-51, 55, 60

MILDMAY, WILLIAM. The Prime Minister succeeding Lord de Terrier. A relative of Lady Laura Standish, and uncle to Barrington Erle. ". . . an old man, nearly worn out in the service of his country, who was known to have been true and honest, and to have loved his country well,—though there were of course they who declared that his hand had been too weak for power, and that his services had been naught" (*Finn* 1:25:208). Most prominent in *Phineas Finn* and *Phineas Redux*; also mentioned frequently in *The Prime Minister*.

MILE END BOROUGH. *See* London

MILES, MRS. Mother of Frank and Philip, and foster-mother of Bessy Pryor. A woman of wealth and social position, who throughout her life had denied herself happiness, and ended by attempting to deny it to Philip and Bessy when they fell in love. One of the principal characters in *The Lady of Launay*.

MILES, FRANK. The estranged older son of Mrs. Miles. *Launay*

MILES, PHILIP. *See* Launay, Philip

MILLBANK PENITENTIARY. Where Alaric Tudor served a six months' sentence for embezzlement. *Clerks* 41-42

MISS MACKENZIE. London, Chapman and Hall, 1865. 2v.

Author's Comment. ". . . written with a desire to prove that a novel may be produced without any love. . . . In order that I might be strong in my purpose, I took for my heroine a very unattractive old maid, who was overwhelmed with money troubles; but even she was in love before the end of the book, and made a romantic marriage with an old man."—*Autobiography*, 1: 10:250.

Notes. Originally titled "The Modern Griselda," this is an amusing example of the way Trollope's characters, as they developed in his mind, contrived to write their own story—in this instance quite against his will.

Plot. Margaret Mackenzie, unattractive and colorless at thirty-five, inherited a small fortune at the death of her brother, and for the first time in her drab existence was free to seek some measure of happiness. To secure this she moved from her gloomy London home to a cheerful apartment in Littlebath where, with an eye on her fortune, she was sought in marriage by the Rev. Jeremiah Maguire, an Evangelical clergyman; by Samuel Rubb, Jr., son of her brother's partner; and by her cousin John Ball, a widower with nine children. She refused them all, but did fall in love with her elderly cousin, and, when it was proved that her fortune was really his, they were married.

MISS OPHELIA GLEDD. In *Lotta Schmidt and Other Stories*, 1867. Originally published in *A Welcome*: original contributions in poetry and prose. London, Emily Faithfull, 1863.

NOTES. Raises, but does not answer, the question whether a talented Boston girl would be considered a "lady" in London. The sleighing incident was drawn from Trollope's own visit to Boston in 1862, and the description of the heroine may have been reminiscent of the author's Boston friend Kate Field.

PLOT. With two lovers, an American and an Englishman, both eminently suitable, Ophelia Gledd hesitated to follow her heart because she feared that her breezy, unconventional manners might not be acceptable to the family of her correct and formal English suitor. She was finally persuaded to take the risk.

MISS SARAH JACK OF SPANISH TOWN, JAMAICA. In *Tales of All Countries* [First Series], 1861.

PLOT. An impoverished young sugar-planter, Maurice Cummings, was induced by his energetic and patriotic aunt, Miss Sarah Jack, to run for the House of Assembly in Jamaica. While in Spanish Town he met and won Marion Leslie, and, despite various misunderstandings, Miss Jack succeeded in smoothing the way for their happy marriage.

MR. SCARBOROUGH'S FAMILY. London, Chatto and Windus, 1883. 3v. Originally published in *All the Year Round*, May 27, 1882-June 16, 1883.

NOTES. ". . . a novel of property . . . cynical and, for its period, daring—shows his [Trollope's] power of sustained and dexterous raillery."—Sadleir, pp. 192, 397.

PLOT. John Scarborough, owner of a large landed property in Hertfordshire, resented the restrictions of the law of entail. He accordingly devised a scheme whereby he was able by a double marriage, one before and one after the birth of his eldest son, to declare him legitimate or not, as the future might make desirable. This eldest son, Mountjoy, was a weak, easily led wastrel who developed into an inveterate gambler, and so encumbered the estate with post-obits that at his father's death it would have gone to the moneylenders. The father, who valued his estate above his honor, then declared Mountjoy illegitimate, producing the certificate of the second marriage in proof. The post-obits now being valueless, he quietly bought them up, once again making the estate unencumbered.

Augustus, the second son, finding himself an heir, soon enraged his father by exhibiting an unseemly haste to enter into his inheritance. To punish him, John made a new will, giving Mountjoy all his property except that covered by the entail, and leaving Augustus only the skeleton of the estate, with no money to maintain it. Not satisfied in thus dashing his younger son's hopes, he then produced the first marriage certificate, making Mountjoy heir under the entail. At his father's death, Mountjoy, again in funds, departed for Monte Carlo, and the assumption is that the estate would once again fall into the hands of the Jews.

MISTLETOE. The seat of the Duke of Mayfair, in Lincolnshire. ". . . an enormous house with a frontage nearly a quarter of a mile long, combining as it does all the offices, coach houses, and stables. There is nothing in England more ugly or perhaps more comfortable" (2:9:89). *Amer. Sen.* 25, 31, 35-36, 40, 44, 60

MISTLETOE, LORD. Son of the Duke of Mayfair, and Arabella Trefoil's cousin, to whom she appealed in her breach-of-promise contest with Lord Rufford. *Amer. Sen.* 48-50, 56, 60, 75

MISTLETOE BOUGH, The. In *Tales of All Countries*, Second Series, 1863. Originally published in *The Illustrated*

London News, Christmas Supplement, Dec. 21, 1861.

PLOT. Elizabeth Garrow, engaged to Godfrey Holmes, a rising young banker in Liverpool, was so determined that she would not allow herself to be carried away by her happiness that she leaned backward to make the affair seem humdrum. Godfrey was deeply and romantically in love with her, and resented her coldness. By mutual consent their engagement was broken, but Godfrey, who was convinced of Elizabeth's love for him, succeeded in convincing her that her self-martyrdom was morbid and their engagement was renewed.

MRS. BRUMBY. In *An Editor's Tales*, 1870. Originally published in *Saint Paul's Magazine*, May 1870.

PLOT. Although totally without talent, Mrs. Brumby attempted to bulldoze the Editor into publication of her manuscript. He refused, but she made herself so disagreeable, finally threatening a lawsuit, that he paid her £10 to get rid of her, and made her an apology for the assault that she alleged had been committed by the Editor's clerk.

MRS. GENERAL TALBOYS. In *Tales of All Countries*, Second Series, 1863. Originally published in *The London Review*, Feb. 2, 1861.

PLOT. The wife of an English general spending the winter in Rome became the center of a literary-artistic and somewhat unconventional coterie. Charles O'Brien, an impressionable young Irish sculptor, made the mistake of assuming that her freedom from prejudice authorized him to make love to her, and was severely snubbed.

MIXET, JOE. A garrulous friend of John Crumb, and his mouthpiece in courting Ruby Ruggles. He was a baker in Bungay. *Way We Live* 33-34, 94

MOFFAT, GUSTAVUS. At one time engaged to Augusta Gresham, he broke the engagement in an effort to marry Martha Dunstable, and was thrashed by Augusta's brother Frank. In the Barchester election he opposed Sir Roger Scatcherd. ". . . a young man of very large fortune, in Parliament, inclined to business, and in every way recommendable [as a husband for Augusta Gresham]. He was not a man of birth to be sure, that was to be lamented. . . . he was the son of a tailor . . . a nice, dapper man, rather above the middle height, and good looking enough had he had a little more expression in his face. He had dark hair, very nicely brushed, small black whiskers, and a small black moustache" (1:4:95; 2:1:8). *Thorne* 4-9, 14-18, 21-22, 24

MOGGS, MR. A West End bootmaker, who objected to his son Ontario's ambition to get into Parliament. *Ralph* 8-9, 16-17, 19-20, 48, 53

MOGGS, ONTARIO. Son of a successful bootmaker, whose attitude toward labor was a great trial to his father. He spoke with vigor at the debating club at the Cheshire Cheese in support of unions and the rights of man, and was asked to stand for the Radical interest at the Percycross election. He was unsuccessful in politics, but his prominence won him the favor of Polly Neefit, whom he had been courting.

"He was a tall, thin, young man, with long straggling hair, a fierce eye, very thick lips, and a flat nose,—a nose which seemed to be all nostril;—and then, below his mouth was a tuft of beard, which he called an imperial. It was the glory of Ontario Moggs to be a politician;—it was his ambition to be a poet; —it was his nature to be a lover;—it was his disgrace to be a bootmaker" (1:8:134).

"He is, it is true, something of a prig, with a solemnity of manner and a pompous pithiness of artificial phrase making him a little absurd. His real cleverness, however, is not below his conceit, his readiness of speech, quickness at the detection of a fallacy and power of argument, justly entitle him to his high reputation at the Cheshire Cheese and other debating clubs."—Escott, p. 254.

One of the principal characters in *Ralph the Heir.*

MOHILL. A village three miles from Ballycloran, ". . . an impoverished town —the property of a non-resident landlord—destitute of anything to give it interest or prosperity—without business, without trade, and without society" (1:9:200). The setting for much of the action in *The Macdermots of Ballycloran.*

MOLESCROFT, MR. The counselor for Phineas Finn when he contested the Tankerville seat. *Redux* 1, 4

MOLK, HERR. A magistrate in Nuremberg, and an old friend of Linda Tressel's father, who, upon learning that Linda was in love with Ludovic Valcarm, urged her to marry Peter Steinmarc, believing Ludovic to be a rascal. *Linda* 7-10, 13-14

MOLLETT, ABRAHAM ("Aby"). Son of Matthew, "surpassing even his father in rascality." "He was a very smart man, with a profusion of dark, much-oiled hair, with dark, copious mustachoes . . . with various rings on his not well-washed hands, with a frilled front to his not lately washed shirt, with a velvet collar to his coat, and patent-leather boots upon his feet" (1:6:105). *Castle Rich.* 6, 13, 15, 17, 20, 23-24, 39, 43

MOLLETT, MARY. Daughter of Matthew Mollett, who called herself "Mary Swan" after her father deserted her and her mother. She supported them both by her needle. *Castle Rich.* 39-40

MOLLETT, MRS. MARY. Matthew Mollett's deserted wife, whose discovery by Mr. Prendergast made Mollett's marriage to Lady Fitzgerald illegal, and cleared the Fitzgerald children of the taint of illegitimacy. ". . . old and sickly looking. . . . Her face was thin and delicate and pale, and not hard and coarse; her voice was low, as a woman's should be, and her hands were white and small. Her clothes, though very poor, were neat, and worn as a poor lady might have worn them" (3:10:199). *Castle Rich.* 39-40

MOLLETT, MATTHEW. After deserting his wife and child in London, he went to Dorsetshire where, under the name of "Talbot," he married Mary Wainright. He soon left her, and after his reported death she married Sir Thomas Fitzgerald. Mollett returned to blackmail Sir Thomas by threatening to prove that his three children were illegitimate. Staggered by the demands made upon him, Sir Thomas died, but his lawyers traced the first wife and proved that the Fitzgerald marriage was legal.

"He was a hale hearty man, of perhaps sixty years of age, who had certainly been handsome, and was even now not the reverse. Or rather, one may say, that he would have been so were it not that there was a low, restless cunning, legible in his mouth and eyes, which robbed his countenance of all manliness. He was a hale man, and well preserved for his time of life; but, nevertheless, the extra rubicundity of his face, and certain incipient pimply excrescences about his nose, gave tokens that he lived too freely" (1:6:104).

One of the principal characters in *Castle Richmond.*

MOLLOY, MICHAEL. A mildly insane man, considering himself to be a neglected and misunderstood writer, who followed the Editor to a Turkish bath, engaged him in conversation and tricked him into a promise to read his worthless manuscripts. Principal character in *The Turkish Bath.*

MOMONT. The butler at Durbellière, who acquitted himself well during the distress of his master's family, but remained jealous of the prowess of his fellow servant Jacques Chapeau, who took a more active part in the campaign. *Vendée* 4, 12, 18-19

MOMSON, MR. The Squire of Buttercup, whose son was a pupil at Dr. Wortle's school. The Squire approved Dr. Wortle's faith in the Peacockes, and supported him against his maligners. *Wortle* 11-12

MOMSON, LADY MARGARET. One of the gossiping women who joined in the campaign against Dr. Wortle, because of his kindness to Mr. and Mrs. Peacocke. *Wortle* 11-12, 14, 24

MONDYON, ARTHUR. The cadet of a noble family in Poitou, who was called "Le petit chevalier." He acted as aide-de-camp to Henri Larochejaquelin during the Vendean revolt. One of the principal characters in *La Vendée.*

MONEYLENDERS in Trollope's works. Few of Trollope's experiences, painful though they might be at the time, went unrecorded in one or another of his novels. As a young man he was frequently in trouble over small debts and his pictures of moneylenders could not have been drawn with such skill had it been otherwise. He knew John and Tom Tozer, and had quaked in his boots when they followed him to the Post Office with their bills. Jabesh M'Ruen, who hounded Charley Tudor, was of the same ilk. And yet, mean and dirty as many of them were, Trollope's genius makes them reasonable. One feels that they believed in themselves, and sympathizes with them when they are bested, as Sexty Parker certainly was by George Vavasor, and Mr. Tyrrwhit by Mr. Scarborough.

Broughton, Dobbs. *Last Chron.*
Clarkson, Mr. *Finn*
Davis, Mr. *Caldigate*
Gurney and Malcolmson. *Scarborough*
Hart, Abraham. *Hotspur*
Hart, Samuel. *Scarborough*
M'Ruen, Jabesh. *Clerks*
Magruin, Mr. *Can You*
Musselboro, Augustus. *Last Chron.*
Parker, Sexty. *Prime Min.*
Sidonia, Mr. *Barchester*
Stubber, Captain. *Hotspur*
Tozer, John and Tom. *Framley*
Tyrrwhit, Mr. *Scarborough*

MONK, LADY. Burgo Fitzgerald's aunt, who provided him with funds, knowing he planned to elope with Lady Glencora. ". . . now about fifty years of age, who had been a great beauty, and who was still handsome in her advanced age. Her figure was very good. She was tall and of fine proportion. . . . She was a comely, handsome, upright dame,—one of whom, as regards her outward appearance, England might be proud. . . . She had come of the family of the Worcestershire Fitzgeralds, of whom it used to be said that there never was one who was not beautiful and worthless" (1:33:258). *Can You* 33, 48-49, 66

MONK, SIR COSMO. A Liberal MP earlier at the Treasury. In Chapter 76 incorrectly called Sir Charles. He did not agree with his wife in her fondness for her nephew Burgo Fitzgerald. "Sir Cosmo had a little party of his own in the House, consisting of four or five other respectable country gentlemen, who troubled themselves little with thinking, and who mostly had bald heads" (1:33:260). *Can You* 33, 66, 76

MONK, JOSHUA. A Radical, representing Pottery Hamlets in Parliament. He was successively President of the

Board of Trade, Chancellor of the Exchequer and Prime Minister. Phineas Finn considered himself Mr. Monk's disciple, and resigned his office in order to vote with him on tenant right. ". . . of all the members of the Cabinet was the most advanced Liberal . . . a thin, tall, gaunt man, who had devoted his whole life to politics hitherto without any personal reward beyond that which came to him from the reputation of his name, and from the honour of a seat in Parliament" (*Finn* 1:14:115). Most prominent in *Phineas Finn* and *Phineas Redux*; briefly in *Duke* 16, 22, 46, 78

MONKHAMS. The seat of Lord Peterborough, ". . . a very grand place in Worcestershire." *He Knew* 3, 16, 96

MONKSHADE. The country place of Sir Cosmo and Lady Monk. *Can You* 33

MONKTON GRANGE. The starting place of the Hamworth Hunt, seven miles from Noningsby, where Felix Graham was injured. *Orley* 28

MONOGRAM, SIR DAMASK. Son of a wealthy contractor and grandson of a butcher, who, by keeping horses for others to ride and breeding pheasants for others to shoot, was accepted in society. *Way We Live* 25, 32, 44, 60-62, 65; *Prime Min.* 9

MONOGRAM, JULIA (Triplex), LADY. An old friend of Georgiana Longestaffe, who had been consistently snubbed and ignored until her marriage to the wealthy Sir Damask made her of use to Georgiana. *Way We Live* 25, 32, 44, 60-62, 65; *Prime Min.* 9

MONSELL, FANNY. *See* Robarts, Mrs. Fanny (Monsell)

MONTAGUE, PAUL. A friend and distant relative of Roger Carbury. He invested his small fortune in a venture in San Francisco, but, not liking the country, returned to England. He won the love of Henrietta Carbury, whom Roger wished to marry. Becoming involved with Augustus Melmotte in his promotion schemes, he vainly tried to warn his fellow directors of the unsoundness of the business, and extricated himself before the crash. One of the principal characters in *The Way We Live Now*.

MONTMORENCI, JOSEPHINE DE. The name assumed by Mrs. Puffle to gain an appointment with the Editor, hoping to persuade him to publish a novel written by her sister-in-law. Principal character in *Josephine de Montmorenci*.

MONTREUIL. A town near Saumur, used as a rendezvous before the battle. *Vendée* 9

MOODY, GREGORY. One of the bedesmen at Hiram's Hospital. *Warden*

MOODY, MAJOR. A professional gambler, who inveigled Mountjoy Scarborough into a card game and fleeced him of all his money—just after Mountjoy had promised his father to give up gambling. *Scarborough* 13

MOONBEAM. A pub at Barnfield, the center of the B B hunt. *Ralph* 27, 46

MOONEY, KIT. One of the ringleaders of the gang of Landleaguers, who prevented Black Tom Daly from hunting at Moytubber. *Land.* 11, 39

MOONEY, TEDDY. Father of Kit, whose business as a cabdriver was ruined when the Landleaguers boycotted all the neighboring "gentry," the only ones who could pay to ride in his cab. He later turned against the Landleaguers, and supplied the evidence that convicted Terry Lax of the murder of Florian Jones. *Land.* 39

"MORNING BREAKFAST TABLE." "A daily newspaper of high character," edited by Nicholas Broune, in which appeared some of the articles written by Lady Carbury. *Way We Live* 11, 35, 44, 54

MORONY. *See* Castle Morony

MORONY, MRS. A troublesome Irishwoman, who caused great grief to Brown, Jones and Robinson by demanding to buy the articles in the show-windows, rather than those "just as good" on the shelves. *Struggles* 14-15

MORRIS, DAN. A brickmaker at Hogglestock, who had the check cashed that Mr. Crawley was accused of stealing. *Last Chron.* 12

MORRIS, GEORGE. A neighbor and friend of the Newtons at Newton Priory, ". . . who devoted a considerable portion of his mental and physical energies to the birth, rearing, education, preservation, and subsequent use of the fox,—thinking that in so doing he employed himself nobly as a country gentleman." *Ralph* 31, 42, 49

MORRIS, The HON. GEORGE. MP for the borough of Loughshane for twenty years. He quarreled with his brother, the Earl of Tulla, and lost the seat to Phineas Finn. *Finn* 1-2, 50

MORRIS, LUCY. The governess in the house of Lady Fawn, and at one time companion to Lady Linlithgow. In love with Frank Greystock, whom she finally married. "She was but a little thing; and it cannot be said of her . . . that she was a beauty. The charm of her face consisted in the peculiar, watery brightness of her eyes,—in the corners of which it would always seem that a diamond of a tear was lurking. . . . Her light brown hair was soft and smooth and pretty. . . . Her mouth was somewhat large. . . . Her forehead was low and broad, with prominent temples. . . . When she smiled there was the daintiest little dimple on her cheek. . . . She was a little, thin, quick, graceful creature" (1:3:35-36). One of the principal characters in *The Eustace Diamonds.*

MORRIS, MATTHEW. A passenger on board the boat for Panama, who warned his friend Ralph Forrest against falling in love with Emily Viner. *Journey*

MORRIS, ROBERT. A benevolent gentleman, magistrate for the counties of Galway and Mayo, and cousin of Black Tom Daly, who was wantonly murdered by one of his disgruntled tenants. His death shocked even the most rabid of the Landleaguers into an understanding of the final outcome of their lawlessness. *Land.* 45

MORRISON, The REV. ALEXANDER. The young Rector of Budcombe, whom Mrs. Miles had selected as a husband for her foster child Bessy Pryor. *Launay*

MORRISON'S HOTEL. *See* Dublin

MORTON, MR. The Duke of Omnium's man of business, to whom Lord Silverbridge was frequently compelled to explain his losses, and ask for funds. *Duke* 14, 44-45

MORTON, The REV. CALEB. The Presbyterian minister in Bermuda who fought with and killed the convict Aaron Trow, after he had attacked Morton's fiancée, Anastasia Bergen. One of the principal characters in *Aaron Trow.*

MORTON, JOHN. The eldest son of the 1st Reginald Morton. ". . . married the daughter of a peer, stood for Parliament, had one son [John the second], and died before he was forty" (1:2:14). *Amer. Sen.* 2

MORTON, JOHN (3rd). The Secretary of the British Legation at Washington, and heir to Bragton Hall. He was engaged to Arabella Trefoil, and at his death forgave her for her attempt to marry Lord Rufford and left her a substantial legacy. The estate went to John's cousin Reginald. One of the principal characters in *The American Senator*.

MORTON, The HON. MRS. JOHN (2nd John). Daughter-in-law of the old Squire, who left Bragton Hall when Reginald (2nd) and his Canadian wife came there to live. She was the daughter of a viscount, a fact that she never forgot for a single moment. Appears frequently in *The American Senator*.

MORTON, MRS. LUCY. The actress mistress of George Hotspur, who supported him, advised him, and whom he eventually married. ". . . a woman who had been handsome,—dark, thin, with great brown eyes and thin lips and a long well-formed nose. She was a clever woman and well read too, and in every respect superior to the man whom she had condescended to love" (11:141). *Hotspur* 5, 11-12, 15, 18, 21-22, 24

MORTON, PETER. A distant relative whom Mrs. Morton sought to make the heir of Bragton because of her hatred for Reginald. *Amer. Sen.* 63-64

MORTON, REGINALD, Squire of Bragton. A generous host and an ardent hunter, but not a good financier. The family fortunes declined under his rule, rather less by his own extravagance than by his indulgence of his two sons, John and Reginald (2nd). *Amer. Sen.* 2

MORTON, REGINALD (2nd). He went to Oxford, then took a commission in the army and was sent to Canada. While there he married "the daughter of a bankrupt innkeeper in Montreal," and on his return to England made his home with his father at Bragton. *Amer. Sen.* 2

MORTON, REGINALD (3rd). Lived a great part of his youth in Germany, but on the death of his grandfather returned to Dillsborough, where he had been left various properties. Among them was Hoppet Hall, where he lived. On the death of his cousin John, he inherited Bragton Hall and married Mary Masters. ". . . a young-looking handsome man, with fair hair, cut short, and a light beard, which was always clipped. Though his mother had been an innkeeper's daughter in Montreal he had the Morton blue eyes and the handsome well-cut Morton nose. He was nearly six feet high, and strongly made" (1:5:50). One of the principal characters in *The American Senator*.

MOSS, MAHOMET M. A Jewish impresario from America, who launched Rachel O'Mahony in opera in London and wished to marry her. One of the principal characters in *The Landleaguers*.

MOULDER, MR. A commercial traveler for Hubbles and Grease, dealers in tea, coffee and brandy. ". . . short and fat;—so fat that he could not have seen his knees for some considerable time past. His face rolled in fat, as also did all his limbs. His eyes were large and bloodshot. He wore no beard, and therefor showed plainly the triple bagging of his fat chin. In spite of his overwhelming fatness, there was something in his face that was masterful and almost vicious" (1:6:39). *Orley* 6, 9, 16, 24, 42-43, 61, 67, 77

MOULDER, MRS. MARY ANNE. Sister of John Kenneby, whom she succeeded in marrying to Mrs. Smiley. "The work of her life consisted in sewing buttons on to Mr. Moulder's shirts, and seeing that his things were properly got up when he was at home" (1:24: 187). *Orley* 24, 43, 61

MOUNT FIDGETT, MARQUIS OF. A highly disreputable nobleman, whose death made it necessary for the Duke of Omnium, as Prime Minister, to recommend someone for the honor of the Garter. *Prime Min.* 64

MOUNT PLEASANT. A Jamaican plantation belonging to Maurice Cummings. *Sarah*

MOUNT STREET. *See* London

MOUNTAINEERS (club). *See* London

MOUNTFIDGET, LORD OF. The suitor for the hand of the gentle Euphemia, whom she nursed to health after he had been shot by a poisoned arrow. Hero of *The Gentle Euphemia.*

MOUNTJOY, LADY. Wife of Sir Magnus, and something of a virago. There were those who said that she was "of all women the most overbearing and impertinent. . . . She was large in figure, and painted well, and wore her diamonds with an air . . . declared to be majestic" (1:10:135). *Scarborough* 10, 15, 30, 46

MOUNTJOY, FLORENCE. Although her mother wished her to marry the rascally Mountjoy Scarborough, Florence had given her heart to the comparatively impecunious Harry Annesley, and after three volumes of constancy finally married him.

"In figure, form, and face she never demanded immediate homage by the sudden flash of her beauty. But when her spell had once fallen on a man's spirit it was not often that he could escape from it quickly. . . . Her voice was soft and low and sweet, and full at all times of harmonious words; but when she laughed it was like soft winds playing among countless silver bells. There was something in her touch which to men was almost divine. Of this she was all unconscious, but was as chary with her fingers as though it seemed that she could ill spare her divinity. In height she was a little above the common, but it was by the grace of her movements that the world was compelled to observe her figure. . . . her eyes were more than ordinarily bright, and when she laughed there seemed to stream from them some heavenly delight. . . . her hair was soft and smooth, and ever well dressed, and never redolent of peculiar odors" (1:10:124-25).

Heroine of *Mr. Scarborough's Family.*

MOUNTJOY, SIR MAGNUS. The British Minister in Brussels, and uncle of Florence Mountjoy, whose aid was sought to separate her from Harry Annesley by entertaining her for a protracted period at the Legation. "He was a stout, tall, portly old gentleman, sixty years of age . . . whom it was a difficulty to place on horseback, but who, when there, looked remarkably well" (1:10: 135). *Scarborough* 10, 12-15, 30, 45-46

MOUNTJOY, MRS. SARAH. Florence's mother, whose ambition was that her daughter should marry Mountjoy Scarborough because of his social position, although she knew he was a scoundrel and a gambler. One of the principal characters in *Mr. Scarborough's Family.*

MOWBRAY and MOPUS. London lawyers, who were considered by their professional brethren to be unscrupulous, as they proved themselves to be in acting for Lizzie Eustace in regard to the diamonds. *Eustace* 2, 4, 10-12, 31, 43

MOYDRUM. The family home of Laurence Fitzgibbon, in Ireland. *Finn* 13

MOYLAN, MR. A scheming lawyer at Dunmore, who was Anty Lynch's agent until bribed by Barry to perjure himself by charging the Kellys with conspiracy to obtain Anty's fortune. "He was an ill-made, ugly, stumpy man, about fifty; with a blotched face, straggling sandy hair, and grey shaggy whiskers. He wore a long, brown greatcoat, buttoned up to his chin, and this was the only article of wearing apparel visible upon him" (2:4:95). *Kellys* 3, 16-18

MOYTUBBER. One of the best coverts in Black Tom Daly's region, where the Landleaguers assembled to make it impossible for the "gentry" to hunt. *Land.* 11

MULREADY, MRS. The keeper of the disreputable inn at Mohill, where the trouble-makers of the countryside met to plan their revenge on the officers of the law. ". . . a strong, red-faced, indomitable-looking woman" (1:9:210). Her inn is frequently mentioned in *The Macdermots of Ballycloran.*

MUNDAY, CAPTAIN. The captain of the "Goldfinder," the boat on which John Caldigate sailed to New South Wales. *Caldigate* 5-7, 42

MUNICH. The location of the banking firm, the House of Heine Brothers, in the story of that name.

MUNSTER COURT. *See* London

MURRAY, ANNA. *See* Lovel, Lady Anna

MURRAY, JOSEPHINE. *See* Lovel, Countess

MUSSELBORO, AUGUSTUS. After the death of her husband, he married Mrs. Broughton. ". . . a sort of partner of Broughton's in the City. He wears a lot of chains, and has elaborate whiskers, and an elaborate waistcoat . . . and he doesn't wash his hands as often as he ought to do" (1:24:205). Appears frequently in *The Last Chronicle of Barset.*

MUTTERS, JOE. ". . . an insufferable clerk . . . at Plumstead Episcopi, who had lost all his teeth." Dr. Grantly tried to place him in Hiram's Hospital because he "hardly knew how to get rid of [him] by other means." *Warden* 2

NAG'S HEAD (inn). *See* Exeter

NANTES. Cathelineau was mortally wounded in the battle at Nantes, where the Vendeans were defeated. *Vendée* 14

NAPPIE, MR. An ardent huntsman, whose horse Frank Greystock rode all day, thinking it was one he had ordered sent to him. Mr. Nappie's indignation was considerable and vocal. *Eustace* 38-39, 41

NEARTHEWINDE, MR. The "celebrated parliamentary agent," who acted for Mr. Moffat when he contested the Barchester seat with Sir Roger Scatcherd. *Thorne* 15-17, 22

NECROPOLIS. The "college" in which those coming under the Fixed Period law spent their last year. *Fixed* 6

NEEFIT, MRS. Polly's mother, strong in the interest of Moggs as a son-in-law. Appears frequently in *Ralph the Heir.*

NEEFIT, POLLY. A strong-minded young woman, determined that her father should not make a "lady" of her through marriage with Ralph, the heir. Her choice of Ontario Moggs showed her good sense. ". . . as pretty a girl as you shall wish to see, in spite of a nose that was almost a pug nose, and a mouth that was a little large . . . her laughing dark eyes were full of good-humour. . . . Her complexion was perfect. . . . She was tall, and well made, —perhaps almost robust. She was good-humoured, somewhat given to frank coquetry and certainly fond of young men" (1:5:92-93). One of the principal characters in *Ralph the Heir*.

NEEFIT, THOMAS. The breeches-maker of Conduit Street to whom Ralph, the heir, was deeply in debt. He tried to buy the young Squire as a husband for his daughter Polly.

". . . a stout little man, with a bald head and somewhat protrusive eyes, whose manners to his customers contained a combination of dictatorial assurance and subservience, which he found to be efficacious in his peculiar business. On general subjects he would rub his hands, and bow his head, and agree most humbly with every word that was uttered. In the same day he would be a Radical and a Conservative, devoted to the Church and a scoffer at parsons, animated on behalf of stag-hounds and a loud censurer of aught in the way of hunting other than the orthodox fox. On all trivial outside subjects he considered it to be his duty as a tradesman simply to ingratiate himself; but in a matter of breeches he gave way to no man" (1:5:77-78).

One of the principal characters in *Ralph the Heir*.

NEGRO SOLDIERS' ORPHAN BAZAAR. A charity bazaar for the orphan children of the American Negro soldiers killed in the Civil War. Trollope fired an angry blast at all such affairs. *Mackenzie* 27

NERONI, JULIA. The only child of Paulo and Madeline Neroni, and granddaughter of the Rev. Dr. Vesey Stanhope. *Barchester* 11, 46

NERONI, SIGNORA MADELINE (Stanhope). The younger daughter of the Rev. Dr. Vesey Stanhope, who had married a dissolute Italian, been cruelly treated by him and returned to her father's house, a cripple, and with a daughter. She was selfish, self-centered and ruthless in her demand for attention from all male admirers.

"The beauty of her face was uninjured, and that beauty was of a peculiar kind. Her copious rich brown hair was worn in Grecian *bandeaux* round her head, displaying as much as possible of her forehead and cheeks. Her forehead, though rather low, was very beautiful from its perfect contour and pearly whiteness. Her eyes were long and large, and marvellously bright. . . . The eyelashes were long and perfect. . . . Her nose and mouth and teeth and chin and neck and bust were perfect" (1:9:125-26).

One of the principal characters in *Barchester Towers*.

NERONI, PAULO. The Italian whom Madeline Stanhope married, and of whom little good was known. ". . . a man of no birth and no property, a mere captain in the pope's guard . . . a man of harsh temper and oily manners, mean in figure, swarthy in face, and so false in words as to be hourly detected" (1:9:123). *Barchester* 9

NETHERCOATS. The small country house owned by John Grey, in Cambridgeshire, in the Isle of Ely. *Can You* 3, 10-11, 14, 30, 36

NEVER, NEVER,—NEVER, NEVER. A condensed novel in three volumes, after the manner of Bret Harte. In *Sheets for the Cradle*, vol. 1, nos. 1-6, Boston, 1875.

NOTES. *Sheets for the Cradle* was edited by Susan Hale in connection with, and for the aid of, the Massachusetts Infant Asylum Fair. Probably the only existing copy of Trollope's contribution is in the Boston Public Library. It is a burlesque on the central theme in *The Small House at Allington* and its continuation in *The Last Chronicle of Bar-*

set. Mary Tompkins is a caricature of Lily Dale, Trollope's favorite heroine; John Thomas of Johnny Eames; and the Rev. Abraham Dribble of Mr. Slope. Mr. Sadleir doubts its authenticity.

Plot. Mary Tompkins was sought in marriage by John Thomas, a young postal clerk who later became Postmaster-General, and by the Rev. Abraham Dribble, "a low-church scoundrel" who became Bishop of Rochester. She refused them both, and designed a coarse gray serge gown—"but up and down the collar and round the waist, and in and out of the plaits a curious device had been worked. The letters were not easy to decipher, but when they were read they ran as follows:—'Old Maid.' "

NEVERBEND, FIDUS. Sent with Alaric Tudor to examine the government interest in the tin mine "Wheal Mary Jane." ". . . an absolute dragon of honesty. His integrity was of that all-pervading nature, that he bristled with it as a porcupine does with its quills. . . . He was a stout reddish-faced gentleman, with round shoulders and huge whiskers, he was nearly bald, and wore spectacles . . ." (1:10:203). *Clerks* 7-10, 25-26, 32, 35-36

NEVERBEND, JACK. Son of President Neverbend, but opposed to him in the matter of the Fixed Period, largely because he was in love with Eva Crasweller, whose father would be the first to be "deposited" under that law. Hero of *The Fixed Period.*

NEVERBEND, JOHN. The President of Britannula, and protagonist of the Fixed Period law. He is the narrator of *The Fixed Period.*

NEVERBEND, LACTIMEL. A spinster sister of Fidus Neverbend, whose theories of social equality did not prevent her from toadying to Mrs. Val Scott "with distressing habitual humility. . . . She was altogether short in stature, and very short below the knee. She had fair hair and a fair skin, small bones and copious soft flesh. She had a trick of sighing gently in the evolutions of the waltz, which young men attributed to her softness of heart, and old ladies to her shortness of breath" (2: 9: 183). *Clerks* 25-26, 35

NEVERBEND, MRS. SARAH. Wife of the President of Britannula, who violently disagreed with him in regard to the Fixed Period, and was a highly competent curtain lecturer. *Fixed* 2, 4, 7, 10

NEVERBEND, UGOLINA. Sister of Fidus and Lactimel. "She was somewhat flat in her figure, looking as though she had been uncomfortably pressed into an unbecoming thinness of substance, and a corresponding breadth of surface. . . . read poetry and professed to write it . . . would have brought mankind back to their original nakedness, and have taught them to feed on the grasses of the field, so that the claims of the body, which so vitally opposed those of the mind, might remain unheeded and despised" (2:9: 182-83). *Clerks* 25-26, 35

NEVILLE, MRS. The widow of a brother of the Earl of Scroope, with whom he had quarreled. However, because of the death of his own son, her sons became the heirs to the title. "She was an old woman, with the relics of great beauty, idolizing her two sons for whom all her life had been a sacrifice, in weak health, and prepared, if necessary, to sit in silent awe at the feet of the Earl who had been so good to her boy" (1:3:54-55). *Eye* 3

NEVILLE, FRED. Nephew of the Earl of Scroope, and, because of the death of the Earl's son, his heir. A lieutenant in the cavalry. He seduced Kate O'Hara and was killed by her mother. ". . . a self-indulgent spoiled young man who had realized to himself no idea of duty in life" (1:12:204). One of the principal characters in *An Eye for an Eye.*

NEVILLE, JACK. Fred Neville's younger brother, in the Royal Engineers. After the death of Fred he became Earl of Scroope and married Sophia Mellerby. ". . . a tall, well-made fellow . . . very dark brown eyes, deeply set in his head, with large dark eyebrows. He wore his black hair very short, and had no beard whatever. His features were hard . . . [but] there was much about him in his gait and manner that claimed attention" (1:4:57-58). *Eye* 1, 4, 10-11, 18-20, 24

NEW BURLINGTON STREET. *See* London

NEW SOUTH WALES. The scene of the mining adventures in *John Caldigate.*

NEWGATE PRISON. *See* London

NEWSPAPERS and MAGAZINES in Trollope's works.

"Barsetshire Conservative Standard." *Thorne*

"Baslehurst Gazette and Totnes Chronicle." *Ray*

"Broughton Gazette." *Wortle*

"Carmarthen Herald." *Cousin*

"Christian Examiner." *Mackenzie*

"Daily Delight." *Clerks*

"Daily Record." *He Knew*

"Evening Pulpit." *Way We Live*

"Everybody's Business." *Wortle*

"Jupiter." *Warden, Barchester, Bertrams, Struggles*

"Leeds and Halifax Chronicle." *Orley*

"Literary Chronicle." *Way We Live*

"Morning Breakfast Table." *Way We Live*

"Panjandrum." *Panjandrum*

"People's Banner." *Finn, Redux, Prime Min.*

"Staines and Egham Gazette." *Duke*

NEWTON, GREGORY. The owner of Newton Priory, who attempted to buy from Ralph, the heir, the reversion of the estate so that he might leave it to his natural son, also named "Ralph." His sudden death on the hunting field prevented the conclusion of the contract. "The Squire himself was a very handsome man, tall, broad-shouldered, square-faced, with hair and whiskers almost snow-white. . . . He was a generous, passionate, persistent, vindictive and unforgiving man, a bitter enemy and a staunch friend" (1:11:192-93). One of the principal characters in *Ralph the Heir.*

NEWTON, The REV. GREGORY. Younger brother of Ralph, the heir, and Rector of Newton Peele. In love with Clarissa Underwood, whom he finally married. "He was a tall, slender man, somewhat narrow-chested, bright-eyed, with a kind-looking sweet mouth, a small well-cut nose, dark but not black hair, and a dimple on his chin. . . . A more generous fellow, who delighted more in giving, hesitated more in asking, more averse to begging though a friend of beggars, less self-arrogant, or self-seeking, or more devoted to his profession, never lived. . . . was loved and respected, and believed in by all men and women, rich and poor, who lived within knowledge of his name" (1: 14: 249-50). One of the principal characters in *Ralph the Heir.*

NEWTON, RALPH (the heir). A weak, charming, self-indulgent, but not essentially bad young man, who was saved from a completely mercenary marriage with Polly Neefit, the breeches-maker's daughter, by the death of his uncle. Principal character in *Ralph the Heir.*

NEWTON, RALPH (not the heir). The illegitimate son of Squire Gregory Newton, and greatly beloved by him. The father's sudden death prevented him from concluding the purchase of the reversion of the estate from Ralph, the heir. However, young Newton received a considerable fortune, and purchased a small place in Norfolk, to which he took Mary Bonner as his wife. "He was tall . . . and broad across the chest, and strong and active . . . had been educated abroad . . . German and French were the same to him as his native tongue" (1:11:194). One of the principal characters in *Ralph the Heir*.

NEWTON PEELE. The parish of which Gregory Newton was the rector; a part of the Newton Priory estate. *Ralph* 8, 10

NEWTON PRIORY. The estate of Gregory Newton, which at his death became the property of Ralph, the heir. The setting for much of *Ralph the Heir*; described in chapter 11.

NICKEM, SAMUEL. The clerk of Mr. Masters at Dillsborough, who collected the evidence against Goarly and Scrobby, accused of poisoning foxes in the Dillsborough Wood. ". . . a little red-haired man about forty, who wrote a good flourishing hand, could endure an immense amount of work, and drink a large amount of alcohol without being drunk. His nose and face were all over blotches, and he looked to be dissipated and disreputable. But, as he often boasted . . . he had not been detected in anything dishonest and . . . he was never too tipsy to do his work" (1:14:149). *Amer. Sen.* 3, 14, 19, 29, 32-33, 41, 48, 69

NIDDERDALE, LORD. The eldest son of the Marquis of Auld Reekie, and a cousin of the Duchess of Omnium. He became one of the directors of the South Central Pacific and Mexican Railroad, and offered to marry Marie Melmotte for half a million down. He refused the match when Marie's father tried to tie up the money, but later renewed his suit, having become attracted to Marie. He later married Lord Cantrip's daughter. ". . . not at all beautiful. He had a common-place rough face, with a turn-up nose, high cheek bones, no especial complexion, sandy-coloured whiskers, and bright laughing eyes" (*Way We Live* 2:57:45). Most prominent in *The Way We Live Now*; appears frequently as an acquaintance of Lord Silverbridge in *The Duke's Children*.

NIMROD CLUB. *See* London

NINA BALATKA; the story of a Maiden of Prague. Edinburgh and London, Blackwood and Sons, 1867. 2v. Originally published in *Blackwood's Magazine*, July 1866-Jan. 1867.

AUTHOR'S COMMENT. "It seemed to me that a name once earned carried with it too much favour. . . . To test this . . . I began a short story called *Nina Balatka*, which in 1866 was published anonymously. . . . [it] never rose sufficiently high in reputation to make its [the author's] detection a matter of any importance."—*Autobiography*, 2: 11: 10-11.

NOTES. "Its scene is laid in Prague, the old Bohemian capital. Here there exists a large Jewish colony. Among its members the distinction between Hebrew and Gentile is marked with such depth and bitterness that an intermarriage between the two races is considered degrading to each."—Escott, p. 231.

PLOT. Nina Balatka, the beautiful daughter of a bankrupt merchant of Prague, was in love with the son of her father's former Jewish partner, Stephen Trendellsohn, who had befriended them during her father's long illness and owned the house in which they lived.

Nina's wealthy relatives were determined to prevent her marriage to Anton and plotted to give him cause to doubt her devotion. The deeds to the Balatka house were in the possession of Karil Zamenoy, Nina's uncle, and when Anton asked for them he was told that Nina held them. Nina denied this and to prove it asked Anton to search her desk. When he found them there, she was overwhelmed by his belief that she had attempted to cheat him, and tried to throw herself from the Karls-brücke, but was rescued. Terrified by this near tragedy, a house servant confessed that he had been bribed to hide the deeds in the desk. Nina and Anton were reconciled and after their marriage moved to the more friendly atmosphere of Frankfurt.

NOBBLE. A mining town in New South Wales near John Caldigate's gold mine, about 300 miles west of Sydney. John lived there, in Henniker's Hotel, for some time. *Caldigate* 9-10

NOBLE JILT, The. A Comedy. London, Constable and Co., 1923. 184p.

Author's Comment. ". . . a comedy, partly in blank verse, and partly in prose. . . . The plot I afterward used in a novel called *Can You Forgive Her?* I believe that I did give the best of my intellect to the play, and I must own that when it was completed it pleased me much. . . . The dialogue . . . I think to be good, and I doubt whether some of the scenes be not the brightest and best work I ever did."—*Autobiography*, 1:5:113, 115.

Notes. Written in 1850, but not published until 1923. The prototype, very much removed, of the story of Alice Vavasor and John Grey. The play was probably never staged, although in *The Eustace Diamonds* Mrs. Carbuncle is reported to have attended a performance.

Plot. Margaret de Wynter, after becoming engaged to Count Upsel, a wealthy, elderly and scholarly gentleman, decided that life with him would be dull, and broke her engagement. At the instigation of his sister Helen, Margaret turned again to Mark Steinmark, a discarded suitor who had become the leader of the rebellious Republicans in Bruges in 1792. Mark, however, was so engrossed with the movement that he had no thought of marrying, and she renewed her engagement to Count Upsel.

Dramatis Personae:

Margaret de Wynter.
De Wynter—Her father.
Madame Brudo—Her aunt—a widow.
Count Upsel—Her betrothed.
Steinmark—Leader of the Republicans in Bruges.
Helen—His sister—friend of Margaret.
Belleroache—His friend.
Van Hoppen — Burgomaster of Bruges.
Jeannette — Servant of Madame Brudo.
Stoffle, Souch, Weazle—Three Republican soldiers.
Two Burgomasters of Bruges.

Scene: Bruges in 1792

NOGO, MR. The M P for Mile End, who promoted the Limehouse Bridge project in which Alaric Tudor lost a considerable amount of the Golightly money. *Clerks* 31-32, 34, 46

NOKES, BILL. A workman discharged by Heathcote and hired by Medlicot, and therefore a cause of enmity between the two men. When Nokes set fire to the sheep-ranch, Medlicot came to his neighbor's aid, and Nokes was driven out of the country. *Heathcote* 2-7, 9-11

NONINGSBY. The home of Judge Staveley, near Alston. The scene of much of the action in *Orley Farm*.

NORFOLK.

Beamington Hall. Bought by Ralph

Newton (not the heir) after the death of his father and his removal from Newton Priory. *Ralph*

OILYMEAD FARM. Owned by Mr. Cheesacre. *Can You*

PLAISTOW. Farm belonging to Will Belton. *Belton*

NORMAN, CUTHBERT. The older brother of Harry Norman, whose death made him the heir to Normansgrove. *Clerks* 37

NORMAN, HENRY ("Harry"). The oldest of the three clerks, and cousin of the Woodwards, to whom he introduced his two friends. He was a competent clerk in the Weights and Measures Office, from which he retired at the death of his older brother, which made him the heir of Normansgrove. He married Linda Woodward. ". . . the second son of a gentleman of small property in the north of England . . . a handsome man . . . tall and thin and dark, muscular in his proportions, and athletic in his habits . . . shy and reserved in his manners . . . nevertheless, frank and confident in those he trusted, and true in his friendships" (1:1:5, 8-9). One of the principal characters in *The Three Clerks.*

NORMAN, MRS. LINDA (Woodward). The second of Mrs. Woodward's daughters, who was in love with Alaric Tudor before his marriage to Gertrude, but came to love Harry Norman, and finally married him. One of the principal characters in *The Three Clerks.*

NORMANDY. Bessy Pryor was sent to Avranches when she refused to give up the idea of marriage with Philip Launay. *Launay*

NORMANSGROVE. The home of the Norman family, to which Harry fell heir on the death of his brother. Mentioned frequently in *The Three Clerks.*

NORTH BROUGHTON. Mr. Low represented the borough in Parliament. *Redux* 6

NORTHAMPTONSHIRE.

GORSE HALL. Lord Hampstead's hunting lodge. *Fay*

RUFFORD HALL. Home of Lord Rufford, where the American Senator was entertained. *Amer. Sen.*

WILLINGFORD BULL. Where Lord Chiltern kept his horses, and used by him as headquarters when hunting. *Finn, Redux*

NORTHCOTE, SIR STAFFORD (real person). Trollope admits in his *Autobiography* that he used "the feebly facetious name" of Sir Warwick West end to designate Sir Stafford, in *The Three Clerks.*

NORTHUMBERLAND STREET. *See* London

NORTON and FLICK. London solicitors for the young Earl Lovel. *Anna* 3, 6

NORWICH. Where Mr. Cheesacre and Captain Bellfield continued their wooing of Mrs. Greenow. *Can You* 19

NOT IF I KNOW IT. N.Y., Munro, 1883. (Seaside Library.) Originally published in *Life,* Christmas number, 1882, pp. 1-4.

PLOT. When Mr. and Mrs. Horton went to visit her brother at Hallam Hall at Christmas time, Mr. Horton asked George Wade, his brother-in-law, for the use of his name on a paper. Without asking the nature of the paper, but assuming it was a financial obligation, his host replied hastily, "Not if I know it." Mr. Horton was very angry, as the favor he asked was simply the signature of some one who had known him for a number of years. He determined to leave the house at once, but was persuaded by his wife that the

Christmas time was one of forgiveness. Under the influence of the Christmas sermon the next day, an apology was made, the request explained, and the two men became reconciled.

"NOT SO BLACK AS IT IS PAINTED." The title of a novel written by Maryanne Puffle. Her pretty sister-in-law, assuming the name "Josephine de Montmorenci," schemed to persuade the editor to publish it. *Josephine*

NUNCOMBE PUTNEY. Mrs. Stanbury and her daughters, Priscilla and Dorothy, lived in the Clock House, and shared it with Mrs. Trevelyan and Nora Rowley when Mrs. Trevelyan was estranged from her husband. The inn was the Stag and Antlers, where the landlady Mrs. Crockett professed to have "two clean bed-rooms." Mentioned frequently in *He Knew He Was Right.*

NUPPER, DR. ". . . a sporting old bachelor doctor who had the reputation of riding after the hounds in order that he might be ready for broken bones and minor accidents" (1:4:37). *Amer. Sen.* 4, 42

NUREMBERG. The setting for *Linda Tressel.*

OAKLEY, CAPT. CHARLES. The name given in *Did He Steal It?* to Major Henry Grantly. His part in the play parallels that in *The Last Chronicle of Barset,* except that he is the son of Mrs. Goshawk, rather than of the Archdeacon.

O'BRIEN, CHARLES. An impressionable young Irish sculptor, who took Mrs. General Talboys' sympathy over his unhappy marriage too literally, and was soundly snubbed. *Talboys*

O'BRIEN, KATE. Mrs. Bell's servant at her boardinghouse in Saratoga Springs. *Courtship*

O'CALLAGHAN, The REV. MR. An evangelical curate, popular with the ladies of the "pious set" at Littlebath. *Bertrams* 22, 29

O'CONNELL, DANIEL (real person). The trial of O'Connell and his associates for conspiracy and sedition is described in chapter 1 of *The Kellys and the O'Kellys.*

O'CONOR, THOMAS. An enthusiastic fox-hunter, father of Jack, Peter, Kate, Eliza and Fanny, who entertained Archibald Green in County Mayo. One of the principal characters in *The O'-Conors of Castle Conor.*

O'CONORS OF CASTLE CONOR, The. In *Tales of All Countries* [First Series], 1861. Originally published in *Harper's New Monthly Magazine,* May 1860.

Author's Comment. "I will not swear to every detail . . . but the main purport . . . is true."—*Autobiography,* 1:4:84.

Notes. "*The O'Conors,* a transcript of his own early Irish observations, had a remarkable American success, partly because a certain adventurous breeziness of movement as of style exactly suited a public whose passing taste had for the moment been more or less formed, not only by Charles Lever, but by those who had been before him, as Fenimore Cooper and Captain Marryat."—Escott, p. 271.

Plot. Archibald Green, on a business trip to County Mayo, contrived, at a fox-hunt, to scrape acquaintance with Thomas O'Conor, well known for his hospitality. The hoped-for invitation was so immediately given that a return to the inn for clothing was impossible, and, on learning that the daughters of the house were planning a dance, Green ordered his dancing pumps sent from the inn. Instead, some clumsy hobnailed boots arrived, which he forced the old butler to exchange for his down-at-the-heel slippers.

The clatter of the boots while the butler served dinner, his grimaces of pain because they were too small, and finally a clatter of broken dishes as the poor servant tripped over his own feet, made an explanation imperative. The family received the story as an excellent joke, and the dancing was postponed until the pumps could be delivered by special messenger.

O'DWYER, MR. Brother of Mick and owner of the Kanturk Hotel in Cork. "He was a fat, thickset man, with a good-humoured face, a flattened nose, and a great aptitude for stable occupations" (1:13:269). *Castle Rich.* 13

O'DWYER, FANNY. A barmaid at Kanturk Hotel in Cork, and at one time attracted by Aby Mollett. Niece of the Rev. Bernard McCarthy. *Castle Rich.* 6, 13, 17, 23

O'DWYER, MICK. The proprietor of a public-house in Kanturk. Mrs. Mick ". . . was fat, very; by no means fair, and perhaps something over forty" (2:3:50). *Castle Rich.* 13, 17, 23

O'HARA, CAPTAIN. Having served a term of imprisonment for swindling in France, he returned to Ireland to cadge from his wife. Learning of Fred Neville's affection for his daughter, he blackmailed Fred's family into giving him a competence for life. One of the principal characters in *An Eye for an Eye.*

O'HARA, MRS. Mother of Kate. After Fred Neville had seduced her daughter and refused to marry her, in a fit of insanity Mrs. O'Hara killed him by pushing him over a cliff. She spent the rest of her life in an asylum where she continually tried to justify her act with the words, "An eye for an eye." One of the principal characters in *An Eye for an Eye.*

O'HARA, KATE. A beautiful and well-educated Irish girl, living with her mother in poverty in County Clare. She fell in love with Fred Neville, but he refused to marry her when he came into a title. Her illegitimate child died, and she went to France, where her scapegrace father was living from money obtained by blackmailing her lover's family. Heroine of *An Eye for an Eye.*

OILYMEAD FARM. The farm belonging to Mr. Cheesacre, in Norfolk, of which he hoped to make Mrs. Greenow the mistress. *Can You* 9, 14, 19, 31, 39-40, 47

O'KELLY, The HON. MRS. Mother of the O'Kellys, ". . . a very small woman, with no particularly developed character, and perhaps no very general utility" (2:7:154). *Kellys* 21, 39

O'KELLY, AUGUSTA and SOPHIA ("Guss" and "Sophy"). Lord Ballindine's sisters. ". . . they were both pretty good-natured girls—one with dark brown and the other light brown hair: they both played the harp badly, sung tolerably, danced well, and were very fond of nice young men" (2:7:155). *Kellys* 21, 39

O'KELLY, FRANCIS JOHN MOUNTMORRIS. *See* Ballindine, Lord

O'LAUGHER, MR. A Dublin attorney, who acted as Mr. O'Malley's assistant in Thady Macdermot's trial for the murder of Myles Ussher. *Macdermots* 29-32

OLD BAILEY CRIMINAL COURT. *See* London

OLD MAN'S LOVE, An. Edinburgh and London, Blackwood and Sons, 1884. 2v.

PLOT. John Gordon, a young man of good birth and education but no money, fell in love with Mary Lawrie, but before he offered himself, Mary's stepmother ordered him from the house, believing that since Mary had no fortune she must marry someone with a proper income. Determined to acquire money so that he might be accepted, Gordon went to South Africa, where in a few years he made a moderate fortune in the diamond mines. On his return to England he learned that the stepmother had died, and that Mary had been given a home with her father's warm friend William Whittlestaff.

Mary had been received with some reluctance, as Mr. Whittlestaff was an elderly bachelor whose pattern of life did not include the presence of a young girl in his staid ménage. However, he soon found himself in love with her and asked her to be his wife. She confessed her love for John Gordon, but admitted that he had never spoken of his love for her and that she had not heard from him for three years.

On the day after she had promised to marry her benefactor, John returned, only to learn that he was too late. Mr. Whittlestaff was reluctant to give her up as he felt that she would be safer with him, but on mature thought he accused himself of selfishness in holding her to her word when he knew that for years she had loved the younger man. Accordingly, he sought John out and told him he would release Mary from her engagement, generously offering his assistance in establishing them in their new life together.

"OLD STICK IN THE MUD." A gold mine at Nobble, New South Wales, owned by Timothy Crinkett. *Caldigate* 9-10, 24

OLDESCHOLE, MR. The Secretary of the Internal Navigation Office. *Clerks* 2, 6, 18, 27-28, 45

O'MAHONY, GERALD. An Irish-American agitator, who believed in the cause of the Landleaguers, but did not approve their methods. He became MP for County Cavan. One of the principal characters in *The Landleaguers.*

O'MAHONY, RACHEL. An American girl with a fine voice, who went to Ireland with her father, who was interested in alleviating the distress of the Irish tenant class. She met and fell in love with Frank Jones, but when she became successful in opera in London, Frank refused to marry her and live on her salary—his own income having been wiped out by the Landleaguers. She lost her voice and, repudiating her later engagement to Lord Castlewell, returned to Frank. "She was very fair, and small and frail . . . and the colour on her face was so evanescent that he who watched her was inclined to think that she herself was like her colour. . . . Her beauty was all but perfect" (1:6:96, 98). Heroine of *The Landleaguers.*

O'MALLEY, MR. The Dublin lawyer for the defense at Thady Macdermot's trial for the murder of Myles Ussher. *Macdermots* 29-32

O'MEAGHER, MR. ". . . the member for Athlone, who had just made a grand speech to the people at Athenry . . . [having] spent three glorious weeks in New York, and, having practiced the art of speaking on board the steamer as he returned . . . the gist of the truths had been chiefly this:—that if a man did not pay his rent, but kept his money in his pocket, he manifestly did two good things; he enriched himself, and he so far pauperized the landlord, who was naturally his enemy." Used by Trollope as an example of the Irish-Americans chiefly responsible for the violence caused by the Landleaguers. *Land.* 11

OMNIUM, DUCHESS OF. Glencora MacCluskie, the charming and irrepressible heiress of the Lord of the Isles, became the wife of Plantagenet Palliser, although she loved the worthless Burgo Fitzgerald. Unhappy in her marriage because of her husband's cold and austere nature, and his preoccupation with political affairs, she did her best, by lavish entertaining at Gatherum Castle and Matching Priory, and formal dinners in town, to aid him in his political career, frequently to his great embarrassment. When the Coalition government fell, she and the Duke, with their three children, Lord Silverbridge, Lord Gerald and Lady Mary Palliser, traveled for a year on the Continent, where she became ill, and died soon after their return.

"She was a fair girl, with bright blue eyes and short wavy flaxen hair, very soft to the eye. Lady Glencora was short in stature, and her happy round face lacked, perhaps, the highest grace of female beauty. But there was ever a smile upon it which it was very pleasant to look at; and the intense interest with which she would dance, and talk, and follow up every amusement that was offered her, was very charming" (*Allington* 2:25:265).

"Lady Glencora is the essence of all that Trollope found adorable in woman. She is small of stature . . . she is beautiful, she is gay, a lively 'rattle' but no fool, a lady with plenty of dignity when she wishes, much spirit and fire and fun, a heart, and not too heavily weighted down with principles."—Walpole, p. 102.

Most prominent in *Can You Forgive Her?, The Eustace Diamonds, Phineas Finn, Phineas Redux* and *The Prime Minister*; briefly in *Allington* 55; *Last Chron.* 38-39; *Amer. Sen.* 36, 38, 40, 44; and *Mackenzie* 27

OMNIUM, DUKE OF. As Plantagenet Palliser, he was a hard-working member of the House of Commons, primarily interested in decimal coinage. By temperament and habit the polar opposite of the old Duke, avoiding society, and deploring the ostentatious display of his wealth so dearly loved by his Duchess. He served under Mr. Gresham and Mr. Mildmay as Chancellor of the Exchequer until the death of the old Duke sent him into the House of Lords, when, to remain in the Cabinet, he became President of the Board of Trade, and later Prime Minister. After the death of the Duchess he struggled with the financial and matrimonial affairs of his three children, and when their careers were established, returned to public service as President of the Council.

"He was a tall thin man . . . with nothing in his appearance that was remarkable. It was a face that you might see and forget . . . [but] showing intellect in the forehead, and much character in the mouth. The eyes too, though not to be called bright, had always something to say for themselves, looking as though they had real meaning. . . . He was born in the purple, noble himself, and heir to the highest rank as well as one of the greatest fortunes in the country . . . and yet he devoted himself to work with the grinding energy of a young penniless barrister labouring for a penniless wife, and did so without any motive more selfish than that of being counted in the roll of the public servants of England" (*Can You* 1:22:177; 1:24:185).

"By no amount of description or asservation could I succeed in making any reader understand how much these characters [Plantagenet Palliser in particular], with their belongings, have been to me . . . or how frequently I have used them for the expression of my political or social convictions. . . . and as I have not been able to speak from the benches of the House of Commons, or to thunder from platforms, or to be efficacious as a lecturer, they have served me as safety-valves by which to deliver my soul."—*Autobiography,* 1: 10:240-41.

Prominent in all six volumes of the Parliamentary series; briefly in *Allington* 23-24, 26, 43, 55

OMNIUM, DUKE OF (The old Duke). Uncle of Plantagenet Palliser, who was his heir. Haughty and unapproachable, he was the embodiment of the ducal tradition.

"He rarely went near the presence of majesty, and when he did so, he did it merely as a disagreeable duty incident to his position. . . . the Queen might be queen so long as he was the Duke of Omnium. Their revenues were about the same, with the exception, that the Duke's were his own. . . . In person he was a plain, thin man, tall, but undistinguished in appearance, except that there was a gleam of pride in his eye which seemed every moment to be saying 'I am the Duke of Omnium.' He was unmarried, and, if report said true, a great debauchee" (*Thorne* 2:1:11-12).

Appears frequently in *Framley Parsonage, Phineas Finn* and *Phineas Redux*; briefly in *Can You* 18, 22-23, 25, 73; *Thorne* 1, 15, 17, 19, 46; *Eustace* 47, 54, 61-62, 80; and *Allington* 23, 43, 55

ONGAR, LORD. A thoroughly disreputable, elderly but wealthy nobleman, who married Julia Brabazon and, after treating her with malicious cruelty, drank himself to death. *Claverings* 1-3

ONGAR, JULIA (Brabazon), LADY. Sister of Lady Hermione Clavering. Although in love with Harry Clavering, she sold herself for wealth and position to an elderly debauchee who, after treating her cruelly, drank himself to death within a year of their marriage. She returned to London, accompanied by Count Pateroff and his sister Sophie Gordeloup, who sponged on her and made her life a burden. Ignoring the fact that Harry Clavering was engaged to marry Florence Burton, she tried to attract him again, but failed.

"Julia was tall, with a high brow, a glorious complexion, a nose as finely modelled as though a Grecian sculptor had cut it, a small mouth, but lovely in its curves, and a chin that finished and made perfect the symmetry of her face. Her neck was long, but graceful as a swan's, her bust was full, and her whole figure like that of a goddess" (1:3:29).

One of the principal characters in *The Claverings.*

ONGAR PARK. A beautiful country estate in Surrey in which, after her husband's death, Lady Ongar had a life interest. She was very unhappy there and returned it to the family. *Claverings* 3, 12-13, 38, 42, 45

ONSLOW, HERBERT. A young Englishman, who failed at Cambridge and was sent by his family to Munich, where, after an apprenticeship, he was to be received as a partner into the firm of the House of Heine Brothers. *Heine*

ONSLOW CRESCENT. *See* London

OPTIMIST, MR. Followed Sir Raffle Buffle as Chairman of the General Committee. "A little man, hardly more than five feet high, with small but honest-looking eyes, and close cut hair . . . an industrious little gentleman, very well-connected, who had served the public all his life" (1:28:285). *Allington* 28, 35, 45, 48, 60

ORIEL, MRS. BEATRICE (Gresham). Frank Gresham's favorite sister, and his confidante in regard to his love for Mary Thorne. *Thorne* 4, 21, 26-27, 33, 42, 47

ORIEL, The REV. CALEB. The Rector at Greshamsbury, with whom all the girls were in love. He married Frank Gresham's sister Beatrice. ". . . not a common, everyday parson, but had points about him which made him quite fit to associate with the Earl's daughter . . . a man of family and fortune . . . dark-haired, good-looking . . . of polished manners, agreeable in society" (*Thorne* 1:6:132; 3:2:19-20). Most prominent in *Doctor Thorne* 6, 32, 42, 45; briefly in *Last Chron.* 50, 54-55, 61, where he sat on the Clerical Commission in the Crawley case.

ORIEL, PATIENCE. Sister of the Rev. Caleb Oriel, with whom she lived. Bridesmaid for Augusta and Beatrice Gresham, and later for Mary Thorne. "Miss Oriel was a very pretty girl. . . . She had dark hair, large round dark eyes, a nose a little too broad, a pretty mouth, a beautiful chin, and, as we have said before, a large fortune. . . . She was goodhumoured, ladylike, lively, neither too clever nor too stupid, belonging to a good family . . ." (1:6:128). *Thorne* 6, 11, 23, 26, 32, 47

ORLEY FARM. The home of Lady Mason and her son Lucius, twenty-five miles from London. The ownership of the farm and the resulting trials are the main theme of *Orley Farm*. The original was the farmhouse in which Trollope lived as a boy.

ORLEY FARM. London, Chapman and Hall, 1862. 2v.

AUTHOR'S COMMENT. "Most of those among my friends who . . . are competent to form an opinion on the subject, say that this is the best I have written. . . . The plot . . . is probably the best I have ever made; but it has the fault of declaring itself, and thus coming to an end too early in the book. . . . The hunting is good. The lawyer's talk is good. Mr. Moulder carves his turkey admirably, and Mr. Kantwise sells his tables and chairs with spirit. I do not know that there is a dull page in the book."—*Autobiography,* 1:9:222-23.

NOTES. While it is primarily a tragedy of misdirected maternal love, the book contains much of the best Trollopian humor, and includes the portrait of his finest gentleman, Sir Peregrine Orme. The legal aspects of the Orley Farm case have been severely and justly criticized.

PLOT. Sir Joseph Mason was an old man when Lucius, son of his second wife, was born. He had lived for some years at Orley Farm, a small property near London, which was left by a codicil to his will to this child. The elder son, not content with the large property that had come to him, contested the will but lost his case.

When Lucius, after studying scientific agriculture in Germany, took over the management of Orley Farm, he canceled certain leases, one of which was held by Samuel Dockwrath, a shyster lawyer and son-in-law of the attorney who had drawn Sir Joseph's will. Incensed at the loss of his leasehold, he re-examined the papers relating to the ownership of the property, and found presumptive evidence that the codicil had been forged. On presenting this evidence to the older son, the suit was renewed.

Lady Mason, mother of Lucius, had been on terms of intimacy with her neighbor Sir Peregrine Orme of The Cleeve and his daughter-in-law Edith Orme. When the case was reopened Sir Peregrine gave Lady Mason his full support and, that he might shield her, asked her to marry him. She was deeply touched, but knowing her guilt could not accept him. When the case came to trial she was acquitted, but Lucius returned Orley Farm to the older son.

ORME, MRS. EDITH. Widow of Sir Peregrine's only son, who lived at The Cleeve, where she was a neighbor and warm friend of Lady Mason of Orley Farm. "She had been a great beauty, very small in size and delicate in limb, fair haired, with soft blue wondering eyes, and a dimpled cheek" (1:3:23). One of the principal characters in *Orley Farm.*

ORME, PEREGRINE. Grandson and heir of Sir Peregrine, sent down from Oxford after releasing a bag of rats in hall at dinner-time. He adored his grandfather and accepted him as a model of all the gentlemanly virtues. An unsuccessful suitor for the hand of Madeline Staveley. One of the principal characters in *Orley Farm.*

ORME, SIR PEREGRINE. One of the finest of Trollope's gentlemen. The lord of the manor and owner of The Cleeve, who befriended Lady Mason and desired to marry her.

"The relations of Sir Peregrine and [Lady Mason] are worked with a fine courtesy and gentleness."—Walpole, p. 129.

"He was a fine, handsome English gentleman with white hair, keen grey eyes, a nose slightly aquiline. . . . He was tall, but had lost something of his height from stooping,—was slight in his form, but well made, and vain of the smallness of his feet and the whiteness of his hands. He was generous, quick-tempered, and opinionated; generally very mild to those who would agree with him and submit to him, but intolerant of contradiction, and conceited as to his experience of the world, and the wisdom which he had thence derived" (1:3:22).

One of the principal characters in *Orley Farm.*

OSBORNE, COL. FREDERIC. A friend of Sir Marmaduke Rowley, who enjoyed a reputation in London of being too interested in the wives of his friends. Louis Trevelyan objected to his acquaintance with his wife, and this jealousy was the principal cause of contention between the two. ". . . a bachelor, a man of fortune, a Member of Parliament, and one who carried his half century of years lightly on his shoulders" (1:1:9). One of the principal characters in *He Knew He Was Right.*

OSTEND. Where Sir Thomas Tringle found his daughter Gertrude after she had eloped with Captain Batsby. *Ayala* 48

OUTERMAN, NATHANIEL. A tailor, whose unpaid bill landed Charley Tudor in the spunginghouse. *Clerks* 28

OUTHOUSE, MRS. Sister of Sir Marmaduke Rowley, who believed no wrong of Mrs. Trevelyan, and cordially hated her husband. *He Knew* 29, 32, 52-53, 60

OUTHOUSE, The REV. OLIPHANT. The poor-spirited Rector of St. Diddulph's-in-the-East, who grudgingly provided a home for his wife's nieces after Emily Trevelyan and her husband had parted. *He Knew* 29, 32, 41, 52-53, 59-60

OVAL, SIR KENNINGTON. A member of the British cricket team playing in Britannula, who fell in love with Eva Crasweller. ". . . a good-looking young aristocrat, with plenty of words, but nothing special to say for himself" (1:5:130). *Fixed* 5-8, 11

OWEN, The REV. WILLIAM. A minor canon in the Hereford Cathedral, who married Isabel Broderick. Her uncle had hoped to leave his estate to a man of his family name, and, when Isabel became heir to Llanfeare, her husband changed his name to Indefer Jones. *Cousin* 2, 4, 11-12, 16, 19, 23-24

OXFORD UNIVERSITY STUDENTS.

Amedroz, Charles. *Beltons*

Arabin, Francis, at Balliol and Lazarus. *Barchester*

Archer, Maurice. *Kirkby*
Barham, Father John. *Way We Live*
Bertram, George, at Trinity. *Bertrams*
Blake, Montague, at Exeter. *Old Man*
Carstairs, Lord. *Wortle*
Crawley, Josiah, at Lazarus. *Last Chron.*
Fenwick, Frank. *Vicar*
Fitzgerald, Herbert. *Castle Rich.*
Forrest, Sergeant. *Heathcote*
Germain, Lord George. *Popenjoy*
Gilmore, Harry. *Vicar*
Gordon, John. *Old Man*
Graham, Felix. *Orley*
Grantly, Theophilus. *Warden, Barchester*
Gwynne, Dr., Master of Lazarus. *Warden, Barchester*
Hampstead, Lord. *Fay*
Harcourt, Sir Henry, at Trinity. *Bertrams*
Jones, Henry. *Cousin*
Lufton, Lord. *Framley*
Mackenzie, Jack. *Mackenzie*
Mackenzie, John. *Mackenzie*
Mainwaring, The Rev. Mr., at Christchurch. *Amer. Sen.*
Maule, Maurice. *Redux*
Mayfair, Duke of, at Christchurch. *Amer. Sen.*
Montague, Paul. *Way We Live*
Morton, Reginald. *Amer. Sen.*
Norman, Henry, at Brazenose. *Clerks*
O'Kelly, Francis (later Lord Ballindine). *Kellys*
Oriel, Caleb. *Thorne*
Orme, Peregrine, at Christchurch. *Orley*
Peacocke, Henry, at Trinity. *Wortle*
Silverbridge, Lord, at Christchurch. *Duke*
Robarts, Mark. *Framley*
Stanbury, Hugh. *He Knew*
Staple, Tom, at Lazarus. *Barchester*
Staveley, Augustus. *Orley*
Tregear, Frank, at Christchurch. *Duke*
Trevelyan, Louis. *He Knew*
Tringle, Tom. *Ayala*
Western, George. *Kept Dark*
Wharton, Everett. *Prime Min.*
Wilkinson, Arthur, at Balliol. *Bertrams*
Wortle, Jeffrey, at Exeter. *Wortle*

OXFORDSHIRE.

LUFTON PARK was in Oxfordshire. *Framley*

George Vavasor had a "little establishment" near Roebury. *Can You*

OXNEY COLNE. A parish in Devonshire, of which the Rev. Saul Woolsworthy was rector. *Parson*

PACKER. Lord Trowbridge's steward at Bullhampton. *Vicar* 35, 38, 43, 57, 60

PAKENHAM VILLAS. *See* Barchester

PALESTINE. The setting for *A Ride Across Palestine*; and chapters 6-11 of *The Bertrams.*

PALLISER, ADELAIDE. A distant relative of Plantagenet Palliser, a member of the least well-endowed branch of the family, who was a great friend of Violet Effingham. She was in love with Gerard Maule, as poor as herself, and was befriended by Mme. Max Goesler, who arranged that a large legacy left to her by the old Duke should be made over to Adelaide, thus allowing the young people to marry. ". . . a tall, fair girl, exquisitely made, and carrying always a warranty of her birth in her appearance . . ." (*Redux* 1:18:142). Most prominent in *Phineas Redux*; briefly, with her husband, as guests of Lord and Lady Chiltern, in *Duke* 62-63

PALLISER, EUPHEMIA and IPHIGENIA THEODATA. Two elderly cousins of Plantagenet Palliser, very proud of their relationship, and of their annual invitation to visit at Matching Priory. In Chapters 69 and 79 Euphemia is called Sophy. *Can You* 22-23, 28, 33, 37, 42, 48, 69, 79

PALLISER, LORD GERALD. The second son of the Duke of Omnium, who was entered at Cambridge but sent down when he attended the Derby without permission, to see his brother's horse "Prime Minister" run. In *The American Senator*, it is reported that ". . . young Palliser is to get Slade's berth at Lisbon" (2:1:1). This is probably Lord Gerald, and the post noted was in the diplomatic service. One of the principal characters in *The Duke's Children*.

PALLISER, LADY GLENCORA. The only reference Trollope makes to her is on one occasion when her father the Duke and Phineas Finn met their two wives, ". . . in a pony carriage, and the little Lady Glencora, the Duchess's eldest daughter, was sitting between them" (*Prime Min.* 4:18:131). In *The Duke's Children* it is stated definitely that there were three children, Lord Silverbridge, Lady Mary Palliser and Lord Gerald Palliser.

PALLISER, LADY GLENCORA (MacCluskie). *See* Omnium, Duchess of

PALLISER, JEFFREY. Cousin of Plantagenet Palliser, who would have been his heir had no son been born to Lady Glencora. *Can You* 22-28, 79

PALLISER, MRS. JEFFREY. At the death of the Duchess of Omnium, Mrs. Palliser offered to act as duenna for Lady Mary Palliser. *Duke* 1

PALLISER, LADY MARY. The Duke of Omnium's youngest child, and only daughter. After the death of her mother she was put in the charge of Mrs. Finn, and later of Lady Cantrip. Her love for Frank Tregear, known to her mother who approved of it, but violently opposed by her father, forms one of the central themes in *The Duke's Children*.

PALLISER, PLANTAGENET. *See* Omnium, Duke of

PALMER, MR. Mrs. Winterfield's Perivale attorney. *Belton* 9-10

PANAMA. The destination of Emily Viner, in *The Journey to Panama*.

Sir Roger Scatcherd was "declared contractor for cutting a canal from sea to sea, through the Isthmus of Panama." (1:9:89) *Thorne* 9

PANDEMONIUM (club). *See* London

PANJANDRUM, The. In *An Editor's Tales*, 1870. Originally published in *Saint Paul's Magazine*, Jan.-Feb., 1870.

Plot. An aspiring literary group planned to publish a review called "The Panjandrum," and met week after week to work out the details, but so many jealousies and misunderstandings arose that the plan was abandoned.

PARADISE ROW. *See* Holloway

PARAGON (apartment house). *See* Littlebath

PARIS. The setting for part of the novel of the French Revolution, *La Vendée*.

PARK LANE. *See* London

PARKER, SEXTUS. A moneylender of dubious connections and shady reputation, with whom Ferdinand Lopez became involved, and whom he finally ruined. *Prime Min.* 1, 13, 25, 30, 45-47, 54, 69

PARKER, MRS. SEXTUS. A vulgar but good-hearted woman, very pitiful in her misfortune when she applied to Emily Lopez to save her husband from Ferdinand Lopez. *Prime Min.* 45-47, 55, 69

PARKER'S HOTEL. *See* London

PARSON'S DAUGHTER OF OXNEY COLNE, The. In *Tales of All Countries*, Second Series, 1863. Originally published in *The London Review*, March 2, 1861.

PLOT. Capt. John Broughton hoped to be the heir of his wealthy aunt Miss Le Smyrger, and journeyed down to Devonshire to make friends with her. While there he met and fell in love with Patience Woolsworthy, the rector's high-spirited but portionless daughter. Patience returned his love, but indignantly broke her engagement when he attempted to teach her that marriage to him would considerably raise her in the social scale.

PATAGONIA. On his return to England from the British Embassy in the United States, Reginald Morton was appointed Ambassador to Patagonia. On his death Mounser Green received the position, and he and Arabella Trefoil went there immediately after their marriage. *Amer. Sen.* 28, 65

PATEROFF, EDOUARD, COUNT. An old friend of Lord Ongar, to whom he falsely declared that he had been intimate with Lady Ongar. After Lord Ongar's death, he followed Lady Julia to England, declaring that it was her husband's wish that they should marry. He and his sister succeeded in making Lady Ongar's life miserable.

"He was a fair man, with a broad, fair face, and very light blue eyes; his forehead was low, but broad; he wore no whiskers, but bore on his lip a heavy moustache, which was not grey, but perfectly white. . . . He was well made, active and somewhat broad in the shoulders, though rather below the middle height. But for a certain ease of manner which he possessed, accompanied by something of restlessness in his eye, anyone would have taken him for an Englishman" (1:14:166).

One of the principal characters in *The Claverings*.

PATTERSON, SIR WILLIAM. The Whig Solicitor-General, leading counsel for the young Earl Lovel. He became convinced that the claim of the Countess was valid and advised a compromise. Appears frequently in *Lady Anna*.

PAUL, The REV. MR. A high-church clergyman in Littlebath, whose "name stank in the nostrils of Mrs. Stumfold." *Mackenzie* 12

PAWKINS'S (hotel). *See* London

PEACOCK. The inn in the Brunnenthal Valley near Innsbruck, owned by Frau Frohmann. *Frohmann*

PEACOCKE, MRS. ELLA (Beaufort). An American girl, who, believing that her despicable husband was dead, married Henry Peacocke. When he came back, she and Mr. Peacocke went to England, where they were employed at Dr. Wortle's school. The first husband's brother followed them and attempted to blackmail them, but finally admitted that his brother had since died. Dr. Wortle performed another ceremony, and they were at last legally married.

"She was a woman something over thirty years of age when she first came to Bowick, in the very pride and bloom of woman's beauty. Her complexion was dark and brown. . . . Her eyes were brown, and her eye-brows black, and perfectly regular. Her hair was dark and very glossy, and always dressed as simply as the nature of a woman's head will allow. Her features were regular, but with a great show of strength" (1:2:27-28).

One of the principal characters in *Dr. Wortle's School*.

PEACOCKE, The REV. HENRY. "An ex-Fellow of Trinity" and an assistant master in Dr. Wortle's school, to which, because of the question as to the legality of his marriage, he brought trouble. ". . . was a small wiry man, anything but robust in appearance, but still capable of great bodily exertion. He was a great walker. Labour in the school never seemed to fatigue him. . . . He was a constant reader, and could pass from one kind of mental work to another without fatigue. . . . Though he was a poor man, his own small classical library was supposed to be a repository of all that was known about Latin and Greek" (1:2:26). One of the principal characters in *Dr. Wortle's School.*

PECKHAM. *See* London

PEGWELL BAY. The seaside resort where Marion Fay died. *Fay* 51, 56-57, 59, 64

PENGE, CAROLINE. *See* Rufford, Caroline (Penge), Lady

PENRITH. The nearest town to Thwaite Hall, in Westmoreland. *Mistletoe*

PENWETHER, ELEANOR, LADY. Wife of Sir George. She made it her duty to provide a suitable (i.e. wealthy) wife for her favorite brother, Lord Rufford. *Amer. Sen.* 17, 21-25, 45, 67-68

PENWETHER, SIR GEORGE. Brother-in-law of Lord Rufford, and his adviser in escaping the matrimonial advances of Arabella Trefoil. "He was a man of moderate wealth, very much respected, and supposed to be possessed of almost infinite wisdom. He was one of those few human beings who seem never to make a mistake" (2:18:194). *Amer. Sen.* 45, 48, 57, 61, 66-69, 74

"PEOPLE'S BANNER." A widely read scandal sheet edited by Quintus Slide, which attacked in turn Phineas Finn, Mr. Kennedy and Plantagenet Palliser. *Finn* 26, 28, 33, 47, 75; *Redux* 22, 27-28, 61, 80; *Prime Min.* 18, 38, 50-51, 56, 62

PEPÉ, CARLO. A young Venetian advocate, who fought under Garibaldi, and refused to give his consent to the engagement of his sister to one of the Austrian officers until the Italians should be victorious. One of the principal characters in *The Last Austrian Who Left Venice.*

PEPÉ, NINA. In love with Hubert von Vincke, an Austrian officer stationed in Venice during the Austrian occupation. When they withdrew and her brother gave his consent to her engagement, she searched through the hospitals until she found her wounded lover, nursed him back to health and eventually married him. Heroine of *The Last Austrian Who Left Venice.*

PEPPERCORN, HICKORY. A brewer in Plumplington, who thought his daughter Polly too good to marry Jack Hollycombe, the malt salesman. One of the principal characters in *Two Heroines of Plumplington.*

PEPPERCORN, POLLY. The favorite daughter of Hickory, and skillful in managing him. One of the principal characters in *Two Heroines of Plumplington.*

PEPPERMINT, MR. An habitué of the Cat and Whistle; a widower with three young children, looking about for a mother for them. He chose Norah Geraghty, the pretty Irish barmaid. *Clerks* 20, 27, 31

PERCIVAL, LORD. Son of Earl Grex and brother of Lady Mabel Grex. He lived on his winnings from the card table. Lord Gerald Palliser once lost £3,400 to him in the course of one house party. *Duke* 9, 19-20, 60

PERCYCROSS (Percy St. Cross). Sir Thomas Underwood contested Percycross in an election largely autobiographical of Trollope's own experience at Beverley. The inn was the Cordwainers' Arms, where Ontario Moggs had his headquarters. *Ralph* 20-32, 39-40, 44, 51

PERIVALE. The home of Mrs. Winterfield, a small town between Taunton and Salisbury, "which I maintain to be the dullest little town in England." Captain Aylmer represented Perivale in Parliament. The setting for many of the scenes in *The Belton Estate.*

PERSIFLAGE, LORD. "He was, above all, a man of the world. He had been Ambassador at St. Petersburg, and was now a member of the Cabinet. He liked the good things of office. . . . He did not expect his order to endure forever. . . . He had no abhorrence for anybody; but he liked pleasant people; he liked to treat everything as a joke; and he liked the labours of his not unlabourious life to be minimized" (1:12:154-55). Appears frequently in *Marion Fay.*

PERSIFLAGE, GERALDINE, LADY. Mother of Lady Amaldina Hauteville, and sister of the Marchioness of Kingsbury. Her friendship and hospitality toward her sister's two stepchildren was a cause of continuous enmity between her and the Marchioness. *Fay* 4, 11-12, 18, 26, 45, 50-53

PERSSE, MR. A hunting man living at Donaraile, near Castle Morony, who persuaded Black Tom Daly not to use his gun against the Landleaguers at Moytubber. *Land.* 9-11, 23

PETERBOROUGH, LORD. Father of Charles Glascock. His illness in Naples brought about the meeting there of his son and Caroline Spaulding. *He Knew* 3, 39, 55

PETERBOROUGH, LORD (Charles Glascock). As Charles Glascock he was a friend of Louis Trevelyan, and fell in love with Nora Rowley, who disappointed all her friends by refusing him. His romance with an American girl, Caroline Spaulding, and his later friendship with Nora Rowley, form one of the subplots of *He Knew He Was Right.*

PETERBOROUGH, CAROLINE (Spaulding), LADY. Niece of the American Minister to Italy, whom she visited in Florence. There she met Charles Glascock, later Lord Peterborough, and married him. Appears frequently in *He Knew He Was Right.*

PETERS, MR. A retired attorney, living at Littlebath, who was a great trial to his daughter Mrs. Stumfold, although he was the source of her "superfluities of comfort." *Mackenzie* 4-5

"PETITE VENDÉE, LA." A group of Royalists under the "Mad Captain," Adolphe Denot, with headquarters at Laval. Later called "the Chouans." *Vendée* 30

PETRIE, WALLACHIA. An American poet in Florence, laughingly called by her friend Caroline Spaulding the "American Browning." She strongly opposed Caroline's marriage to Lord Peterborough. *He Knew* 55-56, 76-77, 80-81

PETTY BAG, LORD. Harold Smith was for a short time Lord Petty Bag. John Robarts was private secretary in this office. *Framley* 10, 18, 32

PHINEAS FINN, THE IRISH MEMBER. London, Virtue and Co., 1869. 2v. Originally published in *Saint Paul's Magazine*, Oct. 1867-May 1869.

AUTHOR'S COMMENT. "It is all fairly good except the ending,—as to which till I got to it I had made no provision. As I fully intended to bring my hero again into the world, I was wrong to marry him to a simple pretty Irish girl, who could only be felt as an encumbrance on such return. When he did return I had no alternative but to kill the simple pretty Irish girl, which was an unpleasant and awkward necessity."—*Autobiography*, 2:17:161.

NOTES. Although not generally reckoned as the first of the Parliamentary series, as some of the characters appeared earlier in *The Eustace Diamonds* and *Can You Forgive Her?*, it is in fact the first in which the affairs of the parliamentary world are of major interest.

PLOT. Phineas Finn, a young Irishman just admitted to the bar, was elected to Parliament from Loughshane through the support of his father's old friend Lord Tulla. His genial temperament soon won him many highly placed friends in London society, among them Lady Laura Standish. Although Phineas was in a sense committed to marry a childhood sweetheart, Mary Jones, he fell in love with Lady Laura. She, however, had sacrificed her fortune to pay the debts of her brother Lord Chiltern, and valued her position in society above her romantic love for Phineas. She was deeply and intelligently interested in politics and the maintenance of a salon needed money and position, and she found both in the person of Robert Kennedy, a wealthy MP representing a group of Scottish boroughs.

In Lady Laura's circle of friends, Violet Effingham stood nearest to her, and when Phineas sought to marry her Lady Laura was bitterly angry, not only because she considered that he was being untrue to her, but that she wished Violet to marry Lord Chiltern. Violet did in fact love him, but his violent temper and manner of life did not seem to insure her happiness. When Lord Chiltern learned that Phineas was his rival, he challenged him and a duel was fought in Belgium, with no serious results. Both men were soon sensible of their folly, and shortly after they became reconciled Violet accepted Chiltern.

Phineas, by taking a government post to enable him to pay his way in London, lost his seat in Loughshane, and through the good offices of Lady Laura was offered Loughton, her father's pocket-borough. His career seemed assured until from a matter of principle he voted against his colleagues on a bill for tenant right in Ireland, and was forced to resign. In the meantime, life with the harsh and priggish Mr. Kennedy had become impossible for the high-spirited Lady Laura. She rejoined her father and eventually, to escape her husband's demand that she return to him, went into exile at Dresden.

Mme. Max Goesler, a wealthy and charming widow, interested herself in securing another seat for Phineas and, when he refused to allow her to finance the cost of the election, offered to put him in possession of her great fortune by their marriage. This he was too proud to accept and, discouraged by the net result of his years in Parliament, returned to Ireland where he married Mary Jones.

PHINEAS REDUX. London, Chapman and Hall, 1874. 2v. Originally published in *The Graphic*, July 19, 1873-Jan. 10, 1874.

NOTES. "There are certain chapters in the middle of *Phineas Redux* that are Trollope at the highest power. . . . It is in these chapters in *Redux* that have to do with Kennedy's growing madness (his attack on Phineas in the lodging is a grand piece of dramatic writing), Laura Kennedy's hopeless love for Phineas, and Phineas' quarrel with Bonteen that Trollope is at his very finest . . . an absolute modern. No post-war-psychoanalytic realist can teach him anything. He seems in these passages to know all the morbid obscurities of the human heart."—Walpole, pp. 108-9.

PLOT. After seven years of exile in Ireland and the death of his wife, Phineas Finn returned to London. Those in power had implied that were he again in Parliament, he would be taken into the government. He accordingly contested the borough of Tankerville and was elected. Lady Laura Kennedy was still in Dresden, where Phineas visited her, and at her request had an interview with her husband when he returned to London. Mr. Kennedy believed that Phineas was responsible for his wife's refusal to return to him, and after hot words attempted unsuccessfully to shoot him. No report was made to the police but relatives took him, completely mad, back to Loughlinter, where he soon died.

At the death of the old Duke, Plantagenet Palliser succeeded to his honors. The Daubeny government fell, Mr. Gresham became Prime Minister and the new Duke Lord Privy Seal. Mr. Bonteen had expected to become Chancellor of the Exchequer, and was angry and disappointed when asked to take the Presidency of the Board of Trade. There had never been friendship between Phineas and Mr. Bonteen, and one night, after a quarrel at their club, Mr. Bonteen was murdered. Suspicion was first directed to the husband of Lizzie Eustace, the converted Jew Emilius, since Mr. Bonteen was attempting to discover evidence that his marriage to Lizzie was bigamous, but Emilius had, seemingly, a perfect alibi. The quarrel at the club had been over heard by a number of members and, on purely circumstantial evidence, reinforced by the hesitating testimony of the blundering Lord Fawn, Phineas was indicted. His friends rallied to his support but the case against him was very strong. New evidence of the duplicity of Emilius was found through the ingenuity of Madame Goesler, and Phineas was acquitted. Unnerved by his sufferings, he resigned his seat, but was immediately re-elected and offered his old place as Undersecretary of the Colonies. He refused, and soon after he and Madame Goesler were married.

The old Duke of Omnium had left valuable jewels and a large sum of money to Madame Goesler in his will. She refused to accept them, and with the consent of the new Duke returned the jewels to the estate and turned over the legacy to Adelaide Palliser, a charming young cousin of the younger Duke, whose love affair with the equally impecunious Gerard Maule was thus brought to a happy conclusion.

PICCADILLY. *See* London

PICKERING, FRED. An aspiring poet, who took his wife to London, hoping to have a literary career. With meager funds, he disdained available jobs as too menial, and at the end of a year, his money exhausted, returned to Manchester where he became an attorney's clerk. Principal character in *The Adventures of Fred Pickering.*

PICKERING PARK. A large estate in Sussex belonging to the Longestaffes, which was purchased and extensively altered by Augustus Melmotte. Before the alterations were complete Melmotte had killed himself, and the estate reverted to its former owners. Frequently mentioned in *The Way We Live Now.*

PIE, SIR OMICRON. A famous London physician, whose name appears in a number of the novels. He was called in as a consultant in the illness of Bishop Grantly and of Dean Trefoil in *Barchester* 31-33; of Sir Roger Scatcherd and Lady Augusta Gresham in *Thorne* 9, 31, 34, 40; the old Duke of Omnium in *Prime Min.* 24; George Bertram, Sr., in *Bertrams* 41; and briefly when Lady de Courcy suggested an appeal to him to send her husband to a German spa in *Allington* 26. There is one reference to him in *Doctor Thorne* as "Sir Simon Omicron."

PIKE, MATTHEW. Peter Prosper's butler, whose chief duty was to keep Harry Annesley from interviewing his uncle. *Scarborough* 25-27, 44-45, 50-51, 57, 64

PILE, MR. A bootmaker at Percycross, a Conservative and very active in the elections. ". . . it must be acknowledged that he was not a pure-minded politician. He loved bribery in his very heart. . . . The idea of purity of election . . . did in truth make him feel very sick" (2:10:179). *Ralph* 20, 23, 25-26, 29, 39, 44, 51

PIPKIN, MRS. Mrs. Hurtle's landlady in Islington, with whom Ruby Ruggles stayed when she followed Felix Carbury to London. Appears frequently in *The Way We Live Now*.

PLAISTOW HALL. A 900-acre farm in Norfolk, the home of Will Belton. *Belton* 2-3, 13, 20

PLANKEN, FRITZ. A handsome young Viennese, whose unkind remarks as to the musicianship, age and appearance of Herr Crippel, Lotta Schmidt's other lover, caused her to dismiss him and marry Herr Crippel. *Lotta*

PLOMACY, MR. The steward of Ullathorne for fifty years, in charge of the party given by Miss Monica Thorne at Ullathorne. *Barchester* 35-39

PLUM-CUM-PIPPINS. A small church near Cambridge, whose rector was the Rev. Augustus Smirkie. *Caldigate* 23

PLUME, AUGUSTE. A baker in Laval, lieutenant of the "Mad Captain" Adolphe Denot. He later became a barber in Paris in the employ of Jacques Chapeau. *Vendée* 30-32, 34

PLUMPLINGTON. A small town in Barsetshire, the scene of *Two Heroines of Plumplington*.

PLUMSTEAD EPISCOPI. A parish in the Barchester diocese, whose rector was the Rev. Theophilus Grantly. Described in chapter 8 of *The Warden*. Most often mentioned in *The Warden* and *Barchester Towers*, but frequently referred to in each of the Barchester novels.

PLUMSTOCK. A parish in Cheshire, of which the Rev. Mr. Granger was rector. *Widow*

PODGENS, MR. and MRS. Grocers at Framley Cross, ". . . great favorites with her ladyship [Lady Lufton], both having been servants up at the house." They lived near the church, Mr. Podgens, "the neat grocer, being the clerk and sexton," and Mrs. Podgens, "the neat grocer's wife, the pew-opener in the church." Their new baby was described by Lucy Robarts as "a duck." *Framley* 2, 16

POGSON and LITTLEBIRD. Commission merchants in King's Court, who employed the Quaker Zachary Fay as chief clerk. *Fay* 15, 25, 32

POITEVINS. A Royalist club in Paris made up of men from the province of Poitou. *Vendée* 1

POITOU. The province in which Lescure, Larochejaquelin and Denot all lived, and which was the battleground for most of the Royalist rebellion described in *La Vendée*.

POKER and HODGE. A London firm, which purchased John Gordon's interest in the "Stick-in-the-Mud" mine. *Old Man* 18, 22

POLLINGTON. The home of Dr. Shand, in Essex, where John Caldigate visited his friend Dick. *Caldigate* 4, 15, 49

POLPENNO. The Cornish borough represented in Parliament by Frank Tregear. The inn was the Cambourne Arms, where Frank's rival had his headquarters. *Duke* 55

POLWENNING. The home of Frank Tregear's parents, in Cornwall. *Duke* 55

POLYEUKA MINE. A gold mine near Nobble, New South Wales, owned first by Timothy Crinkett, and later by John Caldigate, out of which he made a fortune. *Caldigate* 10

POMFRET, JOHN. A young Englishman, who journeyed to Spain to propose marriage to Marie Daguilar, the daughter of his father's partner. His rudeness in examining minutely the dress and ornaments of a Spanish nobleman, thinking him to be an ignorant bullfighter, forms the substance of *John Bull on the Guadalquivir*.

POPE, AGNES. A servant of Farmer Trumbull, suspected of revealing the hiding place of her master's money to his murderer. She married Sam Brattle. *Vicar* 12, 14-15, 73

POPENJOY, LORD. The title of the heir of the Marquis of Brotherton. The question of the legitimacy of his son is the key to the plot of *Is He Popenjoy?*.

POPHAM VILLA. A house in Fulham, Surrey, in which Sir Thomas Underwood established his daughters, but in which he lived very little. The setting for much of *Ralph the Heir*.

POPPINS, TOM. A clerk, and friend of George Robinson, who married Polly Twizzle, Maryanne Brown's best friend. *Struggles* 11-13, 16-19, 22

POPPLECOURT, LORD. Selected by the Duke of Omnium as a husband for his daughter Lady Mary, but with no success. "Lord Popplecourt was a man in possession of a large estate which was unencumbered. His rank in the peerage was not high; but his barony was of an old date. . . . He had good looks of that sort which recommend themselves to pastors and masters, to elders and betters. . . . He looked as though he were steady. He was not impatient nor rollicking. . . . Lord Silverbridge had declared him to be a fool. No one thought him to be bright" (2:8: 91-92). Appears frequently in *The Duke's Children*.

PORCHESTER GARDENS. *See* London

PORLOCK, LORD. The eldest son and heir of Earl de Courcy, but on bad terms with all the family. He married late in life only to spite his younger brothers. *Allington* 17, 23, 26, 43, 47-48, 56; *Thorne* 16

PORT GLASGOW. The district represented by Septimus Traffick in Parliament. *Ayala* 5

PORTMAN SQUARE. *See* London

PORTRAY CASTLE. An estate in Scotland in which Lizzie Eustace had a life interest. The setting for much of the action in *The Eustace Diamonds*; described in chapter 21.

POSSITT, The REV. MR. Mrs. Winterfield's favorite clergyman in Perivale. ". . . a weakly, pale-faced little man, who worked so hard in the parish that on every day, Sundays included, he went to bed as tired in all his bones as a day labourer from the fields" (1:9: 221). *Belton* 8-9

POTT, MR. A wealthy young man traveling with his tutor in the Holy Land, who was one of Miss Todd's guests at her picnic in the Valley of Jehoshaphat. *Bertrams* 6, 8

POTTER, MR. Nathaniel Sowerby's London lawyer. *Framley* 28

POTTERY HAMLETS. Represented in Parliament by Joshua Monk. *Finn* 9

POUNTNER, The REV. DR. A canon of Brotherton Cathedral, who with very little success admonished Dean Lovelace for hunting. *Popenjoy* 10

POUNTNEY, MAJOR. One of the Duchess of Omnium's hangers-on, who wangled an invitation to one of the large political parties at Gatherum Castle. He so offended the Duke by a direct request for the Silverbridge seat that he was asked to leave the Castle. *Prime Min.* 20, 27-28, 48, 50

POWELL, DR. Indefer Jones's physician. *Cousin* 4-7

POWELL, LORD DAVID. The younger brother of the Marquis of Llwddythlw. *Fay* 19, 39

PRAGUE. Where Mme. Max Goesler obtained evidence against Mr. Emilius that freed Phineas Finn from the charge of murdering Mr. Bonteen. *Redux* 57, 64, 66

The setting for *Nina Balatka.*

PRATT, FOWLER. A friend of Adolphus Crosbie, who was a member of Sebright's Club, and stood up with Crosbie at his wedding. *Allington* 25, 27-28, 31, 35, 45; *Last Chron.* 50, 54, 59

PRECIS, ALPHABET. A candidate in the Weights and Measures examination for chief clerk, ". . . who had declared to all his friends that if the pure well of official English undefiled was to count for anything, he ought to be pretty safe" (1:11:236). *Clerks* 11

PRENDERGAST, MR. The friend and London attorney of Sir Thomas Fitzgerald, who acted for Sir Thomas in dealing with the Molletts. "He was short of stature, well made, and in good proportion; he was wiry, strong, and almost robust. . . . His hair was grizzled, and his whiskers were grey, and round about his mouth his face was wrinkled; but with him even these things hardly seemed to be signs of old age. He was said by many . . . to be a stern man. . . . But he had also the reputation of being a very just man. . . . He was a handsome man too, with clear, bright, gray eyes, a well-defined nose, and expressive mouth . . ." (1:9: 83-85). *Castle Rich.* 9, 15-39

PRETTYMAN, ANNABELLA and ANNE. Two sisters, whose school in Silverbridge Grace Crawley attended as a student, and where she was later a teacher. *Last Chron.* 5-7, 9, 14, 20, 41

PRICE, MR. A gentleman-farmer and sportsman, who leased Cross Hall from the Marquis of Brotherton. *Popenjoy* 6-9, 13, 18, 21, 45, 48, 57

PRICE, MRS. A charming and predatory young widow on the boat with Arthur Wilkinson and George Bertram from Suez to Southampton. *Bertrams* 39-40

PRIME, MRS. DOROTHEA (Ray). The elder daughter of Mrs. Ray, a widow wooed by the Rev. Mr. Prong, whose spiritual guidance she revered, but whose interest in her bank account she distrusted. "Her fault was this; that she had taught herself to believe that cheerfullness was a sin, and that the more she became morose, the nearer would she be to the fruition of those hopes of future happiness on which her heart was set" (1:1:6). One of the principal characters in *Rachel Ray.*

PRIME MINISTER, The. London, Chapman and Hall, 1876. 4v.

AUTHOR'S COMMENT. "I had never yet drawn the completed picture of such a statesman as my imagination had conceived. . . . He should have rank, and intellect, and parliamentary habits, by which to bind him to the service of his country; and he should also have unblemished, unextinguishable, inexhaustible love of country . . . as the ruling principle of his life; and it should so rule him that all other things should be made to give way to it. . . . Such a character I endeavoured to depict in describing the triumph, the troubles, and the failure of my Prime Minister."—*Autobiography,* 2:20:214-18.

NOTES. In its major theme a study of the interrelation of two divergent temperaments: the Duchess striving to make her husband the greatest figure of his time, and he conscious only of his duties and responsibilities.

PLOT. The Liberal government fell, and neither Mr. Gresham nor Mr. Daubeny could form a cabinet. Largely through the influence of the Duke of St. Bungay, the Duke of Omnium, very much against his will, consented to lead a Coalition government. Effective as he had been in the House of Commons, he was too thin-skinned, too diffident and unbending, too much inclined to feel that opposition to his views was a personal affront, to be a successful Prime Minister. The Duchess, by abounding and sometimes indiscriminating hospitality at Gatherum Castle and Matching Priory, endeavored to consolidate his supporters, but with indifferent results. Despite all its handicaps the Coalition government endured for three years, and when it fell the Duke retired from politics.

Interwoven with the main theme is the story of Emily Wharton and her disastrous marriage to Ferdinand Lopez. Emily's father, a wealthy barrister, violently objected to her marriage but was eventually won to give a grudging consent. Almost immediately it became evident that Lopez, whose finances were in a precarious condition, had an eye on his father-in-law's purse rather than on his wife's happiness. He ordered her to obtain money for his speculations and when she refused made her life a burden. His social gifts secured for him an invitation to Gatherum Castle and while there the Duchess hinted that he might seek election to Parliament as a member from Silverbridge, the Palliser pocket-borough. When the Duke declined to have anything to do with the election, she was compelled to hedge, but a word to a local politician seemed to indicate that Lopez was the favored candidate. Arthur Fletcher, who had loved Emily Wharton since his boyhood, had entered the contest before Lopez, but when he learned of the identity of his opponent was persuaded, with difficulty, not to withdraw. Lopez was badly beaten, and was loud in his complaints against the Duke and Duchess for what he styled their treachery to him. He succeeded in securing his election expenses of £500 from Mr. Wharton, and later had the incredible effrontery to demand a like sum from the Duke. Learning for the first time of his wife's part in supporting Lopez, and to protect her name, the Duke had the bad judgment to pay the sum demanded. The payment became known and Quintus Slide promptly made it the subject of a withering attack on the Duke in the scandal sheet, the "People's Banner." The affair caused so much gossip that a question was asked in the House, where Phineas Finn, in a graceful speech from which all mention of the Duchess was excluded, brought the matter to an end.

Meanwhile the business affairs of Lopez and of his partner Sexty Parker went from bad to worse. He gave up his pretentious apartment—for which Mr. Wharton had to pay—and forced Emily to secure for them a home with his reluctant father-in-law. Utterly discredited, he secured the promise of the management of a mine in Guatemala and threatened to take Emily into exile with him. Mr. Wharton tried to buy him off through the purchase of shares, the condition of his appointment by the company. When the offer of the position was withdrawn he ended his life by jumping before a fast-moving train. For a year Emily was crushed, but when her brother Everett, who had become heir to the Baronet Sir Alured Wharton, married his cousin Mary, she left off her weeds, and soon after became the wife of Arthur Fletcher.

"PRIME MINISTER." Lord Silverbridge's horse, which failed to win the Leger and caused its owner to lose £70,000. *Duke* 17, 43-44

PRIMERO FAMILY. Neighbors of Roger Carbury, living at Bundlesham, in Sussex. ". . . the young Primeros had three horses apiece, and killed legions of pheasants annually at about ten shillings a head" (1:6:34). *Way We Live* 6

PRITCHETT, MR. The business manager for George Bertram, Sr., who was fond of young George and constantly counseled him for his own good to be more attentive to his wealthy old uncle. Appears frequently in *The Bertrams.*

PRODGERS. A very stuffy detective, employed by Mr. Tyrrwhit, the moneylender, to locate Captain Scarborough. *Scarborough* 5

PROGRESS (club). *See* London

PRONG, The REV. SAMUEL. The vicar of a district in Baslehurst, of the sanctimonious type so often satirized by Trollope. He aspired to the hand of Mrs. Prime, but a difference of opinion on the settlement of her property prevented the match. ". . . a little man, over thirty, with scanty, light-brown hair, with a small, rather upturned nose, with eyes by no means deficient in light and expression, but with a mean mouth. His forehead was good, and had it not been for his mouth his face would have been expressive of intellect and of some firmness. . . . He was deficient in one vital qualification—he was not a gentleman" (1:6:120). *Rachel* 6, 9, 17, 20-21, 24-25

PROSPER, PETER. The owner of Buston, and uncle of Harry Annesley, whom he had named as his heir. Considered generally by those who knew him to be somewhat of a fool. His courtship of Matilda Thoroughbung of the local brewing family supplies comic relief for the novel. "He was somewhat dry . . . and skinny, with high cheekbones and large dull eyes. But he was clean, and grave, and orderly" (2:26:62). One of the principal characters in *Mr. Scarborough's Family.*

PROTEST, LADY SELINA. Associated with Miss Mildmay in the "Disabilities," she championed Dr. Olivia Q. Fleabody in her fight for the management of the organization. ". . . a very little woman with spectacles—of a most severe aspect" (1:17:232). *Popenjoy* 16-18, 27, 30, 33, 60

PROUDIE, MRS. The domineering wife of the Bishop of Barchester, who vies with Lady Glen and Planty Pal as Trollope's greatest character. She won her struggle with Mr. Slope, the Bishop's chaplain, for primacy in the diocese and drove him out of it, but when conquered by Mr. Crawley and Dr. Tempest she died and released the poor Bishop from his thralldom.

". . . one of the greatest figures in the Barsetshire chronicles . . . is sufficient of herself to insure a comparative immortality for any novel."—Walpole, p. 49.

"It was not only that she was a tyrant, a bully, a would-be priestess, a very vulgar woman, and one who would send headlong to the nethermost pit all who disagreed with her; but that at the same time she was conscientious, by no means a hypocrite, really believing in the brimstone which she threatened, and anxious to save the souls around her from its horrors. And as her tyranny increased so did the bitterness of the moments of her repentance increase, in that she knew herself to be a tyrant—till that bitterness killed her." —*Autobiography,* 2:15:109.

Most prominent in *Barchester Towers, Framley Parsonage* and *The Last Chronicle of Barset*; briefly in *Allington* 55; and *Thorne* 15-16

In *Did He Steal It?*, represented by Mrs. Goshawk.

PROUDIE, THOMAS, BISHOP. The Bishop of Barchester, entirely dominated by his wife. "He had been preacher to the royal beef-eaters, curator of theological manuscripts in the Ecclesiastical Courts, chaplain to the Queen's yeomanry guard, and almoner to his Royal Highness the Prince of Rappe-Blankenburg. . . . In person Dr. Proudie is a good looking man, spruce and dapper, and very tidy. He is somewhat below middle height, being about five feet four, but he makes up for the inches which he wants by the dignity with which he carries those which he has. It is no fault of his own if he has not a commanding eye, for he studies hard to assume it. His features are well formed, though perhaps the sharpness of his nose may give to his face . . . an air of insignificance. If so, it is greatly redeemed by his mouth and chin, of which he is justly proud" (*Barchester* 1:30:30, 35).

Most prominent in *Barchester Towers, The Last Chronicle of Barset* and *Framley Parsonage*; briefly in *Thorne* 15-16; and *Allington* 55. In *He Knew* 49, he is mentioned for an appointment on the Ecclesiastical Commission; and in *Claverings* 2, he uses his authority to compel the Rev. Henry Clavering to give up hunting.

In *Did He Steal It?*, represented by Mr. Goshawk, a local magistrate in Silverbridge.

PROUDIE FAMILY. [Dr. Proudie] "has a large family, of which the three eldest are daughters." Only three are named, the two oldest, Olivia and Augusta, and Netta, the youngest. Olivia, after considering herself engaged to Mr. Slope at one time, finally married the Rev. Tobias Tickler, a widower with three children, rector of a district church near Bethnal Green. The Rev. Optimus Grey married one of the others, probably Augusta. They were ". . . fine engaging young ladies . . . tall and robust like their mother, whose high cheekbones, and—, we may say auburn hair, they all inherit" (*Barchester* 1:3:38). Appear, frequently in *Barchester Towers* and *Framley Parsonage.*

PRYOR, BESSY. A dearly loved foster child of Mrs. Miles, who fell in love with Philip Launay and was banished to Normandy until she would promise obedience in giving him up. Philip proved as stubborn in the matter as Bessy, and together they won Mrs. Miles's consent. Heroine of *The Lady of Launay.*

PRYOR, JOHN. The English suitor of Miss Ophelia Gledd, who had some doubt whether the outspoken and unconventional Boston society girl would be sympathetically received in London. *Gledd*

PUCKER, MISS. A friend and coworker with Mrs. Prime in the Dorcas Society at Baslehurst. A woman with a squint and a malignant virtue, a gossip, whom the whole village disliked. *Rachel* 1-2, 9, 14, 20-21

PUDDICOMBE, The REV. MR. The vicar in the neighborhood of Dr. Wortle's school, who frequently gave good but unpalatable advice to the Doctor that was always resented, but invariably acted upon. ". . . a clergyman without a flaw." *Wortle* 5, 9-11, 13, 17, 23

PUDDINGDALE. A parish in the diocese of Barchester, whose vicar was Mr. Quiverful. Mentioned frequently in *The Warden* and *Barchester Towers.*

PUDDLEBRANE, MR. A member of the British cricket team playing in Britannula, who argued against cremation mainly because it would deprive him of a place in the village cemetery with his ancestors. *Fixed* 7

PUDDLEHAM, The REV. MR. A preacher at the Primitive Methodist chapel in Bullhampton, and a protégé of Lord Trowbridge. ". . . an earnest man, who, in spite of the intensity of his ignorance, is efficacious among the poor" (1:2). Appears frequently in *The Vicar of Bullhampton.*

PUDGE. Will Belton's most trusted farmer. *Belton* 20

PUFFLE, MISS. One of the two possibilities in Mr. Prosper's mind when looking for a bride. However, she ran away with young Farmer Tazlehurt. *Scarborough* 27, 44, 51, 57

PUFFLE, MRS. MARYANNE. The author of "Not So Black as It Is Painted," which her attractive sister-in-law attempted to wheedle the Editor into publishing. *Josephine*

PULLBODY, DR. The London physician of the Marquis of Brotherton. *Popenjoy* 47-48

PUREFOY, SIR JOHN. A guest of Lord Rufford, and owner of the horse "Jemima," ridden by Major Caneback when he was killed. *Amer. Sen.* 21-23, 31, 73, 80

PURITAN GRANGE. The home of the Bolton family, near Cambridge. Mentioned frequently in *John Caldigate.*

PUTTOCK, The REV. MR. The Vicar at Bragton, an asthmatic clergyman with a salary of £800 a year and a house, whose duties were performed by his curate for a remuneration of £100 and a pony. The American Senator was loud in his criticism of such cases. *Amer. Sen.* 9, 12

PYCROFT COMMON. A village near Bullhampton, where Carry Brattle took refuge with Mrs. Burrows after being turned out of the house by her father. *Vicar* 25

PYRAMIDS. The setting for *An Unprotected Female at the Pyramids.*

PYRENEES. The hot baths of Vernet are in the Eastern Pyrenees, and are the setting for *La Mère Bauche.*

QUARTPOT ALLEY. *See* London

QUAVERDALE, MR. An unsuccessful hack-writer in London, a friend of Harry Annesley. *Scarborough* 22, 57

QUEEN ANNE STREET. *See* London

QUEEN'S COLLEGE, Galway. Where Frank Jones was educated. *Land.* 1

QUEEN'S GATE. *See* London

QUEENSLAND, Australia. The setting for *Harry Heathcote of Gangoil.*

QUÉTINEAU, GENERAL (real person). The Republican general in command at Saumur, who was captured by the Vendeans and released by them, but later executed by the Convention for failure to hold the town. *Vendée* 9-10

QUICKENHAM, RICHARD, Q.C. A London barrister, brother-in-law to the Vicar of Bullhampton, who produced the evidence that the Methodist chapel opposite the vicarage gates was built on glebe land. ". . . a tall, thin, man, with eager grey eyes, and a long projecting nose, on which, his enemies in the courts of law were wont to say, that his wife could hang a kettle, in order that the unnecessary heat coming from his mouth might not be wasted. His hair was already grizzled, and, in the matter of whiskers, his heavy impatient hand had nearly altogether cut away the only intended ornament to his face" (42:266-67). *Vicar* 9, 37-38, 42, 55

QUIN, LADY MARY. The spinster daughter of the Earl of Kilfenora, living in County Clare and conversant with all the gossip concerning Fred Neville and Kate O'Hara, which she relayed to Lady Scroope. *Eye* 2, 6, 9-10, 13, 19, 21

QUIVERFUL, The REV. MR. The Vicar of Puddingdale, where he tried unsuccessfully to support his family on an annual stipend of £400. His appointment as Warden at Hiram's Hospital to succeed Mr. Harding was the cause of a bitter quarrel between Mrs. Proudie and Mr. Slope. Most prominent in *Barchester Towers* 10, 15, 24-25, 43, 52; briefly in *Warden* 19-20; and *Last Chron.* 54, where he is a member of the Clerical Commission in the Crawley case.

QUIVERFUL, MRS. LETITIA. Wife of the Vicar of Puddingdale. A bedraggled, overworked but plucky mother of fourteen children, who fought for them and for her too meek husband with spirit and tenacity, and with final success. Most prominent in *Barchester Towers* 10, 16, 24-25, 43, 50; briefly in *Framley* 45

RACHEL RAY. London, Chapman and Hall, 1863. 2v.

Notes. "The book lives still because of its delicate little scenes of comedy, the meeting of the lovers, Mrs. Tappitt's ball, the bedroom confidences of the Tappitts, Rachel's talks with her mother."—Walpole, pp. 141-42.

A Trollopian tirade against Evangelical intolerance, the Rev. Mr. Prong and Mrs. Prime substituting for Mr. Slope and Mrs. Proudie. Commissioned by *Good Words*, but rejected as unfit for Sunday reading. It is one of the few instances in all Trollope's stories where he makes a worker, in this case a brewer, his hero.

Plot. Luke Rowan, who had gone to Baslehurst to protect his interests in the Bungall and Tappitt brewery, met Rachel Ray and fell in love with her, to the dismay of Mrs. Tappitt who wished him to marry one of her daughters, and of Rachel's mother and older sister who did not think him sufficiently pious. Luke's struggle to win Rachel and to gain the control of the brewery furnish the plot.

RAG (club). *See* London

RAILWAY INN. *See* Exeter

RALPH THE HEIR. London, Hurst and Blackett, 1871. 3v. Originally published in *Saint Paul's Magazine*, Supplement, Jan. 1870-July 1871.

Author's Comment. "This was the novel of which Charles Reade afterwards took the plot and made on it a play [*Shilly Shally*]. I have always thought it to be one of the worst novels I have written, and almost to have justified that dictum that a novelist after fifty should not write love stories."—*Autobiography*, 2:19:195.

Notes. The account of the Percycross election in which Sir Thomas Underwood was defeated, and of the subsequent petition, is almost autobiographical of Trollope's own experience at Beverley, and is told with humor and spirit.

Plot. The estate of Newton Priory, occupied by Gregory Newton, was entailed to his nephew Ralph, although it was a great grief to him that it could not go to his natural son, also named Ralph, who lived there with him. Ralph, the heir, became involved in debt, and to extricate himself proposed to marry Polly Neefit, daughter of a breechesmaker to whom he was heavily indebted, her father having agreed to cancel the debts and to give £20,000 along with his daughter. Polly firmly refused to become a "lady," preferring her own choice, Ontario Moggs, son of a bootmaker. As an alternative to marriage, Ralph considered selling the reversion of his interest in Newton Priory to his uncle. This plan met the approval of Gregory as it would allow him to leave the estate legally to his son, but the transaction was not complete when Gregory was killed on the hunting field, and Ralph the heir succeeded. The Ralph who was not the heir received £40,000 in his father's will with which he bought a property in Norfolk, where he took his bride, Mary Bonner.

Sir Thomas Underwood, father of Clarissa and Patience, and earlier guardian of Ralph, the heir—a lawyer of note and a former MP—was persuaded to contest Percycross but was defeated. His daughter Clarissa who had thought herself in love with Ralph, the heir, was finally disillusioned by his fickleness and married the Rev. Gregory Newton, Rector of Newton Peele, who for years had loved her devotedly.

RAMSBOTTOM, MR. A Liverpool lawyer, who was adviser to Paul Montague in his dealings with Augustus Melmotte. *Way We Live* 38

RAMSDEN, LORD. Lord Chancellor under Mr. Daubeny and the Duke of Omnium. *Prime Min.* 8, 12, 20, 72

RAPINSKI. The jeweler and pawnbroker in Prague to whom Nina Balatka took her jewels. *Nina* 9, 12

RATTLER, MR. A parliamentary whip, who considered himself a great Liberal, and was at one time Patronage Secretary of the Treasury. Appears frequently in *Phineas Finn, Phineas Redux* and *The Prime Minister.*

RAY, MRS. A gentle, clinging widow of an Exeter ecclesiastical lawyer, much under the domination of her widowed daughter Mrs. Prime. Continual bullying had so soured her outlook on life that when Luke Rowan fell in love with her younger daughter, Rachel, she agreed with Mrs. Prime that all young men were "wolves," and almost ruined the romance of the two young lovers. One of the principal characters of *Rachel Ray.*

RAY, DOROTHEA. *See* Prime, Mrs. Dorothea (Ray)

RAY, RACHEL. The younger daughter of Mrs. Ray, both of them dominated by the evangelical and opinionated older daughter, Mrs. Prime. Rachel fell in love with Luke Rowan, the brewer, and despite all obstacles finally married him. "She was a fair-haired girl, with hair, not flaxen, but of light-brown tint,—thick, and full, and glossy. . . . She was well made, being tall and straight, with great appearance of health and strength. She walked as though the motion was pleasant to her, and easy,—as though the very act of walking was a pleasure" (1:1:16). Heroine of *Rachel Ray.*

READE, CHARLES (real person). His play *Shilly Shally* was pirated from the plot of *Ralph the Heir.*

RECKENTHORPE, MAJOR. A retired United States senator, living at Frankfort, Kentucky, whose two sons violently disagreed on the question of secession, and joined the opposing armies in the Civil War. One of the principal characters in *The Two Generals.*

RECKENTHORPE, FRANK. A young Southerner, educated at West

Point, who became a general in the Union Army during the Civil War. During a skirmish in the Blue Ridge he captured his wounded brother Tom, a general in the Confederate Army, sent him back to a hospital in Alexandria and eventually arranged to have him invalided home. One of the principal characters in *The Two Generals*.

RECKENTHORPE, TOM. Major Reckenthorpe's second son, a general in the Confederate Army. He was badly wounded in battle, and lost a leg, but returned home where he married Ada Forster, with whom both brothers had been in love. One of the principal characters in *The Two Generals*.

RED HOUSE. A house in Nuremberg belonging to Linda Tressel, subject to the life use of her dominating aunt. The setting for much of *Linda Tressel*.

RED LION INN. *See* Courcy

REDDYPALM, MR. The landlord of the Brown Bear, whose vote carried the parliamentary election at Barchester for Sir Roger Scatcherd. *Thorne* 17, 22

REFORM CLUB. *See* London

REGAN, PATRICK. A young Irish barrister in London, who was a member of the Panjandrum Committee. *Panjandrum*

RELICS OF GENERAL CHASSÉ. In *Tales of All Countries* [First Series], 1861. Originally published in *Harper's New Monthly Magazine*, Feb. 1860.

NOTES. "A foolish and laborious joke about trousers, staged in Antwerp and sadly reminiscent of Mrs. Trollope at her worst."—Sadleir, p. 185.

PLOT. The Rev. Augustus Horne, on a holiday in Belgium, visited the former quarters of General Chassé, the defeated leader at the siege of Antwerp, where one of the exhibits was a pair of the General's enormous trousers. Mr. Horne, who was also a large man, in a spirit of mischief decided to see which man was the larger. Removing his own trousers, he was about to step into the General's when a group of English women tourists was heard to approach. He hurriedly escaped into an adjoining room, leaving his own garment behind, which the women cut up for souvenirs.

RERECHILD, DR. A Barchester doctor, "a follower and humble friend of Dr. Fillgrave." Briefly, as Eleanor Bold's physician, in *Barchester* 23, 31; and at Sir Roger Scatcherd's deathbed, in *Thorne* 7, 24

RETURNING HOME. In *Tales of All Countries*, Second Series, 1863. Originally published in *Public Opinion*, Literary Supplement, Nov. 30, 1861.

NOTES. The story is based on an actual incident reported in Trollope's *West Indies and the Spanish Main*.

PLOT. After a ten-year exile in Costa Rica, Mr. and Mrs. Arkwright, with their small child, attempted to take a short cut through the country to catch a boat to England. The difficulties of this trip on donkey-back, through almost impassable forests and down steep mountain sides, were increased by incessant and torrential rains. Mrs. Arkwright, utterly exhausted when they reached the river, was reassured by the sight of the canoes in which they would make the remainder of the trip. She and the baby were made comfortable for their long ride, but before her husband could step into the canoe a sudden storm swept it from the shore, overturned it, and its occupants were drowned. Mr. Arkwright, brokenhearted, abandoned his voyage and returned to his post.

REYNOLDS, JOE. A leader of the illegal potheen distillers, and one of Thady Macdermot's tenants at Ballycloran. "Joe was aware that he was a marked man, and consequently . . . was very well inclined to that or any thing else which might be inimical to gaols, policemen, inspectors, gaugers, or any other recognized authority" (1:4: 60). One of the principal characters in *The Macdermots of Ballycloran.*

REYNOLDS, TIM. Brother of Joe, whom Captain Ussher threw into prison for a crime that he did not commit, thus increasing the hate of the potheen distillers toward Ussher. *Macdermots* 4

RIBBONMEN. A group of tenants revolting against the landlords. ". . . County Leitrim was full of Ribbonmen, and no town so full as Mohill" (1:4: 60). Mentioned frequently throughout *The Macdermots of Ballycloran.*

RIBBS, MR. The butcher at Dillsborough, a very humble and silent member of the Dillsborough Club. *Amer. Sen.* 4

RICHARDS, MRS. The landlady of the house where the three clerks lived. *Clerks* 2-3, 13, 19, 28

RICHMOND. The location of Fawn Court, home of Lord Fawn, his mother and numerous sisters. *Eustace*

RIDE ACROSS PALESTINE, A. In *Tales of All Countries*, Second Series, 1863. Originally published in *The London Review*, Jan. 5, 12, 19, 1861, under the title: *The Banks of the Jordan.*

PLOT. Mr. Jones, journeying alone in Palestine, welcomed the companionship of a young traveler who begged to accompany him. After several days together they were overtaken by an elderly man of no uncertain temper who made it known that he was the guardian of the young traveler, and that nothing short of marriage between the companions would satisfy him. Mr. Jones was much chagrined that he had not discovered for himself that the young person was a girl, masquerading as a young man.

"RIGHTS OF WOMEN INSTITUTE; Established for the Relief of the Disabilities of Females." Disrespectfully known as the "Disabilities." An organization in Marylebone Road sponsored chiefly by Miss Julia Mildmay and Lady Selina Protest. Mentioned frequently in *Is He Popenjoy?*

RING, ABEL. Brother of Fanny Arkwright, and her husband's partner in Costa Rica. One of the principal characters in *Returning Home.*

RIVER COTTAGE, Willesden. Where Trevelyan secreted his son after kidnaping him. *He Knew* 67, 70

ROANOKE, LUCINDA. An American niece of Mrs. Carbuncle, with whom she lived and who trapped her into an engagement with Sir Griffen Tewett whom she hated. On the day of the wedding she refused to go on with it, and went mad. "She looked as though she were four-and-twenty but in truth she was no more than eighteen . . . tall, and was as one used to command, and walked as though she were a young Juno. Her hair was very dark,—almost black,—and very plentiful. Her eyes were large and bright, though too bold for a girl so young. . . . [her] complexion was certainly marvellous. . . . the colour would go and come and shift and change with every word and every thought" (2:36:127). One of the principal characters in *The Eustace Diamonds.*

ROBARTS, DR. Mark Robarts' father, a physician at Exeter, who died leaving but little money, making it necessary for his unmarried daughters to live with relatives—Jane with her sister Mrs. Crowdy, and Lucy with her brother Mark at Framley Parsonage. *Framley* 1, 10-11

ROBARTS, BLANCHE. *See* Crowdy, Mrs. Blanche (Robarts)

ROBARTS, MRS. FANNY (Monsell). Wife of Mark Roberts. ". . . if high principles without asperity, female gentleness without weakness, a love of laughter without malice, and a true loving heart, can qualify a woman to be a parson's wife, then was Fanny Monsell qualified to fill that station" (1:1:7). One of the principal characters in *Framley Parsonage.*

ROBARTS, GERALD. Brother of Mark, for whom a commission in the army had been bought, and who became a captain in the Crimea. *Framley* 10

ROBARTS, JANE. Mark's second sister, who lived with her sister Mrs. Crowdy at Creamclotted Hall, and was designed by the Squire, her brother-in-law, to be the mistress of the neighboring Heavybed House. *Framley* 10

ROBARTS, JOHN (sometimes "Jack"). Mark's youngest brother, ". . . a clerk in the Petty Bag office, and private secretary to Lord Petty Bag himself" (1:10:191). *Framley* 10-11, 18, 32

ROBARTS, LUCY. Mark's youngest sister, who made her home with him at Framley Parsonage. She refused to marry Lord Lufton until his mother should ask her to do so.

". . . what eyes she had! . . . They flashed upon you, not always softly; indeed not often softly if you were a stranger to her; but whether softly or savagely, with a brilliance that dazzled you as you looked at them. . . . was thoroughly a brunette. Sometimes the dark tint of her cheek was exquisitely rich and lovely, and the fringes of her eyes were long and soft, and her small teeth, which one so seldom saw, were white as pearls, and her hair, though short, was beautifully soft—by no means black, but yet of so dark a shade of brown" (1:10:197-98).

"I think myself that Lucy Robarts is, perhaps, the most natural English girl I ever drew."—*Autobiography*, 1:8:191.

"She is the most adorable Cinderella in fiction since the first one. She is independent, brave, filled with wisdom but never a prig, energetic, and ready for any crisis but modest withal, and gentle without too much Victorian prudery."—Walpole, pp. 57-58.

Heroine of *Framley Parsonage.*

ROBARTS, MARK. The Vicar of Framley Church, and for a short time a prebendary at Barchester Cathedral. Educated at Harrow and Oxford with his friend Lord Lufton, who became his brother-in-law.

"In person he was manly, tall, and fair-haired, with a square forehead, denoting intelligence rather than thought, and clear white hands, filbert nails, and a power of dressing himself in such a manner that no one should ever observe of him that his clothes were either good or bad, shabby or smart" (*Framley* 1:1:9).

Most prominent in *Framley Parsonage*, and in *The Last Chronicle of Barset*, where he was on the Clerical Commission in the Crawley case.

ROBERTS, MR. Lord Kingsbury's man of business. *Fay* 33, 37-38, 42, 45, 54

ROBESPIERRE, MAXIMILIAN (real person). He ordered the ruthless suppression of the Vendean Royalists. "The sharp nose, the thin lips, the cold grey eyes, the sallow sunken cheeks, were those of a precise, passionless, self-confident man, little likely to be led into any excess of love or hatred, but little likely also to be shaken in his resolve either for good or evil. . . . His face probably was a true index to his character. . . ." (3:1:13). *Vendée* 22-23

ROBINSON, MR. An Englishman traveling in Italy, who attempted to help a fellow traveler and his family get settled at Lake Como, where he had the misfortune to have one of their boxes taken to his room. Since all their money and the wife's jewels were in that box, his embarrassment when it was found was only equaled by his anger when they accused him of stealing it. Principal character in *The Man Who Kept His Money in a Box.*

ROBINSON, GEORGE. An advertising man, the junior member of the firm in *The Struggles of Brown, Jones and Robinson.*

ROBY, MRS. HARRIET. Sister of Emily Wharton's dead mother; a shallow social-climber who approved Emily's decision to marry Ferdinand Lopez against her father's judgment, and so won Mr. Wharton's hatred. *Prime Min.* 4-5, 9-10, 13, 47, 74

ROBY, RICHARD. Brother of Thomas Roby at the Admiralty, and brother-in-law of Abel Wharton, who disapproved of him heartily. ". . . a florid youth of forty. He had a moderate fortune, inherited from his mother, of which he was sufficiently careful; but he loved races, and read sporting papers; he was addicted to hunting and billiards; he shot pigeons, and,—so Mr. Wharton had declared calumniously more than once to an intimate friend,—had not an H in his vocabulary" (1:4:57). *Prime Min.* 4, 9, 48

ROBY, THOMAS. In the second rank of parliamentary figures, holding successively the posts of Patronage Secretary of the Treasury, Secretary of the Admiralty and Secretary of the Treasury. Appears frequently in *The Prime Minister*; briefly in *Finn* 6; *Redux* 16; and *Duke* 67-68

RODEN, GEORGE. A clerk in the Post Office, and, despite their difference in the social scale, an intimate friend of Lord Hampstead. When Lady Frances Trafford engaged herself to him in the face of violent family objection, the friendship of the two men did not change, and when it was discovered that George was heir to the title of Duca di Crinola, all opposition ceased. "He was certainly a handsome young man, and endowed with all outward gifts of manliness; easy in his gait . . . with motions of his body naturally graceful but never studied, with his head erect, with a laugh in his eye, well-made as to his hands and feet" (1:4:49). One of the principal characters in *Marion Fay.*

RODEN, MRS. MARY. Mother of George, who early in life had married an Italian nobleman who deserted her. She returned to England with her infant son, but told him nothing of his ancestry. At the death of his father they were recalled to Italy, and George learned that he had inherited the title of Duca di Crinola. One of the principal characters in *Marion Fay.*

ROEBURY, in Oxfordshire. Where George Vavasor had a hunting stable. *Can You* 12

ROEHAMPTON. ". . . a suburban Elysium" maintained by Mrs. Montacute Jones so that she might give garden parties for her friends. It was there that Lord Silverbridge first met Isabel Boncassen. *Duke* 28

ROLLAND, The RIGHT REV. MR. The Bishop of Broughton, who admonished Dr. Wortle about his championship of Mr. and Mrs. Peacocke. *Wortle* 1, 3, 5, 8, 10-14, 17

ROME. The Tringles leased the Palazzo Ruperti for their stay in Rome when Ayala Dormer was their guest. *Ayala* 6

The setting for *Mrs. General Talboys.*

ROMER, MR. ". . . a very clever young barrister," who was the assistant to Mr. Closerstill in Sir Roger Scatcherd's parliamentary campaign. *Thorne* 15-17, 22, 25

ROONEY, TERRY. Barry Lynch's manservant, who learned most of his master's affairs by a diligent application of his eye to the keyhole. *Kellys* 5

ROPER, MRS. The keeper of a boardinghouse at Burton Crescent where Johnny Eames and Joseph Cradell lived. Mother of Amelia. Appears frequently in *The Small House at Allington.*

ROPER, AMELIA. The daughter of Johnny Eames's London boardinghouse keeper. She entangled Johnny into a written declaration of love, from which he extricated himself with considerable difficulty, and later married Joseph Cradell. "Her eyes were bright, but then, also, they were mischievous. She could talk fluently enough; but then, also, she could scold. She could assume sometimes the plumage of a dove; but then again she could occasionally ruffle her feathers like an angry kite" (1:5:42). Appears frequently in *The Small House at Allington.*

ROSEBANK. The home of Farmer Lookaloft and his family, near Ullathorne. *Barchester* 35

ROSENHEIM, FRITZ. A carrier in the mountains of Upper Austria, who was unjustly accused of stealing a valuable box that had been entrusted to him. Hero of *Katchen's Caprices.*

ROSS, DICK. A hanger-on of Sir Francis Geraldine, who nevertheless was very frank in his criticism of the baronet's treatment of Cecilia Western. *Kept Dark* 6, 10, 17, 19

ROSSITER, The REV. MR. The Vicar of Beetham, who hoped to have Alice Dugdale as a daughter-in-law. *Dugdale*

ROSSITER, MRS. John's matchmaking mother, who hoped for her son's marriage with Georgiana Wanless. *Dugdale*

ROSSITER, MAJOR JOHN. Deputy Inspector-General of the Cavalry, and a son of the vicar at Beetham, where he had grown up with Alice Dugdale, the doctor's daughter. Lady Wanless considered him a desirable son-in-law, and he found it difficult to escape from the lovely Lady Georgiana, and to marry his childhood sweetheart. Hero of *Alice Dugdale.*

ROTTEN ROW. *See* London

ROUND, MR. Alice Vavasor's London lawyer. *Can You* 57, 61

ROUND and CROOK, "of Bedford Row, London." Attorneys for Joseph Mason in both Orley Farm trials. Appear frequently in *Orley Farm.*

ROWAN, MRS. Luke's mother, who did not consider Rachel Ray a suitable wife for her son, and who connived with Mrs. Ray to prevent their marriage. "A somewhat stately lady, slow in her movements and careful in her speech" (1:6:117). *Rachel* 6, 11, 13, 15, 30

ROWAN, LUKE. Nephew and heir of Mr. Bungall, one of the founders of the Bungall and Tappitt brewery. Luke gave up his study of the law in a determination to improve the quality of the beer made under the old firm name. His contest for the management of the brewery and his courtship of Rachel Ray both ended in success. Hero of *Rachel Ray.*

ROWAN, MARY. Luke's pretty sister, in whose honor the Tappitts gave a ball. ". . . very willing to be pleased, with pleasant, round eager eyes, and a kindly voice" (1:6:117). *Rachel* 6-7, 11, 30

ROWLEY, BESSIE, LADY. Sir Marmaduke's wife. Appears frequently in *He Knew He Was Right.*

ROWLEY, EMILY. *See* Trevelyan, Mrs. Emily (Rowley)

ROWLEY, SIR MARMADUKE. The Governor of the Mandarin Islands, and father of eight daughters. An old-fashioned colonial administrator, much distrusted by the younger men in the Colonial Office. ". . . he was one from whom the effervescence and elasticity and salt of youth had altogether passed away. He was fat and slow, thinking much of his wife and eight daughters, thinking much also of his dinner" (1:1:5). One of the principal characters in *He Knew He Was Right.*

ROWLEY, NORA. Emily's sister, who returned to London as Emily's companion after the latter's marriage to Louis Trevelyan. She was courted by the wealthy Charles Glascock, heir of Lord Peterborough, but chose Hugh Stanbury and love, rather than riches. One of the principal characters in *He Knew He Was Right.*

ROWLEY FAMILY. There were eight daughters, the only ones named being Emily, who married Louis Trevelyan; Nora, who married Hugh Stanbury; and Sophie and Lucy, who accompanied their parents to London. Appear frequently in *He Knew He Was Right.*

RUBB, SAMUEL, JR. Son of Tom Mackenzie's partner, who swindled Margaret Mackenzie out of a large sum of money and then tried to marry her to obtain the rest of her fortune. However, he fell in love with her, and after she had lost her money he still tried to persuade her to marry him. One of the principal characters in *Miss Mackenzie.*

RUDHAM PARK. The home of the De Barons near Cross Manor, where Mr. De Baron entertained a large houseparty in honor of the Marquis of Brotherton. *Popenjoy* 50-53

RUFFORD, LORD. The largest landowner in the Dillsborough region, interested primarily in sport. He narrowly escaped marriage with Arabella Trefoil, but through his sister's machination was finally captured by Caroline Penge. ". . . a stout, ruddy-faced, handsome man of about thirty" (*Amer. Sen.* 1:9:91). Most prominent in *The American Senator*; briefly, as a guest at Stalham, in *Ayala* 23, 26, 50

RUFFORD, CAROLINE (Penge), LADY. A wealthy young friend of Lady Penwether, whom Lord Rufford married as a sort of insurance after his escape from Arabella Trefoil. "Lady Rufford had been a Miss Penge, and the Penges were supposed to be direct descendants of Boadicea" (*Ayala* 49). Most prominent in *The American Senator,* 21-25, 67-68, 74; briefly in *Ayala* 23, 26, 49-51

RUFFORD UNITED HUNT CLUB (the U R U). Supported by the gentlemen and farmers about Dillsborough. It is sometimes called the "Ufford and Rufford Hunt Club." Captain Glomax was M F H in *Amer. Sen.* 8-11, 21-23; and Sir Harry Albury in *Ayala* 22, 24

RUGGLES, DANIEL. A tenant on one of Roger Carbury's farms, and grandfather of Ruby. *Way We Live* 18, 33-34, 39, 43, 46, 87

RUGGLES, RUBY. A pretty country girl, engaged to John Crumb, the local miller. Sir Felix Carbury made love to her and she followed him to London. John Crumb went after her, thrashed Sir Felix soundly in the street, persuaded Ruby to return home, and eventually married her. Appears often in *The Way We Live Now.*

RUMMELSBURG, PRUSSIA. In an elaborate attempt to circumvent the law of entail, John Scarborough went to this small town to marry, concealing the records. He later married the same wife again in Nice. *Scarborough* 54, 56, 58, 63

RUNCE, JOHN. A loyal member of the U R U, who was loud in his denunciation of the American Senator for his criticism of fox-hunting. *Amer. Sen.* 22, 25, 68

RUNCIMAN, MR. The landlord of the Bush Inn at Dillsborough. "He was a hale, good-looking man about fifty, with black hair, now turning grey at the edges, and a clean-shorn chin. . . . He was a masterful, but a pleasant man, very civil to customers and to his friends generally while they took him the right way; but one who could be a Tartar if he were offended. He was a temperate man in the main; but on Saturday nights he would become jovial, and sometimes a little quarrelsome" (1:4: 35-36). Appears frequently in *The American Senator.*

RUNNYMEDE HUNT. Major Tifto was the efficient M F H, with headquarters at the Bobtailed Fox, Egham. Lord Silverbridge hunted with them. *Duke* 6, 36, 49, 57-58

ST. BUNGAY, DUCHESS OF. An aunt of Lady Laura Standish, so convinced of her own importance that she bitterly resented those who did not bow down to her, and embarrassed her distinguished husband with constant complaints of fancied slights. "The Duchess was a woman of about forty, but with no meaning in her beauty, carrying a good fixed colour in her face, which did not look like paint, but which probably had received some little assistance from art. She was a well-built, sizeable woman, with good proportions and fine health,—but a fool" (*Can You* 1:22: 175). Briefly in *Can You* 22-23, 25; and as a patroness of the Negro Soldiers' Orphan Bazaar, in *Mackenzie* 27

ST. BUNGAY, DUKE OF. One of the most distinguished of the top-flight political personages, appearing in each of the six novels in the Parliamentary series. He was most successful as President of the Council, where his broad knowledge of events and personalities made him the ideal mediator. His youngest son was Lord James Fitz Howard.

". . . the very front and head of the aristocratic old Whigs of the country . . . a fussy, popular, clever, conscientious man, whose digestion had been too good to make politics a burden to him, but who had thought seriously about his country, and is one who will be sure to leave memoirs behind him" (*Finn* 1:29:242).

Most important in *The Prime Minister*; appears frequently in *Phineas Finn* and *Phineas Redux*; briefly in *Can You* 23-24, 50; and *Duke* 22, 71

ST. CUTHBERT'S (church). The parish church in Barchester of which Mr. Harding became rector after resigning the wardenship of Hiram's Hospital. Frequently mentioned in *Barchester Towers* and *The Warden*, where it is described in some detail in chapter 21.

ST. CUTHBERT'S (school). ". . . one of the grandest schools in England," in which Harry Clavering was a teacher for a short time after leaving college. *Claverings* 1

ST. DIDDULPH'S-IN-THE-EAST. A parish in London, of which the Rev. Mr. Outhouse was rector, and where for some time Mrs. Trevelyan and her sister Nora made their home. *He Knew* 29, 32

ST. EWOLD'S. A parish just outside Barchester, whose vicars were successively Mr. Goodenough, Mr. Arabin, Mr. Harding and, as the Barchester series ends, Mr. Crawley. The vicarage is described in some detail in *Barchester Towers* 21. Frequently mentioned in *The Warden, Barchester Towers* and *The Last Chronicle of Barset.*

ST. FLORENT. A small town in Anjou, the scene of the first Royalist revolt, forming much of the background for *La Vendée.*

ST. GEORGE, LORD. Son of the Marquis of Trowbridge and much more intelligent than his father, who held him somewhat in awe. He was able to make peace between the Vicar of Bullhampton and his father in their quarrel over the glebe land that the Marquis had given to the Primitive Methodists for their chapel. *Vicar* 26, 43, 48, 56-60, 70, 72

ST. JAMES HALL. *See* London

ST. JAMES'S PLACE. *See* London

ST. JAMES'S STREET. *See* London

ST. JOHN'S WOOD. *See* London

ST. LAUD'S. The church in Poitou from which Father Jerome was banished. *Vendée* 7

ST. LAURENT-SUR-SÈVRE. Where Agnes Larochejaquelin helped to establish a hospital to care for the wounded Royalists, and where Cathelineau died. *Vendée* 14

ST. LOUIS, Missouri. The Rev. Mr. Peacocke was vice-president of a college in St. Louis, where he married Ella Lefroy, believing her to be a widow. *Wortle* 2

ST. PETER'S-CUM-PUMKIN, Exeter. The rector was the Rev. Mr. Gibson, for whose affections the two French sisters were rivals. The name of the church is sometimes spelled "St. Peter's-cum-Pumpkin." *He Knew* 83

ST. QUINTEN, MRS. LYDIA. One of the promoters of the Panjandrum, and weekly hostess to the Committee. *Panjandrum*

SALISBURY. In this cathedral town, Trollope had his first suggestion of the plot of *The Warden.*

THREE HONEST MEN. The inn to which Carry and Sam Brattle were traced when they were in disgrace with their family. *Vicar* 39

SALOP, SIR GILBERT. A friend of Mr. Oldeschole, who recommended Charley Tudor's appointment. *Clerks* 2, 18

SAN FRANCISCO. Where the grave of Ferdinand Lefroy was found by Mr. Peacocke. *Wortle* 21

SANTERRE, ANTOINE-JOSEPH (real person). A Republican friend of Danton, and leader in the assault and capture of Durbellière. "He was a large, rough, burly man, about forty years of age; his brown hair was long and uncombed, his face was coarse. . . . his lips were thick and sensual, and his face was surrounded by huge whiskers, which made him look uncouth and savage" (2:6:163-64). *Vendée* 12, 15, 18-19, 21

SARATOGA SPRINGS, N.Y. The setting for *The Courtship of Susan Bell.*

SAUL, The REV. SAMUEL. The serious and hard-working curate of the Rev. Henry Clavering, who surprised everyone by falling in love with Fanny Clavering, and finally persuading her to return his affections. At the end of the book he was made Rector of Clavering, and they were married.

"Mr. Saul was very tall and very thin, with a tall thin head, and weak eyes, and a sharp, well-cut nose, and, so to say, no lips, and very white teeth, with no beard, and a well-cut chin. His face was so thin that his cheekbones obtruded themselves unpleasantly. He wore a long rusty black coat, and a high rusty black waistcoat, and trousers that were brown with dirty roads and general ill-usage. Nevertheless, it never occurred to any one that Mr. Saul did not look like a gentleman" (1:2:24-25).

One of the principal characters in *The Claverings.*

SAULSBY CASTLE. The estate of Lord Brentford, to which his daughter Lady Laura Kennedy returned after leaving her husband. *Finn* 12-13, 33-34, 55; *Redux* 78

SAUMUR. A fortified town in La Vendée, captured by the Royalists in their first important battle. *Vendée* 9-10

SAWYER, DR. "A very skilful young surgeon from Brotherton," who attended Mrs. Houghton at Cross Hall after her accident on the hunting field. *Popenjoy* 9

SCARBOROUGH, AUGUSTUS. The younger son of John Scarborough, who for a time was considered the heir to Tretton Park. A thoroughly contemptible son and brother, who eventually turned everyone against him. One of the principal characters in *Mr. Scarborough's Family.*

SCARBOROUGH, JOHN. The head of the family. A completely pagan landowner, who held the law of entail in contempt, and to evade it pronounced his eldest son to be illegitimate. "He was luxurious and self-indulgent, and altogether indifferent to the opinion of those around him" (1:1:2). Principal character in *Mr. Scarborough's Family.*

SCARBOROUGH, MARTHA. An unmarried sister of John Scarborough and of Mrs. Mountjoy, who lived with her brother at Tretton Park. *Scarborough* 7-8, 19-21, 38, 53-54, 56

SCARBOROUGH, CAPT. MOUNTJOY. The elder son of John Scarborough, whom his father declared illegitimate in order to save the property from the moneylenders, the Captain having used the property as security for the payment of his debts. A confirmed gambler. ". . . dark-visaged, with coal-black whiskers and moustaches, with sparkling angry eyes, and every feature of his face well cut and finely formed" (3:61:268). One of the principal characters in *Mr. Scarborough's Family.*

SCARROWBY. The Durham estate of Sir Harry Hotspur, on which he wished George Hotspur to undergo a probationary period of two years to prove himself worthy of Emily's hand. *Hotspur* 20-21

SCATCHERD, LADY. A hard-working woman, well-suited to her husband when he was a stonemason, but unfitted for the position of mistress of Boxall Hill, after her husband was knighted. Foster mother of Frank Gresham. Most prominent in *Doctor Thorne* 10, 12, 22-29, 43; briefly in *Framley* 38-39

SCATCHERD, SIR LOUIS PHILIPPE. The only child of Sir Roger, who had determined to make a gentleman of him by sending him to Eton and to Cambridge, from which institutions he was promptly expelled. He tried to marry Mary Thorne, but the match was indignantly repudiated by Dr. Thorne. ". . . strong neither in mind or body . . . he already showed symptoms of his father's vices, but no symptoms of his talents. . . . he had begun life by being dissipated without being generous; and at the age of twenty-one he had already suffered from delirium-tremens. . . . He was a small man, not ill-made by Nature, but reduced to unnatural tenuity by dissipation. . . . His hair was dark red, and he wore red moustaches, and a great deal of red beard beneath his chin, cut in a manner to make him look like an American. His voice also had a Yankee twang, being a cross between that of an American trader and an English groom. . . . his eyes were keen and fixed, and cold and knowing" (2:10:99-100, 194). *Thorne* 10, 24-37, 40, 43

SCATCHERD, MARY. *See* Tomlinson, Mrs. Mary (Scatcherd)

SCATCHERD, SIR ROGER. In early life a stonemason in Barchester, who, to avenge the dishonor of his sister Mary, killed Henry Thorne and served a term of imprisonment. Later he became a great contractor, made a fortune and was made a baronet. He loaned money to Mr. Gresham until he held mortgages on practically the whole estate, and took over Boxall Hill in part payment, erecting there a huge, expensive mansion. A ruthless man, a radical in all his thinking and a heavy drinker. He died of alcoholism, leaving his fortune to his worthless son, who soon followed him. Mary Thorne finally came into possession of the fortune. One of the principal characters in *Doctor Thorne.*

SCATCHERD SERVANTS.

HANNAH. Lady Scatcherd's confidante at Boxall Hill, and practically her only friend. *Thorne* 12

JOE. Louis Scatcherd's valet. He attempted to flirt with Bridget, a maid in Dr. Thorne's home, and suffered a broken nose from a rolling pin with which she defended herself. ". . . he was a little fellow. . . . His out-door dress was a little, tight frockcoat, round which a polished strap was always buckled tightly, a stiff white choker, leather breeches, top-boots, and a hat with a cockade, stuck on one side of his head" (3:4:62-63). *Thorne* 34, 46

SCATTERALL, RICHARD. A "navvy" friend of Charley Tudor in the Internal Navigation Office. *Clerks* 18, 20, 27-28, 31

SCHLESSEN, FRITZ. Frau Frohmann's young lawyer in Innsbruck, who married her daughter Amalia. One of the principal characters in *Why Frau Frohmann Raised Her Prices.*

SCHMIDT, LOTTA. The pretty young Viennese shopgirl with two suitors, Herr Crippel, an elderly musician at the Volksgarten, and the young, handsome, self-confident Fritz Planken. The latter's cruel and unjust criticism of Herr Crippel's musicianship, appearance and age made Lotta decide to marry Crippel. Heroine of *Lotta Schmidt.*

SCHOOLS AND COLLEGES. *See* Bonn, University of; Bowick School; Cambridge University; Cheltenham College; Eton; Harrow; Leipzig, University of; Marlbro' School; Oxford University; Queen's College, Galway; St. Cuthbert's School; Trinity College, Dublin; Winchester College

SCOTLAND.

CASTLE CORRY. Owned by the Earl of Altringham. *Hotspur*

CASTLE REEKIE. Home of the Marquis of Auld Reekie. *Can You*

CAULD-KALE CASTLE. Lord Gaberlunzie's seat in Aberdeenshire. *Clerks*

CRUMMIE-TODDY. Where Lord Silverbridge and Gerald Palliser went for the shooting, in Perthshire. *Duke*

DRUMCALLER. A small cottage owned by Colonel Stubbs, near Inverness. *Ayala*

GLENBOGIE. Sir Thomas Tringle's place in Invernessshire. *Ayala*

INCHARROW. Where Sir Walter Mackenzie lived in Rossshire. *Mackenzie*

KILLANCODLEM. Belonging to Mrs. Montacute Jones. *Duke, Popenjoy*

LOUGHLINTER. Mr. Kennedy's estate in Perthshire. *Finn, Redux*

PORTRAY CASTLE. Lizzie Eustace had a life interest in this property belonging to her husband's family. *Eustace*

SCOTT, UNDECIMUS ("Undy"). The eleventh son of Lord Gaberlunzie, ". . . thrice elected and twice rejected" M P from the Tillietudlum district. A thorough rascal, who became a stock-jobber and induced Alaric Tudor to invest his ward's money in one of his schemes.

". . . stalwart and comely, hirsute with copious red locks, not only over his head, but under his chin and round his mouth. He was well made, six feet high, neither fat nor thin, and he looked like a gentleman. He was careful in his dress, but not so as to betray the care that he took; he was imperturbable in temper, though restless in spirit; and the one strong passion of his life was the desire of a good income at the cost of the public" (1:8:162).

One of the principal characters in *The Three Clerks*.

SCOTT, CAPT. VALENTINE. Brother of Undy, who married the Widow Golightly and her £1000 a year, and attempted to force Alaric Tudor to hand over a considerable portion of Clementina Golightly's fortune. *Clerks* 1, 7, 34, 36, 41

SCOTT, MRS. VALENTINE. The widow of Jonathan Golightly, and mother of Clementina. ". . . a very pushing woman . . . who had in her day encountered, with much patience, a good deal of snubbing, and who had had to be thankful when she was patronized, now felt that her day for being a great lady had come, and that it behoved her to patronize others. She tried her hand upon Gertrude [Tudor] and found the practice so congenial to her spirits, so pleasantly stimulating, so well adapted to afford a gratifying compensation for her former humility, that she continued to give up a good deal of her time to No. 5, Albany Row, Westbourn Terrace . . . [the] house in which the Tudors resided" (2:1:6). *Clerks* 17, 24-26, 29, 32-36

SCOTT FAMILY. "They were a cannie, comely, sensible brood. Their father and mother, if they gave them nothing else, gave them strong bodies and sharp brains. They were very like each other, though always with a difference. Red hair, bright as burnished gold, high, but not very high cheek bones, and small sharp twinkling eyes, were the Gaberlunzie personal characteristics. There were three in the army, two in the navy, and one at a foreign embassy; one was at the diggings, another was chairman of a railway company, and our own particular friend, Undecimus, was picking up crumbs about the world in a manner that satisfied the paternal mind that he was quite able to fly alone" (*Clerks* 1:8:152).

SCROBBY, MR. A retired grocer with a grievance against his landlord Lord Rufford. Because of this he conspired with Goarly to poison the foxes in the U R U Hunt country. Appears frequently in *The American Senator*.

SCROOME, The HON. JOSIAH. The Representative to the American Congress from the state of Mickewa, living at 125 Q St., Minnesota Ave., Washington. A friend of Senator Gotobed, from whom he received letters telling of the Senator's experiences in England. *Amer. Sen.* 29, 51

SCROOPE, EARL OF. The death of his son made his nephew Fred Neville his heir, and when Fred was killed the title and estate fell to his younger brother, Jack. ". . . a tall, thin man, something over seventy. . . . His shoulders were much bent. . . . His hair was nearly white, but his eyes were still bright, and the handsome well-cut features of his fine face were not reduced to shapelessness by any of the ravages of time. . . . In youth he had been a very handsome man, and had shone forth in the world, popular, beloved, respected, with all the good things the world could give" (1:1:14). *Eye* 1, 4, 8-10, 17

SCROOPE, MARY, LADY. The second wife of the Earl, and much younger than he. Although she knew that Fred Neville had betrayed Kate O'Hara, she still insisted that he should not marry her, and induced the Earl to extract a promise from him to that effect. After his death she became a recluse, accusing herself of having condoned his dishonor and for the advice that indirectly led to his murder. One of the principal characters in *An Eye for an Eye.*

SCROOPE MANOR. The seat of the Earl of Scroope in Dorsetshire, described in chapter 1 of *An Eye for an Eye.*

SCRUBY, MR. The grasping and unscrupulous agent for George Vavasor when he contested the Chelsea seat in Parliament. *Can You* 13, 35, 38, 41, 44, 46, 51, 60, 71, 73

SCUMBERG'S HOTEL. *See* London

SCUTTLE, JEM. The postboy from the Dragon of Wantly, Barchester, who stole Mr. Soames's check and emigrated to New Zealand, leaving Mr. Crawley to bear the accusation. *Last Chron.* 29

SEBRIGHT'S (club). *See* London

SEELY, MR. The attorney for John Caldigate in his bigamy trial, who believed his client to be guilty. *Caldigate* 29-30, 34, 37-43, 45, 58, 61

SENTIMENT, MR. POPULAR. An author whose novel, *Almshouse*, attacked Hiram's Hospital and similar institutions. Evidently the novel was published as a serial, as it is spoken of in one place as "the twenty numbers." Possibly Charles Dickens was in Trollope's mind. *Warden* 15

SEPPEL, HERR. A man of all work at the Peacock, who undertook to cart the peasants' produce to Innsbruck when Frau Frohmann refused to pay them the market price. *Frohmann*

SERRAPIQUE. The ship on which Emily Viner made the voyage in *The Journey to Panama.*

SEVILLE. The setting for most of *John Bull on the Guadalquivir.*

SHAND, DR. Dick Shand's father, a physician in a small country town in Essex. Father also of Matilda, Harriet, Maria and Josh. *Caldigate* 4, 14-15, 49-50

SHAND, DICK. A classmate of John Caldigate at Cambridge, and his partner in the gold-mining project in Australia. Dick could not keep from drinking and failed miserably as a miner. He returned to England in time to give testimony that freed John from the charge of bigamy. One of the principal characters in *John Caldigate.*

SHAND, MARIA. Dr. Shand's third daughter, who was in love with John Caldigate. *Caldigate* 4, 6, 14-15, 49-50, 62

SHANDY HALL, The Jamaica home of Marian Leslie, about 18 miles from Spanish Town. *Sarah*

SHAP. A village about five miles from Vavasor Hall, where George Vavasor met his sister Kate at the Lowther Arms when his grandfather had forbidden him the house. *Can You* 38, 54

SHARPIT and LONGFITE. Mr. Hart's Baslehurst lawyers in his contest with Butler Cornbury for the seat in Parliament. *Rachel* 24, 27

SHEEP'S ACRE FARM. Where Ruby Ruggles lived with her grandfather. *Way We Live* 18

SHIRES, Estates in, etc. *See under name of shire*

Barsetshire (fictitious)
Berkshire
Buckinghamshire
Cambridgeshire
Cheshire
Cornwall
Cumberland
Devonshire
Dorsetshire
Durham
Essex
Gloucestershire
Hampshire
Herefordshire
Hertfordshire
Lincolnshire
Middlesex
Norfolk
Northamptonshire
Oxfordshire
Shropshire
Somersetshire
Suffolk
Surrey
Sussex
Westmoreland
Wiltshire
Worcestershire
Yorkshire

SHROPSHIRE.

HARTLEBURY. Seat of the Marquis of Hartletop. *Allington*

TRAFFORD HALL. Estate of the Marquis of Kingsbury. *Fay*

SIDONIA, MR. A Jewish moneylender, from whom Ethelbert Stanhope borrowed a considerable sum, which was repaid, under protest, by his father. *Barchester* 9, 19

SIENA, Italy. After Louis Trevelyan had abducted his son, he went into hiding at Casalunga, near Siena. *He Knew* 78-79

SILVERBRIDGE (borough). The pocket-borough of the Duke of Omnium, represented in Parliament successively by Plantagenet Palliser (*Allington*), John Grey (*Can You, Prime Min.*), Arthur Fletcher (*Prime Min.*) and Lord Silverbridge (*Duke*).

SILVERBRIDGE (town). A small town in Barsetshire frequently mentioned throughout the Barchester and the Parliamentary series. The inn was the George and Vulture, used as headquarters in the elections. *Prime Min.* 29, 34; *Duke* 14

Since the town had no courthouse, the magistrates sat at the inn, and Mr. Crawley appeared before them there. *Last Chron.* 8, 20

SILVERBRIDGE, LORD. The intelligent but wayward eldest son of the Duke of Omnium, who, after he was sent down from Oxford, busied himself with racing, at which he lost £70,000. At his father's suggestion he proposed to Lady Mabel Grex and, when he was refused, turned to Isabel Boncassen, an American girl who was reluctantly accepted by the Duke. Most prominent in *The Duke's Children*; mentioned as an infant in *Can You* 80; as "a fair-haired, curly-pated, bold-faced little boy" in *Finn* 57; and often in *The Prime Minister*.

SING SING. Harry Heathcote's Chinese cook, who deserted him to join the Brownbie gang. *Heathcote* 8, 11

SIR HARRY HOTSPUR OF HUMBLETHWAITE. London, Hurst and Blackett, 1871. Originally published in *Macmillan's Magazine*, May-Dec. 1870.

AUTHOR'S COMMENT. ". . . had for its object the telling of some pathetic incident in life rather than the portraiture of a number of human beings."—*Autobiography*, 2:18:184.

NOTES. "This is one of the little stories, only an episode, a proud, generous, irascible old father, a gentle faithful-unto-death little heroine, and a villain of desperate wickedness."—Walpole, p. 143.

PLOT. The death of his only son and heir made it necessary for Sir Harry Hotspur to make a new will. The title had to go to a distant cousin, George Hotspur, a man of great personal charm but a spendthrift and a gambler. Sir Harry wished the ancestral property to go to his daughter Emily and hoped that when she married, her husband would adopt the family name. George Hotspur schemed to marry her to save himself from financial ruin and succeeded in winning her love. Although she was convinced of his unworthiness, she believed that she alone could save him, but she had promised her father not to marry without his consent and this Sir Harry refused to give. George was bought off by the family lawyers and eventually married his mistress, an actress who had been supporting him. Emily was taken to Italy by her parents, where she died.

SKULPIT, JOB. One of the bedesmen at Hiram's Hospital. *Warden*

SLIDE, QUINTUS. The editor of the "People's Banner," a widely read scandal sheet, who attacked Phineas Finn with great energy, threatened to publish Mr. Kennedy's letter libeling his wife, and upon being refused an invitation to Gatherum Castle bitterly attacked the Duke of Omnium. His paper finally became so involved in lawsuits that he was dismissed.

". . . a young man under thirty, not remarkable for clean linen . . . well-known and not undistinguished member of a powerful class of men. . . . And, though he talked of ' 'ouses' and 'horgans' he wrote good English with great rapidity, and was possessed of that special sort of political fervour which shows itself in a man's work rather than in his conduct" (*Finn* 1:26:217).

An important character in *Phineas Finn, Phineas Redux* and *The Prime Minister.*

SLOPE, The REV. OBADIAH. The domestic chaplain to Bishop Proudie at Barchester. At first a protégé of the Bishop's wife, but later her enemy when he endeavored to wrest the control of the diocese from her hands. He might have married one of the many Proudie daughters, but instead wooed Eleanor Bold, and was for a time enamored of Signora Neroni. At the command of Mrs. Proudie he was finally dismissed, and married a rich widow in London, where he had a church in the vicinity of the New Road.

"I have heard it asserted that he is lineally descended from that eminent physician who assisted at the birth of Mr. T. Shandy, and that in early years he added an 'e' to his name, for the sake of euphony. . . . Mr. Slope is tall, and not ill made. His feet and hands are large . . . but he has a broad chest and wide shoulders to carry off these excrescences, and on the whole his figure is good. His countenance, however, is not specially prepossessing. His hair is lank, and of a dull pale reddish hue. It is always formed into three straight lumpy masses, each brushed with admirable precision, and cemented with much grease. . . . He wears no whiskers, and is always punctiliously shaven. His face is nearly the same colour as his hair, though perhaps a little redder: it is not unlike beef,—beef, however, one would say, of a bad quality. His forehead is capacious and high, but square and heavy, and unpleasantly shining. His mouth is large, though his lips are thin and bloodless; and his big, prominent, pale brown eyes inspire anything but confidence. His nose, however, is his redeeming feature: it is pronounced, straight, and well-formed; though I myself should like it better did it not possess a somewhat spongy, porous appearance, as though it had been cleverly formed out of red coloured cork" (*Barchester* 1:4:47-48).

Most prominent in *Barchester Towers*; briefly in *Framley* 40, 45

Caricatured as the Rev. Abraham Dribble in the burlesque *Never, Never, —Never, Never.*

SLOPE, SIR SIMON. The Solicitor-General who conducted the prosecution at Phineas Finn's trial for the murder of Mr. Bonteen. *Redux* 57, 61-67; briefly in *Eustace* 54

SLOW and BIDEAWHILE. A respectable old firm of lawyers in London, mentioned in many of the novels. They acted for the Greshams in *Thorne* 44-47; Martha Dunstable in *Framley* 42; Margaret Mackenzie in *Mackenzie* 8, 10, 14-29; Louis Trevelyan in *He Knew* 4, 14, 19, 33, 59, 75; the Longestaffes in *Way We Live* 58, 64, 69, 73-77, 81, 86; and Sir Peregrine Orme in *Orley* 20, 38

SMALL HOUSE AT ALLINGTON, The. London, Smith, Elder and Co., 1864. 2v. Originally published in *The Cornhill Magazine*, Sept. 1862-April 1864.

AUTHOR'S COMMENT. "*The Small House at Allington*, is, I think, good. The De Courcy family are alive, as is also Sir Raffle Buffle. . . . There is also an old squire . . . whose life as a country gentleman with rather straightened means is, I think, well described."—*Autobiography*, 1:10:239.

NOTES. Introduces Trollope's favorite heroine Lily Dale, and his two most admired characters, Plantagenet Palliser and his wife Lady Glencora, later the Duke and Duchess of Omnium. It is generally accepted that the character of Johnny Eames is representative of the young Trollope.

PLOT. Lily Dale, her sister Bell and their widowed mother lived in the Small House at Allington, almost as pensioners of old Squire Dale of the Great House. The Squire's nephew and heir Bernard had grown up with the two sisters, and Bell was the Squire's choice for the next mistress of his beloved home. Lily fell deeply in love with one of her cousin's London friends, the handsome Adolphus Crosbie, and promised to marry him. He was a self-seeking social-climber and at a house party at Courcy Castle, despite his engagement to Lily, he proposed to Lady Alexandrina de Courcy and was accepted. Lily was crushed by his faithlessness but tried unsuccessfully to conceal her grief. Johnny Eames, who had loved her since they were children, was so enraged that, on meeting Crosbie at a railway station, he thrashed him soundly. This episode did not add to Crosbie's popularity and, when the affair became known at Allington, Johnny became a hero in the neighborhood. Lord de Guest was much pleased at his prowess, undertook to help him in his career and eventually left him a substantial legacy.

Even before his marriage, Crosbie regretted his choice and within ten weeks after the ceremony, Lady Alexandrina left him to retire to Baden-Baden with her mother, where she soon died. Bell married the doctor in the nearby town of Guestwick, but Lily, despite the unwavering devotion of Johnny Eames, refused to marry him and devoted herself to her mother and the old Squire.

SMALL HOUSE AT ALLINGTON. The home of Mrs. Dale and her daughters, Bell and Lily. "The glory of the Small House at Allington certainly consists of its lawn, which is as smooth, as level, and as much like velvet as grass has ever yet been made to look" (1:2:15). It provides the setting for much of the action in *The Small House at Allington*.

SMILER, MR. One of the two thieves at Carlisle who stole the empty box from which Lizzie Eustace had removed the diamonds. ". . . a gentleman for whom the whole police of London entertained a feeling which approached to veneration" (2:49:300). *Eustace* 49, 57, 74, 78

SMILEY, MRS. MARIA. A widow with £200 a year out of the Kingsland Road brickfields. A friend of Mrs. Moulder, who engineered a marriage between her reluctant brother John Kenneby and the widow. ". . . a firm set, healthy looking woman of—about forty. She had large, dark, glassy eyes, which were bright without sparkling. Her cheeks were very red, having a fixed settled colour that never altered with circumstances. Her black wiry hair was ended in short crisp curls, which sat close to her head. It almost collected like a wig, but the hair was in truth her own. Her mouth was small, and her lips thin . . ." (2:3:20). *Orley* 43, 77

SMIRKIE, The REV. AUGUSTUS. A widower with five children, who married Julia Babington. Rector of Plum-cum-Pippins at a salary of £300. *Caldigate* 23, 32, 41-42, 46, 58

SMIRKIE, MRS. JULIA (Babington). In her youth, she had been in love with her cousin John Caldigate, but on his marriage to Hester Bolton she became his bitter enemy. Appears frequently in *John Caldigate.*

SMITH, The REV. MR. "Smith was a curate of Crabtree [Parva], a gentleman who was maintaining a wife and half a dozen children on the income arising from his profession. . . . It was only worth some £80 a year, and a small house and glebe" (13:207). *Warden* 13, 21

SMITH, BARNEY. Black Tom Daly's huntsman. *Land.* 9-11

SMITH, CHURCHILL. A member of the Panjandrum Committee. *Panjandrum*

SMITH, MRS. EUPHEMIA. An adventuress, whom John Caldigate met on the boat going out to New South Wales, and who, after John's marriage to Hester Bolton, accused him of bigamy. Known on the stage as "Mademoiselle Cettini." One of the principal characters in *John Caldigate.*

SMITH, HAROLD. Brother-in-law of Nathaniel Sowerby, he was an MP holding minor positions in the Treasury and the Admiralty, and, for three short weeks, was Lord Petty Bag. "He was a younger son, and not possessed of any large fortune. Politics as a profession was therefore of importance to him. . . . He was labourious, well-informed, and on the whole, honest: but he was conceited, long-winded, and pompous" (*Framley* 1:2:28-29). Most prominent in *Framley Parsonage*; briefly in *Last Chron.* 52, 59

SMITH, MRS. HAROLD. Nathaniel Sowerby's adoring sister, determined that her husband's position in the world should be of use to her brother. ". . . a clever, bright woman, good-looking for her time of life—and she was now over forty—with a keen sense of the value of all worldly things, and a keen relish for all the world's pleasures. She was neither labourious, nor well-informed, nor perhaps altogether honest . . . but then she was neither dull nor pompous, and if she was conceited, she did not show it" (*Framley* 1:2:29). Most prominent in *Framley Parsonage*; briefly in *Last Chron.* 52, 59

SMITH, MANFRED. The manager of the Negro Soldiers' Orphan Bazaar. *Mackenzie* 27, 29

SNAPE, THOMAS. The senior clerk at the Internal Navigation Office, and the butt of the juniors. "He was not by nature an ill-natured man, but he had become by education harsh to those below him, and timid and cringing with those above" (1:2:30). *Clerks* 2, 17-18, 27-28, 45

SNAPPER, The REV. MR. Bishop Proudie's domestic chaplain, who took over the Hogglestock parish when Mr. Crawley resigned. *Last Chron.* 68-69, 73, 82

SNOW, MR. One of the defense lawyers in Phineas Finn's trial for the murder of Mr. Bonteen, ". . . who was supposed to handle a witness more judiciously than any of the rising men" (2:17:139). *Redux* 57

SNOW, MARY. Daughter of a drunken engraver, from whom Felix Graham rescued her. He planned her education with the idea that he could "mold" her to be his wife. When this proved inexpedient he arranged a marriage for her with Albert Fitzallen, an apothecary who was in love with her. *Orley* 22, 33, 47, 54, 56-57

SOAMES, MR. Lord Lufton's man of business in Barchester, who lost a check for £20 and claimed that he had left it in Mr. Crawley's house. *Last Chron.* 1-12, 18-19, 40, 70-74

SOAMES and SIMPSON. The attorneys at Buntingford who prepared Matilda Thoroughbung's marriage settlement. *Scarborough* 27, 43-44, 48, 50

SOCANI, MADAME. An American girl, a former mistress of Mahomet M. Moss and a member of his opera company in London. She was jealous of Rachel O'Mahony, and tried in every way to injure her. Rachel said of her, "She can sing; she has a delicious soprano voice, soft and powerful; but she has also a temper and temperament such as no woman, nor yet no devil ought to possess" (1:14:233). *Land.* 14, 19, 28

SOMERS, MR. The agent at Castle Richmond, and Chairman of the Relief Committee for the famine sufferers. "He was a large, heavy, consequential man, always very busy, as though aware of being one of the most important wheels that kept the Irish clock agoing; but he was honest, kind-hearted in the main, true as steel to his employers, and good-humoured—as long as he was allowed to have his own way" (1:12:253). Appears frequently in *Castle Richmond*.

SOMERSET HOUSE. *See* London

SOMERSETSHIRE.

BELTON CASTLE. Home of Clara Amedroz, which became the property of Will Belton. *Belton*

LAUNAY. Property owned by Mrs. Miles. *Launay*

PARAGON. In Littlebath, where Miss Baker and Miss Todd lived, and for a time Miss Mackenzie. *Bertrams, Mackenzie*

SOUCHEY. The servant of Josef Balatka. ". . . an old dependant, who, though he was a man, was cook and housemaid, and washerwoman, and servant-of-all-work. . . . but with his fidelity had come a want of reverence toward his master and mistress, and an absence of all respectful demeanour" (1:1:12-13). *Nina* 1-5, 12-16

SOUTH AUDLEY STREET. *See* London

SOUTH CENTRAL PACIFIC AND MEXICAN RAILWAY. A stockjobbing company promoted by Hamilton Fisker in San Francisco, and in London by Augustus Melmotte, that forms the central theme in *The Way We Live Now.*

SOUTHAMPTON BUILDINGS. *See* London

SOWERBY, NATHANIEL. Although an MP and possessed of a high position in society, he was an inveterate spendthrift, a gambler and without conscience in using his friends for his own purposes. He had frittered away his fortune, and had mortgaged his dearest possession, Chaldicotes, until it was lost to him. "He was bald, with a good forehead, and sparkling moist eyes. He was a clever man, and a pleasant companion, and always good-humoured when it so suited him. He was a gentleman, too, of high breeding and good birth" (1:3:43).

"He is the finest possible example of Trollope's understanding of and feeling for scoundrels. Trollope has a true, almost Balzacian genius for all the shabby gentlemen in the City. And Mr. Sowerby is the best of all the shabby gentlemen. His letters to Mark Robarts are masterpieces, his little interview with Tom Tozer a gem, his final decline and ruin a proper and never cruel climax." —Walpole, p. 58.

One of the principal characters in *Framley Parsonage.*

SPANISH TOWN, Jamaica. The setting for *Miss Sarah Jack of Spanish Town.*

SPARKES, MRS. CONWAY. ". . . a literary lady, who had been very handsome, who was still very clever, who was not perhaps very good-natured," and who feuded with the Duchess of St. Bungay at Lady Glencora's house party at Matching Priory. She also appears as a guest at Lady Monk's reception. Briefly in *Can You* 22-26, 48-49; *Finn* 48, and, as a patroness of the Negro Soldiers' Orphan Bazaar, in *Mackenzie* 27

SPAULDING, CAROLINE. *See* Peterborough, Caroline (Spaulding), Lady

SPAULDING, JONAS. The American Minister to Italy, who was the uncle of Caroline and Olivia. *He Knew* 40, 46, 55, 76, 80, 87

SPAULDING, OLIVIA. An American girl from Providence, R.I., who with her sister visited their uncle, the American Minister to Italy, in Florence. *He Knew* 37, 40, 46, 56

SPICER, MR. A mustardmaker at Percycross, who, because he controlled the votes of all his men, was most important to the Conservatives in the election. *Ralph* 20, 25, 29, 39

SPINNEY LANE. *See* London

SPIVEYCOMB, MR. A papermaker at Percycross, who supported the Conservatives largely because of contracts arranged by members of that party. *Ralph* 20, 23, 25, 29, 39, 51

SPONDI, SIGNORA CAMILLA. The old Earl Lovel's mistress, living with him at the time of his death, to whom he attempted to leave his entire fortune. The court finally awarded it to Lady Anna, the Earl's daughter. *Anna* 2

SPOONER, MISS. A neighbor and friend of the Underwoods, at Popham Villa. *Ralph* 3, 7, 15, 57

SPOONER, NED. Thomas Spooner's cousin, who managed his estate while Thomas was unofficial assistant to Lord Chiltern in the hunt club. *Redux* 29, 53

SPOONER, THOMAS PLATTER. A country gentleman and ardent huntsman, whose estate, Spoon Hall, was in the neighborhood of the Chiltern place, Harrington Hall. When Adelaide Palliser visited the Chilterns, Mr. Spooner fell in love with her, and found it difficult to believe that she could be serious in refusing him. He later married Miss Leatherside.

"He was Spooner of Spoon Hall, and had been High Sheriff for his county. He was not so young as he once had been;—but he was still a young man, only just turned forty, and was his own master in everything. He could read, and he always looked at the country newspaper; but a book was a thing that he couldn't bear to handle" (*Redux* 1:18:147).

Redux 15-16, 18-19, 29, 41, 53, 76; *Duke* 62-63

SPOTTED DOG, The. In *An Editor's Tales*, 1870. Originally published in *Saint Paul's Magazine*, March-April 1870.

PLOT. Julius Mackenzie, highly educated but unfortunately married and ruined by drink, appealed to the Editor for work. The Editor had on hand for indexing a manuscript on which a country clergyman had spent many years. Examining Mackenzie as to his fitness to do the work, he recognized his scholarship and decided to trust him with the task. The poor man confessed that it would be unsafe for him to have the material at home, as his wife was a drunkard, and his children undisciplined. He suggested that his friends, the owners of the Spotted Dog, might be willing to keep it for him and allow him to work there. The Editor went with him to the pub, made the arrangements and turned over the manuscript to him. For a time he made good progress, and the Editor began to hope that all was well with him. The drunken wife, however, followed him to the pub, and in the ensuing disturbance the landlord turned them both out. When this was reported to the Editor he hurried to Mackenzie's lodging, where he found the manuscript in the fireplace half-burned by the drink-maddened wife, and her husband a suicide.

SPOTTED DOG (pub). *See* London

SPRIGGS, MATHEW. One of the bedesmen at Hiram's Hospital. *Warden*

SPROUT, MR. A maker of cork soles in Silverbridge, who worked for the election of Ferdinand Lopez as MP. The Duke of Omnium was advised by Lady Rosina de Courcy to have his shoes soled with Mr. Sprout's handiwork. *Prime Min.* 27, 34; *Duke* 14

SPRUCE, SALLY. The ". . . ancient maiden cousin" of Mrs. Roper, who lived in her boardinghouse. *Allington* 5, 10-11, 36, 41, 51, 59

SPRUGEON, MR. The Silverbridge ironmonger who proposed Ferdinand Lopez for representative in Parliament from Silverbridge, but who later threw him over. *Prime Min.* 34; *Duke* 14

SQUERCUM, MR. Dolly Longestaffe's lawyer, who was heartily despised by the family lawyers, Slow and Bideawhile, and greatly feared by Dolly's father. "He was a mean-looking little man, not yet above forty, who always wore a stiff light-coloured cotton cravat, an old dress coat, a coloured dingy waistcoat, and light trousers of some hue different from his waistcoat. He generally had on dirty shoes and gaiters. He was light-haired, with light whiskers, with putty-formed features, a squat nose, a large mouth, and very bright blue eyes" (2:58:46). *Way We Live* 58, 69, 73-75, 77, 81, 86, 88, 96

STACKPOOLE, MR. A racing friend of George Hotspur, who reported to Emily Hotspur that George was at the races, after George had told her that he had not gone to them. *Hotspur* 9, 12-14

STAG AND ANTLERS. *See* Nuncombe Putney

STAINES. Samuel Cohenlupe was MP for Staines. *Way We Live* 9

"STAINES AND EGHAM GAZETTE." A paper that had always supported the Runnymede Hunt, and was very bitter against Major Tifto. *Duke* 57

STALHAM PARK. Sir Harry Albury's country place, where he entertained Ayala Dormer and loaned her the pony "Croppy" to ride. *Ayala* 23-26

STANBURY, MRS., of Nuncombe Putney. The widow of a clergyman who had a small living in Devonshire. Mother of Hugh, Priscilla and Dorothy. Appears frequently in *He Knew He Was Right.*

STANBURY, DOROTHY. Hugh Stanbury's younger sister, who lived with Aunt Stanbury at Exeter. She won the heart of the crabbed old lady, although she refused stoutly to be married off to the Rev. Mr. Gibson, and eventually persuaded her aunt to allow her to marry Brooke Burgess.

". . . light haired, with almost flaxen ringlets, worn after the old-fashioned way. . . . She had very soft grey eyes, which ever seemed to beseech you to do something when they looked at you, and her mouth was a beseeching mouth. . . . Her complexion was pale, but there was always present in it a tint of pink running here and there, changing with every word she spoke, changing indeed with every pulse of her heart. Nothing ever was softer than her cheek. . . . She was rather tall than otherwise . . ." (1:8:63).

One of the principal characters in *He Knew He Was Right.*

STANBURY, HUGH. A brilliant but impecunious young Oxonian, who deserted the law for journalism and thus incurred the anger of his Aunt Stanbury, who had paid for his education. He was a classmate of Louis Trevelyan and became involved with his friend's affairs, helping the young wife and her sister to find a temporary home with his own mother. Although he had a formidable rival for Nora Rowley's hand in Charles Glascock, he won her. One of the principal characters in *He Knew He Was Right.*

STANBURY, JEMIMA ("Aunt Stanbury"). A wealthy spinster, who inherited her fortune from a deceased lover, and whose determination to return it intact to the Burgess family interfered with her desire to help her impecunious relatives. For a time she would not consent to the marriage of her niece Dorothy with Brooke Burgess, whom she had made her heir.

"She was a little woman, now nearly sixty years of age, with bright grey eyes, and a strong Roman nose, and thin lips, and a sharp-cut chin. She wore a headgear that almost amounted to a mobcap, and beneath it her grey hair was always frizzled with the greatest care. Her dress was invariably black silk, and she had five gowns,—one for church, one for evening parties, one for driving out, and one for evenings at home and one for mornings" (1:7:54).

Aunt Stanbury is reminiscent of Trollope's cousin Fanny Bent, whom he visited at Exeter as a boy.

One of the principal characters in *He Knew He Was Right.*

STANBURY, PRISCILLA. Hugh's older sister, ". . . a young woman who read a great deal, and even had some gifts of understanding what she read" (1:14:113). Although she played no large role in the story, she was the character Trollope said he intended as the heroine of *He Knew He Was Right.*

STANDISH, LADY LAURA. *See* Kennedy, Lady Laura (Standish)

STANDISH, OSWALD. *See* Chiltern, Oswald Standish, Lord Chiltern

STANHOPE, MRS. Wife of the Rev. Dr. Vesey Stanhope. "In manner and appearance she was exceedingly prepossessing. She had been a beauty, and even now, at fifty-five, she was a handsome woman. Her dress was always perfect. . . . The structure of her attire was always elaborate, and yet never over laboured. She was rich in apparel, but not bedizened with finery; her ornaments were costly, rare, and such as could not fail to attract notice. . . . But when we have said that Mrs. Stanhope knew how to dress, and used her knowledge daily, we have said all. Other purpose in life she had none" (1:9:118-19). *Barchester* 9

STANHOPE, CHARLOTTE. The eldest child of the Rev. Dr. Vesey Stanhope, who devoted her life to an attempt to maintain an appearance of dignity for the rest of the family. Appears frequently in *Barchester Towers.*

STANHOPE, ETHELBERT ("Bertie"). The only son of the Rev. Dr. Vesey Stanhope, an unscrupulous idler, willing to sponge on his unwilling father, or on an unloved wife if such could be provided for him without undue exertion on his part. Goaded by his sister Charlotte, he proposed to Eleanor Harding, but with no success.

"His great fault was an utter absence of that principle, which should have induced him, as the son of a man without fortune, to earn his own bread. . . . He was habitually addicted to making love to ladies, and did so without any scruples of conscience. . . . He had no principle, no regard for others, no self-respect, no desire to be other than a drone in the hive, if only he could, as a drone, get what honey was sufficient for him. He was certainly very handsome. . . . [his eyes] of so light and clear a blue as to make his face remarkable. . . . His light hair was very long and silky, coming down over his coat. His beard had been prepared in holy land, and was patriarchal. He never shaved, and rarely trimmed it. It was glossy, soft, clean, and altogether not unprepossessing. . . . His complexion was fair and almost pink, he was small in height and slender in limb, but well-made, and his voice was of peculiar sweetness. . . . His costume cannot be described, because it was so various; but it was always totally opposed in every principle of colour and construction to the dress of those with whom he for the time consorted" (1:9:129, 32-34).

One of the principal characters in *Barchester Towers.*

STANHOPE, MADELINE. *See* Neroni, Signora Madeline (Stanhope)

STANHOPE, The REV. DR. VESEY. The Vicar of Crabtree Canonicorum in the diocese of Barchester, who had lived for many years in Italy on the salary derived from his neglected duties. He was recalled by Bishop Proudie at Mr. Slope's insistence, but when that dignitary was dismissed, Dr. Stanhope and his family drifted back to Italy.

". . . the least singular and most estimable of them all and yet such good qualities as he possessed were all negative. . . . He was a good-looking rather plethoric gentleman of about sixty years of age. His hair was snow white, very plentiful, and somewhat like wool of the finest description. His whiskers were very large and very white, and gave to his face the appearance of a benevolent sleepy old lion" (*Barchester* 1:9:117).

Most prominent in *Barchester Towers*; briefly in *Thorne* 19; and *Framley* 26, 45

STANTILOUP, MRS. JULIANA. Worsted in a lawsuit with Dr. Wortle over fees for her son's schooling, she became his bitter enemy, and by her campaign of gossip about Mr. and Mrs. Peacocke nearly ruined Dr. Wortle's school. *Wortle* 1-3, 8-15, 19, 23

STAPLE, TOM. "A great man at Oxford . . . leader of the Oxford tutors," who was called in to reinforce the high-church party at Barchester when they wished to make Mr. Harding Dean of the Cathedral. *Barchester* 34

STAPLEDEAN, MARQUIS OF. The patron of the living at Hurst Staple. A miserly misanthrope, living at Bowes Lodge, in Westmoreland. *Bertrams* 3, 16, 26-27, 42-43

STARTUP FARM. The home of George Brattle, the miller's eldest son. *Vicar* 41

STAUBACH, FRAU CHARLOTTE. The widowed aunt of Linda Tressel, who feared that the joys of this life were too much in the girl's mind, and tried to force her to marry old Peter Steinmarc. ". . . the petticoated pietist of Nuremberg is a kindly woman at heart. Only the iron creed, which makes her whole being so grievous to herself and to those about her, constrains her to see wickedness in joy; in every form of pleasure a species of profligacy; in all love for children a pernicious indulgence, endangering their eternal welfare; and in every woman, Satan's easy prey, until guarded by a middle-aged, respectable, unlovable and austere husband."—Escott, p. 233. One of the principal characters in *Linda Tressel*.

STAVELEY, JUDGE. Father of Madeline, Augustus and Isabella, living at Noningsby, where he was a neighbor of Sir Peregrine Orme and Lady Mason. ". . . one of the best men in the world, revered on the bench, and loved by all men" (1:18:138). Appears frequently in *Orley Farm*.

STAVELEY, AUGUSTUS. Son of the Judge, and brother to Madeline. He was a friend and confidant of Felix Graham, and a half-hearted suitor of Sophia Furnival. ". . . a handsome, clever fellow, who had nearly succeeded in getting the Newdigate, and was now a member of the Middle Temple. He was destined to follow the steps of his father, and become a light at the Common Law bar . . ." (1:18:137). Appears frequently in *Orley Farm*.

STAVELEY, ISABELLA. *See* Arbuthnot, Mrs. Isabella (Staveley)

STAVELEY, LADY ISABELLA. ". . . a good, motherly, warm-hearted woman, who thought a great deal about her flowers and fruit . . . much also about her butter and eggs . . . also a great deal about her children, who were all swans" (1:19:144). Appears frequently in *Orley Farm*.

STAVELEY, MADELINE. Daughter of the Judge, who was sought in marriage by young Peregrine Orme and Felix Graham. She loved the latter, and at the end of the novel became engaged to marry him. In a preface to his description of her, Trollope confides to his readers, "I intend that [she] shall . . . be the most interesting personage in this story."

". . . she was very slight, and appeared to be almost too tall for her form . . . but not the less were all her movements soft, graceful and fawn-like. . . . Her face was oval. . . . her nose was Grecian, but perhaps a little too wide at the nostril to be considered perfect in its chiselling. Her hair was soft and brown . . ." (1:19:145-46). Appears frequently in *Orley Farm*.

STEELYARD, MR. The junior counsel for the prosecution in the Orley Farm case. *Orley* 68, 71

STEIN, ANNOT. Daughter of Michael, and the sweetheart of Jacques Chapeau, whom she married when the Vendean revolt had been put down, and he became a barber in Paris. ". . . she was young and rosy; she had soft hair and bright eyes; she could dance all night, and was known to possess in her own right some mysterious little fortune . . . the comfortable sum of five hundred francs" (1:6:164). *Vendée* 6-7, 20, 26, 29, 33-34

STEIN, MICHAEL. The blacksmith at Echanbroignes, who made rude arms for the Vendeans and considered that his two sons, Jean and Peter, could help the cause most by continuing at their trade. They disagreed with him and became valued soldiers. When driven from his home by the advance of the enemy, Michael also fought gallantly at Laval. *Vendée* 6-7, 12-13, 17, 22, 29, 31, 33

STEINMARC, PETER. An elderly town-clerk in the Nuremberg magistrate's office, who had lived for years as a roomer in the home of Linda Tressel and who finally decided to own the house through marriage with its owner. Linda hated him and, to avoid marrying him, eloped with his scapegrace young cousin Ludovic Valcarm. When Ludovic was arrested before the marriage could take place and Linda returned home alone, Peter repudiated her as being unfit to be his wife. One of the principal characters in *Linda Tressel*

STEINMARK, HELEN. Sister of Mark, and friend and confidante of Margaret de Wynter. One of the principal characters in *The Noble Jilt.*

In *Can You Forgive Her?*, represented by Kate Vavasor.

STEINMARK, MARK. The leader of the revolutionary forces of Bruges in 1792. A former suitor of Margaret de Wynter. One of the principal characters in *The Noble Jilt.*

In *Can You Forgive Her?*, represented by George Vavasor.

STEMM, JOSEPH. Sir Thomas Underwood's law clerk and general factotum. "Stemm was hardly more than five feet high, and was a wizened dry old man, with a very old yellow wig. He delighted in scolding all the world, and his special delight was in scolding his master" (1:10:178). Appears frequently in *Ralph the Heir.*

STEVENAGE, DUCHESS OF. A leader of fashion, living at Castle Albury. Augustus Melmotte secured her presence at his daughter's coming-out ball by rescuing her brother Lord Alfred Grendall from bankruptcy. *Way We Live* 4, 21, 27, 32, 59

"STICK-IN-THE-MUD MINE." The diamond mine in Kimberley owned by John Gordon and Fitzwalker Tookey. *Old Man* 18

STICKATIT, GEORGE. The junior member of the firm of Dry and Stickatit, lawyers, and the executor of the estate of George Bertram, Sr. *Bertrams* 45-46

STIGGS, MRS. The Vicar of Bullhampton arranged for Carry Brattle to board with Mrs. Stiggs while he tried, vainly, to induce her father to allow her to return home. *Vicar* 3, 9-10, 14-15

STISTICK, MR. and MRS. Guests at Sir Harry Harcourt's dinner. Mr. Stistick was M P for Peterloo. *Bertrams* 33

STOBE, HERR. An employee at the Sach brothers' brewery, who informed Peter Steinmarc of his cousin's visits to Linda Tressel. *Linda* 11

STOBEL, CARL. A young Viennese diamond-cutter, who married Marie Weber, intimate friend and fellow clerk of Lotta Schmidt. *Lotta*

STOFFLET, JEAN NICOLAS (real person). A gamekeeper, chosen as one of the first leaders in the Royalist uprising in La Vendée. He was killed at Angers. *Vendée* 9-11

STOGPINGUM (more properly "Stoke Pinquium"). Eiderdown and Stogpingum was a parish held by the Rev. Dr. Vesey Stanhope. *Barchester* 9

STOKES, MR. The Germain family lawyer, whose chief attribute was an attempt to avoid making decisions. *Popenjoy* 24-26, 28, 30-31, 61-62

STOVEY, FARMER. A tenant for a short time on the Belton estate. *Belton* 2-3

STOWTE, CAROLINE and SOPHIE. Daughters of Lord Trowbridge, very stodgy maiden ladies, who patronized the villagers at Bullhampton. *Vicar* 17, 72

STRATHBOGY. A Scottish borough, supposed to be within the gift of the Scotts, that was offered to Alaric Tudor as bait to persuade him to advance money to Undy. *Clerks* 24, 29, 32, 35-36

STRATTON. A small town in rural England, where Harry Clavering began his apprenticeship with Mr. Burton of the firm of Beilby and Burton, civil engineers. *Claverings* 3

STRINGER, DANIEL. The clerk at the Dragon of Wantly, whose testimony cleared Mr. Crawley of the accusation of stealing the Soames check. *Last Chron.* 70, 72-74, 76-77

He also appears as Mick Stringer in the play *Did He Steal It?*.

STRINGER, JOHN. The landlord of the Dragon of Wantly in Barchester, which was owned by Mrs. Arabin. When he paid her his rent with a check stolen from Mr. Soames, and she indorsed it to Mr. Crawley without his knowledge of its nature, the difficulties of Mr. Crawley began. *Last Chron.* 70, 72

STRUGGLES OF BROWN, JONES, and ROBINSON, The. By One of the Firm. N.Y., Harper, 1862. Originally published in *The Cornhill Magazine*, Aug. 1861-March 1862.

AUTHOR'S COMMENT. "It was meant to be funny, was full of slang, and was intended as a satire on the ways of trade. . . . I think that there is some good fun in it, but I have heard no one else express such an opinion."—*Autobiography*, 1:9:214.

NOTES. ". . . a loosely written, satirical sketch . . . which a hostile critic might be excused for describing as Thackeray-and-water."—Escott, p. 160.

PLOT. The story is of the partnership in a haberdashery between Brown, a retired dealer in butter, Jones, his son-in-law, and Robinson, a great believer in advertising. As a result of timidity on the part of Brown, peculation by Jones and extravagance by Robinson, the business soon became bankrupt. Robinson aspired to the hand of Maryanne, Brown's youngest daughter, but her other suitor, Brisket the butcher, seemed more prosperous. Maryanne played off one lover against the other until she was eventually discarded by both, and spent her days nursing her complaining invalid father.

STUART, JACK. The owner of the yacht that took Sir Hugh and Archibald Clavering on the fishing trip to Norway, during which they were both drowned. *Claverings* 35-36, 38-39, 44, 47

STUBBER, CAPTAIN. A money-lender, who held much of George Hotspur's paper. *Hotspur* 8, 10, 12, 18, 22-23

STUBBS, COL. JONATHAN. A staff officer at Aldershot, and a cousin of the Marchesa Baldoni and Lady Albury, both of whom aided him in his courtship of Ayala Dormer. Despite his high character, Ayala did not at first recognize him as her "Angel of light," but he was persistent and at last was accepted. "His hair was ruby red, and very short; and he had a thick red beard; not silky, but bristly, with each hair almost a dagger,—and his mouth was enormous. His eyes were very bright, and there was a smile about him, partly of fun, partly of good humour" (1:16:194). One of the principal characters in *Ayala's Angel.*

STUMFOLD, MRS. Wife of the crusading Mr. Stumfold, whose chief pleasure in life was browbeating her husband's women parishioners. *Mackenzie* 3-5, 9-13, 19, 30

STUMFOLD, The REV. MR. An Evangelical clergyman, very popular with the ladies at Littlebath. "His chief enemies were card-playing and dancing as regarded the weaker sex, and hunting and horse racing . . . as regarded the stronger" (1:2:29). *Mackenzie* 2-5, 9, 12-13, 19

STURT, FARMER, and WIFE. Neighbors and almost the only intimate friends of Mrs. Ray and her daughters at Bragg's End. Appear frequently in *Rachel Ray.*

SUEZ. Where George Walker was offered entertainment intended for a visiting dignitary, Sir George Walker, and was dropped when the distinguished guest appeared. *Walker*

SUFFOLK.

BABINGTON HOUSE. Home of John Caldigate's cousins, the Babingtons. *Caldigate*

BUNDLESHAM. Home of the Primero family. *Way We Live*

CARBURY HALL. Home of Roger Carbury. *Way We Live*

CAVERSHAM. The Longestaffe estate. *Way We Live*

POPPLECOURT. Estate of Lord Popplecourt. *Duke*

TOODLUM. George Whitstable's house. *Way We Live*

SUFFOLK STREET. *See* London

SUPPLEHOUSE, MR. A newspaperman, an intimate friend of Nathaniel Sowerby, and an MP who was backed by the "Jupiter" for a place in the Cabinet. He was greatly hated by Harold Smith, who announced, "There is a man endowed by no great talent, enjoying no public confidence, untrusted as a politician, and unheard of even as a writer by the world at large, and yet, because he is on the staff of the 'Jupiter' he is able to overturn the government and throw the whole country into dismay" (2:7:123). *Framley* 2, 3, 6, 18, 20, 23-24, 28-29

SURBITON COTTAGE. The suburban home of the Woodwards, in Hampton. The setting for much of *The Three Clerks.*

SURREY.

BOLSOVER HOUSE. Home of Mrs. Brownlow. *Ralph*

FAWN COURT. Estate of Lord Fawn. *Eustace*

The Finns had a place in Surrey. *Duke*

THE HORNS. Lady Glencora's wedding present from the old Duke of Omnium. Frequently mentioned throughout the Parliamentary series, and occasionally in the Barchester series.

ONGAR PARK. Lady Ongar had a life interest in the property, but she returned it to the family. *Claverings*

POPHAM VILLA. Where Sir Thomas Underwood took a house for his two daughters. *Ralph*

SURBITON COTTAGE. Home of Mrs. Woodward and her three daughters. *Clerks*

SURTEES, The REV. MR. The curate to the Rev. Mr. Mainwaring, supposed to be a suitor for the hand of Mary Masters. "He was a painstaking, eager, clever young man, with aspirations in church matters which were always being checked by the rector" (1:1:12). *Amer. Sen.* 1, 42

SUSSEX.

MERLE PARK. Sir Thomas Tringle's suburban house. *Ayala*

PICKERING HALL. Purchased by Augustus Melmotte from the Longestaffes. *Way We Live*

SWAN, MARY. *See* Mollett, Mrs. Mary (Swan)

SWANTON, The REV. MR. The Rev. Mr. Boyce's curate at Allington, whose sermons, according to Lily Dale, were much too long. *Last Chron.* 16

SWITZERLAND. Where Alice Vavasor spent a vacation with her cousins Kate and George, and where she later went with Plantagenet Palliser and Lady Glencora. *Can You* 5-6, 68-70, 73-76

TAGMAGGERT, LADY EMILY. A colorless, docile creature, whose chief recommendation was a considerable fortune. She was Lady Aylmer's choice as a wife for her son. *Belton* 32

TALBOT, MR. *See* Mollett, Matthew

TALBOYS, MRS. ARABELLA. An unconventional and voluble Englishwoman, who belonged to an artistic-literary set in Rome. Her unexplained presence there without her husband, and her outspoken rebellion against most social laws, led to embarrassing situations. Principal character in *Mrs. General Talboys.*

TALLOWAX, MISS. Lady George Germain's great-aunt, much impressed by the social position of her niece. "... about sixty, very small, very healthy, with streaky red cheeks, small gray eyes, and a brown front" (1:4:47-48). *Popenjoy* 3-5, 63

TALLOWAX, MR. The wealthy grandfather of Mary Lovelace, whose will, leaving her his fortune, made possible her marriage to Lord George Germain. *Popenjoy* 1

TALLY-HO LODGE. Major Tifto's "box," in the neighborhood of Egham. *Duke* 36

TALMONT, PRINCE OF (real person). One of the leaders in the Royalist uprising in La Vendée. *Vendée* 1-2, 4, 11, 26-27, 33

TANKERVILLE. The borough in Durham that returned Phineas Finn to Parliament after his return from Ireland, and again following his trial. The Lambton Arms was his election headquarters. *Redux* 1-4, 13, 71

TAPPETT, TONY. A huntsman of the Rufford and Ufford pack. *Ayala* 23-24, 50, 64

TAPPITT, MRS. MARGARET. Wife of Thomas, whom she was quite capable of managing. Her enmity against Luke Rowan and Rachel Ray stemmed from her thwarted wish to have Luke as a husband for any one of her three daughters. One of the principal characters in *Rachel Ray.*

TAPPITT, THOMAS. The manager and part-owner of the Bungall and Tappitt brewery, and maker of very bad beer. He bitterly resented Luke Rowan's attempts to improve the beverage as the beer sold well as it was, but he finally lost the management of the business to Luke. One of the principal characters in *Rachel Ray.*

TAPPITT FAMILY. Augusta, Martha and Cherry. They were great friends of Rachel Ray, until she outshone them at their own ball and a coldness resulted between them. ". . . good-humoured, laughing, ordinary girls,—very much alike, with long brown curls, fresh complexions, large mouths, and thick noses." Important characters in *Rachel Ray*.

TAUNTON. The town nearest to Belton Castle, the home of Clara Amedroz. *Belton* 1-3, 6-7

TAVISTOCK.

BEDFORD HOTEL. Where Alaric Tudor and Fidus Neverbend stayed while investigating the "Wheal Mary Jane" tin mine. *Clerks* 9

BLUE DRAGON INN. Where Undy Scott persuaded Alaric Tudor to invest in the "Wheal Mary Jane" tin mine. *Clerks* 9

TAVISTOCK SQUARE. *See* London

TELEGRAPH GIRL, The. In *Why Frau Frohmann Raised Her Prices and Other Stories*, 1882. Originally published in *Good Cheer*, Christmas number of *Good Words*, Dec. 1877. Reprinted in N.Y. by Ogilvie, 1882.

PLOT. Two telegraph girls, Lucy Graham and Sophie Wilson, shared a modest lodging in London. Lucy was distressed at Sophie's frivolity—spending her money on ribbons and looking continually for a husband. Abraham Hall, a widower with a small child, lived in the same house. Lucy admired him for his achievements as an engineer, but Sophie frankly flirted with him and both girls thought he was attracted to her. She became ill and was ordered to the seashore, so that the rent for their room fell on Lucy, who nevertheless managed to send part of her small earnings to help defray Sophie's expenses. Abraham Hall tried to share the burden but Lucy firmly refused his help, and was so selfless and courageous that he fell in love with her, and when he secured another position, they were married. Sophie recovered her health and married a barber at the seaside resort where she had been living.

TEMPEST, The REV. DR. MORTIMER. The old Rector of Silverbridge, who was chairman of the Commission to examine Mr. Crawley as to his possession of the stolen check, and who had a memorable interview with Mrs. Proudie regarding it. "Dr. Tempest was well known among his parishioners to be hard and unsympathetic, some said unfeeling also, and cruel; but it was admitted by those who disliked him most that he was both practical and just, and that he cared for the welfare of many, though he was rarely touched by the misery of one" (*Last Chron.* 2:4:27). Most prominent in *The Last Chronicle of Barset*; briefly, as seconding the nomination of Lord Silverbridge as MP for Silverbridge, in *Duke* 14

TEMPLE, The. *See* London

TENDEL, FRAULEIN, and SISTER. Two impecunious maiden ladies from Innsbruck, who spent their summers at the Peacock. It was partly because of them that Frau Frohmann refused to raise her prices, feeling that she might deprive them of their holidays. *Frohmann*

TENWAY JUNCTION. A railway junction some six or seven miles from London, where Ferdinand Lopez threw himself in front of an express train and was killed. *Prime Min.* 60

TETCHEN. The servant of Frau Staubach, who assisted Ludovic Valcarm in his courtship. One of the principal characters in *Linda Tressel*.

TEWETT, SIR GRIFFIN. A young baronet engaged to Lucinda Roanoke, although she hated him and went mad at the seeming necessity of marrying him. "He was a fair, frail young man, with a bad eye, and a weak mouth, and a thin hand, who was fond of liqueurs, and hated to the death any acquaintance who won a five-pound note of him, or any tradesman who wished to have his bill paid" (2:36:133). One of the principal characters in *The Eustace Diamonds.*

THOMAS, MRS. The woman whom Felix Graham engaged to superintend the education of Mary Snow, so that she might become a suitable wife for him. *Orley* 33, 39, 48, 54

THOMAS, JOHN. A clerk in the Post Office, who became Postmaster-General. A caricature of Johnny Eames in the burlesque *Never, Never,—Never, Never.*

THOMPSON, MRS. The widow of an Indian civil servant, who placed her daughter Lillian in a school at Le Puy while she and her youngest daughter, Mimmy, went to live at an hotel in the same city. She was courted by a kindly gentleman, M. Lacordaire, whom she had heard called a "*marchand.*" Although she considered her station in life something above one "in trade," she accepted him, even after he had told her somewhat diffidently that he was a tailor. Principal character in *The Chateau of Prince Polignac.*

THOMPSON, JANE. The fiancée of Charles Jones. His unconventional meeting with her sister Mrs. Brown was explained at the festivities in *Christmas at Thompson Hall.*

THOMPSON, JOHN. The owner of Thompson Hall, where the Browns and Charles Jones spent the Christmas holidays. *Christmas*

THOMPSON, SARAH. The protégée of Lady Lufton, who insisted that she be a teacher to the parish children, against Mark Robarts' better judgment. *Framley* 1

THOMPSON HALL. The scene of the festivities in *Christmas at Thompson Hall.*

THORNE, HENRY. Father of Mary Thorne, and brother of Dr. Thorne. A black sheep whose conduct forced his relatives to close Ullathorne to him, and so brought about a coldness between Dr. Thorne and the Ullathorne family. He seduced Mary Scatcherd, and was killed by her brother Roger. *Thorne* 2, 7

THORNE, MRS. MARTHA (Dunstable). Daughter of a wealthy patent medicine tycoon, whose business, the "Ointment of Lebanon," she managed after his death. Despite her origin she was much sought-after by those who hoped to profit from her wealth and the place in society she had made for herself. Although she had many suitors, she married Dr. Thorne.

"She has a very high colour, very red cheeks, a large mouth, big white teeth, a broad nose, and bright, small black eyes. Her hair also was black and bright, but very crisp and strong, and was combed close round her face in small crisp black ringlets. Since she had been brought out into the fashionable world some one of her instructors in fashion had given her to understand that curls were not the thing. 'They'll always pass muster,' Miss Dunstable had replied, 'when they are done up with bank-notes' " (*Thorne* 2:2:19).

Most prominent in *Framley Parsonage* and *Doctor Thorne*; briefly in *Last Chron.* 2, 14, 45, 52-53, 59, 76

THORNE, MARY. *See* Gresham, Mrs. Mary (Thorne)

THORNE, MRS. MAUDE (Hippesley). Daughter of the Dean of Exeter Cathedral, and friend of Cecilia Holt. *Kept Dark* 1, 3, 6, 16, 20

THORNE, MONICA. Sister of Wilfred Thorne, ". . . who participated in his prejudices and feelings so strongly, that she was a living caricature of all his foibles. . . . Genealogy was her favorite insanity. . . . Her virtues were too numerous to describe, and not sufficiently interesting to deserve description. . . .

"In her person and dress she was perfect, and well she knew her own perfection. She was a small elegantly made old woman, with a face from which the glow of her youth had not departed without leaving some streaks of a roseate hue. She was proud of her colour, proud of her grey hair which she wore in short crisp curls peering out all around her face from the dainty white lace cap. . . . She was proud of her teeth, which were still white and numerous, proud of her bright cheery eye, proud of her short jaunty step, and very proud of the neat, precise, small feet with which those steps were taken. She was proud also, ay, very proud, of the rich brocaded silk in which it was her custom to ruffle through her drawing-room" (*Barchester* 2:3:56-57).

Most prominent in *Barchester Towers* 22-23, 33-37, 48-49; briefly in *Thorne* 7, 47; and *Last Chron.* 2, 16, 47, 83

THORNE, DR. THOMAS. A doctor in Barchester, later in Greshamsbury, who adopted his brother Henry's illegitimate child Mary, and brought her up as his own. He married Martha Dunstable, and became a country gentleman of Chaldicotes.

"No man plumed himself on good blood more than Dr. Thorne. . . . He had within him an inner, stubborn, self-admiring pride, which made him believe himself to be better and higher than those around him. . . . He was brusque, authoritative, given to contradiction . . . and inclined to indulge in a sort of quiet raillery. . . . People did not always know whether he was laughing at, or with them" (*Thorne* 1:3:57).

Most prominent in *Doctor Thorne*; also in *Framley* 8, 28, 38-39, 47-48; and as a member of the Commission to question Mr. Crawley in *The Last Chronicle of Barset*.

THORNE, WILFRED. The owner of Ullathorne, and Squire of St. Ewold's. A bachelor of fifty years. ". . . a man of considerable literary attainments. . . . His favorite authors were Montaigne and Burton, and he knew more perhaps than any other man in his county, and the next to it of the English essayists of the two last centuries. . . . He was a great proficient in all questions of genealogy" (*Barchester* 2:3:44). Most prominent in *Barchester Towers* 22-23, 35-37, 46, 49; briefly in *Thorne* 2, 7, 47; *Framley* 3, 6; and *Last Chron.* 16, 58, 82-83

THORNE SERVANTS.

BRIDGET. Who defended herself with a rolling pin when Joe, Louis Scatcherd's man, tried to flirt with her. Engaged to "Tummas." *Thorne* 34

JANET. The "senior domestic." *Thorne* 34

THOMAS. The Doctor's groom, engaged to Bridget. *Thorne* 34

THOROUGHBUNG, JOE. A young brewer in Buntingford, who married Harry Annesley's sister Mary. *Scarborough* 22-25, 28-29, 44, 48, 50-51, 59

THOROUGHBUNG, MATILDA. A self-sufficient maiden lady of forty-odd years, who was chosen by Peter Prosper as his bride, but whose canny business sense alienated his somewhat lukewarm affections. Her insistence on managing her own fortune, and on providing a home for her companion Miss Tickle, finally proved too much to endure, and Peter withdrew his offer. *Scarborough* 22-28, 43-44, 48, 50-51, 59

THREE CLERKS, The. London, Bentley, 1858. 3v.

AUTHOR'S COMMENT. "It was certainly the best novel I had yet written. The plot is not so good as that of *The Macdermots*; nor are there any characters in the book equal to those of Mrs. Proudie and the Warden; but the work has a more continued interest, and contains the first well-described love-scene that I ever wrote. The passage in which Kate Woodward, thinking that she will die, tries to take leave of the lad she loves, still brings tears to my eyes when I read it. I had not the heart to kill her. I never could do that. And I do not doubt but that they are living happily together to this day."—*Autobiography*, 1:6:148.

Notes. "I return the *Three Clerks* with our true thanks and appreciation. We both quite agree with you in considering it the best of the three clever novels before the public. [*The Warden* and *Barchester Towers* are probably meant.] My husband, who can seldom get a novel to hold him, has been held by all three, and by this the strongest. Also, it has qualities which the others gave no sign of. For instance, I was wrung to tears by the third volume. What a thoroughly *man's* book it is."—Letter from Elizabeth Barrett Browning to Mrs. T. A. Trollope, dated Casa Guidi, Fiesole. From T. A. Trollope, *What I Remember*, p.402.

Trollope lovers will treasure this book for two reasons—the first appearance of Mr. Chaffanbrass, the lawyer, and the picture of Trollope's own early days in London as shown in the story of Charley Tudor.

Plot. Henry Norman, with his friends Alaric and Charley Tudor, all of them in government service, were frequent visitors at the suburban home of Mrs. Woodward and her three daughters. Henry loved Gertrude, the eldest daughter, but she refused him as she loved Alaric. Alaric won by competitive examination a place to which Henry aspired but for which he was unwilling to compete and, when he became engaged to Gertrude, Henry felt doubly aggrieved and bitterly angry. In a desire to make money quickly, Alaric fell into the hands of Undy Scott, a stockbroker, who induced him to join in several dubious ventures, for one of which he was persuaded to embezzle from a trust fund. He was tried and sentenced to six months' imprisonment.

Henry meantime had succeeded to the family estates and was engaged to marry the second Woodward daughter, Linda. He generously aided Gertrude in clearing up her husband's affairs and, on Alaric's release from prison, helped them to emigrate to Australia.

The third clerk, Charley Tudor, spent several profitless years in the Internal Navigation Office, wasting his time and getting into debt. He became involved with the moneylenders, narrowly escaped marriage with a barmaid and completely lost faith in himself. Alaric's catastrophe, however, brought him to a realization of his danger and, largely through the influence of Katie Woodward, he pulled himself together, secured a better position, and when Katie recovered from a seemingly mortal illness, they were married.

THREE HONEST MEN (inn). *See* Salisbury

THUMBLE, The REV. CALEB. A humble and obsequious pensioner in the train of Mrs. Proudie, to whom she planned to give the living at Hogglestock when Mr. Crawley was ejected. ". . . a little man, about forty years of age . . . who existed on such chance clerical crumbs as might fall from the table of the bishop's patronage. . . . He was a humble, mild-voiced man when within the palace precincts" (1:9:95). Appears frequently in *The Last Chronicle of Barset*.

He plays the same part in the plot of *Did He Steal It?*, but as a schoolmaster rather than a clergyman.

THWAITE, DANIEL. A journeyman tailor, son of old Thomas Thwaite, who was brought up with Lady Anna and had received her promise to marry him. Despite the Countess' rage, and her attempt to murder him, the marriage took place, and the pair left England to live in Sydney, Australia. One of the principal characters in *Lady Anna.*

THWAITE, THOMAS. A tailor in the town of Keswick, somewhat of a freethinker, who, because of his belief in the justice of the Countess Lovel's claim to her title, spent on her his entire fortune. When his son and Lady Anna fell in love, the Countess promptly forgot all his past kindnesses and forbade the marriage. Embittered, he died leaving his son only the accounts showing the debt due him from the Countess. One of the principal characters in *Lady Anna.*

THWAITE HALL. The home of Major Garrow, near Penrith in Westmoreland. The setting for *The Mistletoe Bough.*

TICKLE, JEMIMA. The life-long companion of Miss Thoroughbung, and the final reason for the failure of that lady to marry Peter Prosper. *Scarborough* 23, 26-27, 44, 48, 50

TICKLER, The REV. TOBIAS. The curate of a district church in Bethnal Green, a widower with three children, who married Bishop Proudie's eldest daughter, Olivia. *Framley* 40, 45, 48

TIERNEY, MAT. A guest at Handicap Lodge, and later at Grey Abbey. "He was a fat, jolly fellow, always laughing, and usually in a good humour; he was very fond of what he considered the world; and the world, at least that part of it which knew him, returned the compliment" (1:8:199). *Kellys* 8, 10, 15, 30, 32

TIFTO, MAJOR. The joint owner with Lord Silverbridge of the horse "Prime Minister." Angered because his partner had snubbed him, he lamed the horse just before the Leger and caused Lord Silverbridge a loss of £70,000. "He was a well-made little man, good-looking for those who like such good looks. He was light-haired and blue-eyed, with regular and yet not inexpressive features. But his eyes were small and never tranquil, and rarely capable of looking at the person who was speaking to him. He had small, well-trimmed, glossy whiskers, with the best-kept moustache, and the best-kept tuft on his chin which were to be seen anywhere" (1:6:69). One of the principal characters in *The Duke's Children.*

TILLIETUDLEM. The Scottish borough that returned Undy Scott to Parliament. *Clerks* 8, 24, 29

TINTAGEL. The Cornish town near which Mahala Tringlos and her grandfather lived, and where for a time Mahala went to school. *Malachi*

TODD, MISS SALLY. A friend and fellow traveler of Miss Baker, who lived at the Paragon in Littlebath, and was happiest when giving parties. Two memorable ones were those in the Valley of Jehoshaphat, where she entertained the Bertrams, father and son; and the card party in Littlebath that so annoyed the Stumfoldians. Sir Lionel Bertram was interested in her fortune, and proposed marriage, but with no success.

". . . a maiden lady, fat, fair, and perhaps almost forty; a jolly, jovial lady, intent on seeing the world, and indifferent to many of its prejudices and formal restraints" (*Bertrams* 1:9:162-63).

". . . is said to have been modelled on Frances Power Cobbe, a fat jolly lady who was prominent as a humanitarian and an anti-vivisectionist."—Sadleir, p. 386n.

Prominent in *The Bertrams* 6-13, 21-22, 27-33; and *Miss Mackenzie* 3-5, 9-13, 19

TODD, BREHGERT and GOLDSHEIMER. Augustus Melmotte's London bankers, almost ruined by their association with him. *Way We Live* 45

TOFF, MRS. The managing housekeeper at Manor Cross, a great gossip and a power in the servants' hall. *Popenjoy* 21-24, 31, 46, 56

TOFFY, CONSTABLE. A bumbling country official, who, after many false leads, uncovered the evidence that freed Sam Brattle from the accusation of being the murderer of Farmer Trumbull. *Vicar* 15, 46, 51, 53

TOMBE, MR. Mr. Grey's lawyer, who arranged to supply George Vavasor with money from Mr. Grey's account, rather than from Alice Vavasor's. "Mr. Tombe was a remarkable man in his way. He wore powder to his hair,—was very polite in his bearing,—was somewhat asthmatic, and wheezed in his talking,—and was, moreover, the most obedient of men, though it was said of him that he managed the whole income of the Ely Chapter just as he pleased" (2:11:85). *Can You* 37, 41, 44, 51-52

TOMKINS, MARY. A caricature of Lily Dale in the burlesque *Never, Never,—Never, Never.*

TOMLINSON, MRS. MARY (Scatcherd). Seduced by Henry Thorne, she was the mother of his illegitimate child, Mary. When Dr. Thorne adopted the child, she married a village workman and they emigrated to America. ". . . an apprentice to a straw-bonnet maker . . . a model of female beauty of the strong and robust cast, and had a reputation as being a girl of good character and honest, womanly conduct" (1:2:33). *Thorne* 2, 10, 13

TONEROE. Martin Kelly's farm in County Mayo, *Kellys* 1

TOODLUM. A country house in Suffolk, belonging to George Whitstable. *Way We Live* 78

TOOGOOD, THOMAS. A lawyer at Gray's Inn with a jolly family of twelve children. He was a cousin of Mrs. Crawley, who persuaded her husband to consult him in the matter of the stolen check. Though his help was but grudgingly accepted, he was successful in uncovering the real thief, and so cleared Mr. Crawley's name. "He was a good-humoured, cheery-looking man about fifty years of age, with grizzled hair and sunburnt face, and large whiskers" (*Last Chron.* 1:32:270-71). Most prominent in *The Last Chronicle of Barset*; also in the play *Did He Steal It?*.

TOOKEY, FITZWALKER. An unreliable business associate of John Gordon in his Kimberley diamond mine. *Old Man* 18, 22

TOPPS, MAHOGANY. The chairman of the meeting at the Bobtailed Fox that deposed Major Tifto from his position as M F H of the Runnymede Hunt. *Duke* 57-58

TORRINGTON, MR. One of the executors of the estate of Mr. Martock, whose possession of the original deed, dissolving the partnership of Mason and Martock, made necessary his appearance at the second Orley Farm trial. *Orley* 68

TOWERS, TOM. The newspaperman who wrote indignant articles in the "Jupiter" denouncing the management of the Hiram's Hospital funds. ". . . a very leading genius, and supposed to have high employment on the staff of the *Jupiter*. . . . It is probable that Tom Towers considered himself the most powerful man in Europe; and so he walked on from day to day, studiously striving to look a man, but knowing within his breast that he was a god"

(*Warden* 14:225). *Warden* 10, 14-15; *Barchester* 32, 43; *Framley* 28-29, 31, 37, 47

TOWNSEND, The REV. AENEAS. The Rector of the parish of Drumbarrow, near Castle Richmond. A well-meaning man, but chiefly noted for his hatred of popery. His wife, an intimate friend of Miss Letty Fitzgerald, was even more intolerant than her husband. Of minor importance, but appear frequently throughout *Castle Richmond.*

TOZER, JOHN and TOM. Jewish moneylenders, who held the notes of Lord Lufton and Mark Robarts. *Framley* 12, 19, 27, 42, 44

TRAFFICK, MRS. AUGUSTA (Tringle). The elder daughter of Sir Thomas Tringle, whose large dowry had secured Septimus Traffick as a husband. A selfish, vindictive woman, who hated Ayala Dormer because of her charm and beauty, both of which she lacked. One of the principal characters in *Ayala's Angel.*

TRAFFICK, SEPTIMUS. Son of Lord Boardotrade, and MP for Port Glasgow. He married Augusta Tringle and her £120,000, and became most obnoxious to his father-in-law Sir Thomas, who considered him a very bad investment. "He was somewhat bald, somewhat grey, somewhat fat, and had lost that look of rosy plumpness which is seldom, I fear, compatible with hard work and late hours. He was not particularly ugly, nor was he absurd in appearance. But he looked to be a disciple of business, not of pleasure, nor of art" (1:5:59). One of the principal characters in *Ayala's Angel.*

TRAFFORD, LORD AUGUSTUS, LORD FREDERIC, and LORD GREGORY. The three children of the Marquis of Kingsbury by his second marriage. *Fay* 1, 10, 18, 26, 31, 34, 40

TRAFFORD, LADY FRANCES. Daughter of the Marquis of Kingsbury, who was allowed to marry George Roden after he became acknowledged as Duca di Crinola. One of the principal characters in *Marion Fay.*

TRAFFORD, LIONEL. *See* Kingsbury, Marquis of

TRAFFORD PARK. The country estate of the Marquis of Kingsbury. At different times mentioned as in Yorkshire, and in Shropshire. *Fay* 1, 18-19

TRAVERS, MR. The candidate in opposition to George Vavasor for the Chelsea seat in Parliament. *Can You* 4

TRAVERS and TREASON. A banking firm in the City, of which Sir Thomas Tringle was the senior partner. *Ayala* 1

TREFOIL, MISS. The Dean of Barchester's only child, who kept house for him. ". . . a gaunt spinster . . . very learned in stones, ferns, plants, and vermin, and who had written a book about petals" (1:10:150). *Barchester* 10-11, 31

TREFOIL, The REV. MR. The Dean of the Barchester Cathedral, after whose death Mr. Slope connived to secure the post. It was offered to Mr. Harding who refused it, and finally went to Mr. Arabin. *Barchester* 7, 10, 31-33

TREFOIL, ARABELLA. While engaged to John Morton, she decided that a marriage to Lord Rufford would be more advantageous and used all her wiles to bring it about. When she failed, and John Morton died leaving her a fortune, she married Mounser Green and went with him to a diplomatic post in Patagonia.

"She was a big, fair girl whose copious hair was managed after such a fashion that no one could guess what was her own and what was purchased.

She certainly had fine eyes. . . . They were very large, beautifully blue, but never bright; and the eyebrows over them were perfect. Her cheeks were somewhat too long and the distance from her well-formed nose to her upper lip too great. Her mouth was small and her teeth excellent. But the charm of which men spoke the most was the brilliance of her complexion. . . . Though she was tall and big she never let an awkward movement to escape from her. . . . No young woman could walk across an archery ground with a finer step, or manage a train with more perfect ease, or sit upon her horse with a more complete look of being at home there. . . . She . . . did not care much for pleasure. But she did care to be a great lady,—one who would be allowed to swim out of rooms before others, one who could snub others, one who could show real diamonds when others wore paste, one who might be sure to be asked everywhere even by the people who hated her. She rather liked being hated by women and did not want any man to be in love with her,—except as far as might be sufficient for the purpose of marriage" (1:12:124-26).

In a letter dated Feb. 17, 1877, Trollope writes: "The critics . . . will tell me that she is unwomanly, unnatural, turgid,—the creation of a morbid imagination, striving after effect by laboured abominations. But I swear I have known the woman, not one special woman . . . but all the traits, all the cleverness, all the patience, all the courage, all the self-abnegation—and all the failure. Will such a one as Arabella Trefoil be damned? . . . I think that she will go to a kind of third-class heaven in which she will always be getting third-class husbands."

One of the principal characters in *The American Senator.*

TREFOIL, LADY AUGUSTUS. As unscrupulous as her daughter, but not so clever. Her life was made up of subterfuges and unwanted country visits, in an attempt to arrange a satisfactory marriage for Arabella. One of the principal characters in *The American Senator.*

TREFOIL, LORD AUGUSTUS. Father of Arabella, and younger brother of the Duke of Mayfair, from whom he drew a sufficient dole to enable him to live in comfort, providing he lived alone, with no responsibilities for the debts of his wife and daughter. "He was a handsome fat man, with a long grey beard, who passed his whole life in eating, drinking, and playing whist, and was troubled by no scruples and no principles" (2:22:238). *Amer. Sen.* 49, 56, 60

TREGEAR, MR. The Squire of Polwenning in Cornwall, a country gentleman whose second son, Frank, married Lady Mary Palliser. *Duke* 55

TREGEAR, FRANCIS OLIPHANT ("Frank"). The younger son of a Cornish gentleman, and an Oxford classmate of Lord Silverbridge. Though he was without fortune and had no profession, Lady Mary Palliser married him, despite the opposition of her father, the Duke of Omnium. "He was beautiful to look at. . . . He was dark, with hair that was almost black . . . with clear brown eyes, a nose as regular as Apollo's, and a mouth in which was ever to be found that expression of manliness, which of all characteristics is the one women love best. He was five feet ten in height. He was always well dressed, and yet always so dressed as to seem to show that his outward garniture had not been matter of trouble to him" (1:3:30-31). One of the principal characters in *The Duke's Children.*

TREGOTHNAN HALL. The Docimers' house in Cornwall, to which Imogene Docimer was taken to keep her away from Frank Houston. *Ayala* 59

TREMENHERE, MISS. Jilted George Western to marry Capt. Walter Geraldine. *Kept Dark* 4, 8

TRENDELLSOHN, ANTON. Son of Stephen, carrying the major responsibility for his business. He was in love with Nina Balatka, despite their difference in race, and married her in the face of all opposition. Hero of *Nina Balatka.*

TRENDELLSOHN, STEPHEN. A wealthy old Jewish merchant of Prague, at one time a partner of Josef Balatka. He objected strongly to the marriage of their two children. *Nina* 1, 4, 6

TRESSEL, LINDA. An orphan in Nuremberg, brought up by her aunt Frau Staubach in an atmosphere of repression and false Christianity. To escape a marriage with an old man that was arranged by her aunt, she eloped with a worthless young political agitator, but he was arrested as they stepped from the train and Linda returned home alone. The hated elderly suitor considered her conduct made her unfit to be his wife and repudiated her. Heroine of *Linda Tressel.*

TRETTON PARK. A valuable property in Hertfordshire, belonging to John Scarborough. The setting for most of the action in *Mr. Scarborough's Family.*

TREVELYAN, SIR CHARLES (real person). In his *Autobiography*, Trollope admits that he drew the character of Sir Gregory Hardlines in *The Three Clerks* from his knowledge of Sir Charles Trevelyan.

TREVELYAN, MRS. EMILY (Rowley). The eldest daughter of Sir Marmaduke Rowley, married to Louis Trevelyan. She stubbornly resisted the orders of her jealous husband to forbid Colonel Osborne the house, insisting that to do so would be to justify his charges. She followed Trevelyan to Italy after he had abducted their son, and persuaded him to return to England for medical treatment, where he soon died. One of the principal characters in *He Knew He Was Right.*

TREVELYAN, LOUEY. The infant son of Louis and Emily Trevelyan, who was kidnaped by his half-mad father and taken to Italy. Appears seldom, but spoken of frequently in *He Knew He Was Right.*

TREVELYAN, LOUIS. A wealthy young landowner, who married Emily Rowley. Becoming jealous of Colonel Osborne, a friend of Emily's father, he brooded on his inability to compel his wife to dismiss the Colonel and finally went mad. "The progress of Louis Trevelyan from an idle, rich, good-looking, affectionate husband, to the mad invalid whose death was made premature and miserable by his own weakness is in the grand manner."—Christopher LaFarge, "I Know He Was Right," *Saturday Review of Literature*, Jan. 27, 1940, pp. 12-14. Principal character in *He Knew He Was Right.*

TRIBBLEDALE, DANIEL. A clerk in the employ of Pogson and Littlebird, who married Clara Demijohn. *Fay* 29-30, 32, 41, 57-58, 61

TRIGGER, MR. Mr. Griffenbottom's confidential agent, who tried to manage the election at Percycross for both Conservative candidates. His dishonesty in bribing, if not in the outright buying, of votes caused the borough to be disenfranchised. Appears frequently throughout the election scenes in *Ralph the Heir.*

TRINGLE, AUGUSTA. *See* Traffick, Mrs. Augusta (Tringle)

TRINGLE, EMMELINE, LADY. Wife of Sir Thomas, with two unattractive daughters and a hobbledehoy son. She made a home first for Ayala Dormer, and then Lucy, but her own daughters' jealousy of the attractive cousins made her life burdensome. ". . . with a house at the top of Queen's Gate . . . with a palatial moor in Scotland, with a seat in Sussex and as many carriages and horses as would suit an archduchess. Lady Tringle had everything in the world, an open-handed husband, who was said to have told her that money was a matter of no consideration" (1:1:2). One of the principal characters in *Ayala's Angel.*

TRINGLE, GERTRUDE. The younger daughter of Sir Thomas, whose chances of marriage seemed to hinge on her having the same dowry as her older sister. Her first suitor, Frank Houston, retired on finding that she would have no dowry at all if she married him. Captain Batsby married her in the hope that Sir Thomas would relent. One of the principal characters in *Ayala's Angel.*

TRINGLE, SIR THOMAS. The senior partner in the great banking firm of Travers and Treason, and father of Augusta, Gertrude and Tom, whose matrimonial affairs caused him a great deal of trouble. He was generous to his two nieces, Ayala and Lucy Dormer. ". . . seemed to carry arrogance in his brow and in his paunch" (1:1:5). One of the principal characters in *Ayala's Angel.*

TRINGLE, TOM. The only son and heir of Sir Thomas, whose unrequited love for Ayala Dormer led him into all sorts of scrapes. One of the principal characters in *Ayala's Angel.*

TRINGLOS, MAHALA. Granddaughter of Malachi, who gathered seaweed to earn their precarious living. Heroine of *Malachi's Cove.*

TRINGLOS, MALACHI. A poor old cripple, called "Old Glos," whose long years of gathering seaweed for fertilizer had left him dependent on his granddaughter Mahala. One of the principal characters in *Malachi's Cove.*

TRINITY COLLEGE, Dublin. Phineas Finn graduated from Trinity. *Finn*

The Rev. Mr. Maguire had been a student there. *Mackenzie*

TRISTRAM, MISSES HARRIET and JULIA. Rather horsy young women, members of the Hamworth Hunt. *Orley* 28, 30, 38

TROW, AARON. The escaped convict who attacked Anastasia Bergen when she refused him money, and was later killed by Anastasia's fiancé in a dramatic fight on the cliffs and in the sea. Principal character in *Aaron Trow.*

TROWBRIDGE, MARQUIS OF (John Augustus Stowte). The owner of most of the land in Bullhampton Parish. In a moment of spite at the Vicar, he gave to the Primitive Methodists land, just at the vicarage gate, on which to build a chapel. The land was later found to be part of the glebe belonging to the vicarage, to the great embarrassment of the Marquis.

". . . a man nearer seventy than sixty, but very hale, with few signs of age. He was short and plump, with hardly any beard on his face, and short grey hair, of which nothing could be seen when he wore his hat. . . . he was a silly, weak, ignorant man, whose own capacity would hardly have procured bread for him in any trade or profession, had bread not been so adequately provided for him by his fathers before him" (17:108).

Appears frequently in *The Vicar of Bullhampton.*

TRUMBULL, FARMER. A tenant of Lord Trowbridge at Church Farm, and a neighbor of the Vicar of Bullhampton. It was of his murder that Sam Brattle was unjustly accused. *Vicar* 3, 12, 14, 17

TRUMPETON WOOD. A tract of land belonging to the Duke of Omnium, in which the foxes were not preserved to the satisfaction of Lord Chiltern. *Redux* 2, 14, 75

TUAM, Ireland. A small village near Dunmore, the home of J. Daly, Barry Lynch's lawyer. Mentioned frequently in *The Kellys and the O'Kellys.*

CARNLOUGH, the home of Thomas Blake, was two miles from Tuam. *Land.*

TUDOR, ALARIC. One of the three clerks, who incurred the enmity of Harry Norman when he married Gertrude Woodward, with whom Harry had long been in love. Starting as a junior clerk in the Weights and Measures, he became a favorite of Sir Gregory Hardlines and rose rapidly to become a Civil Service Commissioner. He was induced by Undy Scott to venture his ward's fortune in a stockjobbing scheme that failed. He was tried for embezzlement and, after serving a six months' sentence, emigrated to Australia with his wife and two sons. One of the principal characters in *The Three Clerks.*

TUDOR, CHARLEY. The youngest of the three clerks, tied to an uninteresting job in the Internal Navigation Office, where he acquired bad habits and made second-rate friends. Katie Woodward fell in love with him, and through her influence he eventually found himself, and they were married. Charley's entrance examination to the Navigation Office is reminiscent of Trollope's on entering the Post Office, and many other of his experiences are autobiographical. One of the principal characters in *The Three Clerks.*

TUDOR, MRS. GERTRUDE (Woodward). The oldest of the three Woodward sisters, who refused Harry Norman and married Alaric Tudor. One of the principal characters in *The Three Clerks.*

TULLA, EARL OF. The patron of Phineas Finn, who aided Phineas in getting the seat for the borough of Loughshane. *Finn* 1-2, 50

TURKISH BATH, The. In *An Editor's Tales*, 1870. Originally published in *Saint Paul's Magazine*, Oct. 1869.

PLOT. The Editor describes a visit to a Turkish bath where one Michael Molloy, who later proved to be mentally deranged, succeeded in persuading him to read one of Molloy's entirely worthless manuscripts.

TURNBULL, MR. A radical, although a man of wealth, who deliberately refused to take office, feeling himself better able to serve the people as a private member. ". . . a good-looking robust man about sixty, with long grey hair and a red complexion, with hard eyes, a well-cut nose, and full lips. He was nearly six feet high, stood quite upright, and always wore a black swallow-tail coat, black trousers, and a black silk waistcoat. . . . He was one of the most popular, if not the most popular politician in the country. Poor men believed in him, thinking that he was their most honest public friend; and men who were not poor believed in his power, thinking that his counsels must surely prevail" (*Finn* 1:18:145). Most prominent in *Phineas Finn*; briefly in *Redux* 9, 20, 34-35; *Prime Min.* 12

TURNOVER PARK. The seat of the Marquis of Trowbridge, in Wiltshire. *Vicar* 17, 72

TWENTYMAN, MRS. KATE (Masters). Gregory Masters' second daughter, who was devoted to Larry Twentyman, because as a child he allowed her to ride his pony and squired her on the hunting field. After Mary Masters became the wife of Reginald Morton,

Larry transferred his affections to the adoring Kate and they were married and lived at Chowton Farm. Most prominent in *The American Senator*; briefly in *Ayala* 23-24

TWENTYMAN, LAWRENCE. A gentleman-farmer and sportsman, living at Chowton Farm, who hunted with the U R U. He was a suitor for the hand of Mary Masters, but, when Mary refused him, married her younger sister. "He was a handsome, good looking man of about thirty, and would have been a happy man had he not been too ambitious in his aspirations after gentry" (*Amer. Sen.* 1:1:10). Most prominent in *The American Senator*; appears in *Ayala* 23-24, 26, 39, 47-49, 56 where he led Ayala and Nina Baldoni in a successful day's hunting.

TWIZZLE, POLLY. The best friend of Maryanne Brown, who married Tom Poppins. *Struggles* 3, 8, 21

TWO GENERALS, The. In *Lotta Schmidt and Other Stories*, 1867. Originally published in *Good Words*, Dec. 1863.

Plot. Two brothers, Tom and Frank Reckenthorpe, living near Frankfort, Kentucky, at the beginning of the American Civil War, parted on the issue of secession, Tom becoming a Confederate general and Frank a general in the Union Army. In a battle on the Blue Ridge, Tom, severely injured, was captured by his brother who was in command of the Union forces, and through his influence invalided home, where he married Ada Forster, whom both brothers had loved.

TWO HEROINES OF PLUMPLINGTON, The. In *Good Cheer*, Christmas number of *Good Words*, Dec. 1882.

Notes. The setting of this short story is in a small town in Barsetshire, and mentions the contest regarding Mr. Harding as Warden of Hiram's Hospital.

Plot. Mr. Greenmantle, the bank manager at Plumplington, had a daughter Emily, who was in love with Philip Hughes, cashier at the bank. The banker, a thorough snob, objected to Philip as a son-in-law because he was not his social equal and had no money. On a lower plane a similar situation had developed in the home of Hickory Peppercorn, the local brewer. Jack Hollycombe, a malt salesman, loved Polly Peppercorn, but her father thought she could do better. Polly, who was a very pretty girl and the pride of her father's eye, brought him to terms by wearing her oldest, shabbiest clothes. Emily managed her father by going into a "decline." Both girls had the sympathy and understanding of the village rector, the Rev. Dr. Freeborn, who invited both families and the two suitors to a Christmas dinner, and succeeded in creating such a warm spirit of friendliness that he soon after performed both wedding ceremonies.

TYROL. The background for *Why Frau Frohmann Raised Her Prices.*

TYRONE, MARQUIS OF. The Lord Lieutenant of Ireland, who was unfriendly to Phineas Finn when he became Secretary for Ireland. *Prime Min.* 12

TYRRWHIT, MR. A Jewish moneylender in London, who advanced a large sum of money to Captain Scarborough and expected to become the owner of Tretton Park when the Captain went bankrupt. Appears frequently in *Mr. Scarborough's Family.*

U R U (Ufford and Rufford United Hunt Club). *See* Rufford United Hunt Club

ULLATHORNE COURT. The home of Wilfred and Monica Thorne, just outside Barchester, and the setting for

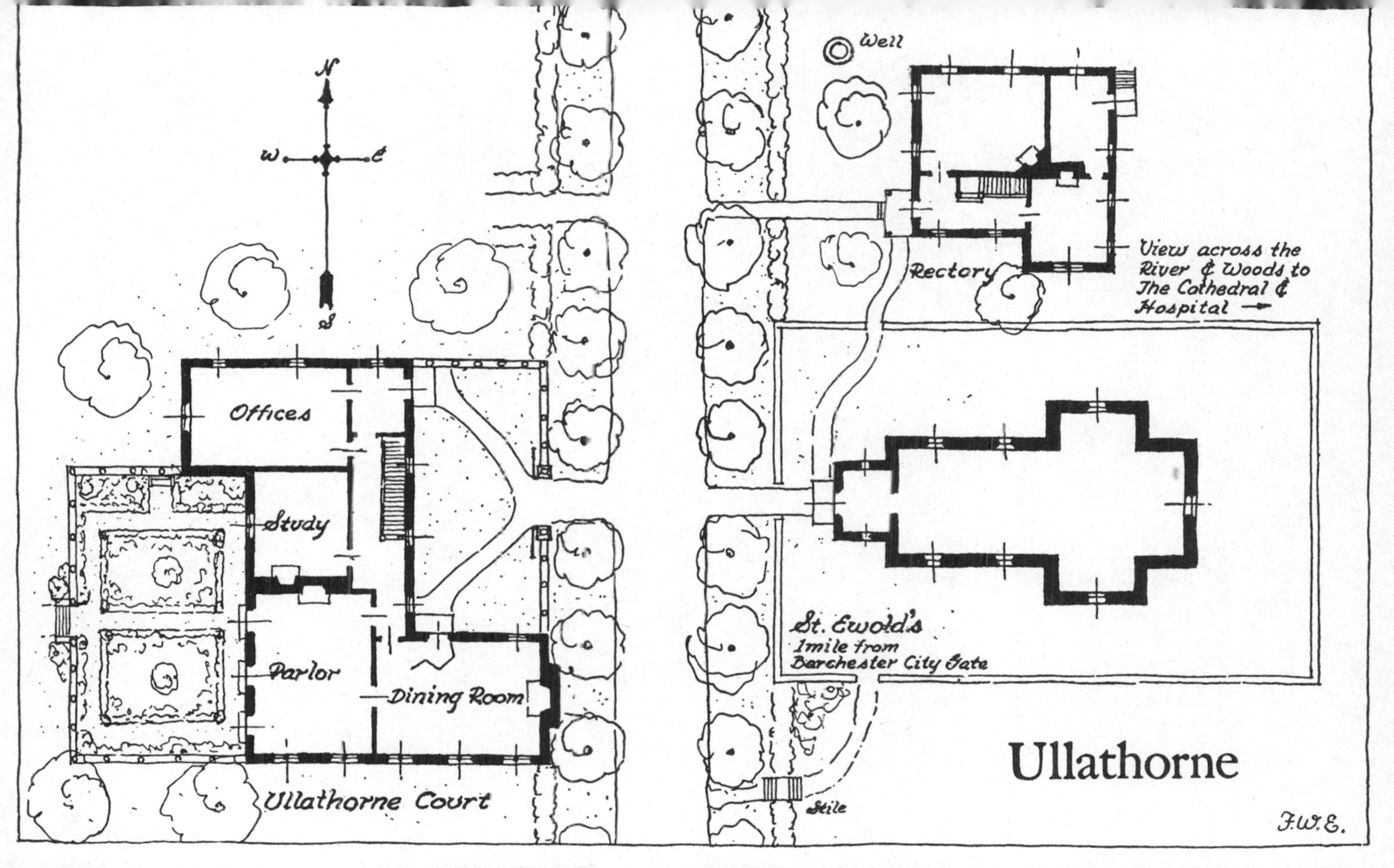
N
W
E
S
Well
Offices
Study
Parlor
Dining Room
Ullathorne Court
Rectory
View across the River & Woods to The Cathedral & Hospital →
St. Ewold's
1 mile from Barchester City Gate
Stile
Ullathorne
F.W.E.

the Ullathorne sports. *Barchester* 22-23, 35-42

ULRICA. Cousin of Count Grandnostrel. *Euphemia*

UMBLEBY, MRS. Wife of Yates, and a village gossip. *Thorne* 2, 25-26, 31-32

UMBLEBY, YATES. The agent and lawyer of the Gresham estate, who mismanaged it so badly that he was replaced by Mortimer Gazebee. *Thorne* 1, 32, 34, 45

UNDERWOOD, CLARISSA. The younger of Sir Thomas' daughters, very gentle, sweet and fragile, who thought herself in love with Ralph, the heir. Despite rumors of his profligacy she refused to censure him, and it was not until he tried to marry Mary Bonner, and later Polly Neefit, that she acknowledged his instability. After some time she engaged herself to his brother Gregory, Rector of Newton Peele, who had loved her devotedly for years. One of the principal characters in *Ralph the Heir*.

UNDERWOOD, PATIENCE. The elder of Sir Thomas' daughters, ". . . a marvel among young women for prudence, conduct, and proper feeling" (1: 2:24). One of the principal characters in *Ralph the Heir*.

UNDERWOOD, SIR THOMAS. Father of Patience and Clarissa, and for some time guardian of Ralph, the heir. After a short service in Parliament and as Solicitor-General, he retired to his chambers in the Southampton Buildings, and devoted years to the preparation of a life of Francis Bacon—of which he never wrote a line. One of the principal characters in *Ralph the Heir*.

U.S. CIVIL WAR. Forms the background of *The Two Generals*.

The Negro Soldiers' Orphan Bazaar, at which Miss Mackenzie assisted, was given to aid the families of Negroes killed in the Civil War. *Mackenzie*

UNIVERSE (club). *See* London

UNPROTECTED FEMALE AT THE PYRAMIDS, An. In *Tales of All Countries* [First Series], 1861. Originally published in *Cassell's Illustrated Family Paper*, Oct. 6, 13, 1860.

Plot. Miss Dawkins proclaimed herself to be an emancipated Englishwoman, free to wander about the world unprotected. She was always watching for the opportunity, however, to join some party that was going to a spot she wished to visit. Having attached herself for a trip to the Pyramids with Mr. Damer and his family, she learned that they were going up the Nile, and, finding Mr. Damer quite breathless after his ascent of the Great Pyramid, told him that she had decided to accept his invitation to join them for the next stage of their journey. Despite his lack of breath, Mr. Damer forced himself to decline the honor, having discovered the lady to be ill-natured and heartily disliked by his wife and daughter.

UNTHANK, JACKSON. An American in Florence, a friend of the American Ambassador, Jonas Spaulding. ". . . a man of wealth and taste, who was resolved on having such a collection of pictures at his house in Baltimore, that no English private collection should in any way come near to it" (1:46:357). Quite possibly refers to William Walters or his son Henry, the founders of the Walters Gallery in Baltimore, both of whom were in Florence during the 70's, and whom Trollope may have met. *He Knew* 46

UPPINALL, MR. One of the clerks in the Weights and Measures Office, who aspired to be chief and entered the examination "as confident as a bantam cock," but was nevertheless unsuccessful. *Clerks* 6, 11

UPSEL, COUNT. A wealthy nobleman, immersed in his books and untouched by the revolutionary movement of the day. He was twice engaged to Margaret de Wynter, whom he finally married. One of the principal characters in *The Noble Jilt.*

In *Can You Forgive Her?*, represented by John Grey.

URMAND, ADRIAN. A linen-buyer from Basle, whom Michel Voss selected as a husband for his niece Marie Bromar. ". . . a pretty man, with black hair, of which he was very careful, with white hands, with bright small dark eyes which were very close together, with a thin regular nose, a small mouth, and a black moustache, which he was always pointing with his fingers" (5:82). One of the principal characters in *The Golden Lion of Granpère.*

USBECK, JONATHAN. The Hamsworth attorney for Sir Joseph Mason whose writing of the codicil to his will was one of the mysteries of the Orley Farm case. *Orley* 1, 7, 12, 16, 32, 71

USBECK, MIRIAM. *See* Dockwrath, Mrs. Miriam (Usbeck)

USHANT, MARGARET, LADY. The widowed daughter of the old Squire of Bragton, who for many years lived with him, making a home for Mary Masters, first as a child and later as a companion. One of the principal characters in *The American Senator.*

USSHER, CAPT. MYLES. A sub-inspector of police, charged with the prevention of distillation of potheen in County Leitrim. He seduced Feemy Macdermot and was killed by her brother Thady. "He had natural abilities, somewhat above par; was good looking, strongly made, and possessed that kind of courage, which arises more from animal spirits, and from not having yet experienced the evil effects of danger, than from real capabilities of enduring its consequences" (1:4:45). One of the principal characters in *The Macdermots of Ballycloran.*

UTTERDEN. The parish in which Folking, the home of John Caldigate, was situated. *Caldigate* 1

VALCARM, LUDOVIC. An attractive young man, perpetually in trouble with the police because of his political activities. In love with Linda Tressel, he persuaded her to elope with him to escape marrying his elderly cousin, whom Linda hated. As they left the train at their destination, Ludovic was arrested and taken off to jail, and Linda returned alone to Nuremberg where her elderly suitor spurned her. One of the principal characters in *Linda Tressel.*

VAN SIEVER, MRS. Concerned in unsavory money dealings with the firm of Broughton and Musselboro. ". . . the widow of a Dutch merchant, who was very rich. She was a ghastly thing to look at, as well from the quantity as from the nature of the wiggeries which she wore. She had not only a false front, but long false curls, as to which it cannot be conceived that she would suppose that any one would be ignorant as to their falseness. She was very thin, too, and very small, and putting aside her wiggeries, you would think her to be all eyes. She was a ghastly old woman to the sight, and not altogether pleasant in her mode of talking" (1:24:210). Appears frequently in *The Last Chronicle of Barset.*

VAN SIEVER, CLARA. She posed as Jael for Conway Dalrymple, whom she later married. ". . . certainly a handsome young woman. She was fair and large. . . . Her features were regular, and her full, clear eyes had a brilliance of their own, looking at you always steadfastly and boldly, though very seldom pleasantly. Her mouth would have been beautiful had it not been too strong for feminine beauty. Her teeth were perfect,—too perfect,—looking like miniature walls of carved ivory. . . . Her nose and chin were finely chiselled, and her head stood well on her shoulders . . . but there was about her nothing of feminine softness" (1:24:212). Appears frequently in *The Last Chronicle of Barset.*

VAVASOR, SQUIRE. Grandfather of Alice, Kate and George. ". . . a stout old man, with a red face and gray eyes, which looked fiercely at you, and with long gray hair, and a rough gray beard, which gave him something of the appearance of an old lion. He was passionate, unreasoning, and specially impatient of all opposition; but he was affectionate, prone to forgive when asked to do so, unselfish and hospitable. He was, moreover, guided by rules, which he believed to be rules of right" (1:31: 241). *Can You* 1, 4, 7, 30-32, 38, 53-54

VAVASOR, ALICE. The heroine of *Can You Forgive Her?*, her fault being that she was twice engaged to and twice jilted her cousin George Vavasor, and twice engaged to John Grey before she finally married him. A cousin of Lady Glencora Palliser, whose confidante she was in Lady Glen's love for Burgo Fitzgerald.

"In person she was tall and well made, rather large in her neck and shoulders, as were all the Vavasors, but by no means fat. Her hair was brown, but very dark, and she wore it rather lower upon her forehead than is customary at the present day. Her eyes, too, were dark, though they were not black, and her complexion, though not quite that of a brunette, was far away from being fair. Her nose was somewhat broad, and retroussé, too, but . . . it was a charming nose, full of character and giving to her whole face at times a look of pleasant humour, which it would otherwise have lacked. Her mouth was large and full of character, and her chin oval, dimpled, and finely chiselled. . . . a fine, handsome, high-spirited young woman" (*Can You* 1:1:6).

Most prominent in *Can You Forgive Her?*; briefly, as Mrs. Grey, a guest at Matching Priory, in *Eustace* 47

In *The Noble Jilt*, represented by Margaret de Wynter.

VAVASOR, GEORGE. Cousin of Alice Vavasor, to whom he was twice engaged. Disinherited by his grandfather, he forced Alice to lend him money to contest a seat in Parliament, which, being won, had to be contested a second time, with more demands for funds. When he lost his seat and the respect of all his friends, quarreled with Alice and tried to kill her fiancé, John Grey, he emigrated to America.

"He would not generally have been called ugly by women, had not one side of his face been dreadfully scarred by a cicatrice, which in healing, had left a dark indented line down from his left eye to his lower jaw. . . . His hair was black, and was parted in the front. His forehead, though low, was broad. His eyes were dark and bright, and his eyebrows were very full, and perfectly black. . . . He wore a thick black moustache, which covered his mouth, but no whiskers. . . . rather low in stature, but well made, with small hands and feet, but broad in the chest and strong in the loins . . ." (*Can You* 1:4:30-31).

One of the principal characters in *Can You Forgive Her?*

In *The Noble Jilt*, represented by Mark Steinmark.

VAVASOR, JOHN. Alice's father, who held a sinecure worth £800 a year that required but little of his time and less of his energy. By common consent he and his daughter, although they lived in the same house and shared its expense, went their own way with no regard for the other's opinion or welfare. ". . . a handsome man, with a fine forehead, round which the hair and beard was only beginning to show itself to be grey. He stood well, with a large person, only now beginning to become corpulent. His eyes were bright and grey, and his mouth and chin were sharply cut, and told of gentle birth" (*Can You* 1:1:4). One of the principal characters in *Can You Forgive Her?*

In *The Noble Jilt*, represented by M. de Wynter.

VAVASOR, KATE. George's adoring sister, who lived with the old Squire at Vavasor Hall. George persuaded her that, after breaking her engagement with him, Alice Vavasor still owed him her financial aid in contesting a seat in Parliament, and Kate arranged the trip to Switzerland on which they succeeded in inducing Alice to furnish the necessary money. One of the principal characters in *Can You Forgive Her?*

In *The Noble Jilt*, represented by Helen Steinmark.

VAVASOR HALL. The estate of Squire Vavasor, in Westmoreland, where Kate lived with her old grandfather. The setting for many of the scenes in *Can You Forgive Her?*.

VENDÉE, LA. An Historical Romance. London, Colburn, 1850. 3v.

AUTHOR'S COMMENT. "The story is certainly inferior to those that had gone before [*The Macdermots of Ballycloran* and *The Kellys and the O'Kellys*];—chiefly because I knew . . . in truth, nothing of life in the La Vendée country, and also because the facts of the present time came more within the limits of my powers of story-telling than those of past years. . . . The conception as to the feeling of the people is, I think, true; the characters are distinct; and the tale is not dull. As far as I can remember, this morsel of criticism is the only one that was ever written on the book." —*Autobiography*, 1:5:107.

NOTES. "It is the true strain of human sympathy running through the book that makes it memorable. . . . it was remarkable that a young unknown novelist should be able to produce anything as sturdily honest and undecorated as this."—Walpole, p. 41.

PLOT. Following the execution of Louis XVI, a Royalist revolt broke out in La Vendée under the leadership of Charles de Lescure and Henri Larochejaquelin, both wealthy landowners in that region. After an initial success in capturing Saumur, the Republican armies invaded the province, sacked and burned the towns and villages and with savage violence destroyed the chateaux of the Royalists. The romance centers on the love of Henri Larochejaquelin and Marie de Lescure, and on the renegade Denot's love for Agatha Larochejaquelin.

VENDÉE, LA. A department formed from the province of Poitou; the scene of the historical novel *La Vendée*.

VENICE. The setting for *The Last Austrian Who Left Venice*.

VEQUE, PETER. A servant at the Lion d'Or. Of minor importance, but appears frequently in *The Golden Lion of Granpère*.

VERNET. In the French village of Vernet, noted for its hot springs, was the inn owned by La Mère Bauche, in the story of that name.

VERONICA JOHN, SISTER. Daughter of Lady Baldock, and cousin of Violet Effingham. Until she became a nun, her name was Hon. Augusta Boreham. *Finn* 11, 22, 34, 42; *Redux* 2

VICAR OF BULLHAMPTON, The. London, Bradbury, Evans and Co., 1870.

AUTHOR'S COMMENT. ". . . written chiefly with the idea of exciting not only pity but sympathy for a fallen woman, and of raising a feeling of forgiveness for such in the minds of other women." —*Autobiography*, 2:18:176.

NOTES. "Ostensibly a novel written in defence of the 'fallen woman,' it has a quaintly solemn preface in which the author apologizes to his public for venturing on ground so delicate. But the book itself fails admirably to fulfill its proclaimed intentions. It is as characteristically Trollopian in plot and staging as the preface in its self-conscious propagandism is uncharacteristic. A vigorous story of village life, *The Vicar of Bullhampton* presents a delightful parson, several charming ladies, a gruff farmer, a pompous marquis and some aggressive nonconformity."—Sadleir, p. 397-98.

PLOT. The parish of Bullhampton, near Salisbury, was largely the property of the Marquis of Trowbridge, though Harry Gilmore owned in it an estate, Hampton Priory. One of the latter's tenants was the miller Brattle, whose daughter Carry had been seduced and had hidden herself in London, and whose son Sam was accused of the murder of Farmer Trumbull. The Marquis demanded that the family be evicted, but Harry indignantly refused. In this he was ably seconded by the Vicar of Bullhampton, who vigorously attacked the Marquis for his uncharitable demand to punish a God-fearing—though bull-headed—father for the sins of his children.

The Marquis resented the Vicar's opposition and to annoy him gave to the Primitive Methodists land for a chapel just opposite the vicarage gates. The hideous building was well on its way to completion when old records disclosed that the property was glebe land. The Marquis was compelled to tear down the offending chapel, to the ill-concealed delight of the victorious Vicar.

When a small boy, Sam Brattle had been one of the Vicar's favorites and, when he was accused of complicity in the murder of the neighboring farmer, the Vicar undertook to befriend him. Through his energy the murderers of Mr. Trumbull were found and Sam was cleared. Carry, discarded by her lover and in want, had returned to the neighborhood, and the old miller was with difficulty induced to let her return to his home.

The Vicar's charming wife tried to arrange a marriage between their neighbor Harry Gilmore and her best friend Mary Lowther. Harry loved her, but Mary was engaged to her distant cousin Walter Marrable, a prospective heir to a property but with small present fortune. Soon after his engagement to Mary, his father succeeded in swindling him out of all his resources and, discouraged as to the future, they broke their engagement. Mary explained all this to Harry before accepting him, but soon after Walter succeeded to his uncle's estate and returned for her. Harry generously released her from their engagement, and the two lovers were married.

VIENNA. The Volksgarten and Sperl's dancing academy on the Leopoldstrasse form the background for *Lotta Schmidt*.

VIGIL, MR. WHIP. The government whip opposed to the Limehouse Bridge project, in which Undy Scott and Alaric Tudor had made a heavy investment. *Clerks* 8, 24, 27, 31-32, 34

VIGNOLLES, CAPTAIN. A professional gambler, who fleeced Captain Scarborough. *Scarborough* 41-42, 49

VIGO, MARY. *See* Askerton, Mrs. Mary (Vigo)

VINCENT, MRS. Cousin of Mrs. Roden, who called on her at Paradise Row regularly each Monday at three o'clock. *Fay* 5, 17, 35, 43, 49-50

VINCKE, CAPT. HUBERT VON. An artillery officer stationed in Venice during the Austrian occupation in 1866. He fell in love with an Italian girl, Nina Pepé, but could not win her brother's consent to the marriage until Venice was freed of her conquerors. Hero of *The Last Austrian Who Left Venice.*

VINER, EMILY. A middle-aged Irish woman, who journeyed to Panama to marry an old sweetheart, only to find on arrival that he had died on the way to meet her boat. Principal character in *The Journey to Panama.*

VIVIAN, MR. A friend of Lord Hampstead, who was junior private secretary to Lord Persiflage, the Secretary of State. Of minor importance, but appears frequently in *Marion Fay.*

VOSS, GEORGE. Son of Michel, whose love for Marie Bromar is the center of the plot of *The Golden Lion of Granpère.* ". . . he had in his eye, and in his beaked nose, and his large mouth, and well-developed chin, that look of command . . . which women, who judge men by their feelings rather than their thoughts, always love to see" (5:82-83).

VOSS, MME. JOSEPHINE. Michel's second wife, and aunt of Marie Bromar. One of the principal characters in *The Golden Lion of Granpère.*

VOSS, MICHEL. The landlord of the Golden Lion of Granpère. ". . . a tall, stout, active, and very handsome man, about fifty years of age. . . . His short, dark, curly hair—that was always kept clipped round his head—was beginning to show a tinge of gray, but the huge moustache on his upper lip was still of a thorough brown, as was also the small morsel of beard which he wore upon his chin. He had bright sharp brown eyes, a nose slightly beaked, and a large mouth. He was on the whole a man of good temper, just withal, and one who loved those who belonged to him; but he chose to be master in his own house, and was apt to think that his superior years enabled him to know what younger people wanted better than they would know themselves" (1:9-10). One of the principal characters in *The Golden Lion of Granpère.*

VOSSNER, HERR. The purveyor of the Beargarden Club, who, after selling the members' I O U's, absconded with the club's funds. *Way We Live* 10, 38, 49, 69, 96

WADDINGTON, CAROLINE. *See* Harcourt, Caroline (Waddington), Lady

WADDLE, MR. The foreman in Mr. Neefit's tailor shop, where he also served as his employer's confidant and adviser. *Ralph* 5, 9, 16-17, 36, 42, 45

WADE, GEORGE. Utterly misunderstanding a request made by his brother-in-law for his name on a paper, he refused hastily. After the Christmas sermon he apologized for his rudeness, only to learn that all he had been asked for was a testimonial that he knew his guest to be a man of property. One of the principal characters in *Not If I Know It.*

WAINWRIGHT, MARY. *See* Fitzgerald, Mary (Wainwright), Lady

WALBECK STREET. *See* London

WALES. The setting for the plot of *Cousin Henry* is Llanfeare, Carmarthenshire.

WALKER, MR. His accident on the hunting field was reported as that of Lord Hampstead. *Fay* 40-42, 46

WALKER, MR. A tenant at Brownriggs Farm, a part of the Newton Priory estate. *Ralph* 11, 18, 23, 28, 34

WALKER, MR. Mr. Wharton's attorney in his dealings with his son-in-law Ferdinand Lopez. *Prime Min.* 53, 55

WALKER, MR. A young man whom George Hotspur cheated at cards. *Hotspur* 12, 15, 18-19, 21-23

WALKER, GEORGE. In Egypt for his health, he was mistaken for a distinguished government official, and accepted an invitation from the local Arab dignitary that was promptly withdrawn when Sir George Walker arrived. Principal character in *George Walker at Suez.*

WALKER, GEORGE. The foremost attorney in Silverbridge, senior member of the firm Walker and Winthrop, which attended to the local business of the Duke of Omnium and was much concerned with the Crawley trial. "He was a man between fifty and sixty years of age, with grey hair, rather short, and somewhat corpulent, but still gifted with that amount of personal comeliness which comfortable position and the respect of others will generally seem to give" (*Last Chron.* 1:1:4). Appears frequently in *The Last Chronicle of Barset*; and proposes Lord Silverbridge's election to Parliament in *Duke* 14

WALKER, GREEN. The MP from Crew Junction, and a staunch supporter of Harold Smith. ". . . a young but rising man . . . a nephew of the Dowager Marchioness of Hartletop" (1:8:142). *Framley* 8, 12, 23, 31

WANLESS, GEORGIANA. Sir Walter's second daughter, designed by her mother as the wife of Major Rossiter, though both young people were indifferent to the scheme. Failing to capture the Major, Lady Wanless arranged for Georgiana's marriage with Mr. Burmiston, a rich young brewer who had originally been marked for the third daughter. ". . . she was wonderfully handsome,—a complexion perfectly clear, a nose cut as out of marble, a mouth delicate as of a goddess, with a waist quite to match it. Her shoulders were white as alabaster. Her dress was at all times perfect" (2:24-25). One of the principal characters in *Alice Dugdale.*

WANLESS, MARGARET, LADY. The matchmaking mother of several daughters, who struggled valiantly to induce Major Rossiter to marry her second daughter, Georgiana. One of the principal characters in *Alice Dugdale.*

WANLESS, SIR WALTER. A baronet with more daughters than money, and a wife determined that all of them should marry. ". . . one of those great men who never do anything great, but achieve their greatness partly by their tailors, partly by a breadth of eyebrow and carriage of the body . . . and partly by outside gifts of fortune" (3:28). Appears frequently in *Alice Dugdale.*

WARBURTON, MR. The Duke of Omnium's private secretary. Appears frequently in *The Prime Minister.*

WARDEN, The. London, Longmans, 1855.

AUTHOR'S COMMENT. "The characters of the bishop, of the archdeacon, of the archdeacon's wife, and especially of the warden, are all well and clearly drawn. I had realized to myself a series of portraits, and had been able so to put them on the canvas that my readers should see that which I meant them to see."—*Autobiography*, 1:5:132.

NOTES. "*The Warden* is essential to every lover of Trollope because it is in these pages that he meets for the first time two of the great figures in English fiction, Mr. Harding and Archdeacon Grantly."—Walpole, p. 45.

PLOT. Hiram's Hospital, a fifteenth century foundation attached to Barchester Cathedral, provided a home for twelve old men. Through the centuries the income of the foundation had greatly increased, and the Wardenship was a handsome sinecure for the Precentor of the Cathedral. The incumbent, the Rev. Septimus Harding, a gentle, 'cello-playing old clergyman, lived near the Hospital, with his younger daughter, Eleanor. John Bold, a young surgeon of Barchester, although in love with Eleanor, became convinced that the financial affairs of the Foundation were mismanaged and demanded a public accounting. Mr. Harding's son-in-law Archdeacon Grantly, enraged at this assault on clerical prerogatives, fought the case bitterly until Bold, distressed by the uproar he had occasioned, withdrew his suit. Nevertheless the Warden resigned, and after Eleanor and John Bold were married left his post and became Rector of St. Cuthbert's, a small parish in the Cathedral Close.

WARWICK SQUARE. *See* London

WATT, WALKER. A member of the Panjandrum Committee. *Panjandrum*

WAY WE LIVE NOW, The. London, Chapman and Hall, 1875. 2v.

AUTHOR'S COMMENT. ". . . to the writing of which I was instigated by what I conceived to be the commercial profligacy of the age. . . . The book has all the fault which is to be attributed to almost all satires. . . . The accusations are exaggerated. The vices are coloured, so as to make effect rather than to represent truth."—*Autobiography*, 2:20:201, 211.

NOTES. ". . . one of the most remarkable of all English novels published between 1860 and 1890. This novel, had it been written by any one else or had it been published anonymously, would never have been allowed to pass out of English fiction, but because it came after a long series of novels by the same hand, and because its author had been for some years before its appearance far too readily 'taken for granted' by the critics, its remarkable qualities remained unperceived."—Walpole, pp. 165-66.

PLOT. Augustus Melmotte, about whose past little was known, established himself in London, bought a large house on Grosvenor Square and soon gained a reputation as "a great financier." With him were his wife and a daughter, Marie, whom he launched on the matrimonial market at a grandiose ball for which, in hope of favors to come, he secured the patronage of several duchesses and other titled personages. A San Francisco stockjobber induced Melmotte to organize a London company for the promotion of a fictitious railroad, the South Central Pacific and Mexican, and to set up a dummy directorate of Englishmen of high social standing. Melmotte's large gifts to charitable organizations and lavish entertainments convinced the public of his financial genius, and money flowed through his hands. He was asked by the Government as a great London merchant to give a dinner for the Emperor of China; the Conservatives called on him to contest Westminster for a seat in Parliament. Shortly before the dinner vague rumors began to float about that Melmotte's finances were not in order, and that one of the papers in the sale of an estate he was purchasing had been forged. Public opinion veered sharply. The great dinner was but sparsely attended, but at the election next day he won the Westminster seat.

Marie, as a reputed heiress of millions, was sought in marriage by several highly placed but uniformly impecunious young noblemen. She fell in love with the most worthless of them all, Sir Felix Carbury, planned an elopement with him and stole enough of her father's money to finance it, but Sir Felix gambled away the money and failed to keep the appointment. She later married Hamilton Fisker, originator of the railroad scheme, and went with him to America. Melmotte, to bolster up his vanishing credit, forged yet another paper that would give him possession of his daughter's trust fund. When this failed, deserted by the men who had fawned upon him, and after disgracing himself by appearing on the floor of the House while intoxicated, he committed suicide.

WEBB, COUNSELLOR. The magistrate of Ardrum, whose championship of Thady Macdermot led to his duel with Jonas Brown. ". . . a much more talented man than his brother magistrate [Jonas Brown], he was, moreover, a kind-hearted landlord—ever anxious to ameliorate the conditions of the poor—and by no means greedy after money, though he was neither very opulent nor very economical. . . . He was . . . too fond of popularity, and of being the favourite among the peasantry; and . . . had become so habituated to oppose Jonas Brown in all his sayings and doings, that he now did so whether he was right or wrong" (3:1:24). *Macdermots* 19, 24-26, 32-33

WEBER, MARIE. A young Viennese shopgirl, the intimate friend of Lotta Schmidt. *Lotta*

WEDNESBURY. Lionel Trafford, later the Marquis of Kingsbury, represented Wednesbury in Parliament. *Fay* 1

WEIGHTS AND MEASURES OFFICE. An unusually efficient government bureau, the pride of Sir Gregory Hardlines, which provided employment for each of the "Three Clerks." Complete name: "Office of the Board of Commissioners for Regulating Weights and Measures." Mentioned frequently in *The Three Clerks.*

WEISS, HERR. A magistrate from Brixen, who, with his wife and daughter, spent his holidays at the Peacock Inn. One of the principal characters in *Why Frau Frohmann Raised Her Prices.*

WELL OF MOSES. An excursion to see the Well was arranged by a local Arab, in compliment to Sir George Walker. By mistake George Walker, a member of a mercantile firm in London, was invited, but was left in the lurch when the important guest appeared. *Walker*

WEST BARSETSHIRE. *See* Barsetshire, West

WEST BROMWICH. Represented in Parliament by Joshua Monk. *Finn* 20

WEST CORK AND BALLYDEHOB BRANCH RAILWAY. One of the get-rich-quick schemes in which Undy Scott persuaded Alaric Tudor to invest. *Clerks* 24, 29, 31, 41

WEST POINT, N.Y. Where Frank Reckenthorpe was educated, and which he left to become a general in the Union Army, during the Civil War. *Generals*

WEST PUTFORD. A parish near Hurst Staple, the home of the Rev. Mr. Gauntlet and his daughter Adela. In one instance it is called "West Putfield." *Bertrams* 3, 16

WESTBOURNE TERRACE. *See* London

WESTEND, SIR WARWICK. One of the examining board of Civil Service. "Sir Warwick Westend was an excellent man, full of the best intentions, and not more than decently anxious to get the good things of Government into his hand" (1:11:232). Trollope calls this a "feebly facetious name" for Sir Stafford Northcote. *Clerks* 11, 27, 36

WESTERMANN, FRANÇOIS-JOSEPH (real person). A general in command of the troops sent to put down the Vendean uprising. "Westermann brought with him a legion of German mercenaries, on whom he could rely for the perpetration of any atrocity. . . . He was a man of indomitable courage and undying perseverance. He was a German, who had been banished from Prussia, and having entered the French army as a private soldier had gradually risen to be an officer. Danton and Santerre had discovered and appreciated his courage and energy, and he soon found himself a leader . . . sent to assist in the fearful work which the tyranny of the democrats required" (2: 6:158, 65-66). *Vendée* 12, 15-17

WESTERN, MR. The MP for East Barsetshire, ". . . a tory of the old school . . . one of the gallant few who dared to vote against Sir Robert Peel's bill for repealing the Corn Laws in 1846" (1:26:220). *Finn* 26

WESTERN, MRS. CECILIA (Holt). After a brief engagement to Sir Francis Geraldine, she met and married George Western without informing him of her earlier engagement. When finally he discovered it, he deserted her, feeling that she had deliberately misled him. His sister Lady Grant followed him to Dresden, and effected a reconciliation. Principal character in *Kept in the Dark*.

WESTERN, GEORGE. Cecilia Western's opinionated and unbending husband, who, because she failed to tell him of a former engagement to Sir Francis Geraldine whom he hated, refused to accept her explanations and left her. He was finally convinced of his unreasonableness, and they were reunited. One of the principal characters in *Kept in the Dark*.

WESTMACOTT, MR. A Radical contesting the Percycross seat with Ontario Moggs, in opposition to Mr. Griffenbottom and Sir Thomas Underwood. *Ralph* 20, 25-26, 29, 37, 39, 44

WESTMINSTER ABBEY. Where Mr. Harding spent the greater part of a day in hiding from the Archdeacon, when he went up to London to see his lawyers. *Warden* 16

WESTMINSTER BOROUGH. The constituency that elected Augustus Melmotte to Parliament. *Way We Live* 35, 44, 52, 54, 63-64

WESTMORELAND.

Bowes Lodge. Owned by the Marquis of Stapledean. *Bertrams*

Grex. The dilapidated country house of Lord Grex. *Duke*

Hauteboy Castle. Country seat of Lord Persiflage. *Fay*

Thwaite Hall. Home of Major Garrow and his family. *Mistletoe*

Vavasor Hall. Squire Vavasor's home. *Can You*

WESTON, JULIA. Disguised as a young man and calling herself "John Smith," she persuaded Mr. Jones to take her on a visit to the holy places in Palestine. They were overtaken by her irate guardian, who attempted to force the astonished Mr. Jones (who had a wife and family in England) to marry her. Heroine of *A Ride Across Palestine*.

WESTON, SIR WILLIAM. The stern and dictatorial uncle and guardian of Julia, from whom she escaped for a trip across Palestine with Mr. Jones. *Ride*

WHARTON, ABEL. A wealthy London lawyer, who adored his two children, but deplored his son Everett's aimless way of life, and was unable to prevent his daughter Emily's marriage with Ferdinand Lopez.

"He was a spare, thin, strongly made man, with spare light brown hair, hardly yet grizzled, with small grey whiskers, clear eyes, bushy eyebrows, with a long ugly nose, on which young barristers had been heard to declare you might hang a small kettle, and with considerable vehemence of talk when he was opposed in argument. . . . certainly a man of whom men were generally afraid. At the whist-table no one would venture to scold him. In court no one ever contradicted him" (1:3:38-39).

One of the principal characters in *The Prime Minister.*

WHARTON, SIR ALURED. The head of the Wharton family, and owner of Wharton Hall. "Sir Alured Wharton was a baronet, with a handsome old family place on the Wye, in Herefordshire, whose forefathers had been baronets since baronets were first created, and whose earlier forefathers had lived at Wharton Hall much before that time. It may be imagined therefore that Sir Alured was proud of his name, of his estate, and of his rank" (1:13:212). Appears frequently in *The Prime Minister.*

WHARTON, EMILY. *See* Lopez, Mrs. Emily (Wharton)

WHARTON, EVERETT. Son of Abel Wharton. A good-natured but rather unformed young man, content to live on his allowance, though having vague yearnings toward a political career. When he fell heir to the Wharton estate and the title, he married his cousin Mary, and became a model country gentleman. ". . . a good-looking, manly fellow, six feet high, with broad shoulders, with light hair, wearing a large silky bushy beard, which made him look older than his years. . . . He was a popular man certainly,—very popular with women, to whom he was always courteous, and generally liked by men, to whom he was genial and good-natured" (1:2:24-25). One of the principal characters in *The Prime Minister.*

WHARTON, MARY. The daughter of Sir Alured, who married her cousin Everett, her father's heir. An intimate friend of Emily Lopez. *Prime Min.* 15-16, 67, 75, 79

WHARTON HALL. The home of Sir Alured Wharton, in Herefordshire. *Prime Min.* 15-17, 70, 79

"WHEAL MARY JANE." The tin mine in Cornwall that Alaric Tudor and Fidus Neverbend went to investigate, and of which Alaric wrote an enthusiastic account. *Clerks* 7-11, 17, 24, 29, 34, 41

WHEREAS, MRS. MARTHA. Herbert Fitzgerald's landlady in London, when he went up to study law. *Castle Rich.* 35

WHISTON, The REV. DR. "That turbulent Dr. Whiston," who objected to the administration of the cathedral funds at Rochester and was denounced by Archdeacon Grantly in letters to the press. *Warden* 2

WHITE, The REV. MR. Mr. Slope's successor as domestic chaplain to Bishop Proudie. *Framley* 7

WHITE HORSE INN. *See* Barchester

WHITSTABLE, GEORGE. A loutish landowner of Toodlum Hall, near Caversham, who married Sophia Longestaffe, much to the disdain of Sophia's younger sister, Georgiana. *Way We Live* 17, 21, 78-79, 96

WHITTLESTAFF, WILLIAM. A middle-aged bachelor, who somewhat reluctantly provided a home for Mary Laurie on the death of her father. When he fell in love with her, she accepted him out of gratitude for his kindness, although she had given her heart to John Gordon in her youth. When John unexpectedly appeared from the diamond mines, Mr. Whittlestaff became convinced that Mary still loved him, and generously released her from the engagement. Principal character in *An Old Man's Love.*

WHY FRAU FROHMANN RAISED HER PRICES. In *Why Frau Frohmann Raised Her Prices and Other Stories.* London, Isbister, 1882. Originally published in *Good Words,* Feb.-May 1877.

PLOT. Frau Frohmann, owner of the Peacock Inn in the Tyrolean Alps, was a very conservative woman who believed that everything should continue as it had been "in the good old days." Although warned by her lawyer that she was losing money at the inn, she refused to raise her prices or to change in any particular the superabundant meals served to her guests. She tried to coerce the peasant women, whose entire output of vegetables and dairy products she had bought for years, to sell to her at the old prices. Her butcher refused to sell meat at the old rate, and the whole valley rose against her, sending their produce at great inconvenience to Innsbruck where prices were higher. After a season of bickering with her old friends and friction within her own household, she learned that the income and the salary of all her guests had been raised, so that they were able and willing to pay higher prices.

WICKERBY, MR. The attorney who defended Phineas Finn at his trial for the murder of Mr. Bonteen. *Redux* 55, 57, 60-67

WIDOW'S MITE, The. In *Lotta Schmidt and Other Stories,* 1867. Originally published in *Good Words,* Jan. 1863.

PLOT. During the cotton famine caused by the Civil War in the United States, the Rev. Mr. Granger was active in collecting funds for the relief of the weavers. Nora Field, his wife's niece who lived at the parsonage, was engaged to marry a wealthy American and, to make herself attractive to her new relatives, had been hoarding her money for a suitable trousseau. Distressed by the suffering of the weavers, she determined instead to give the money for their aid.

WILKINSON, The REV. ARTHUR, JR. A classmate of George Bertram at Oxford, who succeeded his father as Vicar of Hurst Staple with the stipulation that he accept a curate's income and turn over the rest of his salary to his mother. This precluded any hope of his marriage to Adela Gauntlet, and the story of their difficulties forms one of the subplots of *The Bertrams.* Most prominent in *The Bertrams;* briefly, as a guest at Miss Todd's party in Littlebath, in *Mackenzie* 11

WILKINSON, The REV. ARTHUR, SR. The Vicar of Hurst Staple, who befriended George Bertram in his youth. Father of Arthur, Jr., Mary, Sophia, Jane and Fanny. He died leaving them dependent on his son for their living. *Bertrams* 1-3

WILKINSON, MRS. ARTHUR, SR. Mother of Arthur, who, by the stipulation of the Marquis of Stapledean, received the bulk of her son's salary, and soon forgot that it was not her own. *Bertrams* 1, 16, 25-27, 42-43

WILLINGFORD BULL (inn). Lord Chiltern kept his horses there, and used the inn as headquarters during the hunting season. *Finn* 17, 24

WILSON, LEGGE. A friend of Phineas Finn, ". . . a great scholar and a polished gentleman, very proud of his position as a Cabinet Minister" (*Finn* 1:29:243). Appears in most of the political novels: briefly in *Finn* 29, 35; and *Redux* 32, 40; as Secretary for India in *Eustace* 17; and *Way We Live* 4, 54

WILSON, SOPHY. A young telegraph girl, who considered her work only as a preliminary to marriage. She became ill and went to the seashore, living in part on the meager earnings of her roommate Lucy Graham. Although she had thought herself in love with Abraham Hall, with whom Lucy was also in love, she met a hairdresser at the beach and married him. One of the principal characters in *The Telegraph Girl.*

WILTSHIRE.

BULLHAMPTON. Home of the Vicar of Bullhampton. *Vicar*

HAMPTON PRIVETS. Harry Gilmore's house. *Vicar*

TURNOVER PARK. Estate of the Marquis of Trowbridge. *Vicar*

WINCHESTER COLLEGE. Arthur Wilkinson and George Bertram were at Winchester together. *Bertrams* 1

The Rev. Francis Arabin was a student there. *Barchester* 20

WINTERBONES, MR. A confidential clerk for Sir Roger Scatcherd, ". . . a little, withered, dissipated, broken-down man, whom gin and poverty had nearly burnt to a cinder, and dried to an ash." (1:9:198). *Thorne* 9-10

WINTERFIELD, MRS. A wealthy widow, living in Perivale, whose fortune, her friends hoped, would be left to Clara Amedroz, an attentive and obedient niece. The fortune, however, was left to Mrs. Winterfield's nephew Captain Aylmer, with the understanding that he would marry Clara. ". . . an excellent lady—unselfish, given to self-restraint, generous, pious, looking to find in her religion a safe path through life. . . . To fight the devil was her work. . . . [She] always wore a thick black silk dress . . . kept a low, four-wheeled, one-horsed little phaeton, in which she made her pilgrimages among the poor of Perivale" (1:1:20, 22). *Belton* 1-9

WINTHROP, ZACHARY. An attorney in Silverbridge, junior partner in the firm of Walker and Winthrop. He was much admired by the young ladies of the town as he was "a bachelor, and had plenty of money." *Last Chron.* 1, 8

WOODS AND FORESTS OFFICE. Fidus Neverbend was on the staff. *Clerks* 7

WOODWARD, MRS. BESSIE. The widow of a clergyman, who lived with her daughters at Surbiton Cottage, Hampton. She was a cousin of Harry Norman, who introduced the two other clerks to the family. Eventually the three clerks married Mrs. Woodward's three daughters. One of the principal characters in *The Three Clerks.*

WOODWARD, GERTRUDE. *See* Tudor, Mrs. Gertrude (Woodward)

WOODWARD, KATIE. The youngest of the three Woodward girls, who fell in love with Charley Tudor against her mother's opposition and in spite of Charley's reputation. When he proved himself worthy of her, her mother's consent was given, and they were married. One of the principal characters in *The Three Clerks.*

WOODWARD, LINDA. *See* Norman, Mrs. Linda (Woodward)

WOOLSWORTHY, PATIENCE. Daughter of the Rector of Oxney Colne, who broke her engagement to Captain Broughton when he showed plainly that he considered himself above her in the social scale and attempted to teach her her good fortune in marrying him. Heroine of *The Parson's Daughter of Oxney Colne.*

WOOLSWORTHY, The REV. SAUL. The Rector of Oxney Colne, and a fervent antiquarian of Devonshire. One of the principal characters in *The Parson's Daughter of Oxney Colne.*

WORCESTERSHIRE.

DUNRIPPLE PARK. Seat of Sir Gregory Marrable, on the border of Warwickshire and Worcestershire. *Vicar*

MONKHAMS. Estate of Lord Peterborough. *He Knew*

WORTLE, DR. JEFFREY. A headstrong, able and generous clergyman, who was the owner and head of the Bowick School. His friendship and belief in Mr. and Mrs. Peacocke almost wrecked his lifework.

"... a man much esteemed by others ... and by himself. ... He had a broad forehead, with bright grey eyes,—eyes that had always a smile passing round them. ... His nose was aquiline. ... His mouth, for a man, was perhaps a little too small, but was admirably formed, as had been the chin with a deep dimple in it. ... He stood five feet ten in height, with small hands and feet. He was now perhaps somewhat stout" (1:1:1, 15-16).

One of the principal characters in *Dr. Wortle's School.*

WORTLE, MRS. JEFFREY. Dr. Wortle's gentle and self-effacing wife. "She was probably as happy a woman as you shall be likely to meet on a summer's day. She had good health, easy temper, pleasant friends, abundant means, and no ambition" (1:1:13). *Wortle* 1, 9, 11, 13, 15-17, 19, 22-23

WORTLE, MARY. Dr. Wortle's charming daughter, engaged to Lord Carstairs. Of minor importance, but appears frequently in *Dr. Wortle's School.*

WORTS, MR. Mr. Tappitt's foreman at the brewery, whose political independence won the contested seat for Butler Cornbury. This infuriated Mr. Tappitt, who had ordered the matter differently. He "had not himself been ambitious of good beer, but the idea had almost startled him into acquiescence by its brilliancy." *Rachel* 24, 27-28

WRIGHT, The REV. MR. The Rector of Belton parish, who seldom officiated at any of the services. He loved scandal and was very ill-natured in circulating gossip about Colonel and Mrs. Askerton. *Belton* 7

WYNDHAM, FANNY. Niece and ward of Lord Cashel, an heiress in her own right, and later of her brother's fortune. At her guardian's insistence she broke her engagement to Lord Ballindine, but refused to marry Lord Cashel's dissipated son Lord Kilcullen. The story ends happily with her marriage to her first lover.

"Fanny Wyndham was above the usual height, but she did not look tall, for her figure was well-formed and round, and her bust full. She had dark-brown hair, which was never curled, but worn in plain braids, fastened at the back of her head together with the long rich folds which were collected there under a simple comb. Her forehead was high, and beautifully formed. ... Her eyes were full and round, of a hazel colour, bright and soft when she was pleased, but full of pride and displeasure when her temper was ruffled, or her dignity offended. Her nose was slightly *retroussé*. ... The line of her cheeks and chin, was very lovely ... her complexion ... was rich and glowing ..." (1:10:243-44).

One of the two heroines of *The Kellys and the O'Kellys.*

WYNDHAM, HARRY. Fanny's brother, who died leaving her £80,000. *Kellys* 11-12

WYNDHAM STREET. New Road. *See* London

WYNTER, M. DE. Margaret's father. One of the principal characters in *The Noble Jilt.*

In *Can You Forgive Her?*, represented by John Vavasor.

WYNTER, MARGARET DE. Daughter of a noble family in Bruges, and engaged to marry Count Upsel. His scholarly pursuits and seeming indifference to the revolutionary movement of the day repelled her ardent patriotism and induced her to return to a former suitor, Mark Steinmark. He, however, was so engrossed with the political scene that he no longer desired to marry her, and she returned to Count Upsel. Heroine of *The Noble Jilt.*

In *Can You Forgive Her?*, represented by Alice Vavasor.

YARMOUTH. Where Alice Vavasor and her aunt Mrs. Greenow spent a summer holiday, during which Mr. Cheesacre and Captain Bellfield contended for Mrs. Greenow's hand and fortune. *Can You* 7

YELD, BISHOP. The Bishop of Elmham, and neighbor of Roger Carbury in Suffolk. A good-natured but inactive churchman. *Way We Live* 6, 16, 19, 55, 87

YORKSHIRE.

AYLMER CASTLE. Home of Captain Aylmer. *Belton*

GROBY PARK. Estate of Sir John Mason. *Orley*

HUNDLEWICK HALL. Home of Maurice Archer. *Kirkby*

KIRKBY CLIFFE. Home of the Rev. Mr. Lownd. *Kirkby*

MATCHING PRIORY. Plantagenet Palliser's wedding gift from the old Duke of Omnium (*Finn*). It is mentioned in many of the novels in the Parliamentary and Barchester series.

YOXHAM. Home of Sir Charles Lovel. *Anna*

YOUNG, ANNA. The woman who went to England with Euphemia Smith to testify against John Caldigate. When confronted with proof of her own perfidy, she turned state's evidence and helped to clear John of the charge of bigamy. *Caldigate* 24, 29, 41-42, 55

YOUNGLAD, MR. The junior counsel for Alaric Tudor at his trial. *Clerks* 40-41

YOXHAM. The Yorkshire town in which the Rev. Charles Lovel was rector. Here Lady Anna was first accepted as one of the family. *Anna* 5-6, 13, 48

ZAMENOY, KARIL. Nina Balatka's wealthy uncle in Prague, who thought that getting the better of a Jewish competitor was a praiseworthy act, regardless of the means used to accomplish it. *Nina* 1, 6, 11

ZAMENOY, MME. SOPHIE. The virago wife of Karil, leaving no stone unturned to prevent the marriage of her niece Nina Balatka with the Jew Anton Trendellsohn. *Nina* 1-2, 5-7, 14

ZAMENOY, ZISKA. The only son of Karil, in love with his cousin Nina Balatka. *Nina* 1-4, 6-7, 9, 11